Texts and Practices

Texts and Practices provides an essential introduction to the theory and practice of Critical Discourse Analysis. Using insights from this challenging new method of linguistic analysis, the contributors to this collection reveal the ways in which language can be used as a means of social control.

The essays in *Texts and Practices*:

- Demonstrate how Critical Discourse Analysis can be applied to a variety of written and spoken texts.
- Deconstruct data from a range of contexts, countries and disciplines.
- Expose hidden patterns of discrimination and inequalities of power.

Texts and Practices, which includes specially commissioned papers from a range of distinguished authors, provides a state-of-the-art overview of Critical Discourse Analysis. As such it represents an important contribution to this developing field and an essential text for all advanced students of language, media and cultural studies.

Carmen Rosa Caldas-Coulthard is Professor of English and Applied Linguistics at the Federal University of Santa Catarina, Brazil. Her most recent publications are contributions to the edited collections *Techniques of Description* (1993) and *Advances in Written Text Analysis* (1994), both published by Routledge.

Malcolm Coulthard is Professor of English Language and Linguistics at the University of Birmingham. His most recent publications with Routledge are *Advances in Spoken Discourse Analysis* (1992) and *Advances in Written Text Analysis* (1994). He also edits the journal *Forensic Linguistics*.

Texts and Practices

Readings in Critical Discourse Analysis

Edited by
Carmen Rosa Caldas-Coulthard
and Malcolm Coulthard

London and New York

First published 1996
by Routledge
11 New Fetter Lane, London EC4P 4EE

Simultaneously published in the USA and Canada
by Routledge
29 West 35th Street, New York, NY 10001

Editorial selection and material © 1996 Carmen Rosa
Caldas-Coulthard and Malcolm Coulthard; individual
chapters © 1996 the contributors

Transferred to digital printing 2003

British Library Cataloguing in Publication Data
A catalogue record for this book is available from the
British Library

Library of Congress Cataloguing in Publication Data
A catalogue record for this book has been requested

ISBN 0–415–12142–6 (hbk)
    0–415–12143–4 (pbk)

Printed and bound by Antony Rowe Ltd, Eastbourne

Contents

Notes on contributors   vii
Preface   xi

Part I Critical discourse theory

1 On critical linguistics   3
   Roger Fowler

2 Representational resources and the production of subjectivity:
   Questions for the theoretical development of Critical Discourse
   Analysis in a multicultural society   15
   Gunther Kress

3 The representation of social actors   32
   Theo van Leeuwen

4 Technologisation of discourse   71
   Norman Fairclough

5 Discourse, power and access   84
   Teun A. van Dijk

Part II Texts and practices: Critical approaches

6 The genesis of racist discourse in Austria since 1989   107
   Ruth Wodak

7 Ethnic, racial and tribal: The language of racism?   129
   Ramesh Krishnamurthy

8 A clause-relational analysis of selected dictionary entries:
   Contrast and compatibility in the definitions of 'man' and
   'woman'   150
   Michael Hoey

9 The official version: Audience manipulation in police
  records of interviews with suspects   166
  Malcolm Coulthard

10 Conflict talk in a psychiatric discharge interview: Struggling
   between personal and official footings   179
   Branca Telles Ribeiro

11 Problems with the representation of face and its manifestations
   in the discourse of the 'old-old'   194
   Dino Preti

12 'Guilt over games boys play': Coherence as a focus for
   examining the constitution of heterosexual subjectivity
   on a problem page   214
   Val Gough and Mary Talbot

13 Barking up the wrong tree? Male hegemony, discrimination
   against women and the reporting of bestiality in the
   Zimbabwean press   231
   Andrew Morrison

14 'Women who pay for sex. And enjoy it': Transgression versus
   morality in women's magazines   250
   Carmen Rosa Caldas-Coulthard

   Bibliography   271
   Index   285

Notes on contributors

Carmen Rosa Caldas-Coulthard is Professor of English and Applied Linguistics at the Federal University of Santa Catarina, Brazil. Her latest publications are (with M. Coulthard, eds, 1991) *Tradução: Teoria e Prática* and contributions to *Techniques of Description* (edited by J. McH. Sinclair, M. Hoey and G. Fox, 1993), *Advances in Written Text Analysis* (edited by M. Coulthard, 1994) and *Language and Gender* (edited by S. Mills, 1994).

Malcolm Coulthard is Professor of English Language and Linguistics at the University of Birmingham, England. His publications include *Linguagem e Sexo* (1991) and five edited collections, *Talking about Text* (1986), *Discussing Discourse* (1987), *Tradução: Teoria e Prática* (with C. R. Caldas-Coulthard, 1991), *Advances in Spoken Discourse Analysis* (1992) and *Advances in Written Text Analysis* (1994).

Norman Fairclough is Reader in Linguistics in the Department of Linguistic and Modern English Language at the University of Lancaster, England. Among his publications are *Language and Power* (1989), *Discourse and Social Change* (1992) and as editor, *Critical Language Awareness* (1992).

Roger Fowler is Professor of Linguistics at the University of East Anglia, England. He has been Visiting Professor at Brown University and at the University of California, Berkeley. Among his major publications are the jointly authored book *Language and Control* (1979), *A Dictionary of Modern Critical Terms* (2nd edn, 1987) and *Language in the News: Discourse and Ideology in the Press* (1991).

Val Gough is Lecturer in English at the University of Liverpool, England, where she teaches courses on women writers, feminist literary theory, feminist science fiction and language and gender. She is currently working on writing and mysticism in the work of Virginia Woolf and Hélène Cixous, and has published articles on Charlotte Perkins Gilman and Virginia Woolf.

Michael Hoey is Professor of English Language at the University of Liverpool, England. His major publications are *Signalling in Discourse* (1979), *On the Surface of Discourse* (1983/1991), *Patterns of Lexis in Text* (1991) and the edited collections *Data, Description, Discourse* (1993) and *Techniques of Description* (with J. McH. Sinclair and G. Fox, 1993).

Gunther Kress is Professor of Education with special reference to the Teaching of English at the Institute of Education, University of London, England. His publications include *Social Semiotics* (with R. Hodge, 1988), *Reading Images* (with T. van Leeuwen, 1990), *Language as Ideology* (with R. Hodge, 1993) and *Learning to Write* (1994).

Ramesh Krishnamurthy is the Development Manager of COBUILD, at the University of Birmingham, England. He has worked on most of the COBUILD publications and teaches corpus lexicography to postgraduates. He is also the author of the Supplement on Indian Names in the *Oxford Dictionary of First Names*.

Andrew Morrison is a Lecturer in the Linguistics Department at the University of Zimbabwe. He has published on news photography in Zimbabwe, critical language awareness for academic study in the humanities and questions in letters to the editor (with Alison Love). He is currently working on a textbook on communication skills for law and completing a novel.

Dino Preti is Professor of Portuguese at the University of São Paulo, Brazil. Among his books are *A Linguagem Falada Culta na Cidade de São Paulo* (4 vols, 1986–90), *A Linguagem dos Idosos* (1991) and the edited book *Análise de Textos Orais* (1993).

Branca Telles Ribeiro is an Associate Professor in the Graduate Programme in Applied Linguistics at the Federal University of Rio de Janeiro, Brazil. Her major publications are *Coherence in Psychotic Discourse* (1994) and 'Framing in psychotic discourse' in *Framing in Discourse* (edited by D. Tannen, 1993).

Mary Talbot is a Lecturer in the Institute of Language and Communication at Odense University, Denmark. Her publications include *Fictions at Work: Language and Social Practice* (1995) and 'A synthetic sisterhood: false friends in a teenage magazine' in *Gender Articulated: Arrangements of Language and the Socially Constructed Self* (edited by K. Hall and M. Bucholtz, 1994)

Teun A. van Dijk is Professor of Discourse Studies at the University of Amsterdam, the Netherlands. He is the founder-editor of the international journals *Text* and *Discourse and Society*. His works include the four edited volumes of the *Handbook of Discourse Analysis* (1985), *News as Discourse*

(1988), *Racism and the Press* (1991) and *Elite Discourse and Racism* (1993).

Theo van Leeuwen worked as a scriptwriter and film and television director and taught communications and media studies at Macquarie University in Sydney. He is currently Principal Lecturer in communication theory at the School of Media of the London College of Printing and Distributive Trades, England. He is joint author of *Reading Images* (with G. Kress, 1990) and of *The Media Interview* (with P. Bell, 1994).

Ruth Wodak is Professor and Head of the Department of Applied Linguistics at the University of Vienna, Austria. Among her publications are *Language, Power and Ideology* (ed., 1989); *Sprache in der Politik: Politik in der Sprache* (with F. Menz, eds, 1990) and *Die Sprachen der Vergangenheiten: Öffentliches Gedenken in österreichischen und deutschen Medien* (with F. Menz, R. Mitten and F. Stern, 1994).

Preface

One of the paradoxes of modern linguistics is that its most distinguished practitioner, Noam Chomsky, although world-famous as a political activist and campaigner, professes no professional interest in language in use – neither in analysing the speeches, committee meetings, letters, memos and books which he claims are subverting the democratic process, nor in reflecting on his own highly effective rhetoric.

Discourse is a major instrument of power and control and Critical Discourse Analysts, unlike Chomsky, feel that it is indeed part of their professional role to investigate, reveal and clarify how power and discriminatory value are inscribed in and mediated through the linguistic system: Critical Discourse Analysis is essentially political in intent with its practitioners acting upon the world in order to transform it and thereby help create a world where people are not discriminated against because of sex, colour, creed, age or social class.

The initial stimulus for this book was the need we felt as teachers to make more easily accessible to students in a single text the most recent theoretical statements of the major thinkers along with illustrative analyses of a variety of texts and situations selected from a variety of countries. However, in choosing the authors and topics we were always conscious of the other audience of fellow professionals. We hope that they agree both that there is a great deal that is new here in the theoretical chapters and that the analytical chapters offer new methods of analysis applied in novel areas.

As a help to both readerships we have collected together the references from all the chapters at the end of the book and then supplemented them with any major items which were missing; we hope that the Bibliography can now be used as a first resource for those intending to undertake research in the area.

The book itself is divided into two parts, Theory and Practice. In the first, theoretical section we have collected together contributions from the leading names in the field, and in the practical section we have set out to cover a variety not only of topic areas but also of countries, because we think that meaning belongs to culture rather than to language and different countries have different experiences. The strength of the volume is that, although there is no single methodology, all of the chapters have one thing in common, that they view social practices and their linguistic realisation as inseparable.

Carmen Rosa Caldas-Coulthard
Malcolm Coulthard
Florianópolis
March 1995

Part I

Critical discourse theory

Chapter 1

On critical linguistics[1]

Roger Fowler

'Functional linguistics' is 'functional' in two senses: it is based on the pre-miss that the form of language responds to the functions of language use; and it assumes that linguistics, as well as language, has different functions, different jobs to do, so the form of linguistics responds to the functions of linguistics. The first paper in *Explorations in the Functions of Language* (Halliday, 1973) makes this point about requests for a definition of lan-guage: 'In a sense the only satisfactory response is "why do you want to know?", since unless we know what lies beneath the question we cannot hope to answer it in a way which will suit the questioner' (Halliday, 1973: 9). In the interview with Herman Parret, Halliday accepts that there may be an 'instrumental linguistics . . . the study of language for understanding something else' and that an instrumental linguistics will have characteris-tics relevant to the purpose for which it is to be used. In doing instrumental linguistics, though, one is also learning about the nature of Language as a whole phenomenon, so there is no conflict or contradiction with 'autonomous linguistics' (Halliday, 1978: 36).

'Critical linguistics' emerged from our writing of *Language and Control* (Fowler *et al.*, 1979) as an instrumental linguistics very much of that descrip-tion. We formulated an analysis of public discourse, an analysis designed to get at the ideology coded implicitly behind the overt propositions, to examine it particularly in the context of social formations. The tools for this analysis were an eclectic selection of descriptive categories suited to the purpose: especially those structures identified by Halliday as ideational and interpersonal, of course, but we also drew on other linguistic traditions, as for example when we needed to talk about speech acts or transformations. Our conception of instrumentality or purpose was quite complicated, and perhaps not fully enough discussed in the book. We were concerned to the-orise language as a social practice, a 'practice' in the sense that word has acquired in English adaptations of Althusser: an intervention in the social and economic order, and one which in this case works by the reproduction of (socially originating) ideology (Kress and Hodge, 1979). In this way the book was intended as a contribution to a general understanding of language. But why 'critical'? Here two models were relevant. It has to be said (and I hope that this will not be regarded as a damaging admission) that our education and working context made us familiar with the hermeneutic side to literary criticism, and we, like the literary critics, were working on the interpretation of discourse – though equipped with a better tool-kit! Contemporary Marxist, post-structuralist and deconstructionist criticism is actually of more use to us (see Belsey, 1980; Eagleton, 1976; Harari, 1979; Norris, 1982) and more in line with the important influence of what was the sense of 'critique' established in the social sciences under the influence of the Frankfurt School:

> 'Critique' ... denotes reflection on a system of constraints which are humanly produced: distorting pressures to which individuals, or a group of individuals, or the human race as a whole, succumb in their process of self-formation. ...
>
> Criticism ... is brought to bear on objects of experience whose 'objectivity' is called into question; criticism supposes that there is a degree of inbuilt deformity which masquerades as reality. It seeks to remove this distortion and thereby to make possible the liberation of what has been distorted. Hence it entails a conception of emancipation.
>
> (Connerton, 1976: 18, 20)

These definitions are worded somewhat negatively, or militantly; I shall return to the question of negativity in criticism in a moment. Imagine them stripped of the negative implications, and it will emerge that they fit well with the concerns of critical linguistics. The first paragraph relates to the social determination of ideology, and the constraining role of language in socialisation. The second paragraph relates to the central preoccupation of critical linguistics with the theory and practice of representation. Critical linguistics insists that all representation is mediated, moulded by the value-systems that are ingrained in the medium (language in this case) used for representation; it challenges common sense by pointing out that something could have been represented some other way, with a very different significance. This is not, in fact, simply a question of 'distortion' or 'bias': there is not necessarily any true reality that can be unveiled by critical practice, there are simply relatively varying representations.

Although the theory of critical linguistics is a value-free theory of representation, of 'language as social semiotic', in practice the instrumentality of the model is reformative. The goals are parallel to those of 'critical sociology', again admirably summarised by Connerton:

> Criticism ... aims at changing or even removing the conditions of what is considered to be a false or distorted consciousness. ... Criticism ... renders transparent what had previously been hidden, and in doing so

it initiates a process of self-reflection, in individuals or in groups, designed to achieve a liberation from the domination of past constraints. Here a change in practice is therefore a constitutive element of a change in theory.

(Connerton, 1976: 20)

The proponents of the linguistic model occupy a variety of socialist positions, and are concerned to use linguistic analysis to expose misrepresentation and discrimination in a variety of modes of public discourse: they offer critical readings of newspapers, political propaganda, official documents, regulations, formal genres such as the interview, and so on. Topics examined include sexism, racism; inequality in education, employment, the courts and so on; war, nuclear weapons and nuclear power; political strategies; and commercial practices. In relation to public discourse on such matters, the goals of the critical linguists are in general terms defamiliarisation or consciousness-raising.

In terms of 'autonomous linguistics' (e.g. transformational-generative grammar), critical linguistics is not linguistics at all, and it is certainly not fair play. In the more liberal world of functional linguistics, however, which allows both applications and the tailoring of the theory to the requirements of those applications, critical linguistics is a legitimate practice which does not need any special defence. So functional linguistics not only provides the theoretical underpinning for critical linguistics, but also offers a supportive intellectual and political climate for this work. This is a tolerance for which I am exceedingly grateful; one can imagine the difficulty of trying to make a career, get published, in circumstances which were less tolerant of pluralism and of comment.

It is not that critical linguistics is marginalised or embattled anyway. The model has attracted considerable interest and recognition at least in Great Britain and some other European academic circles (notably the Netherlands, former West Germany and Spain) and of course Australia. Particular centres of interest would include the universities of East Anglia, Lancaster, Warwick, Murdoch, Amsterdam and Utrecht. Papers inspired or provoked by the model appear regularly at diverse conferences, such as the Utrecht Summer School of Critical Theory in 1984 and the Lancaster conference on Linguistics and Politics in 1986. The label 'critical linguistics' and the book *Language and Control* are frequently used as reference points (see e.g. Chilton, 1985: *passim* and especially p. 215; Fairclough, 1985, especially p. 747). On the other hand, certain aspects of critical linguistics have been subjected to interesting critique (e.g. Chilton 1984; Pateman, 1981). A kind of institutional recognition has been implied in my being invited to contribute a long entry on 'critical linguistics' for *The Linguistics Encyclopaedia* (Malmkjær, 1992).

If linguistic criticism now enjoys a certain academic standing, that is not to say that it is completed as a theory of language or an instrumentality of linguistics – or even half-way satisfactory. Before 1979 the co-authors of *Language and Control* had dispersed to other continents, cities and employments, and this made even the final editing of the book very difficult, and of course prohibited further teamwork on the development of the model. My own work has prevented sustained concentration on the theory and practice of critical linguistics. Returning to the subject in 1986, I found myself troubled by an awareness of difficulties, unclarities, and by the lack of a plan for further development. The original linguistic model, for all its loose ends, at least possessed a certain theoretical and methodological compactness, and I think it is important now to consolidate and develop this (essentially Hallidayan) model. If this is not done, the danger is that 'critical linguistics' in the hands of practitioners of diverse intellectual persuasions will come to mean loosely any politically well-intentioned analytic work on language and ideology, regardless of method, technical grasp of linguistic theory, or historical validity of interpretations.

One is grateful, then, that in two excellent publications, Gunther Kress (1985a; 1985b) has both raised some radical questions about the state of the art, and valuably clarified some central aspects of the theory which were not at all well elaborated in *Language and Control*. These papers take the model several stages on, without distorting the original intellectual base; but they do not raise all the problems which I feel ought to be considered.

Kress opens his contribution to the Chilton volume on nukespeak with a challenging question:

> There is now a significant and large body of work which enables us to see the operation of ideology in language and which provides at least a partial understanding of that operation. Some, perhaps the major, problems remain. I take these to be around the question 'what now?'. Having established that texts are everywhere and inescapably ideologically structured, and that the ideological structuring of both language and texts can be related readily enough to the social structures and processes of the origins of particular texts, where do we go from here?
>
> (Kress, 1985a: 65)

The context makes it clear that the motives for posing this question are essentially strategic: how are we to go ahead and use this model as an instrument of social change? But clearing the way necessitates an improvement to the theory. The effectiveness of critical linguistics, if it could be measured, would be seen primarily in its capacity to equip readers for demystificatory readings of ideology-laden texts (thus the main activity of critical linguistics is inevitably within the educational system). But as Kress points out, the original theory – all traditional linguistic theory, it might be observed – privileges the source of texts, ascribing little power to the reader because the reader simply is not theorised. In response to this problem, Kress elucidates what might be called a 'post-structuralist', more specifically 'Foucaultian', position on the interrelated set of concepts discourse, writer (author), reader.

> Discourses are systematically-organised sets of statements which give expression to the meanings and values of an institution. . . . A discourse provides a set of possible statements about a given area, and organises and gives structure to the manner in which a particular topic, object, process is to be talked about.
>
> (Kress, 1985b: 6–7)

'Discourse' relates to the more recent Hallidayan formulation of register as 'the configuration of semantic resources that the member of a culture typically associates with a situation type. It is the meaning potential that is accessible in a given social context' (Halliday, 1978: 111). But its status is crucially different. Whereas a register is a variety of language, a discourse is a system of meanings within the culture, pre-existing language. Again, one speaks of a text as being 'in' some register R_1, whereas several discourses D_1 to D_n may be 'in' a text.

Writers and readers are constituted by the discourses that are accessible to them. A writer can make texts only out of the available discourses, and so, *qua* writer, is socio-culturally constituted. Authors are writers 'who own their own texts' (Kress, 1985b: 49), but this does not make them any less discursively constructed. Texts construct 'reading positions' for readers, that is, they suggest what ideological formations it is appropriate for readers to bring to texts. But the reader, in this theory, is not the passive recipient of fixed meanings: the reader, remember, is discursively equipped prior to the encounter with the text, and reconstructs the text as a system of meanings which may be more or less congruent with the ideology which informs the text. In modern literary theory this discursive activity of the reader is known as 'productive consumption'.

Intertextuality, dialogue and contradiction are some other important parts of this discursive view of communication, but it is not necessary to discuss these concepts here.

This more dynamic and egalitarian view of the processes of reading is a great advance over the original source-centred theory, and a distinct advantage for educational practice: by giving more power to the reader, it promotes the confidence that is needed for the production of readers (and interlocutors) who are not only communicatively competent, but also critically aware of the discursive formations and contradictions of texts, and able to enter into dialogue with their sources. The dialogue might be internal, for a reader, in which case s/he will learn something about society and its values by becoming aware of alternative beliefs. For a speaker, the dialogue may be real and manifest in interaction with an other, or internal, as a lecturer or writer, say, achieves consciousness of his or her relationship with the other values of the audience or reader- ship (as I did here, in writing 's/he' and 'his or her', acknowledging an ideological problematic to which I would have given no thought some years ago). In all these areas of communication, critical linguistics could give strategic guidance. No doubt the concept of genre of discourse (inter- view, sermon, etc.), which Kress also foregrounds, will be instructive in establishing appropriate strategies. These are pedagogic questions which I cannot take on board here, but they are important for the extension of critical linguistics, since practice can develop theory: experiments with dis- course strategies, for example, would almost certainly help refine the presently unclear definitions of discursive genres.

There is, however, the question of whether we are trying to run before we have learned to walk. I agree with Kress that major problems remain with critical linguistics, but I do not agree that these are principally at the level of strategic utilisation. It seems to me that further work is needed on both theory and method, as well as application. It is one thing to demonstrate the general principle that ideology is omnipresent in texts – I agree with Kress that that principle has been demonstrated. But doing the analyses remains quite difficult, and those analyses that have been published are not as substantial as Kress implies. A small number of prac- titioners have become adept at uncovering ideology in texts; and a smaller number still (mainly the authors of *Language and Control* and their asso- ciates) employ anything approaching a standard, consistent apparatus. Although demonstrations have focused on a good range of types of texts, they tend to be fragmentary, exemplificatory, and they usually take too much for granted in the way of method and of context. As for method, it has to be said that functional linguistics is a complicated subject not well provided with straightforward short textbooks. For the purposes of critical linguistics, Halliday's *An Introduction to Functional Grammar* (1985/94) offers both more and less than is required. More, because crit- ical linguists do not need all the detail; in practice, critical linguists get a very high mileage out of a small selection of linguistic concepts such as transitivity and nominalisation. Yet these fundamental concepts are abstract and difficult, and need to be explained more clearly than they are in Halliday's own writings. Less, because certain methodological areas referred to by critical linguists are better covered in other models: for instance, speech-act theory and Gricean conversational analysis are impor- tant aids to understanding aspects of performative and pragmatic trans- actions. A comprehensive methodological guide, tailored to the needs of the discipline, on the lines of the last chapter of *Language and Control*, is needed, but of course more formal and more extensive than that early 'check-list': a textbook specifically designed for the teaching of critical linguistics. Meanwhile, there is a need for published analyses to be more explicit, less allusive, about the tools they are employing. What I am saying is that we need to be more formal about method, both in order to improve the analytic technique, and to increase the population of competent practitioners. At the moment, students do not find the practice easy.

There is another substantial omission in the published literature, which I want to connect with the question of history and context. Apart from the nukespeak volume (Chilton, 1985) – which is methodologically diverse – there is as yet no book-length study of one topic, or one mode of discourse, genre, or large corpus. A large study would allow the critical linguist to specify historical context in detail. The fragmentary analyses published so far have tended to sketch the background to the text, or assume the reader's prior knowledge of contexts and genre. This is in my view a dangerous economy because of the inevitable transience of the materials treated: who, in the late 1990s, will remember the sacked Cabinet Ministers of the 1980s, or the leaders of the Campaign for Nuclear Disarmament, or the main protagonists in the 'Miners' Strike' (what miners' strike?)? I think that there is a great danger that the writings of critical linguistics will rapidly become opaque through historical supercession.

But the problem is more fundamental than the awkwardness of transience and consequential opacity. The theory of critical linguistics acknowledges that there is a lack of invariance between linguistic structures and their significances. This premiss should be affirmed more clearly and insistently than has been the case. Significance (ideology) cannot simply be read off the linguistic forms that description has identified in the text, because the same form (nominalisation, for example) has different significances in different contexts (scientific writing versus regulations, for example). This is the whole point of our insistence on the dialectical inseparability of two concepts 'language' and 'society' that happen to be separately lexicalised in English (Kress, 1985b: 1), the reason for Halliday's use of portmanteau words such as 'sociosemantic'. One implication of this interdependence of language and context is a considerable procedural difficulty for students: they are likely to believe that the descriptive tools of linguistics provide some privilege of access to the interpretation of the text, but of course this is not so, and thus students find themselves not knowing where to start. By the theory of productive consumption, you can understand the text only if you can bring to it relevant experience of discourse and of context. Linguistic description comes at a later stage, as a means of getting some purchase on the significances that one has heuristically assigned to the text. Teachers often make the mistake of overestimating the discursive experience of young students, who turn out to have no intuitions about a particular text, and therefore cannot get started on the analysis. When teaching, it is necessary to be quite open about the fact that linguistics is not a discovery procedure, and also to specify context in some detail, indicating relevant historical, economic and institutional circumstances.

A healthily provocative way of generalising about these problems would be to assert that critical linguistics is a form of history-writing or historiography. This characterisation would suitably reflect the central interest of the subject, which is not Language as traditionally understood by linguists. As we have seen, critical linguistics is an 'instrumental' linguistics looking beyond the formal structure of Language as an abstract system, towards the practical interaction of language and context. I link critical linguistics with history rather than, say, sociology (as disciplines devoted to what from the traditional linguist's point of view constitutes 'context') because the broadest possible frame of reference is needed: there is no knowing what the critical linguist will be interested in next. But there are more specific connections of aim and method with history. Like the historian, the critical linguist aims to understand the values which underpin social, economic and political formations, and, diachronically, changes in values and changes in formations. As for method, one aspect at any rate, the critical linguist, like the historian, treats texts both as types of discursive practice (charters, letters, proclamations, Acts of Parliament) and as documents (sources for the beliefs of institutions, for example). Like the historiographer, the critical linguist is crucially concerned with the ideological relativity of representation.

In passing it should be observed that critical linguistics is a useful tool for the historian (several students at the University of East Anglia have creatively combined the subjects), but that is not the main point. The important consideration is for the critical linguist to take a professionally responsible attitude towards the analysis of context. Up to now, the majority of the texts analysed have been supposed to relate to a social context well known to both the analyst and to her or his readers: contemporary popular newspapers, advertisements, political speeches of the current scene, classroom discourse, and so on. The plausibility of the ideological ascriptions has had to rest on intersubjective intuitions supposedly shared by writer and reader in a common discursive competence, backed up by informal accounts of relevant contexts and institutions. As was noted in my comments about young students' difficulties, this informal presentation cannot be relied on to prove the point. I think it is about time we stopped saying 'lack of space prevents a full account ...'. What are needed are, exactly, full descriptions of context and its implications for beliefs and relationships.

My final general query concerns the status of ideology as a theoretical concept in critical linguistics. In a sense it is not the definition of the term that is at fault or inadequate. Critical linguists have always been very careful to avoid the definition of ideology as 'false consciousness' (it is a pity that Connerton's very serviceable definitions of 'criticism' quoted above contain pejorative words like 'distortion' and 'deformity'), making it clear that they mean something more neutral: a society's implicit theory of what types of objects exist in their world (categorisation); of the way that world works (causation); and of the values to be assigned to objects and processes (general propositions or paradigms). These implicit beliefs constitute 'common sense', which provides a normative base to discourse. Just as it is not the basic definition that is at fault, so also the existing ideological analyses are adequately illuminating as far as they go. There have been some excellent demonstrations of the structuring power of ideology in the areas of categorisation and of causation (see e.g. Kress, 1985b: ch. 4, and several of his earlier writings; Trew, 1979). My observation is that progress in the linguistic analysis of ideology has been greatest in those two areas where Halliday's ideational function has given the clearest methodological inspiration, namely lexical classification and transitivity. The question that urgently needs to be asked is whether the structural characteristics of the systemic-functional model of grammar have not unduly constrained the range of statements made about ideology in critical linguistics up to now. Function determines form, says the general premiss, and I feel that critical interest so far has been largely centred on those ide-ological functions which are most clearly mapped by observable and well-described linguistic forms, namely vocabulary structure, and the structure of the clause. We need to take a more inclusive view of what constitutes ideology in language, and in particular, give consideration to those implicit meanings which do not have direct surface structure representation.

Numerous methodological and theoretical proposals exist; it is just a question of bringing them within the critical linguistics model, and sub-mitting them to methodological development in the service of that model. I am thinking of the various proposals to the effect that the interpreta-tion of discourse hinges on 'shared knowledge' or 'shared beliefs'. In dis-course analysis, there are the 'general propositions' of Labov and Fanshel (1977), which are relevant beliefs, of a high level of generality, which participants bring to the activity of conversation; they may be equivalent to the 'conventional implicatures' of Grice (1975), whose 'conversational implicatures' are of course also relevant. (In this context it may be noted that the undoubted applicability of Sperber and Wilson's (1986) theory of 'relevance' awaits detailed assessment.) If, following the proposals of Kress, we give the reader a more prominent role in our model, it will be appropriate to look to the various kinds of schemata (see Rumelhart, 1980) which have been developed in cognitive psychology and Artificial Intelligence: 'frames', 'scripts', and 'plans' (Minsky, 1975; Schank and Abelson, 1977); from cognitive semantics we might adopt the notion of 'prototype' (Rosch, 1975); from literary criticism, the concept of 'metaphor' (cf. Kress, 1985b: 70ff).

University Press.

Kress, G. and Hodge, R. (1979) *Language as Ideology*, London: Routledge & Kegan Paul.

Labov, W. and Fanshel, D. (1977) *Therapeutic Discourse: Psychotherapy as Conversation*, New York: Academic Press.

Malmkjær, K. (1992) *The Linguistic Encyclopaedia*, London: Routledge.

Minsky, M. L. (1975) 'Framework for representing knowledge', in P. H. Winston (ed.) *The Psychology of Computer Vision*, New York: McGraw-Hill.

Norris, C. (1982) *Deconstruction: Theory and Practice*, London: Methuen.

Pateman, T. (1981) 'Linguistics as a branch of critical theory', *University of East Anglia Papers in Linguistics* 14–15: 1–29.

Rosch, E. (1975) 'Cognitive representation of semantic categories', *Journal of Experimental Psychology* 104, 3: 192–233.

Rumelhart, D. E. (1980) 'Schemata: the building blocks of cognition', in R. J. Spiro, B. C. Bruce and W. F. Brewer (eds) *Theoretical Issues in Reading Comprehension*, Hillsdale, NJ: Erlbaum.

Schank, R. and Abelson, R. (1977) *Scripts, Plans, Goals and Understanding*, Hillsdale, NJ: Erlbaum.

Sperber, D. and Wilson, D. (1986) *Relevance: Communication and Cognition*, Oxford: Basil Blackwell.

Trew, T. (1979) 'Theory and ideology at work', in R. Fowler, R. Hodge, G. Kress and T. Trew, *Language and Control*, London: Routledge & Kegan Paul, 94–116.

Chapter 2

Representational resources and the production of subjectivity

Questions for the theoretical development of Critical Discourse Analysis in a multicultural society

Gunther Kress

Critical studies of language, Critical Linguistics (CL) and Critical Discourse Analysis (CDA) have from the beginning had a political project: broadly speaking that of altering inequitable distributions of economic, cultural and political goods in contemporary societies. The intention has been to bring a system of excessive inequalities of power into crisis by uncovering its workings and its effects through the analysis of potent cultural objects – texts – and thereby to help in achieving a more equitable social order. The issue has thus been one of transformation, unsettling the existing order, and transforming its elements into an arrangement less harmful to some, and perhaps more beneficial to all the members of a society.

In the process the various critical language projects have developed an impressive range of analytic/critical procedures, and have provided, in the analyses developed, clear insights into the social, political and ideological processes at work.

There are two developments implicit in the project which I wish to highlight as they have so far remained largely implicit. One is the crucial matter of moving beyond the client status of critical language projects in relation to other disciplines – whether linguistics, or psychology, or social theories of various kinds, by taking categories developed in these and applying them in this project. It has become essential to take the decisive step towards the articulation of the theory of language, or communication, of semiosis, which is implied in these critical language activities, to develop an apt theory of language.

The second is closely related. Critical language projects have remained just that: critiques of texts and of the social practices implied by or realised in those texts, uncovering, revealing, inequitable, dehumanising and deleterious states of affairs. I wish to suggest that if critical language projects were to develop apt, plausible theories of this domain, they would be able to move from critical reading, from analysis, from deconstructive activity, to productive activity. One fundamental critique of linguistics has been that it has been a heavily production-oriented enterprise, with no theorised, integrated account of readings or of readers; yet a similar critique might be made of CL or CDA to the effect that they are heavily reception/reading oriented, with no strongly explicit account of production, or of producers. Of course this is an overstatement, but in one crucial respect I believe the criticism stands; CL or CDA have not offered (productive) accounts of alternative forms of social organisation, nor of social subjects, other than by implication.

If linguistic, cultural and economic resources are at present unequally distributed along the lines of class, gender, age, profession, ethnicity, race, religion, and so on, with the consequent formations of subjectivities (one might say deformations, in relation to what might be) then it behoves critical language projects, I believe, to begin to turn their attention to this enterprise. It may be that my present professional location forces this view on me with particular urgency, although I have felt this for some time and articulated it in one or two articles I wrote when I was still living and working in Australia. Allow me then briefly to state my present position, and how it arises. I am now located in an Institute of Education – a pedagogical institution. My job requires of me that I think about and concern myself with the school curriculum, specifically the English curriculum. A curriculum is a design for a future social subject, and via that envisioned subject a design for a future society. That is, the curriculum puts forward knowledges, skills, meanings, values in the present which will be telling in the lives of those who experience the curriculum, ten or twenty years later. Forms of pedagogy experienced by children now in school suggest to them forms of social relations which they are encouraged to adopt, adapt, modify and treat as models. The curriculum, and its associated pedagogy, puts forward a set of cultural, linguistic and social resources which students have available as resources for their own transformation, in relation to which (among others) students constantly construct, reconstruct and transform their subjectivity.

Such a view of the curriculum and of pedagogy requires, however (though this seems, in Britain at least, not the common assumption), that those who construct the curriculum have a vision of the future in which this subject, here and now experiencing the curriculum, will lead her or his life – a culturally, personally, socially productive life, one hopes. It behoves me therefore to state my vision of that future in relation to which I imagine the curriculum. My span of prediction is about twenty years; a period at the end of which a child now entering school will be about 25 years old. I want to have a part in the construction of a positive future, and so I imagine a society which has been willing to continue to learn to deal with several fundamentally significant issues: the issue of multiculturalism first and foremost; the issues of appropriately productive forms of sociality; the issues of the economy and of technology in an age which will be even more deeply transnational than our present period is; and by no means last, the issues arising out of the massive technological and economic transformations of what used to be called the mass media.

My vision therefore focuses on the kind of curriculum – its contents, as well as the form in which its contents are made available – which will be essential in achieving such a vision. More than that, however, I focus on the kind of subject required to carry this task of acting in that society, to construct it, to make it productive in personal, cultural, social, economic ways. My concern is to imagine what resources the curriculum needs to make available to children who are now in schools in order for them to be able to achieve for themselves that task of transformation. I imagine that the citizen of the society of twenty years' hence will have to be confident in the face of difference of all kinds, to see it as a major personal, cultural and economic resource; that they will have to be at ease with constant and continuing change.

In envisaging the tasks of transformations which will lead to such subjectivities I find Bourdieu's category of *habitus*, as embodied practice, most helpful. In the introduction to (the English edition of essays of Bourdieu's) *Language and Symbolic Power* the editor, John Thompson, glosses the term as follows:

> The habitus is a set of *dispositions* which incline agents to act and react in certain ways. The dispositions generate practices, perceptions and attitudes which are 'regular' without being consciously co-ordinated or governed by any 'rule'. The dispositions which constitute the habitus are inculcated, structured, durable, generative and transposable ... [they] are acquired through a gradual process of inculcation in which early childhood experiences are particularly important. Through a myriad of mundane processes of training and learning, such as those involved in the inculcation of table matter ('sit up straight', 'don't talk with your mouth full', etc.) the individual acquires a set of dispositions which literally mould the body and become second nature. The dispositions produced thereby are also *structured* in the sense that they unavoidably reflect the social conditions within which they were acquired. An individual from a working-class background, for instance, will have acquired dispositions which are different in certain respects from those acquired by individuals who were brought up in a middle-class milieu. ... Structured dispositions are also *durable* ... they endure through the life history of the individual ... [they] are *generative* and *transposable* in the sense that they are capable of generating a multiplicity of practices and perceptions in fields other than those in which they were originally acquired.
>
> (Thompson, 1991: 12–13)

In my view the set of representational resources and the practices associated with each of these, that is, the (formal) means and practices by which we represent ourselves to ourselves and to others, play an absolutely crucial role in the formation of an individual's habitus. On the one hand, these are the resources which are available to an individual as the means whereby she or he can effect the transformation of her or his subjectivity, to produce a particular habitus. On the other hand, the representational resources are not highly plastic, that is, they represent, realise, embody in themselves, the content of their form, rich social histories. The media of representation (e.g. language, whether written or spoken; the visual, whether as painting, drawing, photography; the gestural, etc.) have inherent possibilities and limitations as media of communication. That is, the representational resources constitute a highly specific technology, among other things, which is enabling in certain directions, and which impedes in others.

One essential and urgent task in a multicultural society is therefore to conduct an ethnography of representational resources, across all the major identifiable groups in a society. This ethnography would include descriptions of social valuations which attach to the representational resources used by various groups. Such a description would be accompanied by a semiotic analysis of these resources, and of the media of representation through which they were realised.

So for instance, in the domain of language, it will be important to know the semiotic potential of the grammars used by all the ethnic/linguistic groups in a society; to know the characteristic forms of text of all the groups; to know, for instance, what valuations attach to speech as against writing, and to know also how this distinction is articulated and valued. Beyond language, one would want to know about all the other media of public communication which the various groups in a society have at their disposal, and what meanings are characteristically carried by these, with greater or lesser ease, and with what social recognition, valuation and effect.

In this view the issue of equity, for instance, takes on a quite specific character: whereas until now it has generally been seen as a matter of making concessions to marginal groups, allowing them access to goods which the dominant or mainstream group(s) enjoy, of being 'nice' to those less fortunate than oneself, it will, rather, have to be treated as a matter which works reciprocally, in *all* directions. A truly equitable society is one in which the mainstream groups see it as essential to have access to the linguistic and cultural resources of minority groups and demand such access as a matter of equity. Equity cannot be left as a matter of making concessions; it has to be seen as a matter of equality of cultural trade, where each social group is seen as having contributions of equal value to make to all other social groups in the larger social unit.

But for that to be a possibility, we need precisely that inventory of the larger linguistic, semiotic, cultural, social economy. We need to know with great precision what are 'the myriad of mundane processes of training and learning ... which literally mould the body and become second nature'. My assumption is that the potentials in the processes of representation – how cultural groups and their individual members can and do represent themselves, what kinds of representations they receive – are likely to be crucial in the inculcation of representational 'table manners', and are crucial in moulding bodies. In this context, the embodiment of semiotic/cultural practices is much more than a mere metaphor; I think, for instance, of the minute neuro-muscular 'settings' which are learned and become entirely naturalised as a part of learning a first (and less frequently a second) language.

It is here, precisely, where the impressive range of procedures, of skills, of analyses developed in the critical language project, need to be employed; where, in a sense, the emphasis of CL, CDA, or of Social Semiotics must be turned around to become an enterprise focused, engaged on *making*. Or rather, for I am not advocating the abandoning of the project of critique at all, where the critical language project can pursue both aims through the recognition of the need for its own reconstitution as a fully theory of communication, of cultural, social, semiosis. If I am not mistaken, a quite similar direction is evident in Teun van Dijk's proposals and articulations, of a comprehensive theory of Discourse and Discourse Practices, in outlining the theoretical elements which in his view will need to enter into that reconceptualisation. And, as I mentioned earlier, the work of all the people engaged in the project of CDA implicitly or explicitly not only contains the methodological, theoretical and political wherewithal for that enterprise, but also frequently acts in precisely the fashion I am advocating. My pleas then may be no more or no other than a plea for the overt recognition of this task, and a decision to put it formally on the agenda for the further development of this joint project.

At the very least both the questions of representational resources and of representational processes will have to form a part of this new project. The latter seems to me particularly important to mention, as the technological developments in the media of production and dissemination (have already and) are about to put what seemed until now settled practices of production and reception into crisis, and to constitute them in what has seemed until now a paradoxical fashion. So for instance, what have seemed the settled distinctions of reading and writing, of consumption and production generally; of speech and writing; of reference and signification; of the common-sense notion of the monomedial text (e.g. the 'print media'); many of these are even now being undone and altered in ways and directions which are dimly discernible but by no means fully settled. So for

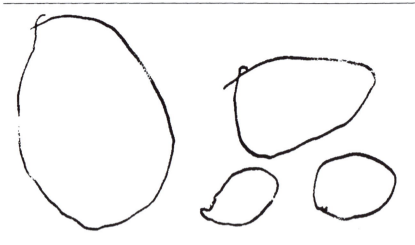

Figure 2.2 Circles

new sign which is produced out of the reader's own interest at that moment.

The history of the child's own development of the representational resources which led him to the production of the sign of the car is relatively well recoverable; and here are some markers along that micro-historical path. This achievement of circles underpinned his ability to produce the representation of the car (see Figure 2.2). That is, as he developed a particular representational resource, the circle, it enabled him to move to a further level of representational capacity, in producing the more complex sign of the car. The production of the representational resources, the changed possibilities of him as a subject in relation to the world, in this case representing/transforming the world seems strongly evident to me. Even earlier stages are recoverable, when the signs produced were quite different – when, perhaps, expression as gesture, and formal production are very closely interrelated (see Figure 2.3).

My point is one about the reciprocal relations between subjectivity; the subject's production of representational resources; the transformation by the subject of, in this case, his subjectivity via the newly produced representational resources; the transformative power of the subject in and on the world as a consequence of this prior transformation; and the subject's renewed transformation of the representational resources, etc. In this instance the process is perhaps relatively clear because it is *relatively* free of the cultural and the social forms of representation; though it is of course the social and cultural world itself which has prompted this sequence of production.

Transformation by the subject of her or his subjectivity in relation to the available representational resources is my central point. *Interest* is

Figure 2.3 Circular 'gestures'

for me a category that allows me to express the momentary focusing, condensation, of subjectivity, the response to the whole host of contingent social factors and past histories which accompany the making of signs.

I shall take a huge metaphoric step and move to a discussion of a series of images, all of them from the front pages of newspapers. Now I am again engaging in the practised performance of CDA or Social Semiotics – reading critically, reading with a particular point of view in mind. My first example is the front page of the *Frankfurter Allgemeine*: a somewhat unusual newspaper now in western Europe (though *Le Monde* is quite similar in one respect) in its continued insistence on the prominence of the representational resource of verbal language (see Figure 2.4). All texts are multi-semiotic and here I shall focus on aspects of layout, on typographical features (e.g. densely spaced print; use of certain typefaces to distinguish genres, for instance report from opinion; the length of items, and so on). The typographical and layout features are, broadly, homologous with this paper's insistence on the dominance of the verbal: the dense spacing suggests a reader who can and will take the time, make the effort,

Frankfurter Allgemeine

ZEITUNG FÜR DEUTSCHLAND

Russische Truppen stürmen Milizgebäude in Tschetschenien

Fünf Tote und hundert Verletzte bei einer Bombenexplosion in Jerusalem

Arafat verurteilt das Attentat / Ministerpräsident Rabin suspendiert die Verhandlungen mit der PLO

Die Koalitionsparteien streiten über das Kruzifix-Urteil

Gerhardt: Entscheidungen des Verfassungsgerichts akzeptieren / Auftrag zu zivilem Ungehorsam

Und wenn das Urteil falsch wäre?
Von Friedrich Karl Fromme

UN gegen Abschiebung von Abdić-Anhängern nach Bosnien

Flucht von Moslimen aus Kroatien nach Banja Luka geht weiter / Vorwürfe gegen Kroatien

China hilft weiter nach dem neuen Pantschen Lama eschen

Rühe sagt Litauen deutsche Hilfe zu

Amnestie in Südkorea angekündigt

Herzog unterzeichnet das neue Abtreibungsgesetz

Manfred Donike gestorben

Figure 2.4 Front page of Frankfurter Allgemeine

have the concentration to read this text. The length of items suggests that this is a reader who would not wish to be 'short-changed', who wishes to have a serious treatment of an issue. The use of different typefaces – and the gothic typeface, with its suggestion of (temporal) distance – suggests the wish to be clear about signalling the ontological status of the different genres. In short, this set of semiotic features, of representational resources, suggests and implies, and I would wish to say, over the longer term *produces* a particular disposition, a particular habitus and, in so doing, plays its part in the production of a particular kind of subjectivity, a subjectivity with certain orientations to 'rationality'.

Clearly, this paper speaks to, and is read by, a particular kind of reader. It would be a complete mistake to treat these aspects as merely formal, as marginal, as not of the core of the matter. On the contrary I would say that it is these formal matters as much as the 'lexis' of the front page which characterise this particular reader/subject (as well as the producer/subject). Features such as these sustain this subjectivity, as well as having their part in forming it. Even though the reciprocal effect between representational resources and subjectivity seems highly static, conservative, its transformative potential on the world and on the reading subject cannot be overestimated. The effort required to attempt to keep the world as it is, the mythic/ideological effort required day after day to maintain a stasis, is every bit as enormous as the efforts required to change the world. The semiotic as well as the political lesson here is that conservatism is an energetic enterprise.

The habitual reader of the *Frankfurter Allgemeine* (*FA*) is happy and comfortable with this paper precisely because there is a broad homology between the structure of the subjectivity of the reader, and the semiotic organisation of this text. It is, for him (or her?) a reader-friendly publication: even though it may not be our preferred notion of friendliness.

If we move, by contrast, to an English tabloid, the *Sun*, we are met by quite different representational resources: the prominence of the verbal has gone, or rather, it has been fundamentally transformed into 'display' rather than 'information' in the traditional sense (see Figure 2.5). Language has become, largely, a visual element. The very large photograph is in this sense, self-explanatory: that is, it signals directly the prominence of the visual in this paper. Language in the conventional sense is a minor, a nearly insignificant element. The introduction of colour is of course significant: rigorously avoided by the *FA* (though not, for instance, by the *Süddeutsche Zeitung*, which has small elements of colour – a sign of a transformation in progress): but it too signals a shift in the projected subjectivity of the reader. This is a reader, so the organisation of the representational resources imply, who does not have the time, the skill, the concentration or willingness to read in a focused fashion. This is a reader who just wants to get her or his perceptions immediately, directly.

Figure 2.5 Front page of the *Sun*

Information must be presented in a pleasurable fashion – hence the image, and hence particularly the colour.

It may be that the appearance of colour signals particularly strongly the shift in the implied and projected subject – the move from rationality information and *work* to entertainment, pleasure. Whereas the *FA* usually has about twelve textual items on its front page, the *Sun* has one. Here too lies a huge difference. The resources with which the world is approached, which are available for the transformation of the world, are fundamentally different. The *Sun* is totally synthetic: there is one account of what the world is today; the *FA* by comparison is analytic; there is a multiplicity of accounts of what the world is. This positions or constructs the reader's subjectivity in a radically different fashion. The transformative potential of the representational resources in each case is different. In the case of the *Sun*, synthesis at the 'lexical' ('what the world is about') level precludes, nearly, the possibility of transformation – though I leave out of account here the issue of the appearance of two distinct semiotic modes and their distinctive representations of content and of the effect of that. In the case of the *FA* analysis at the semiotic level (layout, typographical features) is combined with analysis at the lexical level. At best (and this is clearly said from a particular social, political and moral view) analysis at the semiotic level (the verbal, the visual, colour) in the *Sun* is combined with synthesis at the lexical level; the reader is given fewer resources for analysis and therefore for critique.

I wish to pause here just for a moment, to reflect again on the question of representational resources, their potentialities and limitations, and their effects on subjectivity. It seems to me that radically different resources are employed in the two cases; radically different transformative potentials made available; radically different subjectivities projected. If the *FA* feels friendly to its habituated reader, then we must assume that the *Sun* feels at least equally friendly to its readers also. But these are very different kinds of friends; if you can tell someone's character by the friends they have, then we have here fundamentally different social subjects.

Lest it be thought that this is a matter of 'the political message' and its divergence, here is an illustration of a paper with a totally divergent message from that of the *Sun*, the *Socialist Worker* (see Figure 2.6). In my view, this makes available representational resources which are very close to those of the *Sun*. For me the question is precisely that about subjectivity: which will have the *telling* effect, the configurations of the representational resources, or the 'lexis', the content, the material at the discursive level? There must, at the very least, be a huge question mark here.

The two issues here, those of representational resources and the production (transformation) of subjectivity and the huge issue of multiculturalism are for me brought together at the moment through the question of an apt curriculum. However that is, I think the question for us all in the CDA project is: the apt cultural, social curriculum, pursued in education, in the home and family, in the media, in churches. Let me draw your attention to two last examples, to make the point about cultural

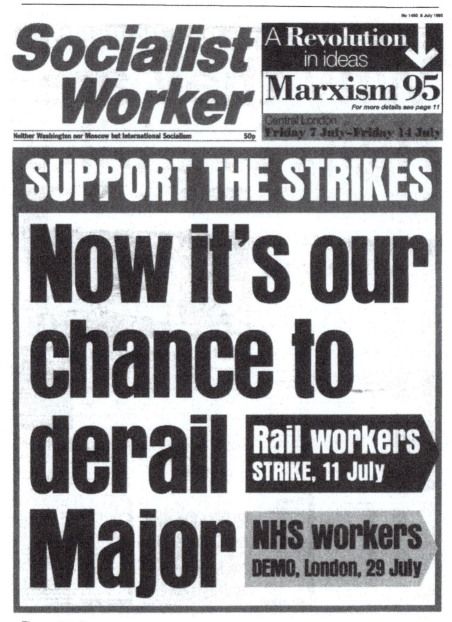

Figure 2.6 Front page of the *Socialist Worker*

Figure 2.7 Front page of the *Bild-Zeitung*

'Contras' tentam bloquear revisão

PT e PDT prometem criar dificuldades e na terça encaminham à Justiça novo recurso contra reforma da Carta

Figure 2.8 Front page of the *Folha de São Paulo*

difference, and to raise the question of production once again: how do we produce, how can we produce, a social subject able to reconcile these differences, contradictions, and transform them for himself or for herself into a multicultural subjectivity.

Class is clearly significant: and one difference between the *FA* and the *Sun*, rests precisely on that. Some of you will know the German equivalent of the *Sun* in terms of type of readership; it looks very different: it makes available representational resources of a different kind, in a different manner (see Figure 2.7). If the *Sun* editor's assumption about the subjectivities of his readership are correct, how can the *Bild* editor's assumptions about his audience also be correct? For one thing of course, there is precisely the question of habitus, as the product of myriad of practice: the *Sun*, as the *Bild* reader are habituated into adopting, transforming themselves into particular kinds of readers. But beyond that I imagine that there looms the much larger question of culture. There is an affinity between the *FA* and the *Bild-Zeitung*, which mirrors an affinity between the *Guardian* and the *Sun*. The former offer plurality, heterogeneity: *Bild* to an extreme that becomes chaotic. The latter offer reduction, simplification: the *Sun*, to an extreme that becomes the stasis of total synthesis. My question is: how does one construct a multicultural, a European subject, given this difference?

This is my question. I have no answer, though I have another example. Here is the front page of the *Folha de São Paulo* (see Figure 2.8). It is a middle-class intellectual paper. The front page suggests a subjectivity somewhere between the *Bild* and the *FA*, but with aspects of the *Sun* also (appeals to pleasure, for example). I cannot decide whether this is an instance of false middle-class intellectual assumption of populist values, or a real attempt at integration, at a first step in a series of transformations.

At any rate it seems to me that these are issues that our project needs to address: and it will need all our collaborative effort to develop a theory which can provide answers or, perhaps even solutions.

REFERENCES

Kress, G. (1993) 'Against arbitrariness: the social production of the sign as a foundational issue in Critical Discourse Analysis', *Discourse and Society* 4, 2: 169–91.
Thompson, J. (1991) *Ideology and Modern Culture*, Cambridge: Polity.

Chapter 3

The representation of social actors

Theo van Leeuwen

1 INTRODUCTION

The question I shall attempt to answer in this chapter can be formulated simply: what are the ways in which social actors can be represented in English discourse? Which choices does the English language give us for referring to people? In addition I shall address another, more specific question: how are the relevant social actors represented in an instance of a particular kind of racist discourse – a discourse which represents immigration in a way that is founded on fear – the fear of loss of livelihood and the fear of loss of cultural identity as a result of the 'influx' of immigrants who are perceived as 'other', 'different' and 'threatening'.

The first of these two questions is a grammatical one, if, with Halliday, we take a grammar to be a 'meaning potential' ('what *can* be said') rather than a set of rules ('what *must* be said'). Yet, unlike many other linguistically oriented forms of Critical Discourse Analysis, I shall not start out from linguistic operations such as nominalisation and passive agent deletion, or from linguistic categories such as the categories of transitivity, but instead seek to draw up a *sociosemantic* inventory of the ways in which social actors can be represented, and to establish the sociological and critical relevance of my categories before I turn to the question of how they are realised linguistically.

There are two reasons for doing so. The first stems from the lack of bi-uniqueness of language. Agency, for instance, as a *sociological* concept, is of major and classic importance in Critical Discourse Analysis: in which contexts are which social actors represented as 'agents' and which as 'patients'? But sociological agency is not always realised by linguistic agency, by the grammatical role of 'Agent'; it can also be realised in many other ways, for instance by possessive pronouns (as in 'our intake of migrants') or by a prepositional phrase with 'from', as in example 1.1, in which the grammatical Agent is sociologically 'patient':

1.1 People of Asian descent say they received a sudden cold-shoulder from neighbours and co-workers.

There is no neat fit between sociological and linguistic categories, and if Critical Discourse Analysis, in investigating for instance the representation of agency, ties itself in too closely to specific linguistic operations or categories, many relevant instances of agency might be overlooked. One cannot, it seems, have it both ways with language. Either theory and method are formally neat but semantically messy (as in the dictionary: one form, many meanings), or they are semantically neat but formally messy (as in the thesaurus: one concept, many possible realisations). Linguists tend towards preserving the unity of formal categories. I shall here attempt the opposite approach, hoping to provide a set of relevant categories for investigating the representation of social actors in discourse.

Halliday (1985: ch. 10) has approached the problem of the lack of bi-uniqueness in another way, through his theory of grammatical metaphor: certain linguistic realisations are 'literal' or 'congruent', others 'metaphorical' or 'incongruent'. But in Halliday's account 'congruent' would seem to mean 'congruent with the grammatical system', rather than 'congruent with reality', the kind of congruence which, in the end, underlies most definitions of metaphor. For Halliday a clause like 'The report confirms ...' would not be a metaphor, because it does not violate the criterion that verbal processes do not require a human 'Sayer' as their subject (cf. Halliday, 1985: 129). I would prefer to see 'the report confirms ...' as just one of the ways in which we can refer to social actors in their role as 'Sayers', as metaphorical or unmetaphorical as any other way, but endowed with its own specific sociosemantic import and hence social distribution: it is likely to be found in contexts where the authority of utterances is bound up with the official status or role of 'Sayers' and/or the official status of genres. In the context of literature, on the other hand, it would be less likely to occur, because there the authority of utterances is bound up with the charismatic personality of the writer, so that we would expect 'Shakespeare says ...' rather than 'the play says ...', for instance. I would therefore prefer to ask: how can 'Sayers' be represented – impersonally or personally, individually or collectively, by reference to their person or their utterance, etc. – without privileging any of these choices as more 'literal' than others, and without thereby also privileging the context or contexts in which one or the other tends to occur as more normative than others.

The second reason is somewhat different, and follows from the assumption that meaning belongs to culture rather than to language and cannot be tied to any specific semiotic. Language can represent social actions impersonally, as in this headline:

1.2 Allied air activity over battlefield intensifies

but so can pictures – think of the difference between, on the one hand, 'personalised' pictures of bombardments, say in feature film sequences showing, in close up, the faces of the crew as they drop the bombs, as well as the faces of the villagers down below as they are about to be bombed, and, on the other hand, diagrams of the same event, for instance maps with large arrows pointing at the targets and schematic drawings representing the explosions.

There is no space here to explore this point in detail (cf. van Leeuwen, 1987, for the representation of social actors in music; Kress and van Leeuwen, 1990, and van Leeuwen, 1993a, for parallels between language and images). Nevertheless, the categories I shall propose in this chapter should, in principle, be seen as pan-semiotic: a given culture (or a given context within a culture) has not only its own, specific array of ways of representing the social world, but also its own specific ways of mapping the different semiotics on to this array, of prescribing, with greater or lesser strictness, what can be realised verbally as well as visually, what only verbally, what only visually, and so on. And these arrangements will also be subject to historical change, sometimes even violent change, as in iconoclasms. The point is important for Critical Discourse Analysis, for, with the increasing use of visual representation in a wide range of contexts, it becomes more and more pressing to be able to ask the same critical questions with regard to both verbal and visual representations, indeed, with regard to representations in all the 'media' that form part of contemporary 'multimedia' texts.

Despite all this, this chapter still attempts to be grounded in linguistics. Each of the representational choices I shall propose will be tied to specific linguistic or rhetorical realisations. To return to my earlier examples, in the case of 'Shakespeare' the representational choice is that of 'nomination' and the realisation the use of a proper name, while in the case of 'the report confirms ...' the representational choice is that of 'utterance autonomisation' (see section 11 below) and the realisation the substitution of the utterance for its Sayer, hence a form of metonymical reference. The difference is that my primary focus is on sociological categories ('nomination', 'agency', etc.) rather than on linguistic categories ('nominalisation', 'passive agent deletion', etc.) and that the system network, the 'array of choices', I shall present in section 13 will range over a variety of linguistic and rhetorical phenomena, and find its unity in the concept of 'social actor', rather than in a linguistic concept such as, for instance, 'the nominal group'.

Finally, the chapter is part of a larger project (see van Leeuwen, 1993a; 1993b) in which I am attempting in addition to map how other elements of social practices (the social activities that constitute them, the times when and the locations where they occur, the dress and body grooming that go with them, etc.) are represented, and how representations add further elements to this, for instance the purposes and legitimations of the social practices, and the sentiments that accompany them. In short, the question addressed in this chapter is part of a larger question: how are social practices transformed into discourses about social practices – and this both in the sense of what means we have for doing so, and in the sense of how we actually do it in specific institutional contexts which have specific relations with the social practices of which they produce representations.

2 'OUR RACE ODYSSEY'

Below I reproduce the first three sections of 'Our Race Odyssey', the text from which I shall draw most of my examples, and which I use to demonstrate how the categories I propose may be used in text analysis. It was published as the leading feature article in 'Spectrum', the Saturday supplement of the *Sydney Morning Herald*, a conservative broadsheet newspaper, on 12 May 1990.

The descriptive framework I shall present in the following sections was worked out with the aid of a much larger and generically diverse corpus of texts which included fictional narratives, comic strips, news stories, newspaper editorials, advertisements, textbooks and scholarly essays, all dealing, in some form or other, with the subject of schooling, and more specifically with the transition from home to school (van Leeuwen, 1993b). As one text can never provide instances of all the categories and modes of representation, I shall, throughout the chapter, also use examples from this corpus.

1   2001: Our Race Odyssey.
2   This country will be vastly different next century if Australians feel they cannot voice legitimate fears about immigration without being branded racists, argues David Jenkins.
3   In Florence last month 80 young white thugs, many wearing costume masks and armed with iron bars, roamed the narrow cobbled streets attacking African street vendors.
4   In France, where non-European immigrants make up 6.5 per cent of the population, former president Valéry Giscard d'Estaing proposed a total halt to immigration.
5   In Japan, a nation with a strong tradition of keeping foreigners at arm's length, similar concerns are being expressed about a mere trickle of Third World immigrants.
6   Japan's National Police Agency had to apologise recently for circulating an internal memo to police stations claiming that Pakistanis

working in Japan 'have a unique body odour', carry infectious skin diseases and tell lies 'under the name of Allah'.

7 The mayor of Kawaguchi has 'joked' that with so many dark-skinned foreigners in town, Japanese are having trouble seeing them at night.

8 In Peru, where the son of Japanese immigrants is a presidential front-runner, the situation is reversed.

9 A racist backlash against ethnic Asians has been unleashed by those who resent the prominence of centrist candidate Alberto Fujimori.

10 People of Asian descent say they have been insulted in the street, denied entry to elegant restaurants and received a sudden cold-shoulder from neighbours and co-workers.

11 In Canada, where the 250,000-strong Sikh community has pressed for the right to have Mounties in turbans and where 22,000 Hong Kong Chinese arrived last year, bringing bulging wallets to cities like Vancouver, racial tolerance is wearing thin.

12 'Native Vancouverites will be made to feel like strangers in their own city as the influx of Asians and their capital freezes them out', wrote one reader of *The Province* newspaper in Vancouver.

13 If you were sitting in Canberra and doing no more than reading the daily newspapers you would be entitled to be a bit concerned by these developments.

14 They italicise the lesson that people, whatever their race, display their less attractive characteristics when they feel threatened and unable to cope with rapid change in the society around them.

15 They highlight the fact that racism is seldom far below the surface – whether it is in Western Europe, in Asia, in North or South America.

16 They may even call into question some aspects of Australia's immigration programme, which is now running at close to record levels, with annual net migration of about 150,000, including 60,000 migrants from Asia.

17 Is the Australian Government concerned?

18 Not a bit.

19 Prime Minister Bob Hawke says he is 'philosophically' a high-migration man.

20 He thinks our current intake is about right.

21 'I hope that as we go on,' he said recently, 'that we may be able to look at higher levels of immigration.'

22 Is the Prime Minister entitled to be quite so confident that we have got our immigration policy settings right?

23 Is he entitled to believe that this nation, which only recently shed the White Australia Policy, is somehow impervious to racist sentiment?

24 On the evidence to date there is some reason to suppose that he is.

25 We have had one of the most successful immigration programmes in the world.

possible. It requires that the regimes and their agents be put constantly in the role of promoters of progress, law and order, concerned to eliminate social evil and conflict, but never responsible for it.

(Trew, 1979: 106)

Some exclusions leave no traces in the representation, excluding both the social actors and their activities. Such radical exclusion can play a role in a critical comparison of different representations of the same social practice, but not in an analysis of a single text, for the simple reason that it leaves no traces behind. In my study of the representation of schooling (van Leeuwen, 1993b), for instance, I found that fathers were radically excluded in texts addressing teachers, but included in many children's stories, even if often only briefly, during the breakfast preceding the first school day, or as givers of satchels, pencil cases and other school necessities. Children's stories aimed at a mass market sometimes included school support staff, but excluded the headmistress, while more 'upmarket' children's stories included the headmistress but excluded people lower than teachers in the school hierarchy, in what is clearly a class-related pattern of inclusion and exclusion.

When the activities (e.g. the killing of demonstrators) are included, but some or all of the social actors involved in it (e.g. the police) are excluded, the exclusion does leave a trace. We can ask 'but who did the killing?' or 'but who was killed?', even though the text does not provide the answers. In this case a further distinction should perhaps be made, the distinction between *suppression* and *backgrounding*. In the case of suppression, there is no reference to the social actor(s) in question anywhere in the text. Thus we learn, in the 'Race Odyssey' text, that someone or some institution surveyed the opinions of the public, but we do not find out which individual or company or other institution did it, which takes away at least one possible avenue of contesting the results of the 'surveys'. In the case of backgrounding, the exclusion is less radical: the excluded social actors may not be mentioned in relation to a given activity, but they are mentioned elsewhere in the text, and we can infer with reasonable (though never total) certainty who they are. They are not so much excluded as de-emphasised, pushed into the background.

How is suppression realised? First there is, of course, the classic realisation through passive agent deletion. Example 3.1 tells us that 'concerns are being expressed', but not who expresses them:

3.1 In Japan similar concerns are being expressed about a mere trickle of Third World immigrants.

Suppression can also be realised through non-finite clauses which function as a grammatical participant. In example 3.2 the infinitival clause 'to maintain this policy' is embedded to function as the Carrier of an attributive clause, and this allows the social actor(s) responsible for the 'maintenance' of the policy to be excluded – and they *could* have been included, for instance, as 'for local education authorities'. The downranking of the process ('maintain') makes the fact that exclusion has taken place a little less accessible, the trace a little less clear:

3.2 To maintain this policy is hard.

It is almost always possible to delete 'Beneficiaries', social actors who benefit from an activity. Example 3.3, for instance, does not include those to whom the 'National Police Agency' apologised (the Pakistanis who had been offended?):

3.3 Japan's National Police Agency had to apologise recently for circulating an internal memo to police stations claiming that Pakistanis working in Japan 'have a unique body odour', carry infectious skin diseases and tell lies 'under the name of Allah'.

Nominalisations and process nouns similarly allow the exclusion of social actors. 'Support' and 'stopping', in example 3.4, function as nominals, although they refer to activities. The same applies to 'immigration'. Again the excluded social actors *could* have been included, for instance through postmodifying phrases with *by, of, from*, etc., but they haven't been:

3.4 The level of support for stopping immigration altogether was at a postwar high.

Processes may also be realised as adjectives, as is the case with 'legitimate' in example 3.5. Who 'legitimises' the 'fear'? The writer? We cannot be sure. The fears simply *are* legitimate, according to this representation:

3.5 Australians feel they cannot voice legitimate fears about immigration.

The activity in example 3.6 involves a human actor, the teacher who opens the door. But coding the activity in middle voice (Halliday, 1985: 150–1) necessitates the exclusion of the agentive participant. The context may lead us to infer that the teacher was involved, but there can be no certainty – it might, for instance, have been the wind. The clause invites a reading in which the opening of the door, the intrusion of the teacher in the child's world of play, is given the force of a natural event.

3.6 The door of the playhouse opened and the teacher looked in.

It is often difficult to know whether suppressed social actors are or are not supposed to be retrievable by the reader, or, indeed, the writer. Example 3.4, for instance, does not tell us who is involved in the act of 'stopping immigration'. Is this because readers are assumed to know already, so that more detailed reference would be overcommunicative, or is it to block access to detailed knowledge of a practice which, if represented in detail, might arouse compassion for those who are 'stopped'? The point is that the practice is here represented as something not to be further examined or contested.

Backgrounding can result from simple ellipses in non-finite clauses with *-ing* and *-ed* participles, in infinitival clauses with *to*, and in paratactic clauses. In all these cases the excluded social actor is *in*cluded elsewhere in the same clause or clause complex. It can also be realised in the same way as suppression, but with respect to social actors who *are* included elsewhere in the text. The two realisations background social actors to different degrees, but both play a part in reducing the number of times specific social actors are explicitly referred to.

To discuss the pattern of inclusion and exclusion in the 'Race Odyssey' text, it is necessary to bring the various ways in which each category of social actor is represented under a common denominator. These common denominators do not, of course, form a more transparent or congruent way of referring to them. They merely serve as an anchor for the analysis, a kind of calibration. For the purposes of analysis, then, I shall call 'racists' those social actors who, actively or otherwise, oppose immigration and immigrants in countries other than Australia, and I shall refer to those who do the same in Australia as 'us'. Again, this is not to say that the latter are *not* racist, but merely to follow the distinction that underlies the way the author argues his case. I shall refer to the immigrants themselves as 'them', to the (Australian) Government as 'government', to the various experts invoked by the writer as 'experts', to the writer himself as 'writer', and to his readers, who are sometimes addressed directly, as 'addressees'. Bruce Ruxton, the 'racist' Australians love to hate, is a category on his own ('our racist'), and finally there are a few minor characters who appear only once, the 'anti-racists' who 'brand as racist' the 'legitimate fears of Australians', 'Allah', 'European Governments' and (Japanese) 'police stations'. Table 3.1 displays the patterns of inclusion and exclusion.

Although the differences are not dramatic, it is clear that the most frequently included social actors are the Australian Government and 'us', Australians, who voice 'legitimate fears', while the most frequently backgrounded or suppressed social actors are, on the one hand, the immigrants, and on the other hand those in other countries who commit such

Table 3.1 Inclusion and exclusion in the 'Race Odyssey' text

	Included %	Backgrounded %	Suppressed %
'racists' (N=24)	67.25	20.25	12.5
'us' (N=46)	72	24	4
'them' (N=98)	61	38	1
'government' (N=32)	73	18	9

racist acts as 'insulting' and 'denying entry to elegant restaurants', and, indeed, people in general, as they are 'naturally inclined to racism' and will 'display unpleasant characteristics when they feel threatened'. In short, those who do not take part in the 'debate' between the Australian people and its government which the writer stages for us in his argument form to some extent a backdrop to this debate.

I do not want to make great claims for treating texts statistically. On the contrary, it is important to realise that the frequencies may shift with the stages in the writer's argument. In the first section of the text, where the writer discusses racism in other countries, migrants are backgrounded in 17 per cent of cases. As soon as the writer moves to his discussion of Australian immigration policy, this increases to 36 per cent. In other words, the migrants close to home are backgrounded more often. In any case, the pattern of inclusion and exclusion must be integrated with the *way in which* they are represented, which I shall discuss in the remainder of this chapter.

What, finally, remains most opaque in this text? First, the voice of the opposition – those who 'brand as racist' Australians 'who voice legitimate fears' are fully suppressed. Second, many of the 'racists' in other countries: we are not told who exactly is responsible for 'insulting people of Asian descent' or 'denying them entry to elegant restaurants', for example. Third, the voice of legitimation, which 'legitimises fears', and which 'entitles' Hawke and 'us' to the view which, by virtue of their sheer prominence in the text, the writer obliquely favours. And finally, those who have to do the dirty work of actually 'stopping' ('halting', 'cutting', etc.) the immigrants.

4 ROLE ALLOCATION

I shall now consider the roles that social actors are given to play in representations, an aspect of representation which also plays a significant part in the work of many critical linguists (e.g. Fairclough, 1989; Fowler, 1991; Fowler *et al.*, 1979; Kress and Hodge, 1979; van Dijk, 1991): who is represented as 'agent' ('Actor'), who as 'patient' ('Goal') with respect to a given action? This question remains important, for there need not be congruence between the roles that social actors actually play in social practices and the grammatical roles they are given in texts. Representations can reallocate roles, rearrange the social relations between the participants. Here is an example, from the field of television studies:

4.1 Children seek out aspects of commercial television as a consolidation and confirmation of their everyday lives. . . . The kids use it [television] subversively against the rule-bound culture and institution of the school.
(Curthoys and Docker, 1989: 68)

4.2 Television affects children's sex-role attitudes. . . . Furthermore, television has been shown to influence more subtle areas such as racial attitudes and cultural views.
(Tuchman *et al.*, 1978: 232)

Leaving aside aspects of the representation of social actors we have not yet discussed (objectivations such as 'television' and 'subtle areas'; abstractions such as 'aspects of commercial television') and the exclusions (e.g. in 'racial attitudes and cultural views'), the two major categories of social actor represented are 'children' and 'television'. In Example 4.1, 'children' and 'the kids' are, grammatically, Actor in relation to activities such as 'seeking out' and 'using' (and also, if one ignores the backgrounding, of 'consolidating' and 'confirming'), while 'television' ('aspects of commercial television' and 'it') is the Goal of both these processes. In 4.2, 'television' is Actor of 'affect' and 'influence', while 'children' ('children's sex-role attitudes'; 'subtle areas such as racial attitudes and cultural views') are Goal. In other words, in one of the representations (that of a populist, 'active audience' theory) the active role is given to children, the passive role to television, while in the other (that of the 'effects' or 'hypodermic needle' theory of mass communication) the active role is given to television and the passive role to children. The two examples deal, in the end, with the same reality, but which of them corresponds best to that reality is of course a problem text analysis cannot solve. What we *can* do, however, is investigate which options are chosen in which institutional and social contexts, and why these choices should have been taken up, what interests are served by them, and what purposes achieved.

I shall say, then, that representations can endow social actors with either active or passive roles. *Activation* occurs when social actors are represented as the active, dynamic forces in an activity, *passivation* when they are represented as 'undergoing' the activity, or as being 'at the receiving end of it'. This may be realised by grammatical participant roles, by transitivity structures in which activated social actors are coded as Actor in material processes, Behaver in behavioural processes, Senser in mental processes, Sayer in verbal processes or Assigner in relational processes (Halliday, 1985: ch. 5). In 4.3, for example, 'they' (i.e. 'us', Australians) are Actor in relation to the process of 'feeling', but 'immigration' (i.e. 'immigrants'; 'them') is activated in relation to 'besieging'. In 4.4, on the other hand, 'young white thugs' are activated and 'African street vendors' passivated. In other words, while in other countries there may be active racists, in Australia the migrants play the active (and 'threatening') role, and 'we' are at best activated as 'Sensers' in relation to mental processes such as 'feeling'.

4.3 They felt 'besieged' by immigration.

4.4 80 young white thugs attacked African street vendors.

When, as in these cases, activation is realised by 'participation' (grammatical participant roles), the active role of the social actor in question is most clearly foregrounded; note how, in examples 4.1 and 4.2, active roles are realised by participation, passive roles in other, more highly transformed ways. But activation can also be realised in other ways, for example through 'circumstantialisation', that is by prepositional circumstantials with *by* or *from*, as with 'from neighbours and co-workers' in:

4.5 People of Asian descent suddenly received a cold-shoulder from neighbours and co-workers.

Premodification (e.g. 'public' in 'public support') or postmodification (e.g. 'of Asians' in 'the influx of Asians') of nominalisations or process nouns can also realise activation. A frequent form of this is 'possessivation', the use of a possessive pronoun to activate (e.g. 'our intake') or passivate (e.g. 'my teacher') a social actor. By comparison to participation this backgrounds agency, changing it into the 'possession' of a process which has itself been transformed into a 'thing'.

Passivation necessitates a further distinction: the passivated social actor can be *subjected* or *beneficialised*. Subjected social actors are treated as objects in the representation, for instance as objects of exchange (immigrants 'taken in' in return for the skill or the money they bring). Beneficialised social actors form a third party which, positively or negatively, benefits from it. In 4.6, for instance, 'about 70,000 migrants' are subjected to the activity of 'bringing in'; in 4.7 'cities like Vancouver' are beneficialised in relation to 'bringing':

4.6 Australia was bringing in about 70,000 migrants a year.

4.7 22,000 Hong Kong Chinese arrived last year, bringing bulging wallets to cities like Vancouver.

There is a cryptogrammatical criterion for considering both these roles passivations: Goals as well as Beneficiaries can become subjects in passive clauses. But there is of course also a grammatical criterion for distinguishing them: Beneficiaries can take a preposition (although they do not have to: see Halliday, 1985: 132ff), Goals cannot (with the exception of very few cases, such as 'What did John do with the dinner?').

Like activation, subjection can be realised in various ways. It is realised by 'participation' when the passivated social actor is Goal in a material process, Phenomenon in a mental process, or Carrier in an effective attributive process (Halliday, 1985: 143) – 'African street vendors' in 4.4 is an example. It can also be realised by 'circumstantialisation' through a prepositional phrase with, for instance, *against*, as in 4.8, where 'ethnic Asians' are passivated:

4.8 A racist backlash against ethnic Asians has been unleashed by those who resent the prominence of centrist candidate Alberto Fujimori.

And it can also be realised by 'possessivation', usually in the form of a prepositional phrase with *of* postmodifying a nominalisation or process noun, as with 'of some 54,000 skilled immigrants' in 4.9:

4.9 An intake of some 54,000 skilled immigrants is expected this year.

Finally, adjectival premodification can also passivate, as, for example, with 'racial' in 'racial tolerance', where (people of different) races are passivated; the example also *abstracts* the social actors represented.

Beneficialisation may be realised either by participation, in which case the beneficialised participant is Recipient or Client in relation to a material process, or Receiver in relation to a verbal process (Halliday, 1985: 132–3). Table 3.2 shows how the 'Race Odyssey' text allocates roles to the most frequently represented social actors.

It is clear that 'racists', 'government' and 'us' most often act upon the immigrants, be it materially or symbolically, and that the immigrants themselves are activated only, or almost only, in relation to one action, the act of immigrating ('influx', 'arriving', etc.), and this mostly in nominalised and deeply embedded form.

Table 3.2 Role allocation in the 'Race Odyssey' text

	Activated %	Subjected %	Beneficialised %
'racists' (N=21)	81	14	5
'us' (N=40)	85	12.5	2.5
'them' (N=66)	53	45	2
'government' (N=29)	86	7	7

5 GENERICISATION AND SPECIFICATION

The choice between generic and specific reference is another important factor in the representation of social actors; they can be represented as classes or as specific, identifiable individuals. Compare, for instance, the following two texts:

5.1. The reference is specific since we have in mind specific specimens of the class tiger.

(Quirk *et al.*, 1972: 147)

5.2. Classification is an instrument of control in two directions: control over the flux of experience of physical and social reality ... and society's control over conceptions of that reality.

(Kress and Hodge, 1979: 63)

The first example betrays a view of reality in which generalised essences, classes, constitute the real, and in which specific participants are 'specimens' of those classes. In the second example the real is constituted by the 'flux of experience', by a specific, concrete world, populated with specific, concrete people, places, things and actions, and 'classification' is seen as an operation upon this reality, which creates a kind of second order reality, a 'conception of reality'.

Sociologists have linked such concepts of reality to social class. For Bourdieu (1986) concrete reference to immediate experience is linked to the habitus of the working class, that is, to the principles that lie behind their appreciation of art, music and literature, behind their moral and political judgements and so on. 'Distance, height, the overview of the observer who places himself above the hurly-burly' (Bourdieu, 1986: 444), on the other hand, is linked to the habitus of the dominant class, the bourgeoisie, and Bourdieu approvingly quotes Virginia Woolf's dictum that 'general ideas are always Generals' ideas'. From this perspective, he says, specific reference is a 'blind, narrow, partial vision' (Bourdieu, 1986: 444). In a similar vein, Bernstein (e.g. 1971: 197) has argued that 'elaborated codes' give access to 'universalistic orders of meaning', while restricted codes give access to 'particularistic orders of meaning', and that access to these codes is class-determined.

The difference can be observed, for instance, in the way that social actors are represented by different sectors of the press. In middle-class oriented newspapers government agents and experts tend to be referred to specifically, and 'ordinary people' generically: the point of identification, the world in which one's specifics exist, is here, not the world of the governed, but the world of the governors, the 'generals'. In working-class oriented newspapers, on the other hand, 'ordinary people' are frequently referred to specifically. The following two examples illustrate the difference. They deal with the same topic and the articles from which they are taken appeared on the same day, their news value deriving from the same statement by Australia's Minister for Sport and Recreation. The first comes from the *Sydney Morning Herald*, a middle-class oriented newspaper, the second from the *Daily Telegraph*, a working-class oriented newspaper:

5.3 Australia has one of the highest childhood drowning rates in the world, with children under 5 making up a quarter of the toll, this is the grim news from Government studies of Australia's high incidence of drowning. The studies show over 500 people drown in Australia every year, with backyard swimming pools the biggest killers for children under 15. The Minister for Sport and Recreation, Mr Brown, said the childhood drowning rate was higher than developed countries such as Britain and the US and comparable with many Asian countries. He said children should be encouraged to swim and parents should learn resuscitation techniques.

5.4 The tragic drowning of a toddler in a backyard swimming pool has mystified his family. Matthew Harding, two, one of twin boys, had to climb over a one-metre 'child-proof' fence before he fell into the pool. Mrs Desley Harding found Matthew floating in the pool when she went to call the twins in for tea yesterday. 'I have got no idea how he got in the pool', said Mrs Harding at her home in Wentworthville South today.

Genericisation may be realised by the plural without article, as in 5.5:

5.5 Non-European immigrants make up 6.5 per cent of the population.

and it may also be realised by the singular with a definite article (5.6) or indefinite article (5.7):

5.6 Allow the child to cling to something familiar during times of distress.

5.7 Maybe a child senses that from her mother.

If mass nouns are used for generic reference to a group of participants, the article will be absent, but this form can also be used for specific reference: generic reference is clearly dependent on a complex of factors, including also tense, and 5.8 has been interpreted as specific mainly because of the absence of habitual or universal present tense:

5.8 Staff in both playgroups and nurseries expressed willingness to supply information if asked and regretted that their opinions were not valued more.

The presence of a Numerative, finally, has been interpreted as realising specific reference.

Even though one expects a certain amount of generic reference in a general argument, which is what the 'Race Odyssey' text purports to be, this does not mean that all categories of social actor are equally often genericised. 'Racists' in other countries, and 'them', the immigrants, are genericised most often (32 and 48 per cent respectively) and so symbolically removed from the readers' world of immediate experience, treated as distant 'others' rather than as people 'we' have to deal with in our everyday lives. The 'government' and 'us', on the other hand, are less often genericised (17 and 15 per cent respectively).

6 ASSIMILATION

Social actors can be referred to as individuals, in which case I shall speak of *individualisation*, or as groups, in which case I shall speak of *assimilation*. Given the great value which is placed on individuality in many spheres of our society (and the value placed on conformity in others) these categories would have to be of primary significance in Critical Discourse Analysis. Examples 5.3 and 5.4 already showed that middle-class oriented newspapers tend to individualise elite persons and assimilate 'ordinary people', while working-class oriented newspapers quite often individualise 'ordinary people'. In my study of 'schooling texts' (van Leeuwen, 1993b) I analysed an item from the ABC (Australian Broadcasting Corporation) radio programme 'Offspring', which deals with issues of interest to parents. One of the expert panellists in the programme made an explicit plea for individualisation, but – experts will be experts, and schools schools – individualisation was, itself, assimilated. The children, despite the emphasis on difference, were represented as groups:

6.1 However you manipulate the age of entry into school, you are always going to have the situation where you have children of different kinds of development and with different skills coming into a school programme. And the important thing is to make sure that the programme is adapted to meet the needs of all these children coming in.

I shall distinguish two major kinds of assimilation, *aggregation* and *collectivisation*. The former quantifies groups of participants, treating them as 'statistics', the latter does not. Aggregation plays a crucial role in many contexts. In our society the majority rules, not just in contexts in which formal democratic procedures are used to arrive at decisions, but also and especially in others, through mechanisms such as opinion polls, surveys, marketing research, etc. Even legislative reform is increasingly based on 'what most people consider legitimate'. For this reason aggregation is often used to regulate practice and to manufacture consensus opinion, even though it presents itself as merely recording facts. Example 6.2 can be seen as an instance of this use of aggregation:

6.2 This concern, the report noted, was reflected in surveys which showed that the level of support for stopping migration altogether was at a postwar high.

Individualisation is realised by singularity, and assimilation by plurality, as with 'Australians' and 'Muslims' in 6.3:

6.3 Australians tend to be sceptical about admitting 'Muslims'.

Alternatively, assimilation may be realised by a mass noun or a noun denoting a group of people, as, for instance, with 'this nation' in 6.4 and 'the community' in 6.5:

6.4 Is he [i.e. Prime Minister Hawke] entitled to believe that this nation, which only recently shed the White Australia Policy, is somehow impervious to racist sentiment?

6.5 The 250,000-strong Sikh community has pressed for the right to have Mounties in turbans.

Aggregation is realised by the presence of definite or indefinite quantifiers, which either function as the Numerative or as the Head of the nominal group, as with 'a number of critics' in 6.6 and 'forty per cent of Australians' in 6.7:

6.6 A number of critics want to see our intake halved to 70,000.

6.7 Forty per cent of Australians were born overseas.

The 'Race Odyssey' text individualises 'racists' and 'immigrants' only when they are also elite persons (Valéry Giscard d'Estaing, the mayor of Kawaguchi, and the presidential candidate (son of immigrants) from Peru, the only 'immigrant' in this category). The individualisation of racism within Australia, in the person of Bruce Ruxton, 'our racist', shows that, in the press, notoriety confers as much elite status as does high office.

'We', the people of Australia, are of course mostly collectivised, not only through the first person plural, but also through terms like 'Australia', 'this nation', 'the community', etc. The government, on the other hand, is mostly individualised – the leader as a strong individual, the people as a homogeneous, consensual group.

'Experts' are collectivised ('the committee', 'surveys'), which helps to signal their agreement. In the remainder of the article, however, they are often individualised, which allows their titles, credentials and institutional affiliations to be showcased.

As indicated already, immigrants are most frequently aggregated, treated as 'statistics', and rather than that this is used to realise frequency modality (as in 'many Australians'), it makes them not only the object of 'rational' economic calculation, but also that large horde 'legitimately feared' by Australians.

7 ASSOCIATION AND DISSOCIATION

There is another way in which social actors can be represented as groups: *association*. Association, in the sense in which I shall use the term here, refers to groups formed by social actors and/or groups of social actors (either generically or specifically referred to) which are never labelled in the text (although the actors or groups who make up the association may of course themselves be named and/or categorised). The most common realisation of association is parataxis, as in this example:

7.1 They believed that the immigration program existed for the benefit of politicians, bureaucrats, and the ethnic minorities, not for Australians as a whole.

Here 'politicians, bureaucrats and ethnic minorities' are associated to form a group opposed to the interests of 'Australians as a whole'. But, rather than being represented as stable and institutionalised, the group is represented as an alliance which exists only in relation to a specific activity or set of activities, in this case their beneficiary role in relation to immigration.

Association may also be realised by 'circumstances of accompaniment' (Halliday, 1985: 141), as in:

7.2 They played 'higher and higher' with the other children.

In this case the association is, perhaps, even more fleeting and unstable.

Possessive pronouns and possessive attributive clauses with verbs like 'have' and 'belong' can make an association explicit without naming the resulting social grouping. In this case, however, the association is represented as more stable and enduring, and, indeed, 'possessive', as in this example, where 'problems' is clearly an abstract reference to a specific kind of immigrant: with other kinds of immigrants an association may be formed, with this kind of immigrant it must be 'avoided':

7.3 We have avoided most of the problems that bedevil Western Europe because few of our non-European migrants have been poor, black, unskilled, Muslim or illegal.

In many texts associations are formed and unformed ('dissociation') as the text proceeds. In one children's story I studied, for instance, there existed, prior to entering school for the first time, an association between two children from the same neighbourhood. As they walked to school and shared their worries, they were always referred to as 'Mark and Mandy'. But the association was disbanded as soon as they entered the classroom. From that moment they were referred to either separately, or as part of the collective of the 'class'.

There are only a few associations in the 'Race Odyssey' text: the lines between the parties are sharply drawn. Two of the associations lump different ethnic origins together ('Asia and the Middle East', 'Lebanese, Turks and Vietnamese'), another associates the 'neighbours and co-workers' who give 'ethnic Asians' the cold-shoulder. The cases of 'our non-European migrants', 'politicians, bureaucrats and ethnic minorities' I have already mentioned.

8 INDETERMINATION AND DIFFERENTIATION

Indetermination occurs when social actors are represented as unspecified, 'anonymous' individuals or groups, *determination* when their identity is, one way or another, specified. Indetermination is typically realised by indefinite pronouns ('somebody', 'someone', 'some', 'some people') used in nominal function, as in this example from a children's book, where a member of the school support staff is indeterminated:

8.1 Someone had put flowers on the teacher's desk.

Here indetermination *anonymises* a social actor. The writer treats his or her identity as irrelevant to the reader. Indetermination can also be realised by generalised exophoric reference, and in this case it endows social actors with a kind of impersonal authority, a sense of unseen, yet powerfully felt coercive force:

8.2 They won't let you go to school until you're five years old.

Indetermination can also be aggregated, as, for example, in: 'many believe ...', 'some say ...', etc.

Differentiation explicitly differentiates an individual social actor or group of social actors from a similar actor or group, creating the difference between the 'self' and the 'other', or between 'us' and 'them', as with 'others' in:

8.3 And though many of the new migrants are educated high-achievers from places like Singapore and Hong Kong – 'uptown' people in American terminology – others are 'downtown' people from places like Vietnam, the Philippines and Lebanon.

There are only two cases of this in the 'Race Odyssey' text, the one just quoted, and the 'other community leaders' (i.e. other than 'politicians and bureaucrats').

When I compared middle-class oriented and mass-market oriented children's stories about the 'first day at school' (van Leeuwen, 1993b), I found that differentiation plays an important role in the former, but does not occur much in the latter. Middle-class children are apparently encouraged to see themselves as individuals, different from 'the other children', and much of the trauma of 'the first day', as represented in these stories, consists in a kind of identity crisis, the child's discovery that she is not unique:

8.4. Mummy, did you know there is another Mary in my class?

The readers of the mass-market oriented stories, on the other hand, are encouraged to take pleasure in their ability to conform successfully.

9 NOMINATION AND CATEGORISATION

Social actors can be represented either in terms of their unique identity, by being *nominated*, or in terms of identities and functions they share with others (*categorisation*), and it is, again, always of interest to investigate which social actors are, in a given discourse, categorised and which nominated. In stories, for instance, nameless characters fulfil only passing, functional roles, and do not become points of identification for the reader or listener. In press 'stories' something similar occurs. We saw, for instance, how a middle-class newspaper nominated only a high-status person, a government minister, while a working-class oriented newspaper, in an article on the same topic, nominated 'ordinary people' (examples 5.3 and 5.4). The press, and not only the press, also tends to nominate men and women in different ways (cf. the types of nomination discussed below). The following sets of examples were taken from the same *Guardian* articles:

9.1 Dwight Harris, aged 32 . . . his wife Beverley, aged 33.

9.2 Carole Maychill, a 32-year-old captain . . . Colonel Robert Pepper.

Nomination is typically realised by proper nouns, which can be *formal* (surname only, with or without honorifics), *semi-formal* (given name and surname, as with 'Dwight Harris' in 9.1) or *informal* (given name only, as with 'Beverley' in 9.1). Occasionally what we might call 'name obscuration' occurs: letters or numbers replace names (e.g. 'Mr X') so that nomination can be signified while the name is, at the same time, withheld. All nominations can be used as vocatives and do not occur with a possessive pronoun, except in contexts of special endearment (e.g. 'My Cathy . . .') at least in English – in other languages the possessive pronoun does not necessarily suggest special endearment (cf. the French 'Mon Capitaine', 'Mon Général').

Items other than proper names may be used for nomination, especially when, in a given context, only one social actor occupies a certain rank or fulfils a certain function. Nominations of this kind in fact blur the dividing line between nomination and categorisation. They are common in stories for young children, with characters referred to as 'The Little Boy', 'The Giant', 'Rabbit', etc., even in vocatives:

9.3 Turkish Sultan, give me back my diamond button.

Nominations may be titulated, either in the form of honorification, the addition of standard titles, ranks, etc. as with 'Dr' in 9.4, or in the form of affiliations, the addition of a personal or kinship relation term, as with 'Auntie Barbara' in 9.5:

9.4 In 50 years, Dr Price says, 26 per cent of the Australian population will be Asian.

9.5 They started out, Auntie Barbara pushing Debbie in her pram.

Press journalists often use what Bell (1985: 98) has called 'pseudo titles', such as 'controversial cancer therapist Milan Brych'. As in standard titles, the definite article is absent in such pseudo titles, but otherwise categorisation and nomination are mixed here, or rather, categorisations are used as unique identities, much as in the children's stories quote above.

The 'Race Odyssey' text nominates heads of government (Valéry Giscard d'Estaing, Prime Minister Bob Hawke), 'our racist' Bruce Ruxton, 'experts' (especially in the section that follows the excerpt in section 2 above, where four different experts are quoted extensively, all in favour of cutting back immigration, and all nominated and titulated), and the writer, who thereby places himself in high company. Not nominated (and absences are as significant in critical discourse analysis as presences) are 'racists' in other countries, 'us' Australians, and, of course, the immigrants, with the exception of that high-status immigrants' son, Alberto Fujimori, the Peruvian presidential candidate.

10 FUNCTIONALISATION AND IDENTIFICATION

I shall distinguish two key types of categorisation, *functionalisation* and *identification*. Functionalisation occurs when social actors are referred to in terms of an activity, in terms of something they do, for instance an occupation or role. It is typically realised in one of the following ways: first, by a noun, formed from a verb, through suffixes such as *-er, -ant, -ent, -ian, -ee*, e.g. 'interviewer', 'celebrant', 'correspondent', 'guardian', 'payee'; second, by a noun formed from another noun which denotes a place or tool closely associated with an activity (a noun which, in Halliday's terms (1985: 134ff) forms the 'Range' of that activity) through suffixes such as *-ist, -eer*, e.g. 'pianist', 'mountaineer'; third, by the compounding of nouns denoting places or tools closely associated with an activity and highly generalised categorisations such as 'man', 'woman', 'person', 'people' (occasionally functionalisations such as 'assistant'), as in 'cameraman', 'chairperson'.

Identification occurs when social actors are defined, not in terms of what they do, but in terms of what they, more or less permanently, or unavoidably, are. I have distinguished three types: *classification, relational identification* and *physical identification*.

In the case of classification, social actors are referred to in terms of the major categories by means of which a given society or institution differentiates between classes of people. In our society these include age, gender, provenance, class, wealth, race, ethnicity, religion, sexual orientation, and so on. But classification categories are historically and culturally variable. What in one period or culture is represented as 'doing', as a more or less impermanent role, may in another be represented as 'being', as a more or less fixed identity. Foucault (1981) has described how, in the late nineteenth century, the discourse of sexology introduced a new classification category, 'sexual orientation'. Social actors who previously were functionalised ('sodomites') were now, increasingly, classified:

> Homosexuality appeared as one of the forms of sexuality when it was transposed from the practice of sodomy onto a kind of interior androgyny, a hermaphrodism of the soul. The sodomite had been a temporary aberration; the homosexual was now a species.
>
> (Foucault, 1981: 42)

At present the category of 'belonging to a company or organisation' begins to play a more important role in identification (cf. 'a Warwick University scientist', 'a Hambro Countrywide Chain spokesman').

The extent to which functionalisation and classification are distinct is also historically and culturally variable. Sociological role theory goes a long way in blurring the two types of categorisation:

> Every role in society has attached to it a certain identity. As we have seen, some of these identities are trivial and temporary ones, as in some occupations that demand little modification in the being of their practitioners. It is not difficult to change from garbage collector to night watchman. It is considerably more difficult to change from clergyman to officer. It is very, very difficult to change from negro to white. And it is almost impossible to change from man to woman. These differences in the ease of role changing ought not to blind us to the fact that even identities we consider to be our essential selves have been socially assigned.
>
> (P. L. Berger, 1966: 115)

Psychological or psychologising discourses, on the other hand, stress the boundaries strongly, as in this question from interviewer Caroline Jones's series of Australian Broadcasting Commission radio programmes *The Search for Meaning*:

> So what would you want to say about that split we seem to have made in our habit of thinking between that which we are (our being) and how we value that; and our doing, all our performance, our work? There's a real split there, isn't there, in our society.
>
> (Jones, 1989: 136)

Do we have an identity beneath the many roles we play? Or is our identity the sum of the roles we have learnt to play? My concern here is not to solve this problem, but to point out that the English language allows us to make a choice between functionalisation and identification, and that the use of this choice in discourse is of critical importance for discourse analysis.

That the choice has a grammatical base, a base in the language itself, can be seen from the rank order of the two types of categorisation in nominal groups. Identifications can be, and frequently are, Classifiers in nominal groups, functionalisations only rarely. One can, for example, say 'the Asian teacher', 'the homosexual musician', 'the woman doctor', but not (or only in a derogatory sense) 'the teacher Asian', 'the musician homosexual', 'the doctor woman'. Only relational identifications (see below) occasionally allow functionalisations to become Classifiers, as, for example, in 'your teacher friend'. Also, classifications and physical identifications cannot be possessivated, except, again, in a derogatory sense (cf. my use of 'our racist'). Relational identifications, on the other hand, are almost always possessivated. But possessivation does not play the same role here as in functionalisation: possessivated functionalisations signify the activation (as in 'his victim') or subjection (as in 'my attacker') of the possessing participant, while possessivated relational identifications signify the 'belonging together', the 'relationality' of the possessivated and possessing social actors (as in 'my daughter' or 'my mother').

Relational identification represents social actors in terms of their personal, kinship or work relation to each other, and it is realised by a closed set of nouns denoting such relations: 'friend', 'aunt', 'colleague', etc. Typically they are possessivated, either by means of a possessive pronoun ('her friend'), or by means of a genitive ('the child's mother'), or postmodifying prepositional phrase with *of* ('a mother of five').

The role of relational identification is, in our society, less important than that of classification and functionalisation, especially where personal and kinship relations are concerned. The intrusion of such relations into the sphere of public activities may be branded as 'nepotism' or 'corruption' (unless you are a monarch). In other societies, however, it plays a key role. Von Sturmer (1981) has described how Australian Aborigines, when they first meet, introduce themselves primarily in terms of relational identification. They 'search for relations whom they share and then establish their relationship on that basis' (1981: 13). This differs from western introductions, where nomination and functionalisation ('What do you do?') are the key to establishing a relation, and where classification ('Where are you from?') comes in only when a social actor displays signs of differing from the social norm, for instance a foreign accent, or a dark skin. Not so among Aborigines:

Mareeba man:	'Where you from?'
Mickey:	'I'm Edward River man. Where you from?'
Mareeba man:	'I'm Lama Lama man ... do you know X?'
Mickey:	'No. Do you know Y?'
Mareeba man:	'No. Do you know Z?'
Mickey:	'Yes, she's my auntie.'

Mareeba man: 'That old lady's my granny. I must call you daddy.'
Mickey: 'I must call you boy. You give me a cigarette.'

(von Sturmer, 1981: 13)

Where kinship relations continue to be functionally important in our society, as is the case especially with the relation between mothers and children, the relevant terms become polyvalent: 'mother' can be used as a
functionalisation ('mothering' is not the act of bringing a child into the
world, but the act of giving care to a child, while 'fathering' signifies only
the act of begetting a child!), as a nomination ('Mother . . .') and as
a relational identification ('my mother . . .'); similarly, 'child' can be a
classification as well as a relational identification.

We might also note that, by the criteria developed here, terms like
'lover' and 'caregiver' (as synonym for 'parent') introduce a measure of
functionalisation into the sphere of personal and kinship relations.
Projections of the future development of personal and kinship relations
in our society, such as those in Alvin Toffler's *Futureshock* (1970) do
indeed predict increasing functionalisation, for example the institutionalisation of 'professional families', couples bringing up other people's
children for money, to allow these children's parents to devote themselves
to their careers.

Physical identification represents social actors in terms of physical
characteristics which uniquely identify them in a given context. It can be
realised by nouns denoting physical characteristics ('blonde', 'redhead',
'cripple', and so on) or by adjectives ('bearded', 'tall') or prepositional
phrases with *with* or *without* postmodifying highly generalised classifications such as 'man', 'woman', etc.:

*10.1 A little girl with a long, fair pigtail came and stood next to Mary
Kate.*

*10.2 'What are you doing there?', shouted the man with the large
moustache.*

Physical identification occurs a good deal in stories, sometimes only when
a character is introduced, as in 10.1, sometimes throughout, as in the story
from which 10.2 is taken. It provides social actors with a unique identity
in the temporary or permanent absence of nomination, and does so by
means of a salient detail. But it also, and at the same time, focuses the
reader or listener on the social actor's physical characteristics, and this
may be done selectively, for instance on the basis of age or gender, as in
these examples from the (Australian) *Daily Mirror*: 'stunning blonde
singer Toby Bishop', 'chubby-cheeked Laura Vezey, 2'.

In contrast to nomination, physical identification is always overdetermined (see section 12): physical attributes tend to have connotations, and these can be used to obliquely classify or functionalise social actors. 'Large moustaches', for example (see example 10.2), derive, perhaps, from the moustaches of Prussian army officers, connoting a sense of rigid disciplinarianism, not only in armies and schools, but also in other contexts. The borderline between physical identification and classification is therefore far from clearcut, as is obvious from the use of skin colour for classification, or from the connotations that cling to such representations of women as 'blonde' or 'redhead'. However, even when used for the purposes of classification, the category of physical identification remains distinct, because of its obliqueness, its overdetermination, and its apparent 'empirical' innocence.

Finally, social actors can be referred to in interpersonal, rather than experiential terms. For these instances I use the term appraisement: social actors are appraised when they are referred to in terms which evaluate them, as good or bad, loved or hated, admired or pitied. This is realised by the set of nouns and idioms that denote such appraisal (and only such appraisal), as, for instance, 'the darling', 'the bastard', 'the wretch' – or 'thugs' in:

10.3 80 young white thugs attacked African street vendors.

It would appear, incidentally, that negative appraisements are more plentiful than positive ones, especially in some registers, such as that spoken by Miles Davis in his ghostwritten autobiography:

10.4 I told the motherfucker as he was going out of the door 'I told you not to go in there, stupid'.
                                                    (Davis, 1990: 13)

As can be expected, the 'Race Odyssey' text does not categorise the individuals and groups it represents to the same degree. 'Racists' and 'immigrants' are categorised a good deal more than are 'we', Australians. And when 'we' are categorised, it is in terms of our shared national identity ('Australians') – the single instance of functionalisation is 'critics'.

'Racists' are classified by provenance and ethnicity ('Japanese', 'native Vancouverites', etc.) and in one case by age and race (the case of the 'young white thugs'). 'Immigrants' are classified by provenance or ethnicity in 50 per cent of cases, by class (e.g. the 'downtown' and 'uptown' immigrants) in 20 per cent of cases, by race ('dark-skinned', 'black') in 13 per cent of cases, by education or skilledness in 10 per cent of cases, and once each by wealth ('poor') and religion ('Muslim'). By and large their treatment in the representation is not all that different from that of the 'racists'. 'Racists' and 'immigrants' also are the only categories of social actor that are occasionally represented in terms of relational identity. Both constitute, in this discourse, the main 'others' for 'us', Australians, and therefore also the main object of classification.

High-status social actors, on the other hand, such as 'government' and 'experts', are always functionalised (the few instances of functionalisation of 'racists' and 'immigrants' also concern high-status persons, such as the 'mayor of Kawaguchi' and the Peruvian presidential candidate. It is a pattern which, I would think, is by no means specific to this text.

11 PERSONALISATION AND IMPERSONALISATION

So far I have discussed representational choices which *personalise* social actors, represent them as human beings, as realised by personal or possessive pronouns, proper names or nouns (sometimes adjectives, as, for example, in 'maternal care') whose meaning includes the feature 'human'. But social actors can also be *impersonalised*, represented by other means, for instance by abstract nouns, or by concrete nouns whose meaning does not include the semantic feature 'human'. I shall distinguish two types of impersonalisation: abstraction and objectivation. Abstraction occurs when social actors are represented by means of a quality assigned to them by the representation. One example is the way in which 'poor, black, unskilled, Muslim or illegal' migrants are referred to by means of the term 'problems' in 11.1: they are being assigned the quality of being problematic, and this quality is then used to denote them. Another example is the substitution of 'the changing face of Australia' for 'the new migrants' in 11.2:

11.1 Australia is in danger of saddling itself up with a lot of unwanted problems.

11.2 Many Australians ... were 'bewildered' by the changing face of Australia.

Objectivation occurs when social actors are represented by means of reference to a place or thing closely associated either with their person or with the activity they are represented as being engaged in. In other words, objectivation is realised by metonymical reference. A number of types of objectivation are particularly common: *spatialisation, utterance autonomisation, instrumentalisation* and *somatisation*.

Spatialisation is a form of objectivation in which social actors are represented by means of reference to a place with which they are, in the given context, closely associated. This happens, for instance, when 'Australians' are substituted by 'Australia', as in 11.3:

11.3 Australia was bringing in about 70,000 migrants a year.

Utterance autonomisation is a form of objectivation in which social actors are represented by means of reference to their utterances. This is the case, for instance, with 'the report' and 'surveys' in 11.4, and because it lends a kind of impersonal authority to the utterances, it is often used in connection with the utterances of high-status and 'official' spokespeople:

11.4 This concern, the report noted, was reflected in surveys which showed that the level of support for stopping immigration altogether was at a postwar high.

Instrumentalisation is a form of objectivation in which social actors are represented by means of reference to the instrument with which they carry out the activity which they are represented as being engaged in:

11.5 A 120 mm mortar shell slammed into Sarajevo's marketplace.

Somatisation, finally, is a form of objectivation in which social actors are represented by means of reference to a part of their body, as in:

11.6 She put her hand on Mary Kate's shoulder.

The noun denoting the body part is almost always premodified by a possessive pronoun or genitive referring to the 'owner' of the body part, and perhaps we should, in such cases, speak of 'semi-objectivation'. Nevertheless, possessivated somatisation still adds a touch of alienation, of Mary Kate not being involved herself: not Mary Kate, but Mary Kate's *body* is being touched, in an unwanted and intimidating intrusion.

More generally, impersonalisation can have one or more of the following effects: it can background the identity and/or role of social actors; it can lend impersonal authority or force to an activity or quality of a social actor; and it can add positive or negative connotations to an activity or utterance of a social actor. When, for instance, 'Australia' is activated in relation to the activity of 'bringing in migrants' (example 11.3), the text does not tell the reader who is responsible for the activity, just as in the case of nominalisations and passive agent deletions. For this reason impersonalisation abounds in the language of bureaucracy, a form of the organisation of human activity which is constituted on the denial of responsibility, and governed by impersonal procedures which, once put in place, are wellnigh impermeable to human agency. Abstractions, finally, add connotative meanings: the qualities abstracted from their bearers serve, in part, to interpret and evaluate them.

The 'Race Odyssey' text impersonalises 'immigrants' often (eighteen times), most of the other categories of social actor only rarely – 'racists' are impersonalised once, 'us', Australians three times, the 'government' once, and 'experts' twice. The writer of the article, on the other hand, impersonalises himself every time he refers to his activities ('italicising', 'highlighting', 'calling into question', etc.) and the only personalised reference to him is the byline ('David Jenkins argues . . .').

Most of the impersonalisations of 'immigrants' are abstractions (83 per cent), and what is abstracted is, in eight out of fifteen cases, quantity: 'immigrants' are referred to as 'levels', 'settings', etc. The qualities of being 'problematic' (see 11.1), of 'changing Australia' (11.2) and of 'race' (as in 'racial tolerance') account for the other cases.

Utterance autonomisation occurs in relation to 'experts' and also in relation to the writer of the article, who represents himself every single time as though, through his person, 'the facts speak for themselves', as realised by the substitution of anaphoric reference to preceding sections of text for reference to his person:

11.7 They [i.e. these developments] highlight the fact that racism is seldom far below the surface.

12 OVERDETERMINATION

Overdetermination occurs when social actors are represented as participating, at the same time, in more than one social practice. One of the children's stories that I analysed, a Dutch story called *De Metro van Magnus* (van Leeuwen, 1981), features a character called 'The Unknown Soldier'. Magnus, the hero of the story, finds The Unknown Soldier (who is 'maybe 18 years old' but 'looks more like a boy than like a man') in the Unknown Soldier Square, where he sits, rather forlorn, at the foot of a huge abstract monument dedicated to The Unknown Soldier. As this monument bears little resemblance to a soldier, Magnus assumes that the 'man-boy' must be The Unknown Soldier. The latter, after some hesitation, agrees. He is glad to get a name, because he himself does not know who he is (he is 'unknown'). Magnus and The Unknown Soldier then go to a place 'rather like a school', where The Unknown Soldier fails miserably at answering the questions asked by 'the man with the large moustache' (already featured in example 10.2). Thus The Unknown Soldier is connected to at least two social practices, warfare and schooling, and comes to symbolise the subjected participant in both these practices, and indeed in all practices that produce victims and underdogs. Magnus's own name is also overdetermined, since he is both little, a child, and 'magnus': through his name he transcends the difference between 'what adults (can) do' and 'what children (can) do'.

I have distinguished four major categories of overdetermination: *inversion, symbolisation, connotation* and *distillation*.

Inversion is a form of overdetermination in which social actors are connected to two practices which are, in a sense, each other's opposites. This happens, for instance, in the well-known comic strip *The Flintstones*. The activities of the Flintstones are very much those of a twentieth-century American suburban family. The Flintstones themselves, however, are overdetermined: they *do* things twentieth-century families do, but they *look like*, and are nominated as, prehistoric cavedwellers. In other words, they have been transformed from [+ contemporary] to [– contemporary] – while still involved in contemporary activities. Reference thus broadens to include prehistoric as well as contemporary practices, perhaps in order that the latter may be viewed as 'natural', as transcending history and culture: overdetermination is one of the ways in which texts can legitimise practices. The 'Magnus' example above is also a case of inversion: Magnus has been transformed from [+ child] to [– child], while still involved in childlike activities.

Symbolisation, as I use the term here, occurs when a 'fictional' social actor or group of social actors stands for actors or groups in non-fictional social practices. The 'fictional' actor often belongs to a mythical, distant past. This distance then allows the actors and the activities in which they engage to refer to several non-fictional actors and practices. Will Wright (1975), in a study of Westerns, has shown how the participants and activities in Westerns changed in the early 1960s towards a pattern which he calls the 'professional plot'. Characteristic of this kind of plot is the transition from individualisation (the lone gunfighter who arrives in town on his horse) to collectivisation, the team of fiercely independent men who work for money rather than for love, justice or honour, are technically competent and highly organised, and form a tightly knit elite with a strong code of solidarity within the group. Wright then shows how these 'professional heroes' and their exploits can be linked to a number of social practices and the social actors involved in them, noting, for instance, how in business the individual entrepreneur has made way for the executive team, in science the individual genius for the efficient research team, and so on, and how the values of such teams are very similar to the values of the heroes of 'professional Westerns': here, too, one finds high technical competence, work for financial rewards, group solidarity against outsiders, and so on. Thus the 'professional heroes' in Westerns can stand for a variety of social actors in actual social practices: doctors, scientists, politicians, business executives, etc. The township, the 'weak society' for which the 'professional heroes' work, can stand for such social actors as the doctor's patients, the corporation's consumers, the politician's voters, etc. In other words, the social actors, and, indeed, the other elements of 'professional Westerns' are overdetermined. Bruno Bettelheim (1979) has similarly mapped the social actors and activities in fairy tales on to contemporary and actual social practices, notably those of the modern middle-class family.

Connotation occurs when a unique determination (a nomination or physical identification) stands for a classification or functionalization. This definition essentially accords with the way Barthes (1967; 1970; 1977) defined 'myth' or 'connotation'. Connotations, said Barthes (1977: 50) are 'discontinuous', 'scattered traits', the knowledge of which is established by cultural tradition:

> A 'historical grammar' of iconographic connotation ought thus to look for its material in painting, theatre, associations of ideas, stock metaphors, that is to say, precisely, in 'culture'.
>
> (Barthes, 1977: 22)

We have already come across an example when we discussed the case of the 'man with the large moustache' (example 10.2): the reader's knowledge of popular culture associates such moustaches with the Prussian military, and then projects into the 'man with the large moustache' all the qualities which the popular culture tradition associates with the Prussian military. Such knowledge is not necessarily conscious. It is 'mythical' knowledge. The signs 'are not understandable, but merely reminiscent of cultural lessons half-learnt' (J. Berger, 1972: 140) – perhaps most frequently learnt from the mass media, movies, comic strips, and so on.

Distillation realises overdetermination through a combination of generalisation and abstraction. It is perhaps best explained by means of an example. A section of a chapter from Ivan Illich's *Deschooling Society* (1971), which I have analysed in some detail elsewhere (van Leeuwen, 1993b), establishes, in the course of the text, the following taxonomy:

professionals who offer therapy

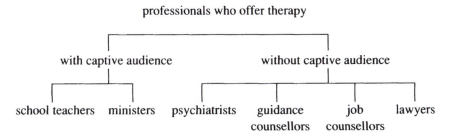

Three observations can be made about this taxonomy. First, while 'psychiatrist', and perhaps also 'guidance counsellor', can be seen as true hyponyms of 'therapist', the professions of 'schoolteacher', 'minister', 'job counsellor' and 'lawyer' are not usually classified as therapeutic. Practitioners may adopt some of the values and manners of therapists, but therapy is not a central aspect of their activities. In other words, Illich has abstracted what would normally be regarded as peripheral qualities and then elevated them to the status of generalisations. This is borne out by the way he formulates the superordinate term: 'professional' can be regarded as a true generalisation of 'schoolteachers', 'ministers', etc., and it is this term which is used as Head of the nominal group.

Second, 'therapy' features only in the Qualifier of the nominal group. The term cannot, by itself, be used to refer to teachers. In other formulations Illich uses 'therapist' as Circumstance of Role ('the teacher-as-therapist') – again, 'therapist' is a circumstantial rather than a central feature. The same can be said for 'with captive audience' and 'without captive audience': in relation to 'schoolteacher', 'minister', etc. this is circumstantial, and hence an abstraction rather than a generalisation. One cannot say that schoolteachers are a kind of 'with captive audience'.

Third, and most importantly in the present context, the taxonomy is not exhaustive. It is not constructed in order to chart the field of therapy, but in order to de-legitimise the activities of teachers by means of a comparison (the intrusion of fields other than those that form the main topic of a text for the sake of comparison always has a legitimising or de-legitimising function). Illich compares the activities of schoolteachers to the activities of ministers and priests. The church is an institution which, in the eyes of the 'radical' readers Illich is addressing, has already been de-legitimised long ago. The de-legitimation of schools, on the other hand, is a more controversial matter. Through overdetermining teachers, through connecting them to both school and church, some of the already achieved de-legitimation of the church can be transferred to the school, to teachers and their activities: 'Children are protected by neither the First, nor the Fifth Amendment when they stand before that secular priest, the teacher' (Illich, 1971: 38).

Distillation, then, is a form of overdetermination which connects social actors to several social practices by abstracting the same feature from the social actors involved in these several practices.

Finally I shall briefly discuss the two most common forms of inversion, *anachronism* and *deviation*. Of the former we have already encountered an example, that of the Flintstones; science fiction can provide another example. Here social actors are projected into the future (and, perhaps, on to another planet as well) – but their activities often bear a remarkable resemblance to contemporary practices. Anachronism is often used to say things that cannot be said straightforwardly, for instance to offer social and political criticism in circumstances where this is proscribed by official or commercial censorship, or to naturalise ideological discourses.

In the case of deviation social actors involved in certain activities are represented by means of reference to social actors who would not normally be eligible to engage in these activities. In children's stories about the first day at school, for instance, reference to children might be replaced by reference to animals, a transformation of the feature [+ human] into [– human]:

12.1   The teacher wrote the name down in the register: NOIL.
Then she finished calling the register.
'Betty Small', she said.
'Yes', said the little girl.
'Noil', said the teacher.
'Yes', said the lion. He sat next to the little girl, as good as gold.

This overdetermination fuses 'what children (can) do' and 'what animals (can) do', and so causes the child to be represented as, at the same time, human and animal, 'civilised' and 'uncivilised', and also as at the same time weak ('small', 'little') and strong. The deviation lies in the transgression of the rule that animals cannot go to school: more naturalistic stories about the first day at school invariably include the episode of the dog who wants to come to school too, but is not allowed to, and then feels sad and abandoned, while the child does not, or at least not initially, understand why his or her dog may not come to school. When, in a fantasy story like the one quoted in 12.1, animals transgress the eligibility rule and do go to school, they must necessarily fail. In the case of Noil, the lion, this does not happen, however, until after Noil has scared off the little boy who teases Betty Small in the playground.

Deviation almost always serves the purpose of legitimation: the failure of the deviant social actor confirms the norms. In the case of Noil and Betty Small it justifies the eligibility rule and so legitimises school as the necessary transition from a state of being in which children 'are at one with the animals', to a state of being in which they 'rise above animals', a state of being in which paradoxically, they are represented as 'small', 'little', and timid, rather than confident and assertive in their new status.

The 'Race Odyssey' text features only one overdetermination, the title, which overdetermines a process, rather than the social actors involved in it, the process of 'coming home after a long journey', of finding 'our' ('racial') identity. If I had chosen to exemplify my account of the representation of the social actors involved in the immigration process with a fictional example, I would probably have had a greater number of instances of overdetermination to discuss.

13 CONCLUSION

Figure 3.1 summarises, in the form of a system network, my answer to the question with which I started out: what are the principal ways in which social actors can be represented in discourse. The square brackets in the diagram stand for either/or choices (e.g. social actors must be either

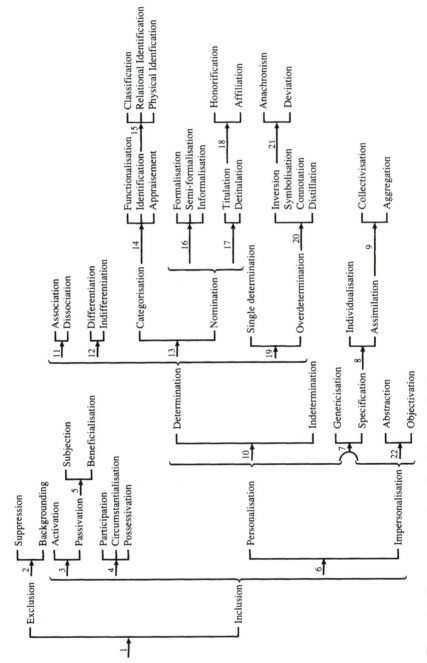

Figure 3.1 The representation of social actors in discourse: system network

'activated' or 'passivated'), the curly brackets stand for simultaneous choices (e.g. social actors can be both 'activated' and 'personalised', or both 'passivated' and 'personalised' and so on). I hope that my discussion of the various categories in the network has made it clear that, in actual discursive practices, the choices need not always be rigidly 'either/or'. Boundaries can be blurred deliberately, for the purpose of achieving specific representational effects, and social actors can be, for instance, both classified and functionalised. In such cases the categories remain nevertheless useful for making explicit how the social actors are represented.

The network brings together what linguists tend to keep separate: it involves a number of distinct lexicogrammatical and discourse-level linguistic systems, transitivity, reference, the nominal group, rhetorical figures, and so on, because all these systems are involved in the realisation of representations of social actors. Nevertheless, there is some linguistic consistency in the network. Initially, it involves three of the major types of transformation, deletion (systems 1 and 2), rearrangement (systems 3–5) and substitution (systems 6–22). Each type of transformation involves distinct linguistic systems: deletion involves voice, and also nominalisation and adjectivalisation, rearrangement principally involves transitivity, while substitution is initially realised by aspects of the structure of the nominal group – the Deictic and Postdeictic, that is, the system of reference (systems 7, 8, 10 and 12), and the Numerative (system 9) (Halliday, 1985, ch. 6; Matthiessen, 1992, ch. 3.2) and then by lexis, different classes of noun, including aspects of morphological structure (systems 13–18). Systems 19–22, finally, involve various forms of metaphor and metonym. More globally, the three sections, 7–12, 13–18 and 19–22, involve, respectively, reference, lexis (the field of nouns referring to human beings) and metaphor.

I shall, finally, summarise my discussion of the 'Race Odyssey' text, which, of course, has restricted itself to the representation of social actors, and therefore not dealt with many other salient and critically relevant features of this text.

Those who, in some way or other, are represented as being 'concerned about' or actually opposing immigration and immigrants in countries other than Australia, I have referred to as 'racists': in the article they are unfavourably compared to opponents of ('high') migration in Australia, who have 'reasonable' rather than 'racist' concerns about immigration. As we have seen, representation of these 'racists' is relatively often suppressed or backgrounded. This has to be offset against the fact that the exclusions follow very definite categorisations, such as '80 young white thugs'. It can be argued that the article invites us to interpret these vague or missing representations in the light of this initial categorisation, which has no equivalent in the representation of Australian opponents of immigration. 'Racists' are also often referred to generically, and they are individualised and nominated only when elite persons are concerned. On the other hand, they are frequently activated in relation to (passivated) immigrants, and this with respect to both material and verbal processes such as 'denying entry' and 'insulting' and mental processes such as 'being concerned'. When they are classified they are most frequently classified in much the same way as are immigrants, by 'where they are from', so that they have at least this in common with those other undesirables, the immigrants themselves. The only negative appraisement, finally, occurs in connection with this category of social actors, and it occurs the very first time they are referred to (again, the case of the '80 young white thugs').

Bruce Ruxton, the home-grown 'racist', is represented as equally un-desirable. But, unlike 'racists' abroad, he is never backgrounded, and individualised as well as nominated. Like other 'racists', he is highly activated in relation to (passive) immigrants. In other words, at home one can easily single out the few deviant individuals who, unlike 'us', Australians, deserve the epithet 'racist', and then turn them into the notorious personifications of prejudice and bigotry which 'we' all (and especially the media) love to hate. Abroad, on the other hand, racism is much more pervasive.

Another group of social actors who oppose or worry about immigrants and immigration is formed by 'us', the Australian people 'as a whole'. This group is more sympathetically treated – less often backgrounded, less often referred to generically, and classified, if at all, only as 'Australians'. If they are activated, it is in relation to mental processes such as being 'bewildered' and 'not understanding', 'feeling unable to cope', and so on, rather than in relation to material and verbal processes, as in the case of the 'racists'. And finally, they form a collective, which underlines their supposed consensus about immigration issues.

The immigrants themselves I have referred to as 'them', and 'they' are relatively often backgrounded, and often referred to generically, which helps to distance the reader from them. They are either assimilated or aggregated, and the aggregations help to represent them as a large 'horde' about to invade 'us', and as the object of 'rational' calculation, rather than as fellow human beings. They are also represented abstractly, and this, again, frequently involves the abstraction of their number. More than any other category of social actors they are classified, by 'ethnic origin', class, race, level of education, wealth, and so on – differences which are not made in relation to 'us', Australians. And immigrants from different ethnic origins are sometimes lumped together in what I have called 'asso-ciations', to create further categories of migrant. If they are activated, finally, it is almost always in relation to one activity, that of 'immigrat-ing': in every other respect they are acted *upon* by others.

The government is rarely backgrounded or referred to generically, and often individualised and nominated, that is, personified in the person of the Prime Minister. It also transcends classification and is always functionalised and playing a highly active role in relation to the immigrants. The social actors who form the executive arm of the government, however, those who must actually 'stop' the immigrants, are suppressed: the article keeps the reality of 'cutting back immigration' at a comfortable distance from the reader.

'Experts' are represented in two ways. Either they are treated like elite persons (highly activated, functionalised, individualised, nominated and titulated) or their utterances are autonomised and/or collectivised, to imbue them with impersonal authority and a sense of consensus among experts.

The writer of the article also refers to himself, and to his readers. The latter are addressed directly, the former makes 'the facts' speak in his stead ('They [i.e. these developments] highlight the fact that racism is seldom below the surface'). Whether or not the writer is also the social actor who legitimates the 'fears' of 'us', Australians, and 'entitles' 'us' (and Prime Minister Hawke) to our feelings of pride, concern, etc., is not clear: although the legitimising social actor plays an important role in the process of immigration, reference to him or her is always suppressed. Perhaps we are not too far from the truth if we recognise here, through traces in the text itself, the active role of the media in this social process, despite the careful stance of neutrality suggested by the way in which most of the representation is attributed to sources other than the writer himself.

REFERENCES

Barthes, R. (1967) *Elements of Semiology*, New York: Hill & Wang.
Barthes, R. (1970) *Mythologies*, London: Paladin.
Barthes, R. (1977) *Image-Music-Text*, London: Fontana.
Bell, A. (1985) 'One rule of news English: geographical, social and historical spread', *Te Reo*, 28, 95–117.
Berger, J. (1972) *Ways of Seeing*, Harmondsworth: Penguin.
Berger, P. L. (1966) *Invitation to Sociology*, Harmondsworth: Penguin.
Bernstein, B. (1971) *Class, Codes and Control, vol. 1, Theoretical Studies towards a Sociology of Language*, London: Routledge.
Bettelheim, B. (1979) *The Uses of Enchantment*, Harmondsworth: Penguin.
Bourdieu, P. (1986) *Distinction: A Social Critique of the Judgment of Taste*, Cambridge: Polity.
Curthoys, A. and Docker, J. (1989) 'In praise of prisoner', in J. Tulloch and G. Turner (eds) *Australian Television: Programs, Pleasures and Politics*, Sydney: Allen & Unwin.
Davis, M. (1990) *Miles: The Autobiography*, London: Macmillan.
Fairclough, N. (1989) *Language and Power*, London: Longman.
Foucault, M. (1981) *A History of Sexuality, vol. 1*, Harmondsworth: Penguin.
Fowler, R. (1991) *Language in the News: Discourse and Ideology in the Press*, London: Routledge.

Fowler, R., Hodge, R., Kress, G. and Trew, T. (1979) *Language and Control*, London: Routledge & Kegan Paul.

Halliday, M. A. K. (1985) *An Introduction to Functional Grammar*, London: Edward Arnold.

Illich, I. (1971) *Deschooling Society*, Harmondsworth: Penguin.

Jones, C. (1989) *The Search for Meaning, vol. 2*, Sydney: ABC Publications.

Kress, G. and Hodge, R. (1979) *Language as Ideology*, London: Routledge.

Kress, G. and van Leeuwen, T. (1990) *Reading Images*, Victoria: Deakin University Press.

Martin, J. R. (1992) *English Text: System and Structure*, Amsterdam: Benjamins.

Matthiessen, C. (1992) *Lexicogrammatical Cartography: English Systems*, Sydney: Department of Linguistics, University of Sydney.

Quirk, R., Greenbaum, S., Leech, G. and Svartvik, J. (1972) *A Grammar of Contemporary English*, London: Longman.

Toffler, A. (1970) *Futureshock*, London: Bodley Head.

Trew, T. (1979) 'Theory and ideology at work', in R. Fowler, R. Hodge, G. Kress and T. Trew, *Language and Control*, London: Routledge & Kegan Paul, 94–116.

Tuchman, G., Kaplan Daniels, A. and Benet, J. (1978) *Hearth and Home: Images of Women in the Mass Media*, New York: Oxford University Press.

van Dijk, T. A. (1977) *Text and Context: Explorations in the Semantics and Pragmatics of Discourse*, London: Longman.

van Dijk, T. A. (1991) *Racism and the Press*, London: Routledge.

van Leeuwen, J. (1981) *De Metro van Magnus*, The Hague: Omniboek.

van Leeuwen, T. (1987) 'Music and ideology: notes towards a sociosemiotics of mass media music', Sydney Association for the Study of Society and Culture, *SASSC Working Papers*, 2, 1–2, 19–45.

van Leeuwen, T. (1993a) 'Genre and field in Critical Discourse Analysis: a synopsis', *Discourse and Society*, 4, 2, 193–225.

van Leeuwen, T. (1993b) 'Language and representation: the recontextualization of participants, activities and reactions', unpub. PhD, University of Sydney.

von Sturmer, J. (1981) 'Talking with Aborigines', *Australian Institute of Aboriginal Studies Newsletter*, 15, 13–30.

Wright, W. (1975) *Sixguns and Society: A Structural Study of the Western*, Berkeley, CA: University of California Press.

Chapter 4

Technologisation of discourse

Norman Fairclough

In this chapter I use 'discourse' to refer to any spoken or written language use conceived as social practice, a position I have elaborated elsewhere (Fairclough, 1989a), and 'order of discourse' (a term adapted from Foucault) for the overall configuration of discourse practices of a society or one of its institutions.[1] I want to suggest that contemporary 'orders of discourse' have a property which distinguishes them from earlier orders of discourse, or which at least has not been manifested in earlier orders of discourse to anything like the same degree; and that this property is of particular significance for the orders of discourse of various types of work, specifically because it is an important factor in changes which are currently taking place in workplace practices and 'workplace culture'. I focus below upon workplace culture, and the constitution of social and professional relations and identities at work.

Contemporary orders of discourse are, I think, becoming deeply and distinctively affected by what I want to call a *technologisation of discourse*, whose central and defining characteristic is the embodiment in institutional forms and practices of circuits or networks which systematically chain together three domains of practice: research into the discoursal practices of workplaces and institutions, design of discoursal practices in accordance with institutional strategies and objectives, and training of personnel in such designed discoursal practices. I am characterising an emergent tendency, whose contours are only becoming clear, and are more clearly defined in some places than in others. Elements of this development can easily be attested in earlier orders of discourse, but it is their tendency towards systematic and institutionalised configuration that justifies seeing technologisation of discourse as a distinctively contemporary process. My main point of reference will be contemporary Britain, and a few particular types of work therein; I refer most to one domain of professional work, higher education. But technologisation of discourse is, I suspect, a widespread accompaniment of changes in workplaces, in industry as well as professions and services, and no doubt on an international scale.

This chapter will address the following questions in turn: what are the characteristics of technologisation of discourse? How does technologisation of discourse relate to wider processes of social and cultural change? What in particular is the connection between technologisation of discourse and changes in 'workplace culture' – in social relations and identities at work? How might technologisation of discourse affect actual discoursal practices? What relationship does technologisation of discourse have to current changes in language education and training?

CHARACTERISTICS OF DISCOURSE TECHNOLOGISATION

My use of the term 'technology' derives ultimately from Foucault's analyses of the alliance between social sciences and structures of power which constitutes modern 'bio-power', which has 'brought life and its mechanisms into the realm of explicit calculations and made knowledge/power an agent of transformation of human life' (Foucault, 1981). Technologies of discourse are more specifically a variety of what Rose and Miller (1989) call 'technologies of government': 'The strategies, techniques and procedures by means of which different forces seek to render programmes operable, the networks and relays that connect the aspirations of authorities with the activities of individuals and groups' (Rose and Miller, 1989). Referring to liberalism as a mode of government, these authors see the 'deployment' of 'political rationalities and the programmes of government' as 'action at a distance', involving the 'enrolment' of those they seek to govern through 'networks of power' incorporating diverse agents and 'the complex assemblage of diverse forces – laws, buildings, professions, routines, norms'. Discourse is, I would suggest, one such 'force', which becomes operative within specific 'assemblages' with other forces.

The technologisation of discourse has, I think, been accelerating and taking on firmer contours since the mid-1980s, but its lineage is longer. For example, 'social skills training' (Argyle, 1978) is a well-established application of social psychological research, and technology of government, which has a partially discoursal nature. Large units of practice such as interviews are assumed to be composed of sequences of smaller units which are produced through the automatic application of skills which are selected on the basis of the contribution to the achievement of goals. It is assumed that these skills can be isolated and described, and that inadequacies in social (including discoursal) practice can be overcome by training people to draw upon these skills. Social skills training has been widely implemented for training mental patients, social workers, health workers, counsellors, managers, salespeople and public officials. One example given by Argyle is training in the 'personnel interview' (used for instance for disciplinary interviews in workplaces), which (and this quotation points to the design element) 'can make it a pleasanter and more effective occasion' (Argyle, 1978).

I have defined technologisation of discourse as an institutionalisation of circuits connecting research, design and training. Training and language education are discussed separately below. I shall use the following list of five characteristics of technologisation of discourse as a framework for elaborating that definition:

1 the emergence of expert 'discourse technologists'
2 a shift in the 'policing' of discourse practices
3 the design and projection of context-free discourse techniques
4 strategically motivated simulation in discourse
5 the pressure towards standardisation of discourse practices.

There have long been specialists in persuasive and manipulative discourse, but what we might call contemporary 'technologists of discourse' have certain distinguishing features. One is their relationship to knowledge. They are social scientists, or other sorts of expert or consultant with privileged access to scientific information, and their interventions into discoursal practice therefore carry the aura of 'truth'. Another is their relationship to institutions. They are likely to hold accredited roles associated with accredited practices and routines in institutions, either as direct employees or as expert consultants brought in from outside for particular projects. For example, *staff development* and *staff appraisal* are two recent additions to the institutional practices of British universities. Both the training of staff and the training of appraisers are partly training in a variety of discourse practices – lecturing, organising seminars, interviewing, designing publishing materials, writing research proposals, and both directly employed staff and outside management consultants are being drawn into specialised institutional roles and practices, partly as discourse technologists.

Discourse practices are, I think, normally 'policed' – subjected to checks, corrections and sanctions – though there is a great deal of variation in how overtly or how rigorously. One effect of the technologisation of discourse is, I suggest, to shift the policing of discourse practices from a local institutional level to a trans-institutional level, and from categories of agent within particular institutions (be it education, law, medicine) to discourse technologists as outsiders. In addition to a shift in the location of policing agents, there is a shift in the basis of their legitimacy. It has traditionally been on the basis of their power and prestige within the profession or institution that certain categories of agent claimed the right to police its practices; now it is increasingly on the grounds of science, knowledge and truth. The discourse technologist as expert as well as outsider. An example would be the discoursal dimensions of the shift in universities from the practices of academics being judged by their peers to their practices being measured and evaluated according to externally generated criteria.

Discourse technologists design and redesign what I shall call 'discoursal techniques', such as interviewing, lecturing or counselling, to maximise their effectiveness and change them affectively – recall the objective of making a disciplinary interview 'a pleasanter and more effective occasion'. Argyle recommends that an interview should end with a review of what has been agreed and 'on as friendly a note as possible', suggestions about design which involve the design of particular utterances (to be 'friendly') as well as the overall organisation of the interview. I suspect that the tendency is for techniques to be increasingly designed and projected as 'context-free', as usable in any relevant context. This tendency is evident in training, where there is a focus upon the transferability of skills – 'teaching for transfer' is now a prominent theme in vocational education for example. Moreover, the projection of such context-free techniques into a variety of institutional contexts contributes to a widespread effect of 'colonisation' of local institutional orders of discourse by a few culturally salient discourse types – advertising and managerial and marketing discourse, counselling, and, of course, interviewing (Fairclough, 1989a).

The redesign of discourse techniques involves extensive *simulation*, by which I mean the conscious and systematic grafting on to a discourse technique of discourse practices originating elsewhere, on the basis of a strategic calculation of their effectivity. I have in mind particularly the simulation of meanings and forms which appertain to the discoursal constitution of social relationships and social identities – which have 'interpersonal' functions in systemicist terminology (Halliday, 1978). The recommendation that an interview end on a friendly note is an invitation to the interviewer to simulate the meanings and forms (those of language but also other semiotic modalities) of 'friendliness', meanings and forms which imply and implicitly claim social relations and identities associated more with domains of private life than with institutional events like interviews. Opening frontiers between the private and the institutional; institutional appropriation of the resources of conversation; 'conversationalisation' and apparent democratisation of institutional discourse: these are pervasive features of the technologisation of discourse. But they are tendencies rooted in broader currents of contemporary cultural change – democratisation, consumerisation – which we can regard as being exploited for strategic and instrumental ends in the technologisation of discourse. This makes the cultural values attaching to informal, conversationalised institutional discourse profoundly ambivalent.

The final characteristic of discourse technologisation in my list is that it constitutes a powerful impetus towards standardisation and normalisation of discourse practices, across as well as within institutions and different types of work. The importance of expert outsiders as discourse technologists, the shifting of the policing of discourse to a transcendent position 'above' particular institutions, and the trend towards context-free discourse techniques – all of these are centralising and standardising pressures upon discourse practice. Pressures which meet with resistance, however, as I shall suggest below.

TECHNOLOGISATION OF DISCOURSE AND WIDER PROCESSES OF CHANGE

One can relate technologisation as a tendential characteristic of contemporary orders of discourse to changes affecting modern social life in various periodicities. One such change is the long-term shift in the pre-eminence of 'government' over other types of power (Foucault, 1979) which gives general salience to technologies of government. Another on a quite different time scale is the set of major upheavals and restructurings which have been affecting various domains of work, especially since the mid-1980s. These seem to have highlighted to an unprecedented degree discoursal and communicative skills in work, exposed widespread 'skill' deficits in this regard, and given sharper definition and contours to the technologisation of discourse. Let me refer to upheavals in two domains of work which seem to me to have discoursal dimensions of this order.

The first is industry, and specifically 'post-Fordist' developments in industry. In post-Fordist production, workers no longer function as individuals performing repetitive routines within an invariant process, but as teams in a flexible relation to a fast-changing production process. In this context traditional employee–firm relations have been seen as dysfunctional by managements, and they have attempted to transform 'workplace culture', setting up for example various institutions which place employees in a more participatory relation with management, such as 'quality circles'. The description of these changes by managements themselves as 'cultural' is not just modish rhetoric: the aim is new cultural values, workers who are 'enterprising', self-motivating and self-disciplining.[2] These changes point to new discoursal practices in the workplace, a qualitative shift in the discoursal competence of the workforce, a shift of emphasis towards, for example, speaking and listening skills in group discussion and decision-making, techniques for elicitation and exchange of information, etc. A role for discourse technologists in engineering such changes is suggested from a training perspective by the 'communication skills' elements of British pre-vocational education programmes which I discuss below.

There are also upheavals affecting professional work which seem to favour an intensification of discourse technologisation. British universities for example have experienced major externally imposed changes (cuts in government finance, imposition of market conditions of operation, mechanisms to ensure answerability and 'relevance') and internal organisational changes ('cash economy', training and appraisal of staff, institutional plans, 'enterprise units' as part of degree schemes, etc.) which have been seen as requiring new skills in teaching, management, counselling, and so on, entailing access to knowledges and techniques from outside higher education. The decreasing autonomy of universities has no doubt made them more 'permeable' to such external influences. In part, it is externally designed discourse techniques (for lecturing, tutoring, interviewing, counselling, etc.) that are being imported.

TECHNOLOGISATION OF DISCOURSE AND CHANGING 'WORKPLACE CULTURE'

I have suggested that the technologisation of discourse is a factor in changing 'workplace culture', a dimension of the application of technologies of government in implementing programmes for change in the culture of the workplace – change in social relationships at work, change in social and professional identities. Of particular relevance here are my comments on the simulation of interpersonal meanings and forms as one characteristic of the technologisation of discourse, and the suggestion of a 'conversationalisation' and apparent democratisation of institutional discourse – a widespread appropriation and simulation of informal conversational interaction. One can distinguish two broad categories of shift in social relationships at work that are discernible across many types of work, in which conversationalisation of discourse appears to be an important factor. One is a shift in a more 'participatory', egalitarian direction in relationships between managers and workers, and in a general sense between those in higher and lower positions within hierarchies – the shift from the 'vertical' to the 'horizontal' firm.[3] The other is a similar shift in relationships between professionals and non-professionals, 'clients' in a broad sense – between teachers and pupils or students, doctors and patients, lawyers and clients, and so forth. The latter merges into shifting relationships between institutions and their 'publics', in the media and advertising.

Borzeix and Linhart (1988) refer to the ironing out of differences between hierarchically different categories of employees as the 'unification' of the enterprise, and point out that unification is the (only apparently paradoxical) complement of the 'atomisation' and 'individualisation' of the enterprise as an effect of the reworking of social identities at work. What Borzeix and Linhart are pointing to here seems to be a variant of what Rose (1989) identifies as broad changes in the cultural constitution of the self in the direction of a more autonomous, self-motivating or 'self-steering' self. It strikes me that conversationalisation of discourse serves both unification and atomisation, which are in any case two sides of the same coin; first, since conversation is a 'lifeworld' discourse type which we all have access to, the effect of conversationalisation of institutional orders of discourse is to help equalise discoursal resources; second, in so doing conversationalisation helps generalise one element of the resources necessary for greater autonomy in work – access to an institutionally accepted discourse repertoire.

Another dimension of changing identities in work is changes in professional identities. Many domains of work are undergoing processes of deprofessionalisation and reprofessionalisation. In the case of university teachers, for example, the process appears actually to involve a decrease in autonomy. Traditional constructions of professional identity which centred upon relatively autonomous (and supposedly disinterested) research and scholarship are under pressure from new models which construct the academic as multiskilled, dispersed across a complex set of duties and functions each of which involves training in specific skills – including research, teaching, administrative, promotional and counselling skills. In terms of the technologisation of discourse, these changes in professional identity seem to go along with an impetus to train academics in the range of externally designed discoursal techniques I have already referred to.

The shift in relationships between professionals and non-professionals (clients) referred to above is not simply in a more egalitarian direction. Such relationships are being pervasively reconstructed on a market model as producer–consumer relationships, and discourse technologists appear to be playing an important part in this process of reconstruction: the discourse techniques of marketing and advertising are being widely projected as models as well as being the focus of training, and as I noted earlier are colonising institutional orders of discourse on a large scale. And it is noteworthy that these discourse techniques are themselves already substantially conversationalised.

A final observation is that the technologisation of discourse as an instrument for cultural change may well have pathological consequences. The designed and strategic nature of more 'natural', 'ordinary', informal and conversational ways of relating to others and 'being oneself' may become patent. And a pathological consequence may be a sort of crisis of sincerity – a disorienting uncertainty about whether these culturally valued qualities of discourse are real or simulated in any given instance.

IMPACT ON DISCOURSAL PRACTICES

People in their actual discoursal practice may react in various ways to pressures for change emanating from the technologisation of discourse: they may comply, they may tactically appear to comply, they may refuse to be budged, or they may arrive at all sorts of accommodations and compromises between existing practices and new techniques. The latter is perhaps the most common and certainly the most interesting case. Study of such accommodations in the discoursal practice of workplaces strikes me as a likely source of insight into the actual impact of technologies of government on practice, and into ongoing processes of change in social relations and social identities.

I want to suggest that the production of discourse under such conditions of change places producers in 'dilemmas' (Billig *et al.*, 1988) which are an effect of trying to operate simultaneously in accordance with divergent constructions of social relationships and social identities, and that these dilemmas lead to accommodations and compromises which are manifested in the ambivalence and heterogeneity of spoken or written texts.

Let me relate these suggestions to a specific example, an extract from a British university prospectus (Figure 4.1). The evolution of university prospectuses clearly reflects pressures on universities to operate under market conditions, and to 'sell' their courses, using discoursal techniques borrowed from advertising. Some of the changes that have occurred are immediately evident in the physical appearance of prospectuses: the typical course entry has shifted since the mid-1980s from a couple of pages of quite dense writing to a mixture of written text, colour photographs, and sophisticated graphics. But prospectuses also show how academics have responded to the dilemmas that these pressures have placed them in by accommodation and compromise. These dilemmas centre upon the contradiction between a traditional professional-(or 'producer'-) oriented relationship between university and applicant, where the university is the 'authoritor' admitting or rejecting applicants according to its criteria for entry; and a 'consumer-oriented' relationship being forced upon universities by the economic position they have been placed in, where the applicant is the authoritor choosing (as consumers do) among the range of goods on offer. On the former model, a prospectus would focally give information about courses and conditions of entry, on the latter model it would 'sell' courses. In fact, contemporary prospectuses attempt a balancing act between the two: in terms of professional identities, they show academics trying to reconcile being academics and being salespeople.

This dilemma shows up in the heterogeneity of the text, and in particular in how its heterogeneity in terms of modalities and genres (written text and photograph on the left, list of courses and graphic display on the right) relates to its heterogeneity in terms of meanings, or more precisely speech functions (the main ones are informing, regulating and persuading). Let me begin with regulating. It strikes me as significant that everything to do with requirements imposed by the university upon the applicant – entry requirements, course requirements – is located in the synoptic right-hand section of the entry. This allows requirements to

AMERICAN STUDIES

Enquiries to Director of Admissions
Teaching staff members of appropriate departments

Lancaster students have always shown lively interest in American subjects, whether in the English, History, Politics or other departments. Now it is possible to take a specialised degree in American Studies. This degree combines different disciplinary approaches to the study of the United States and offers options covering American history, literature, and politics from the earliest colonial settlements to the present day.

In addition, American Studies majors will spend their second year at an American university, such as the University of Massachusetts at Amherst or another selected American university. Lancaster's close American connections make it possible to integrate the year abroad into the degree, so that, unusually in British universities, the American Studies degree can be completed in three years. Special counselling will ensure close integration between the year abroad and the two years at Lancaster.

Degree studies at Lancaster call on specialists in a number

of departments, and, as with most Lancaster degrees students will gain valuable experience in more than one discipline. But a substantial degree of flexibility is maintained, and it is possible for students to concentrate substantially on either history or literature or politics if they so choose.

The first year is largely devoted to providing a disciplinary grounding, and students pursue the normal first year courses in the History, English, and Politics departments, taking American options where they exist. Thereafter the course of study is almost exclusively devoted to American topics, and may include the writing of a dissertation on an American theme.

American Studies graduates pursue careers normally associated with a humanities or social science education: education, business, journalism, publishing, librarianship, and social service, with the wider opportunities which may come from students' transatlantic experience and perspective.

B A Hons American Studies Q400

First Year

History (American options)
English
Politics

Second Year

Four of five courses in American subjects taken at a United States university, including at least one interdisciplinary course.

Third Year

Four or five courses, normally from:

History:
The History of the United States of America

Religion in America from Jamestown to Appomattox, 1607-1865
From Puritan to Yankee: New England, 1630-1730
The Great Alliance: Britain, Russia and the United States, 1941-1945
Cold War America: The United States from Truman to Kennedy

English:
American Literature, 1620-1865
American Literature, 1865-1940
American Literature, 1940-1980

Politics:
The Politics of Race
United States Government: The Politics of the Presidency
The American Policy Process
United States Foreign Policy since 1945

Assessment: see under appropriate subject.

YOU WILL NEED

Amer St	A-level	O-level/GCSE
	BBB/BCC normally incl. English	A pass in a foreign language

or other qualifications (IB, EB, Scottish Highers) at a comparable standard.
AS-levels: will be accepted
Interview policy: special cases only.
Open days: candidates who are offered places will be invited.

Figure 4.1 University undergraduate prospectus

be separated from any source or authoritor, so that the problematic meaning (problematic, that is, in the consumer-oriented model) of the university imposing requirements upon applicants does not have to be overtly expressed. This occlusion is evident in the wording of the graphic display: *you will need* rather than, for instance, *we require* shifts the onus on to the student, and the agentless passives (*will be accepted, candidates who are offered places will be invited*). In the written text, requiring is avoided, and aspects of the degree scheme which might normally be seen as requirements are semanticised in other terms. For example, in paragraph 3 taking courses in several disciplines comes across as an assurance (*students will gain valuable experience*) rather than a requirement; similarly in paragraph 4, taking the three specified courses in the first year comes across as a description (*students pursue* ... (grounded by the preceding clause).

Let me turn from 'requiring' to the other two speech functions, 'informing' and 'persuading'. The most fully persuasive modality is the photograph, which positions the applicant in some unspecified but most attractive 'American' scene, co-constructing the potential student, the programme and the university within a mythical 'America'. The sentences of the written text, on the other hand, are in many cases ambivalent between informing and persuading – persuasion is certainly a significant speech function, but in a mainly covert form which anticipates substantial inferential work on the part of the reader (as of course does the photograph). The opening paragraph for instance appears, on the face of it, to consist of three bits of information (with *lively* as a transparently persuasive lexicalisation) – about the tradition of American Studies at the university, the introduction of a specialised degree, and the content of the degree. The first two sentences are in an overtly temporal relationship marked by the contrast between present perfective and simple present verb forms, and the temporal conjunct *now*. A little inferential work on the part of the reader can construct these markers and bits of information into a persuasive narrative according to which the degree is the culmination of a cross-disciplinary tradition. Similarly in other paragraphs, persuasion is mainly covert. The academic's dilemma appears to be resolved through a compromise; the written text is designed to persuade while appearing to be merely informative.

There are many variants of such accommodations and compromises between 'telling' and 'selling', reflecting the dilemmas of professionals in various domains faced with commodification and marketisation and pressure to use the associated discourse techniques. Elsewhere (Fairclough, 1988), I have analysed the effect of contradictory producer- and consumer-orientations and authoritor–authoritee relations on the modality of a brochure about a bank's financial services. Also (Fairclough, 1989c), I have analysed the compromises effected by a medical practitioner in attempting to adopt a patient-oriented counselling or therapeutic style of medical interview while maintaining control over medically important aspects of the interview. Similarly, Candlin and Lucas (1986) have shown how a family-planning counsellor tries to reconcile contradictory pressures to control clients' behaviour and yet to refrain as counsellors from any form of direction, through the indirect linguistic realisation of speech acts. In all such cases, people are using discourse as one medium in which they can attempt to negotiate their identities and their relationships with others in problematical circumstances of change.

There is, however, a significant gap between such practices of accommodation and compromise, and the impetus within the technologisation of discourse towards more standardised and context-free discourse practices; technologies of government generate strategies of resistance. What appear in a social psychological perspective as attempts to resolve dilemmas, appear in the perspective of a politics of discourse as discoursal facets of processes of hegemonic struggle in which the structuring of orders of discourse and of relationships between orders of discourse is at stake. The outcomes are restructured orders of discourse, innovative mixing of genres, and the emergence of new genres and sub-genres. (Such a hegemonic view of discoursal change is discussed in Fairclough, 1989b.)

LANGUAGE EDUCATION AND TRAINING

Important changes are taking place in language education and training in Britain – for example in the national curriculum for schools and in the 'communication' elements of pre-vocational education programmes – which seem to be closely linked to technologisation of discourse. There is a new emphasis on oracy and spoken language education, on face-to-face interaction and interaction in small groups, sometimes explicitly justified in terms of changing communicative requirements in work. And there is an extension to language of competence-based models of education which see knowledge operationally in terms of what people can do, and see education as training in skills. The syllabus for the Certificate of Pre-Vocational Education illustrates these developments. It is set out as a series of 'core competences ... which are essential to the students' chances of making a success in adult life, including work', each of which is divided into more specific competences (glossed as 'skills, knowledges and attitudes'). Communication is one of the core competences, whose aim is 'to develop communication skills as a way of structuring relationships between people in a changing and multicultural society'. It is divided into the five 'aims' of listening, speaking, reading, writing, and communication and interpretation, each of which is further broken down into more specific skills, including for example: 'talking effectively in a variety of styles and range of contexts – one-to-one/group, familiar/unfamiliar, formal/informal'; 'formulating and conveying requests and instructions clearly and concisely'; 'initiating and sustaining conversations in a range of contexts' (Further Education Unit, 1987: 30). 'Competence' is understood to include the ability to transfer existing skills and knowledge to new situations.

These new priorities and approaches contrast with more traditional emphases on written Standard English. Their emergence can, I think, be interpreted as the spread of a technologising orientation to discourse into the general educational system, most obviously into vocationally oriented programmes, but also to a degree into the general school curriculum. The Cox Report (Department of Education and Science, 1989) on the teaching of English in schools attempts a compromise between these newer and the more traditional priorities, which depends as I have argued (Fairclough, 1992) on the sociolinguistically suspect notion of 'appropriacy'. The competence- and skills-based approach harmonises with the technologisation of discourse in a number of ways: it focuses on training in context-free techniques (skills), it is a pressure for standardisation of practices, it fits with autonomous notions of the self, each individual being construed as housing a configuration of skills which can be worked upon and improved.

NOTES

1 This chapter has arisen out of discussions about interdisciplinary study of institutional discourse at Lancaster University. I am grateful to Paul Bagguley, Romy Clark, Susan Condor, Mick Dillon, Peter Goodrich, Scott Lash, and Celia Lury for responses to earlier versions.
2 I am grateful to Paul Bagguley and Scott Lash for discussions on industrial change.
3 I owe this formulation to Scott Lash.

REFERENCES

Argyle, M. (1978) *The Psychology of Interpersonal Behaviour*, 3rd edn, Harmondsworth: Penguin.
Billig, M., Condor, S., Edwards, D., Gane, M. and Middleton, D. (1988) *Ideological Dilemmas*, London: Sage.
Borzeix, A. and Linhart, D. (1988) 'La participation un clair-obscur', *Sociologie du Travail*, 88, 1, 37–48.
Candlin, C. and Lucas, J. L. (1986) 'Interpretation and explanation in discourse: modes of "advising" in family planning', in T. Ensink, A. van Essen and T. van der Geest (eds) *Discourse Analysis and Public Life*, Dordrecht: Foris, 13–38.
Department of Education and Science (1989) *English for Ages 5 to 16* (Cox Report), London: HMSO.
Fairclough, N. (1988) 'Register, power and sociosemantic change', in D. Birch and M. O'Toole (eds) *Functions of Style*, London: Frances Pinter, 111–25.
Fairclough, N. (1989a) *Language and Power*, London: Longman.

Fairclough, N. (1989b) 'Language and ideology', *English Language Research Journal*, University of Birmingham, 3, 9–28.

Fairclough, N. (1989c) 'Discoursal and social change: a conflictual view', paper delivered at ISA RCS (International Sociological Association Research Committee on Sociolinguistics) conference, Dublin.

Fairclough, N. (1992b) 'The appropriacy of "appropriateness" ', in N. Fairclough (ed.) *Critical Language Awareness*, London: Longman, 33–56.

Foucault, M. (1979) 'Governmentality', *Ideology and Consciousness*, 6, 5–21.

Foucault, M. (1981) *A History of Sexuality, vol. 1*, Harmondsworth: Penguin.

Further Education Unit (1987) *Relevance, Flexibility and Competence*, London: HMSO.

Halliday, M. A. K. (1978) *Language as Social Semiotic*, London: Edward Arnold.

Rose, N. (1989) 'Governing the enterprising self', paper given at conference on Values of the Enterprise Culture, University of Lancaster, September.

Rose, N. and Miller, R. (1989) 'Rethinking the state: governing economic, social and personal life', MS, University of Lancaster.

Chapter 5

Discourse, power and access

Teun A. van Dijk

DIMENSIONS OF DOMINANCE

One of the crucial tasks of Critical Discourse Analysis (CDA) is to account for the relationships between discourse and social power. More specifically, such an analysis should describe and explain how power abuse is enacted, reproduced or legitimised by the text and talk of dominant groups or institutions. Within the framework of such an account of discursively mediated dominance and inequality this chapter focuses on an important dimension of such dominance, that is, patterns of *access* to discourse.

A critical analysis of properties of access to public discourse and communication presupposes insight into more general political, socio-cultural and economic aspects of dominance. This chapter merely gives a succinct summary of this broader conceptual framework. Leaving aside a detailed discussion of numerous philosophical and theoretical complexities, the major presuppositions of this framework are, for example, the following (see, e.g., Clegg, 1989; Lukes, 1974; 1986; Wrong, 1979):

1 Power is a property of relations between social groups, institutions or organisations. Hence, only *social power*, and not individual power, is considered here.
2 Social power is defined in terms of the *control* exercised by one group or organisation (or its members) over the *actions* and/or the *minds* of (the members of) another group, thus limiting the freedom of action of the others, or influencing their knowledge, attitudes or ideologies.
3 Power of a specific group or institution may be 'distributed', and may be restricted to a specific social *domain* or *scope*, such as that of politics, the media, law and order, education or corporate business, thus resulting in different 'centres' of power and elite groups that control such centres.
4 *Dominance* is here understood as a form of social power *abuse*, that is, as a legally or morally illegitimate exercise of control over others in one's own interests, often resulting in social inequality.

5 Power is *based* on privileged access to valued social resources, such as wealth, jobs, status, or indeed, a preferential access to public discourse and communication.
6 Social power and dominance are often *organised* and *institutionalised*, so as to allow more effective control, and to enable routine forms of power reproduction.
7 Dominance is seldom absolute; it is often *gradual*, and may be met by more or less *resistance* or counter-power by dominated groups.

For the discussion in this chapter, it is important to stress one element in these short definitions of power and dominance, that is, the relevance of the *cognitive* dimension of control. Power abuse not only involves the abuse of force, for example in police aggression against black youths, and may result not merely in limiting the freedom of action of a specific group, but also and more crucially may affect the *minds* of people. That is, through special access to, and control over the means of public discourse and communication, dominant groups or institutions may influence the structures of text and talk in such a way that, as a result, the knowledge, attitudes, norms, values and ideologies of recipients are – more or less indirectly – affected in the interest of the dominant group.

Much 'modern' power in democratic societies is persuasive and manip-ulative rather than coercive (using of force), or incentive, such as the explicit issuing of commands, orders, threats or economic sanctions. Obviously, discourse plays a crucial role in thus 'manufacturing the consent' of others (Herman and Chomsky, 1988). It is therefore an impor-tant task of CDA to also study the precise cognitive structures and strate-gies involved in these processes affecting the *social cognitions* of groups (for details on social cognition, see e.g. Fiske and Taylor, 1991). Generally speaking, what is involved here, is the manipulation of *mental models* of social events through the use of specific discourse structures, such as thematic structures, headlines, style, rhetorical figures, semantic strategies, and so on (for details, see van Dijk, 1990; van Dijk and Kintsch, 1983). Unless the readers or listeners have access to alternative information, or mental resources to oppose such persuasive messages, the result of such manipulation may be the formation of *preferred models* of specific situa-tions (e.g., of a 'race riot'), which may in turn be generalised to more general, preferred knowledge, attitudes or ideologies (e.g. about blacks, or about youths).

DISCOURSE AND ACCESS

One major element in the discursive reproduction of power and dominance is the very *access* to discourse and communicative events. In this respect discourse is similar to other valued social resources that form the basis of power and to which there is unequally distributed access. For instance, not everyone has equal access to the media or to medical, legal, political, bureaucratic or scholarly text and talk. That is, we need to explore the implications of the complex question *Who may speak or write to whom, about what, when, and in what context*, or *Who may participate in such communicative events in various recipient roles*, for instance as addressees, audience, bystanders and overhearers. Access may even be analysed in terms of the topics or referents of discourse, that is, who is written or spoken *about*. We may assume, as for other social resources, that *more* access according to these several participant roles, corresponds with *more* social power. In other words, measures of discourse access may be rather faithful indicators of the power of social groups and their members.

Patterns and strategies of discursive access may be spelled out for virtually all social domains, institutions, professions, situations and genres. Thus, in the *political* realm, only ministers have active access to Cabinet meetings, and only parliamentarians to parliamentary debates. Secretaries or clerks may have passive access to Cabinet meetings, that is, only in their roles as people who take notes or carry out orders; they speak only when invited to do so. In public sessions of parliaments, members of the public may have passive access, but only as listeners (or rather, as 'over-hearers'). Similar patterns of access exist also in *business corporations*, for board meetings or in boss–employee interaction.

In *education*, teachers usually control communicative events, distribute speaking turns, and otherwise have special access to, and hence control over educational discourse. On the other hand, students have in principle access to talk in classrooms only when talked to and invited to speak. In some cases, also in other domains, such limited access may be voluntary, in others it may be obligatory, for example, when students must answer exam questions, when citizens are ordered to speak in hearings, defendants in police interrogations or when in court. Similarly, in *medical* encounters, doctors may control many parts of the conversations with their clients, such as the setting (time, place and circumstances, e.g. after 'appointment' only), topics (medical problems only) and style.

Most obvious and consequential are the patterns of access to the mass *media*: who has preferential access to journalists, who will be interviewed, quoted and described in news reports, and whose opinions will thus be able to influence the public? That is, through access to the mass media, dominant groups also may have access to, and hence partial control over the public at large. Except for letters to the editor, the public generally has passive media access only as readers or viewers.

Finally, in everyday *conversations*, there may be culturally different patterns of access based on age, gender, class, education or other criteria that define dominance and discrimination: women may have less access than men, blacks less than whites, young people less than adults.

Thus, for each social domain, profession, organisation or situation, we may sketch a discursive and communicative *schema of conditions and strategies of access* for the various social groups involved: indeed, who may say/write what, how, to whom in what circumstances?

ANALYSING PATTERNS OF ACCESS

The examples informally discussed show different patterns of access, depending on various social or institutional roles, gender, age, position, context or topicality. In order to examine such conditions and strategies of access more explicitly, a number of analytical distinctions need to be made. Although it is a relevant concept in the study of discourse and power, 'access' is a rather vague notion, and therefore needs further specification. It may involve the way people take the initiative for communicative events, the modalities of their participation, as well as the ways they control the various other properties of discourse, such as turn taking, sequencing, topics, or even the ways they are being represented, as referents or topics, in discourse. Let us briefly discuss some of these dimensions of access.

Planning

Patterns of discourse access already begin with taking the initiative, the preparation or the *planning* of a communicative event. Thus a chairperson may 'call' a meeting, a judge may issue a warrant to appear in court, and a professor may decide to hold an exam. Such plans will usually imply decisions about the setting (time, place) and an 'agenda' for talk, as well as the participants being invited or ordered to appear. For medical or educational encounters, patients or students may take the initiative, but doctors and professors usually decide about the setting. Such is also the case for most service encounters, such as with bureaucratic agencies. In media encounters, the relative position and power of news actors and journalists usually determines who may access whom: who has access to a press conference or who 'gives' an interview.

Setting

There are many elements of the setting of communicative events that may be controlled by different participants. First of all, who is allowed or obliged to participate, and in what role, may be decided by the chairperson or by other powerful participants who control the interaction. We have already seen that time, place and circumstances of text and talk may similarly be controlled by powerful actors. Also other circumstances, such as distance, positioning and the presence of 'props of power' (the bench and the robes of a judge, the uniform of police officers, or the 'head' of the table for chairs), may involve differential patterns of access for different participants.

Controlling communicative events

The crucial form of access consists of the power to control various dimensions of speech and talk itself: which mode of communication may/must be used (spoken, written), which language may/must be used by whom (dominant or standard language, a dialect, etc.), which genres of discourse are allowed, which types of speech acts, or who may begin or interrupt turns at talk or discursive sequences. Besides these overall constraints, participants may have differential access to topics, style or rhetoric. Thus, defendants in court may be required to speak the standard language, to answer questions only (and only when required to speak), to speak only about the topic being discussed, and using a polite, deferential style. Similar constraints may exist for subordinates in business companies or students in school. That is, virtually all levels and dimensions of text and talk may have obligatory, optional or preferential access for different participants, for example, as a function of their institutional or social power. Or rather, such power and dominance may be enacted, confirmed and reproduced by such differential patterns of access to various forms of discourse in different social situations. Thus, having access to the speech act of a command presupposes as well as enacts and confirms the social power of the speaker.

Scope and audience control

For dialogues such as formal meetings, sessions or debates, initiators or participants may allow or require specific participants to be present (or absent), or to allow or require these others to listen and/or to speak. Beyond the control of content or style, thus, speakers may also control audiences. That is, discourse access, especially in public forms of discourse, also and most crucially implies audience access. At public meetings or through the mass media, discourses and their speakers or authors may thus have a greater or lesser power scope. Full access to a major newspaper or television network thus also implies access to a large audience: obviously, access to the *New York Times* or CBS signals more power than access to a local newspaper or local radio station. The same is true for writers, teachers, professors or politicians and the relative sizes of their audiences.

Although the scope of access, in terms of the size of the audience of one's discourse, is an important criterion of power, control is much more effective if the minds of the audience can also be successfully 'accessed'.

When speakers are able to influence the mental models, knowledge, attitudes and eventually even the ideologies of recipients, they may indirectly control their future actions. That is, mentally mediated control of the actions of others is the ultimate form of power, especially when the audience is hardly aware of such control, as is the case in manipulation. Indeed, most forms of discursive and communicative access we discussed above, such as control of setting, interaction, topic or style will be geared towards the control of the minds of participants, recipients or the audience at large, in such a way that the resulting mental changes are those preferred by those in power, and generally in their interest.

Synthesising criteria of access

After this discussion of the various types of access, we are now able to spell out – for each type of discourse or communicative event, and for each social group or institution – the various access patterns that establish one of the relationships between discourse and social power. For a court trial, for instance, we might specify the following schema of access, in terms of who control(s) what aspect of such a trial, as informally discussed above (the schema is not complete; for conversational details, see e.g. Atkinson and Drew, 1979; for style, see Erickson *et al.*, 1978; O'Barr, 1982; for access to specific genres, Wodak, 1985; note also that all variation and control is limited by the overall socio-cultural constraints of the legal context and the speech situation).

Initiative: judge
Setting (time, place, participants): judge, prosecutor, barristers
Communicative event
    Participants: judge (e.g. judge may exclude prosecution witnesses)
    Turn allocation and distribution: judge
    Sequencing (e.g. opening and closing the session): judge
    Speech acts:
        Verdict, sentencing, commands, requests, questions, assertions: judge
        Verdict: jury (e.g. in British and US legal systems)
        Indictment, accusations, questions, assertions: prosecutor
        Defence, requests, questions, assertions: defence counsel
        Assertions (as answers to questions): defendant, witnesses
    Topic(s): judge, prosecutor, defence counsel
    Style: judge
    Recording: clerks
    Audience/scope: immediate: usually small; mass mediated: large.
    Result: possibly serious for defendant (loss of money, freedom, or life).

Conversely, we may examine the power of social groups or professions, such as judges, by analysing their range and patterns of access (as judges), and we see that they control most properties of the court trial. However, since (important) trials are often routinely covered by the media, judges also have relatively easy media access as described above, although such access is not total: judges may not control what exactly is written or said about them (Anderson *et al.*, 1988; Chibnall, 1977; Graber, 1980; Hariman, 1990). Although the normal access range and scope of judges is only the legal domain, that is legal discourse in general (e.g. when writing a verdict), and trials in particular, judges may also have access to education and research when giving lectures or writing textbooks, or to politics or finance when they are appointed as members of committees or boards because of their legal expertise or influence. In sum, judges appear to have a medium range of access, corresponding to their relative power. However, since they are, in principle, the only ones who decide about freedom or even about life and death, the consequences of their other-wise moderate power may be tremendous. This is, of course, especially the case for judges of courts of appeal and Supreme Courts, which may even have the last word in deciding on major socio-political issues affecting a whole nation, such as abortion or civil rights. That is, beyond the scope and the range of their discourse access, the power of judges should especially also be measured by the personal, social and political consequences of such access. Indeed, in the legal domain, their discourse may *be* law.

Similar analyses may be made, each for their own domain of power, for more or less powerful presidents, Cabinet ministers, members of parliament or congress, popes and priests, chief executive officers, professors, newspaper editors or union leaders, among others, but also, at lower levels of the power hierarchy, for 'ordinary' citizens, bureaucrats, police officers, teachers or shopkeepers. It is our contention that there should generally be a rather close interdependence between power (and hence access to valued social resources), on the one hand, and access to – control over – the conditions, structural properties and consequences of discourse, on the other hand. In other words, if discourse access is a measure of power, Critical Discourse Analysis becomes an important diagnostic tool for the assessment of social and political dominance.

DISCOURSE, POWER AND RACISM

To further illustrate the analysis of discursive social power and access patterns presented above, let us finally examine in somewhat more detail some of the ways social power is being enacted, legitimised and repro-duced in one major domain of dominance, that by white (European) groups over ethnic or racial minorities, refugees or other immigrants.

Empirical data that form the backdrop of this discussion are derived from our extensive research project on discourse and racism, carried out at the University of Amsterdam since 1980 (van Dijk, 1984; 1987; 1991; 1993a). The various discourses studied for this project were everyday conversations, high school textbooks, news reports in the press, parliamentary debates, scientific discourse, and corporate discourse, among others.

The aim of our discussion here is only to show how ethnic-racial dominance, or racism, is also reproduced through differential patterns of discourse access for majority and minority groups, and not only because of differential access to residence, jobs, housing, education or welfare. This dominance may take two forms: the discursive reproduction of ethnic prejudice and racism within the dominant white group itself, on the one hand, and forms of everyday racism in talk between majority and minority members (e.g. slurs, impoliteness, unfounded accusations), on the other hand (Essed, 1991).

One strategy of such dominant discourse is to persuasively define the ethnic status quo as 'natural', 'just', 'inevitable' or even as 'democratic', for instance through denials of discrimination or racism, or by de-racialising inequality through redefinitions in terms of class, cultural difference or the special (unique, temporary) consequences of immigrant status. The persuasive or manipulatory success of such dominant discourse is partly due to the patterns of access of such text and talk. That is, most power elites are themselves white, and their power implies preferential access to the means of mass communication, political decision-making discourse, the discourses of the bureaucracy, and the legal system. That is, relative to minority groups, dominance is duplicated: it is the white group as a whole that has special privileges and access to social resources, including the symbolic resources of communication, whereas the white power elites additionally control the white group at large, by their persuasive influence on the mental conditions (stereotypes, prejudices, ideologies) of the discriminatory practices of white group members.

The opposite is true for ethnic minority groups, whose subordination is further exacerbated by their (generally) lower class position. That is, their lack of access is not merely defined in terms of racial or ethnic exclusion, but also by their class-dependent lack of access to good education, status, employment or capital, shared with poor whites. The exclusion and marginalisation that result from limited socio-economic and symbolic (discursive, communicative) access hardly need to be spelled out (for details, see Essed, 1991; Jaynes and Williams, 1989). Thus, minorities or immigrants generally have less or no access to the following crucial communicative contexts, as analysed above:

1 Government and legislative discourses of decision-making, information, persuasion and legitimation, especially at the national/state levels.

2 Bureaucratic discourses of higher level policy-making and policy implementation.
3 Mass media discourse of major news media.
4 Scholarly or scientific discourse.
5 Corporate discourse.

Politics

Especially in Europe, virtually no minority group members are members of national governments, and only very few are members of the legislature (for the UK, see Solomos, 1989). In some countries, such as the Netherlands, some minorities that do not have Dutch nationality, but have been residents for five years, have active and passive access to local elections, and thus have a (minimal) voice in city councils, a small 'privilege' fiercely opposed in, say, France and Germany. Due to the size of ethnic minority groups in the USA, there is at least some political representation of minorities and hence access to political decision-making, especially at the local level, for example in cities with a large minority population (Ben-Tovim *et al.*, 1986; Jaynes and Williams, 1989; Marable, 1985). Since most 'ethnic' policies, however, are national or federal, minorities are more or less effectively excluded from more influential text and talk about their own position. On the other hand, minorities are frequent topics of political talk and text, but this form of passive access is hardly controlled by them: they have virtually no influence on this 'representation' in political discourse (van Dijk, 1993a).

Media

The access of minorities to the mass media is a critical condition for their participation in the public definition of their situation. Despite the generally liberal self-definitions of many journalists, lack of media access by minorities is one of the most conspicuous properties of the symbolic dominance of white elites (Hujanen, 1984; Mazingo, 1988; *Minority Participation in the Media*, 1983; Wilson and Gutiérrez, 1985). In Europe, there are virtually no minority journalists, least of all in controlling editorial positions. Major quality newspapers may have just one or two token minorities, often in non-tenured contract or freelance positions. Even in the USA, 51 per cent of the newspapers have no minority journalists, and promotions to higher positions are notoriously problematic. Television has limited access only for some (very 'moderate') visible token minorities. As a result, the newsroom staff are virtually wholly white, and this will of course have serious consequences for news production, writing style, source access and general perspective of news discourse or television programmes

(Hartmann and Husband, 1974; Martindale, 1986; Smitherman-Donaldson and van Dijk, 1988; van Dijk, 1991).

Moreover, due to their limited social and economic power, minority groups and organisations also lack the usual forms of organised media access, such as press conferences, press releases and public relations departments (Fedler, 1973). Conversely, most white journalists are known to routinely prefer (white) institutional sources (Tuchman, 1978), and generally find minorities less credible, especially when these are providing critical opinions about dominant white elites. Communication problems and differences of style between white journalists and minority sources may further limit minority access to the media (Kochman, 1981).

Differential access of majority elites and minorities to the media predictably results in differential access to the structures of news reports as well. Selection and prominence of news *issues* and *topics* are those stereotypical and negative ones preferred by the white political, corporate, social or scholarly elites and their institutions. Thus, the frequent issue of immigration will be primarily defined as an invasion and as essentially problematic, and seldom as a welcome contribution to the economy or the culture of the country. Crime, drugs, violence and cultural deviance are other preferred issues of 'ethnic' news coverage. Conversely, due to limited minority access to the definition of the situation, issues and topics that are directly relevant for minorities are less covered or made less prominent. This is the case for issues such as discrimination, racism, police brutality, shortage of jobs, miserable working conditions, the failures of minority education, and so on, especially when the white elites are to blame for the situation. On the other hand, the actions of white elites that are defined as 'positive' for minorities are usually covered prominently. As in the coverage of North–South relations, 'our' helping 'them' is a very newsworthy topic. Thus, news topic selection and prominence is a direct function of the differential access, interests and perspectives of majority and minority news actors.

Similarly, lack of access to journalists also predicts that minority speakers will be less *quoted* than white majority speakers, as is indeed the case (van Dijk, 1991). If they are quoted at all, then either moderate spokespersons will be quoted who share the opinions or perspective of the majority, or radicals or extremists will be quoted in order to facilitate ridicule or attack (Downing, 1980). Minorities are especially quoted on 'soft' and less 'risky' topics, such as religion, the arts, folklore, or culture more generally (Hartmann and Husband, 1974; Johnson, 1987; van Dijk, 1991). Also, unlike majority group speakers, minorities are seldom allowed to speak alone. Their accusations of the host society and its elites, when quoted at all, *never* go unchallenged.

Similar observations may be made for all properties and levels of news reports. *Headline* content and syntactic structure systematically favour 'us' and problematise 'them', as is also the case for lexical *style* (e.g. 'riots' instead of 'disturbances'), *rhetoric*, disclaimers and other strategic semantic *moves* ('We have nothing against Turks, but . . .'; 'We are a tolerant society, but . . .'), as well as other discursive properties. Thus, on the whole, 'their' negative actions are made more prominent (e.g. by topicalisation, first page coverage, headlining, rhetorical emphasis), whereas 'our' negative actions are de-emphasised by denials, euphemism, mitigation or other strategies for avoiding negative self-presentation (van Dijk, 1991; 1992). Because of a lack of alternative information sources about ethnic relations, the effects of such daily reporting of the models and attitudes of many white readers are predictable: widespread prejudice and xenophobia. Thus, minorities and their representatives have little access to the general public, unless by protests and disruptive behaviour that will precisely be defined as a confirmation of prevailing stereotypes and prejudices.

Academia

Rather similar remarks may be made about patterns of access to educational and scholarly discourse (for details, see van Dijk, 1993a). Minorities, especially in Europe, generally have little access to universities, and even less to the active control of scholarly discourse, even in 'ethnic' studies about them. In the Netherlands, for instance, more than 95 per cent of all 'ethnic' research is carried out by white Dutch researchers, and even more is under white Dutch supervision. Ethnic studies departments, if any, are usually largely white. The topics of such 'ethnic' research are surprisingly similar to those in the mass media: cultural difference and deviance, crime, educational problems, etc. With the usual delays, high school textbooks typically reproduce prevailing scholarly stereotypes about minorities. Not surprisingly, the media will in turn pay special attention to those research results that nicely fit the prevailing stereotypes, such as about youth gangs, drugs, crime or the cultural problems of young immigrant women.

Critical issues, such as discrimination and especially racism, are as little studied as they are covered in the press. Moreover, the few studies of these issues tend to be ignored, denied, marginalised and attacked as 'unscientific' or 'political' scholarship (Essed, 1987).

Thus, ethnic groups, and even their scholarly elites, have virtually no access to, let alone control over, the ways the ethnic situation is defined in the social sciences. Since much of this research is also used as a source for national policies (and for media accounts), we see how dominant white elites jointly collude in preventing access to the hegemonic basis of power, that of knowledge and beliefs and the manufacture of the consensus. It needs no further argument that curricula, scholarly journals, conferences, and other vehicles of scholarly discourse are also usually dominated by white scholars, except for small 'niches' of 'black' journals that have virtually no influence on the scholarly establishment in the social sciences as a whole. The hype, especially in the USA, about what is defined as 'political correctness' in academia reflects an overreaction of dominant white elites against minor and local cultural shifts and minority resistance, rather than a fundamental change in prevailing academic discourse and access patterns (Aufderheide, 1992; Berman, 1992).

Business

Corporate discourse is usually less public, and hence only indirectly involved in manufacturing consent. However, it is ultimately vastly influential through its consequences for the socio-economic implications of the ethnic status quo. If corporate discourse explains high minority unemployment especially in terms that blame the victim (language deficiencies, lack of skills, lower education, failing work ethos, etc.), this discourse will also have easy access to the press and to political decision-making (Fernandez, 1981; Jenkins, 1986; van Dijk, 1993a). Managerial talk about affirmative action and other forms of social responsibility may be associated with many negative properties, such as loss of competition, social unfairness, and so on. Also this feature of prominent corporate discourse, especially in Europe, will indirectly become public, for instance through politicians or journalists repeating or emphasising this point of view.

Few minority group members have leading managerial positions, and when they do, they make sure not to speak too radically about the claims or complaints of their own group, unless they want to lose their jobs. Thus, minorities have very little influence on dominant corporate discourse. That is, they are unable to successfully challenge the ideologies that underlie discrimination and marginalisation of minorities in employment, business and finance in the first place. On the contrary, blaming the victim is a major strategy of white elite dominance, also in corporate discourse: charges of discrimination will be reversed by accusing minorities (especially blacks) of causing their own predicament, as noted above.

SOME EXAMPLES

After the more theoretical analysis of the relations between discourse, power and access, and the review of access patterns for discourse on ethnic relations, let us finally discuss some concrete examples. These will be taken from the coverage of ethnic affairs in the British press, during the first six months of 1989. Many reports during these months dealt with the Salman Rushdie affair, and – as usual in the press – with 'illegal' immigration.

Example 1

Thus the *Sun* begins one of its articles (23 January 1989) on immigration as follows:

GET LOST, SPONGERS

By Victor Chapple

A BLITZ on illegal immigration is being launched by the Government.

The number of staff dealing with foreign spongers will be more than **DOUBLED** and **TOUGH** new curbs are planned against bogus overseas students.

Key targets will be phoney colleges which enrol youngsters, but provide no courses.

When immigration officers raided one in East London last year, they found that 990 of the 1000 'students' had no right to be in Britain. Home secretary Douglas Hurd is considering law changes to stop foreign visitors switching to student status while here.

The huge (23 × 3cm) banner headline of this article represents the evaluative comment of the *Sun* on the plans of the government. The same is true for the use of 'bogus' and 'phoney', when describing students and colleges. These evaluative terms are not likely to be those used by the British government or Home Secretary Mr Douglas Hurd. It is at this point that the power, the autonomy and hence the responsibility of the newspaper are obvious: they could hardly blame the 'politicians' for the racist language they use to influence the readers. In terms of our analysis of patterns of access, the style of reporting is accessible only to the reporter (Victor Chapple) or the editors of the *Sun*, and so is the persuasive effect such negative other-presentation may have on the minds of the readers. The direct contribution to the confirmation of well-known ethnic prejudices in the UK, that is, of immigrants as 'spongers', is thus within the scope of the responsibility of the tabloid.

At the same time, however, we need to emphasise the 'collusion' between the press elites on the one hand, and the political elites on the other. After all, the policies and political actions written *about* are those of the British authorities: they will do anything to reduce what they define as 'illegal' immigration. The tabloid does not merely report such actions, however, but supports them, and even fabricates their reasons (students will be expelled because they are 'spongers'). Thus, in many ways, the right-wing press supports conservative immigration policies, while at the same time framing them in a popular rhetorical style ('get lost', 'spongers', 'phoney', etc.) that makes such policies seem to respond to popular demand and resentment against immigration, thereby legitimising them.

Besides the direct access of the newsmakers to the style (size, lexicalisation, etc.) of the headlines and the style of the rest of the article, we also witness some degree of access of a prominent politician, that of the Home Secretary, whose picture is reproduced, whose actions are covered (positively) and whose future policies are mentioned. In the rest of the article, not quoted here, about a Sri Lankan refugee, Mr Viraj Mendis (described as an 'activist') – who had sought refuge in a church but was arrested in a police raid and expelled after many years of residence in the UK – Douglas Hurd is also quoted, as is a Tory Member of Parliament (MP), both protesting against the action of churches in hiding refugees. The churches have no access to the press here: no spokespersons are quoted. Viraj Mendis, in a separate small article, is quoted as wanting to 'expose the racism of the British government', and a picture of him is also shown. However, the framing of *his* words is dramatically different from that of Hurd. He is portrayed, in the text, as 'sip[ping] mineral water in an exclusive club in Colombo', which implies that someone who is in such a situation can hardly be a serious refugee, and hence not a credible speaker. The very fact that he accuses the British government of racism is so preposterous for the *Sun* that such an accusation hardly needs further discrediting of Mendis, as the tabloid had done during the whole Mendis affair (for a more detailed analysis of right-wing reporting in the UK on the Viraj Mendis case, see van Dijk, 1993b).

In sum, we find several modes of access here. First, access of media elites: tabloid reporters and editors themselves, who chose the topic as being newsworthy, and control its style and rhetoric, layout, photos, and who thus also have direct and persuasive access to the 'minds' of the readers.

Second, access of political elites: Mr Hurd as main actor has access to the topic, the quotations and the visual images of a tabloid read by about 5 million British readers.

Third, access of other politicians: access of a Tory MP, supporting Mr Hurd (or rather being critical of him for not having acted fast enough) and hence also sustaining the negative evaluation of the *Sun*.

Fourth, access of a refugee: passive access of Viraj Mendis to a secondary topic of this article (and to the main topic of a related short story), to quotation and photographs, but embedded in a negative framework so as to invalidate his credibility.

Example 2

The next example is also taken from the *Sun*, and was published a few days later (2 February 1989):

BRITAIN INVADED BY AN ARMY OF ILLEGALS

SUN News Special

By John Kay and Alison Bowyer

Britain is being swamped by a tide of illegal immigrants so desperate for a job that they will work for a pittance in our restaurants, cafes and nightclubs.

Immigration officers are being overwhelmed with work. Last year, 2,191 'illegals' were being nabbed and sent back home. But there are tens of thousands more, slaving behind bars, cleaning hotel rooms and working in kitchens. . . .

Illegals sneak in by:

- **DECEIVING** immigration officers when they are quizzed at airports.
- **DISAPPEARING** after their entry visas run out.
- **FORGING** work permits and other documents.
- **RUNNING** away from immigrant detention centres.

We again find the familiar picture of a huge banner headline, featuring three major negative expressions, usually associated with immigrants and refugees: 'invaded', 'army', and 'illegals'. This style of describing undocumented immigrants is fully under the control (and access) of the *Sun* journalists, with the probable consequences for the access to the public mind, as described above. Note the special semantic implications and associations of the use of 'invasion' and 'army', which explicitly relates immigration with violence and threats to 'Britain': Immigration is War.

Since this is a 'News Special', the responsibility seems to be even more that of the tabloid: they do not report a news event, such as a political action, as is the case in the previous example, but they bring a 'report' based on their own journalistic 'investigations'. The 'facts' thus constructed by the tabloid are as familiar as their metaphorical style, by which refugees and other immigrants are routinely compared to a 'tide' that 'swamps' the country. The term 'swamped' is familiar. It was also used by Margaret Thatcher before she was elected prime minister, when she said that she feared that Britain would be 'rather swamped' by people of an alien culture. Hence, the metaphors, though under full access and control of the journalists, are as such hardly new, and belong to the stock in trade of racist conservatives speaking about immigration. Obviously, as is the case with the use of 'invaded' and 'army', being 'swamped' by a 'tide' of 'illegals' is just as threatening for the (white) British population, which is the primary audience for such style. The rest of the article shows the same style, for example when the police actions are called a 'battle to hunt down the furtive workforce'. This is indeed what it is: a war to keep Britain white.

Immigration officers also have (passive, topical) access to this article, and are duly pitied as being 'overwhelmed' by the task. No harsh word will be found in the *Sun* about the ways that immigration officers accomplish their task of 'tracking' down 'illegals'. Note though that there seems to be a suggestion of commiseration with the immigrants as well, as may be inferred from the use of 'working for a pittance' and 'slaving'. At the same time, the style of the rest of the article does not seem to confirm this journalistic mood in favour of the immigrants. Rather 'working for a pittance' also implies that since immigrants will do any job for any wage, they compete with white British workers. Thus, such a representation supports the familiar racist conclusion: 'They take away our jobs!' Indeed, nowhere is it stressed in the article that most white British no longer want such work.

The next fragment, emphasised by bold capitals and attention-seeking 'bullets', summarises the various forms of deviance, violation and crime attributed to immigrants: they are liars and frauds. The rest of the article is similar (they do not pay taxes, etc.), but also focuses on the businesses that are being 'raided' by the police. However, the focus of illegality is *not* on employers, businesses and all those others who exploit immigrants and pay sub-standard wages. Indeed, the headline of the article is *not* BRITAIN THREATENED BY A GANG OF IMMIGRANT-EXPLOITING BUSI-NESSES. Even the use of the passive voice in the syntax of the sentences hides those who do illegal hiring: 'They [immigration officials] ended up taking away **THIRTEEN** Nigerians, all employed illegally', of which the last clause hides the agent of illegal hiring.

As for the relations of power and access involved, we first of all find the reporters (and possibly the editors) of the *Sun* again responsible for the selection of the topic of this 'special report', for its style and the focus on certain dimensions (immigrants as threat and criminals) and not on others (employers engaging in illegal hiring and exploiting minorities). That is, the media elites have exclusive and active access to, and control over a large part of this text, and such is also their responsibility in manipulating the minds of the readers: the 'facts' of immigration are not to be blamed (as the reporters would undoubtedly say), but the journalistic ways of fabricating, representing and persuasively formulating such 'facts'.

At the same time, other news actors are involved and have various measures of access. Positively represented, as could be expected, are the immigration officers (in ethnic reporting in the right-wing press, the officers of law and order are *always* presented positively, as the guardians of Britain, who valiantly struggle in the racial war). One of them is also introduced in a later quote which tells the readers that he doesn't know how many illegals there are (apparently, the *Sun* does know) but that the officials are stepping up 'their efforts to track them down'. Employers, we have seen, are stylistically absent: their businesses may be raided, but they are literally out of the picture; only 'illegals' (that is immigrants, not managers) are found there. Yet, at the end, and in a small separate article, some bosses may talk; however, they affirm that they hire only legal immigrants (from the EU), a claim that is not presented as at all doubtful by the *Sun*. Not a single negative word about employers is found in this article, despite the fact that the 'illegal' immigrants are working for a pittance. On the contrary, they are represented as victims, who are sometimes 'tricked by false credentials'.

In sum, also throughout this special report, 'we' or 'our' people (officials, business, Britain), are consequently represented in a positive way, and 'they' in a very negative way, as an invading army or as a swamping tide, people who, in the *Sun*'s words, must be 'nabbed' and 'carted off' by the immigration officials.

We see that patterns of access (who is written about, who is allowed to speak, who may address whom, and who may use what style, etc.) are closely related to modes of self- and other-presentation in public discourse on ethnic affairs. Access to the press, through access to the journalists, also presupposes group-membership: those who belong to 'us' will have more access, especially the elites, but at the same time, they will also be represented more positively. The inverse is true for 'them'. Indeed, not a single 'illegal immigrant' is quoted in this 'special report': their views, experiences, backgrounds are irrelevant. With a foreign army, that is, the enemy, one does not talk: one 'hunts them down' and 'carts them off'.

Other examples

Many similar examples may be given: in the tabloid press most reporting has the same overall structures and strategies of access to selection, topicality, style and quotation, along the familiar US–THEM schema of racist representations. For the right-wing tabloids, this also means that 'them' immigrants are associated with 'them' of the 'loony left', another familiar target of tabloid attacks, as in the first of the following banner headlines and text fragments:

LEFTIES HAND £20,000 TO ILLEGAL IMMIGRANT
(Sun, 6 February 1989)

BE BRITISH, HURD TELLS IMMIGRANTS

A DIRECT warning to Britain's 750,000 Moslems will be issued by Home Secretary Douglas Hurd today.
He will tell them they must learn to live with British laws and customs – particularly for the sake of their children. The alternative would be growing public anger and resentment and renewed social conflict.
(Daily Mail, 24 February 1989)

NO RACIALISM IN TORY PARTY, SAYS THATCHER
(Daily Telegraph, 23 June 1989)

Thus, immigrants and the left share the familiar accusations of 'fraud' exposed by the tabloids, as in the first headline. Indeed, 'ratepayers' money', as is often stressed, is thus presented as 'squandered' by loony left councils or programmes, a topic obviously popular with many tabloid readers.

In the second example, Home Secretary Hurd, responsible for immigration and ethnic relations, appears again, this time with a full account of a speech he *will* give (some news is not about the past, but about the near future), and which is worth an immense headline in 3 cm high capitals. That is, after the Rushdie affair, Muslims have become fair game both for paternalistic, if not threatening, political action, as well as for the press (and not only the right-wing tabloids), which associates *all* Muslims with the radical fundamentalists among them. If cultural autonomy was occasionally an official policy of western governments, the words now being spoken by Hurd and emphasised by the *Mail* leave no doubt about the real, assimilationist goals of ethnic relation policies: adapt to us, or get out. Worse, as is the case in much tabloid reporting and editorials, as soon as immigrants or minorities are represented as violating the law (as in 'riots') or trespassing the norms of cultural adaptation, popular 'resentment' (or even the fascists) are made to appear as a threat. Ironically, if not cynically, we need to realise that this resentment is created and fed by the tabloids themselves. Similarly, the threat of 'racial conflict' is not attributed to white racists, but to immigrants themselves, a familiar move of strategic reversal in the attribution of responsibilities.

The third example speaks for itself. As prime minister, Margaret Thatcher obviously had most privileged access to the media, thus being allowed to define the ethnic situation, and thus, of course, to deny racism (while at the same time using the familiar conservative mitigation 'racialism'). Notice, that if (well-founded) accusations of racism are reported at all, the conservative press will routinely use the distance- or doubt-implying term 'claim' (for details, see van Dijk, 1991). Not so when Thatcher 'flatly denies', during a parliamentary debate, that there is no racism in the Conservative party, a claim met with derision from the Labour benches, here represented, however, as less credible than Thatcher. Indeed, the denial of racism is one of the hallmarks of elite racism (see van Dijk, 1993c).

Again we find the familiar patterns of access: Hurd, as a conservative politician, and by castigating Muslims, has ample access to the tabloid, its topic selection, its headline, and quote, and so has Thatcher. The immigrants and Muslims have passive access (as topics), but *they* do not control their representation, and their spokespersons are not quoted, unless it is a radical fundamentalist who will gladly oblige by confirming the prejudices of the reporter about the threat posed by Muslims and Arabs.

CONCLUSIONS

The conclusions of this chapter may be brief. Within the framework of a critical analysis of discourses, the study of the reproduction of power and dominance through discourse is a primary objective. One element in this reproduction process is the structures and strategies of 'access': who controls the preparation, the participants, the goals, the language, the genre, the speech acts, the topics, the schemata (e.g. headlines, quotes), the style, and the rhetoric, among other text features, of communicative events. That is, who can/may/must say what, to whom, how, in what circumstances and with what effects on the recipients?

Among the resources that form the power base of dominant groups, also the preferential access to public discourse is an increasingly important asset, because it allows access to the control mechanisms of the public mind. In modern societies, discourse access is a primary condition for the manufacture of consent, and therefore the most effective way to exercise power and dominance.

Our brief analysis of some examples from the British press shows how the tabloids, conservative politicians and the forces of law and order have preferential access to the public definition of immigration and minorities, as well as to their derogation as criminals, frauds, invading armies, and radical assassins, among many other other-descriptions of 'them', while at the same time presenting 'us' as tolerant, tough and valiant, if not as victims. That is, the power of preferential access to the media is intimately related to the power of dominant groups to define the ethnic situation, and to contribute to the reproduction of racism, that is, the power of the white group.

REFERENCES

Anderson, D. A., Milner, J. W. and Galician, M. L. (1988) 'How editors view legal issues and the Rehnquist Court', *Journalism Quarterly*, 65, 294–8.

Atkinson, M. and Drew, P. (1979) *Order in Court: The Organisation of Verbal Interaction in Judicial Settings*, London: Macmillan.

Aufderheide, P. (1992) *Beyond PC: Toward a Politics of Understanding*, Saint Paul, MN: Graywolf Press.

Ben-Tovim, G., Gabriel, J., Law, I. and Stredder, K. (1986) *The Local Politics of Race*, London: Macmillan.

Berman, P. (1992) *Debating PC: The Controversy over Political Correctness on College Campuses*, New York: Bantam-Dell.

Chibnall, S. (1977) *Law and Order News: An Analysis of Crime Reporting in the British Press*, London: Tavistock.

Clegg, S. R. (1989) *Frameworks of Power*, London: Sage.

Downing, J. D. H. (1980) *The Media Machine*, London: Pluto.

Erickson, B., Lind, A. A., Johnson, B. C. and O'Barr, W. M. (1978) 'Speech style and impression formation in a court setting: the effects of "powerful" and "powerless" speech', *Journal of Experimental Social Psychology*, 14, 266–79.

Essed, P. J. M. (1987) *Academic Racism: Common Sense in the Social Sciences*, University of Amsterdam: Centre for Race and Ethnic Studies, CRES Publications, no. 5.

Essed, P. J. M. (1991) *Understanding Everyday Racism*, Newbury Park, CA: Sage.

Fedler, F. (1973) 'The media and minority groups: a study of adequacy of access', *Journalism Quarterly*, 50, 1, 109–17.

Fernandez, J. P. (1981) *Racism and Sexism in Corporate Life*, Lexington, MA: Lexington Books.

Fiske, S. T. and Taylor, S. E. (1991) *Social Cognition*, 2nd edn, New York: McGraw-Hill.

Graber, D. A. (1980) *Crime News and the Public*, New York: Praeger.

Hariman, R. (ed.) (1990) *Popular Trials: Rhetoric, Mass Media, and the Law*, Tuscaloosa, AL: University of Alabama Press.

Hartmann, P. and Husband, C. (1974) *Racism and the Mass Media*, London: Davis-Poynter.

Herman, E. S. and Chomsky, N. (1988) *Manufacturing Consent: The Political Economy of the Mass Media*, New York: Pantheon.

Hujanen, T. (ed.) (1984) *The Role of Information in the Realization of the Human Rights of Migrant Workers*, report of international conference, Tampere (Finland), University of Tampere: Dept of Journalism and Mass Communication.

Jaynes, G. D. and Williams, R. M. (eds) (1989) *A Common Destiny: Blacks and American Society*, Washington, DC: National Academy Press.

Jenkins, R. (1986) *Racism and Recruitment: Managers, Organisations and Equal Opportunity in the Labour Market*, Cambridge: Cambridge University Press.

Johnson, K. A. (1987) *Media Images of Boston's Black Community*, William Monroe Trotter Institute, Research Report, Boston MA: University of Massachusetts.

Kochman, T. (1981) *Black and White Styles in Conflict*, Chicago: University of Chicago Press.

Lukes, S. (1974) *Power: A Radical View*, London: Macmillan.

Lukes, S. (ed.) (1986) *Power*, Oxford: Blackwell.

Marable, M. (1985) *Black American Politics*, London: Verso.

Martindale, C. (1986) *The White Press and Black America*, New York: Greenwood Press.

Mazingo, S. (1988) 'Minorities and social control in the newsroom: thirty years after Breed', in G. Smitherman-Donaldson and T. A. van Dijk (eds) *Discourse and Discrimination*, Detroit, MI: Wayne State University Press, 93–130.

Minority Participation in the Media (1983) Hearings before the Subcommittee on Telecommunications, Consumer Protection and Finance, of the Committee on Energy and Commerce, House of Representatives, 98th Congress, 19 and 23 September, 1983.

O'Barr, W. M. (1982) *Linguistic Evidence: Language, Power and Strategy in the Courtroom*, New York: Academic Press.

Smitherman-Donaldson, G. and van Dijk, T. A. (eds) (1988) *Discourse and Discrimination*, Detroit, MI: Wayne State University Press.

Solomos, J. (1989) *Race and Racism in Contemporary Britain*, London: Macmillan.

Tuchman, G. (1978) *Making News: A Study in the Construction of Reality*, New York: Free Press.

van Dijk, T. A. (1984) *Prejudice in Discourse*, Amsterdam: Benjamins.

van Dijk, T. A. (1987) *Communicating Racism*, Newbury Park, CA: Sage.

van Dijk, T. A. (1990) 'Social cognition and discourse', in H. Giles and R. P.

Robinson (eds) *Handbook of Social Psychology and Language*, Chichester: Wiley, 163–83.

van Dijk, T. A. (1991) *Racism and the Press*, London: Routledge.

van Dijk, T. A. (1992) 'Discourse and the denial of racism', *Discourse and Society*, 3, 87–118.

van Dijk, T. A. (1993a) *Elite Discourse and Racism*, Newbury Park, CA: Sage.

van Dijk, T. A. (1993b) 'Discourse and cognition in society', in D. Crowley and D. Mitchell (eds) *Communication Theory Today*, Oxford: Pergamon, 104–26.

van Dijk, T. A. (1993c) 'Principles of critical discourse analysis', *Discourse and Society*, 4, 249–83.

van Dijk, T. A. and Kintsch, W. (1983) *Strategies of Discourse Comprehension*, New York: Academic Press.

Wilson, C. C. and Gutiérrez, F. (1985) *Minorities and the Media*, London: Sage.

Wodak, R. (1985) 'The interaction between judge and defendant', in T. A. van Dijk (ed.) *Handbook of Discourse Analysis, vol. 4, Discourse Analysis in Society*, London: Academic Press, 181–91.

Wrong, D. H. (1979) *Power: Its Forms, Bases and Uses*, Oxford: Blackwell.

Part II

Texts and practices: Critical approaches

The genesis of racist discourse in Austria since 1989

Ruth Wodak

Whenever one comes to Vienna, one is met on the way into the city by a barrage of colourful posters proclaiming 'Vienna is different'. This 'difference' compared to other European capital cities is said to lie in Vienna's being less dirty, noisy and crowded. The Austrian government apparently wishes to keep it so – that is, less crowded: the new residency law that came into effect on 1 July 1993 not only closes the door to many potential immigrants, but also effectively empowers the immigration authorities to expatriate any number of those who have lived legally in Austria for years. Alas, Austria's increasingly restrictive residency requirements have narrowed Vienna's 'difference' with other European capitals considerably.

Prospective immigrants not only must be, as the law states, 'capable of being integrated and willing to integrate', but also are now required to file their application for residency in Austria from their native land, irrespective of where they might currently reside. Moreover, the application, filed from abroad, must show proof of permanent employment in Austria, and show that one has arranged for housing sufficient to provide a minimum of 10 square metres per person.

The potential for abuse is most acute for those who wish to extend their temporary residency permits. According to the new law, if the Austrian immigration authorities fail to complete work on the request by the end of six weeks after the expiration of the current permit, applicants lose their authorisation to remain in the country, even if the delay is due only to the slowness or inefficiency of the immigration authorities themselves. And without any legal right to remain in the country, applicants may be expelled at the authorities' discretion.

It is, of course, utopian to believe that any country, especially one with a population of less than 8 million, could open its doors to unrestricted immigration. Yet the provisions of the new law – everywhere understood and widely hailed as a measure designed to crack down on illegal immigration – appear even to some of the politicians who voted for it as inhumane. The provision about the size of flat is particularly ironic: not only would thousands of guest workers be affected, but also several thousand native citizens live in apartments with fewer than 10 square metres' space per person.

The six-week deadline that the law sets has become the focus of heated political debate in Austria. Politicians who only months previously had voted for the law (the only members of parliament who voted against it were the Greens), doubtless concerned that resident guest workers indispensable to the economy might fall victim to the bureaucratic arbitrariness the law encourages, have called for the law's speedy change.

Perhaps the most grotesque aspect of this debate to date has been the nearly Pauline conversion by Michael Graff, the Christian Democratic People's party spokesperson and head of the parliamentary judiciary committee. Graff, who voted for the measure in both committee and the house, claimed that he would have voted differently, if he had only taken the trouble to read the law before the votes.

Prior to the law's passage, the debate in Austria was characterised by the climate of fear aroused by the prospect of millions of potential immigrants ready to 'inundate helpless Austria'. Although some of the elites seem to have lost the courage of their earlier conviction, there is no real chance of the law's being changed in any fundamental way: no votes are to be won in Austria, as elsewhere, by appearing to be 'soft on economic refugees'. The traditional pre- and post-Waldheim stereotypes about Austria – Mozart, Lippizaner stallions and *Gemütlichkeit* (pleasure) (Mitten, 1992; Wodak *et al.*, 1990) – may be only so much public relations drivel, but the government's pre-emptive exclusionary hardline against foreigners may go some way towards explaining why Austria still connotes these clichés, rather than names like Hoyoswerde, Mölln, Rostock and Solingen. The only foreigners entitled to *Gemütlichkeit* these days, it seems, are those who do not come from eastern and southern Europe, and who come to spend money.

I would like to place my chapter in the newly established paradigm of study of the discourses of racism and prejudice (e.g. van Dijk, 1993; Wodak and Matouschek, 1993). It is in this connection that the debate on the residency law is relevant: for the arguments advanced in favour of such laws, though frequently implicitly racist, are none the less equally frequently disguised as straightforwardly economic good sense. Thus I would like to discuss some discursive forms of racist talk, taking the Austrian case as my point of departure and as the source of my examples. My aims are threefold: first, to say a bit about the general theory and methodology of discourse analysis in relationship to the study of prejudice and racism, specifically on the theory of 'discourses of difference'. My second aim is to explain the discourse-historical approach in discourse analysis. This methodological approach, which we developed in the course of a two-year study of postwar anti-semitism in Austria, cite but one example, in general Hung_____ _____ ed more positively in Austria than are Romanians and _____ traceable to some extent to perceived cultural affinities with these former groups dating from the time of the Austro-Hungarian empire, and to some extent to a kind of residual historical memory in Austria of Hungarians and Czechs as onetime heroic fighters against Soviet tanks. At the same time, and somewhat anomalously, the fall of the 'iron curtain' and the accompanying end of the Cold War marked a major caesura in attitudes inside Austria towards potential immigrants from eastern Europe, transforming former heroic escapees from communist tyranny into contemporary 'criminal tourists' (Matouschek *et al.,* 1995; Mitten and Wodak, 1993). Media images have been instrumental in constructing and reinforcing the prejudiced terms of the debate on the so-called 'foreigner problem'.

It is essential in this connection to reiterate the significance and influence of the choice of topics by social elites such as politicians, journalists, etc on the formation of prejudice among the broader political public. As Teun van Dijk writes, summarising his many years of research on prejudiced discourse:

> most ethnic news stories are not reproductions of conversational stories. On the contrary, everyday stories often reproduce media stories. It is in this sense (only) that the media (claim to) provide what the public 'wants'.... Against this background, we have reasons, and empirical evidence, to assume that elite groups provide the initial (pre)-formulations of ethnic prejudices in society, and that the media are the major channel and the communicative context for such discourse.
>
> (van Dijk, 1989: 361)

SOME FACTS ABOUT AUSTRIA

The Austrian First Republic, established in 1918, issued from the collapsing multi-ethnic and multicultural Habsburg monarchy (Burger,

1990). During the final years of the monarchy, language conflicts had dominated public and political discourse, although legally all languages were said to be equal and were to be taught in primary schools. Following the First World War, Austria's tense relations with the other Habsburg successor states were in no small measure due to the political antagonisms these language conflicts had engendered.

Between 1938 and 1945, Austria was occupied by the Nazis and became a part of the Third Reich. The Nazi Aryan *Volksgemeinschaft* (nation) required and received a language policy consistent with its exclusionary ethos (Wodak, 1993). Since 1945, Austria has undergone many political and sociological changes: occupied by Allied forces for ten years after the war, in 1955 Austria became an independent and neutral country, though its political institutions owed more to western than to eastern European influence. An 'economic miracle' was accompanied by the creation of an advanced welfare state on the Swedish model. In 1956, during the anti-Stalinist uprising, 160,000 Hungarians entered Austria, most on their way elsewhere, and were heartily welcomed, though the economic situation in Austria was not particularly favourable. In 1968, nearly 100,000 Czechs came to Austria after the crushing of the 'Prague Spring', and again there were no complaints. In the early 1980s, almost 50,000 Poles fled to Austria after the declaration of martial law, and these, too, were greeted with varying degrees of enthusiasm. The big change occurred in 1989 and 1990, when the 'iron curtain' fell and thousands of citizens from former Warsaw Pact countries travelled to Austria.

In the 1990s Austria contains several different types of foreigners and minorities: autochthonous minorities (Slovenes, Croats, Hungarians, Jews, Gypsies, Czechs and Slovaks); immigrant workers (mainly Turks and Yugoslavs who began arriving in the 1970s); political refugees (including Iranians, Vietnamese, Hungarians, Czechs, Poles, Albanians, Bosnians, and so on); and, since 1989, the so-called 'economic refugees' (predominantly Hungarians, Poles, Czechs, Romanians and Russians). Each of these categories has a different legal status: some non-native citizens of other countries have become naturalised citizens; some have acquired refugee status; others are permanent or temporary residents (Fassmann and Münz, 1992).

By 1991, approximately 400,000 foreigners were living in Austria, around 5.3 per cent of the total population. This corresponds roughly to the percentage of foreign workers and their family members who lived in Austria in the 1970s. Thus, when comparing percentages, nothing much has changed since the mid-1970s. Yet the perception of change is pervasive, as is constantly implied by the reporting of the press about the huge masses of immigrants having entered recently or being about to enter.

NEO-RACISM IN CONTEMPORARY AUSTRIA: A DISCOURSE-HISTORICAL STUDY

In 1991, the Department of Applied Linguistics at the University of Vienna began a pilot study entitled 'Austria's Attitudes towards its East-Central European Neighbours: Studies on Xenophobic Public Discourse'. The aim of the study was to discern the attitudes that Austrians had towards Hungarians, Czechs and Slovaks, Poles and Romanians in the years 1988–90 and to investigate in what ways they had altered both historically as well as more recently. Specifically, the study examined – both quantitatively and qualitatively – neo-racist utterances and discursive strategies in regional and national newspapers, weekly news magazines (2,000 articles), and television and radio news and features broadcasts (20 hours of video). In addition, interviews were conducted with politicians and with randomly selected respondents (Matouschek et al., 1995). As in an earlier study on postwar anti-semitism (Wodak et al., 1990), sociolinguistic, psycholinguistic and text-linguistic approaches were applied in a 'discourse-historical' way: original sources, the precise social and political contexts and social psychological factors were integrated into the analysis.

The discourse-historical approach concentrates on three dimensions of prejudiced language use: the content of prejudiced remarks (which varies according to the targeted social group); argumentation strategies (cohesive devices in texts which serve specific argumentative aims); and linguistic forms of realisation (generalisations, stories, etc.). I shall illustrate each of these three dimensions below.

THE DISCOURSES OF DIFFERENCE

In research on racism, 'discourses of difference' are understood to be racist practice when they serve 'to establish social, political and economic practices that preclude certain groups from material and symbolic resources' (Hall, 1989: 913). Stuart Hall argues that the association of a differentialist production of meaning with issues of power constitutes, or can constitute, a practice of exclusion.

We, however, believe that it is necessary to give a more precise definition of 'racist' discourse. 'Racism', like 'hostility to foreigners', is first of all a concept with a negative connotation. Yet there is no unanimity on whether both imply the same thing or whether both are manifestations of a more profound syndrome to which hostility to foreigners and minorities, marginalisation of handicapped persons, hostility to women, anti-semitism, etc. belong. It is thus essential to differentiate the various phenomena at issue.

According to Taguieff (1991) 'racism' implies three different forms of racism, namely ideological racism (as structured cluster of representations and views), prejudice-based racism (sphere of opinions, attitudes, beliefs) and behavioural racism (racism as practices of discrimination, persecution and even annihilation). The confusing array of ideas circulating as racism has resulted in two central reductions, between racism (anti-semitism) as a negative attitude towards 'the other' and racism (anti-semitism) as a system of extermination. The popular use of the word shows hybrid forms which, according to Taguieff, become concrete in one general synthetic definition:

> racism is an ideology, the hard core of which consists of an asserted inequality. This is founded on natural differences between groups (races). An assumption implying the practices of exclusion, discrimination, persecution and annihilation is ushered in, and accompanied by, forms of hate and disdain.
>
> (Taguieff, 1991: 225)

Regarding the term 'race', Guillaumin (1991; 1992) believes that the word lacks 'semantic boundaries', be it in ideologies or in the sciences. However, for her its 'field of perception' has not become obsolete. It 'resurfaces in different verbal forms, that is in different words or in circumlocutions or equivalents' (Guillaumin, 1992: 80).

Like Guillaumin (who differentiates between four general groups of traits) we can list the following examples of distinguishing features:

- physical traits (real or attributed ones such as skin and hair colour, sex, physiognomy, etc.), e.g. the darker skin and hair colour of some Romanians or Jews
- spiritual-cultural (socio-historically acquired) traits
- religion ('the Muslims', 'the Jews')
- nationality in the sense of belonging to a specific ethnic group ('the Slovenes' in Austria)
- nationality in the sense of belonging to a certain national state ('the Americans', 'the Israelis')
- social traits
- socio-economic ones (economic system, prosperity) (the economic refugees, e.g. 'the Ossis' from East Germany)
- political (power system) ('the Communists').

All of these traits [attributed to a group of people] merge to form an ensemble that can be defined syncretically. If causal relations can sometimes be established between these various elements, as is the case for instance, in racist doctrines and theories, it is merely a secondary process [an attempt to rationalise or warrant racial thinking].

(Guillaumin, 1992: 83)

According to Guillaumin the elements could be distinguished in analytical terms, but in social perception the ensemble of elements merges to form a singular reality, with the group becoming a singular entity. Such an object of perception could be referred to as 'race'. Of course, various types of traits could appear in clusters, as, for instance, in the anti-semitism of Nazis. In this particular case there is a predominance of anti-semitism based on doctrinary genetic-racist arguments. However, there has always been a more or less pronounced blend of negatively assesssed socio-cultural traits (compare, for example, Hitler's statement 'The Jewish race is above all a community of the intellect ...' and the sad 'proof of the superiority of the intellect over flesh', cited from Taguieff, 1991: 247). The potentially *syncretic nature* of anti-semitism and racism become clear in that inherently contradictory distinctive elements are used for ideological legitimation of exclusion and genocide (cf. 'syncretic anti-semitism' after Mitten, 1993).

It is important to note that there are also other, seemingly restricted groups of characteristics. The hostility of West German citizens *vis-à-vis* the so-called 'Ossis' cannot, for instance, be accounted for on the basis of physical or religious characteristics. And, of course, no recourse can be taken to nationality, since it is taboo to question the unity of the German nation. Thus primarily the traits related to the social and political structure of former East Germany result in discursive exclusion. Here it becomes clear that an analytical distinction can be drawn between 'ethnic' and 'racist' (i.e. racial-biologistic) prejudices.

What individual traits can be selected within a racist discourse or a discourse of difference and what consequences this involves for those affected depends on the greatest variety of historical, social, psychological and social-ideological factors. The different consequences of the marginalisation of the 'Ossis' (East Germans) from the 'Wessis' (West Germans), of the eastern 'economic refugees' from the Austrians and the marginalisation of 'coloured persons' from 'whites' in the United States or South Africa will, of course, be different in each particular case. The Austrian discourse on Jews shows that there are even various types of differences on different public levels. In the public at large, mainly ethnic and cultural traits are used for marginalisation whereas on the public level of politics and the media there are primarily socio-economic and religious criteria.

Discourses of difference in Hall's sense (1989) are thus discourses in the widest (even Foucauldian) sense – as we understand them; ones that make a distinction between 'us' and another group. This distinction is made on the basis of a selection of specific traits attributed to one group, traits which are seen, in some sense, as being significant.

THE DEVELOPMENT OF TOPICS IN THE MEDIA AS AN INDICATOR OF CHANGE IN ATTITUDES TOWARDS AUSTRIA'S EAST CENTRAL EUROPEAN NEIGHBOURS

In general, communication about minorities is centred thematically around a few elements such as difference, deviance and perceived threat. According to a frequently occurring generalisation, foreigners damage the host country's socio-economic interests. The emphasis here is on the threat to economic interests due to competition, particularly the unfair competition offered by the shadow labour market. Another such generalisation holds that 'they' (i.e. foreigners) are also different in terms of culture, mentality, etc. In this case, the emphasis is on the perceived threat to the dominant cultural order. Foreigners are also said to be involved in activities that are viewed negatively (e.g. loudness) or are said to be criminally inclined. The emphasis in this latter prejudice is on the threat that deviance poses to the established social order.

In our study tracing the development of public discourse in Austria on the so-called 'foreigner and refugee problem', we found a strong temporal correlation between the new freedom of travel and emigration in the former 'iron curtain' countries and the evident change of attitude towards our eastern neighbours. With the first great wave of travellers beginning in 1988 came a major increase in the applications for political asylum. The 'refugee problem' and the fears accompanying it thus became one of the most important issues of public life in Austria.

The public discussion about foreigners, beginning in 1989, initially yielded a discourse of sympathy for those freeing themselves from the Communist yoke. This discourse then developed into what I have termed a discourse of tutelage, and in the end evolved into an aggressive discourse of defensive self-justification. Throughout, however, the content of many of the prejudices remained constant, but were employed and redeployed to accommodate the discursive demands of an altered political situation. The range of linguistic realisations (our third dimension) is very broad; it reaches from allusions and insinuations to blatant and crudely racist statements. The new residency law, and the widespread assent it has met, may indeed be seen as a culmination of sorts, but this assent could build upon a specific history and evolution of discursive practices about the 'foreigner problem'.

The absurd lengths to which this discourse led may be illustrated by an unintentionally humorous aspect of party electoral propaganda. During the campaign prior to the 1990 elections to the Austrian National Assembly, public discourse in the print media and by several leading politicians became fully dominated by the subject of foreigners. Playing on the increasing hostility towards foreigners, the Vienna chapter of the Freedom Party of Austria (FPO), a party sharing many features with Le Pen in France, put up a campaign poster declaring 'Vienna must not be allowed to become Chicago!'. This slogan apparently had the intended effect, for the FPO was able to more than double its previous number of votes (Plasser and Ulram, 1991). But what does this bewildering slogan mean?

At first glance, it does seem to evoke associations with criminality identified in the popular imagination with large US cities in general, and, because Chicago was chosen, possibly alludes to filmic and television depictions of Al Capone and his ilk. However, one fact about Chicago does suggest another element of meaning that this poster might have been designed to elicit, namely, that Chicago is the city with the largest concentration of people of Polish heritage outside Poland. If this pattern were related discursively, as it was temporally, to the dominant campaign issue of 'foreign criminality', there seems to be little doubt that the Freedom Party slogan about Chicago was a characteristic allusive formula designed to trigger just the kind of xenophobic resentment the new wave of 'criminal tourism' had unleashed. The leader of the Freedom Party in Vienna, I note here in passing, is one Werner Pawkowicz, a man whose name does not exactly teem with Teutonic associations.

In an opinion poll published in 1991 (GFK-Fessel, 1991), 84 per cent of those questioned reported having had no negative experiences with foreigners in the months prior to the poll, 69 per cent had had no contact with foreigners in their neighbourhoods, and 70 per cent counted no foreigners among their friends or acquaintances. Yet it was precisely among respondents with the least direct contact with foreigners that fear and hatred of foreigners were the most pronounced. This dissonance between personal experience and negative attitude is known to be the most fertile territory for the formation and reproduction of neo-racist prejudice against ethnic minorities.

Of course, political leaders on the right do their best to promote such images. Jörg Haider, the leader of the Freedom Party, the party with the aversion to Chicago, addressed a group of police officers serving in the district in Vienna with the highest concentration of foreigners, thus:

> Here at home we have, you might say, the South American mafia, which has specialised in pick-pocketing and at their own training camps in Italy received the introductory course from the Mafia before they were released to Austria. We have Poles who have organised themselves and concentrated on auto theft. We have citizens of former Yugoslavia who are experts in breaking into private homes, and if you should ever lose your house keys, call on them to get back into your houses really fast. We have Turks who have set up excellent organisations in the field of Heroin and we have Russians, who today are proven experts in the area of extortion and of muggings.
>
> (Jörg Haider's talk on the topic of 'security' 1992)

ARGUMENTATION STRATEGIES IN PREJUDICED DISCOURSE

I would like to turn to our second dimension of analysis, strategies of argumentation. If we accept the kind of open appeals to racism characteristic of Haider, we see that such strategies involve the linking of discrete but related contents in a given text which convey prejudice (in the present context, neo-racist prejudice) while simultaneously seeking to disguise it (Wodak, 1991; Wodak *et al.*, 1990). Of the many such strategies available, I would like to mention two sets.

The first consists of strategies of group definition and construction, strategies which assist in constituting a 'we discourse' (the first step of a discourse of difference). The linguistic forms of realising this constitution of an ingroup and outgroup (our third dimension) include the use of grammatically cohesive elements, such as personal pronouns, depersonalisation (*Anonymisierung*), generalisation and equation of incommensurable phenomena (*Gleichsetzung*); the use of vague characterisations; and the substantive definition of groups. An essential function of 'we discourse' is the denial of personal responsibility and its displacement on to the group as a whole, in the sense that what many people believe cannot be wrong.

In a similar vein, strategies of self-justification enable speakers to make normative evaluations of the outgroup and to assign guilt or responsibility to members of that group or to the group as a whole. The aim of such a discourse of self-justification, which is closely wound up with 'we discourse', is to allow the speaker to present herself or himself as free of prejudice or even as a victim of so-called 'reverse' prejudice.

THE DEVELOPMENT OF A PUBLIC RACIST DISCOURSE: MEDIA DISCOURSE ABOUT ROMANIA AND ROMANIANS

Anonymous letters

To illustrate these strategies, I would like to turn to media discourse proper about Romania and Romanians. I should start by stating the obvious. In public situations where anonymity is assured, speakers exhibit little or no inhibitions in expressing their prejudices.

For example, in an anonymous letter to the Austrian Interior Minister dated 5 March 1991, a 70-year-old female Viennese (based on the internal evidence in the letter) complained of the negligence, corruption and hypocrisy of the politicians currently in power in relation to the problems of foreigners and refugees:

> 'Scandals' and 'asylum policies' are the trademarks of this government. You are incapable of getting a grip on the stream of asylum seekers.

A mandatory visa requirement for Romanians should be introduced. Why should an Austrian citizen be robbed by these thieving elements?

Politicians would not understand the fears of the population living in the working-class districts, the letter continued, because they all live in wealthy neighbourhoods. The author also provided an example: 'Of the sixty families living in one house, forty are Turks with lots of children. These people spend most of their time in the corridors. Dirt wherever one looks. They must have lived in pig sties.' Later on, the author blames the politicians for being the cause of 'hostility towards foreigners'. These politicians, she stated, do not want to recognise 'that only a minority, really only those who take part in demonstrations, are friendly towards those seeking asylum, and you give them anything they [asylum seekers] want'.

In this letter, Romanians were characterised explicitly as 'thieving elements', while the 'stream of asylum seekers' (note the metaphorical use of stream, flood), of which the Romanians are at least partly the cause, represents a threat to the Austrians. Turks are described as having many children. Loud and dirty, they swarm together in masses (forty out of sixty). Their lifestyle is equated with that of pigs. The substantial content of the complaint, presented in the form of explicit prejudices, is these people's alleged criminality and their insufficient ability to assimilate. In addition, particularly noticeable is the author's equation of foreign workers with refugees: 'foreigners' (Turks) are put in the same category as 'asylum seekers' (Romanians). The negative attitudes are quite explicit here, though the responsibility for these attitudes is placed squarely on the shoulders of the foreigners themselves or on those of the politicians. The self-justification strategies of victim–victimiser reversal and disavowal of all personal guilt displaces the responsibility on to foreigners and politicians.

The discourses of sympathy, tutelage and justification

As our analytical focus moves away from such discursive situations into settings and contexts of increasing personal exposure, however, we are confronted with a much more complex array of strategic discursive features employed to express the same or similar prejudices. This is, in our view, traceable to an increasing intrusion into a speaker's consciousness of the normative expectations associated with these various public settings.

The most significant example concerns the development of forms of racist discourse I mentioned above: the discourses of sympathy, of tutelage and of defensive justification; the point of departure of every form of prejudiced discourse is the constitution of groups (see Chapter 4). Events in the former Warsaw Pact countries led to an increasing media presence of Poles, Hungarians, Czechs, Slovaks and Romanians, but, and this was the most important development, presented as members of their respective national communities rather than ethnically interchangeable victims of Communism.

The reporting of the fall of Ceauşescu at Christmas 1989 represented an initial climax of public discourse about Romanians. The stories in the media focused on poverty, illness, and violence as well as on the assistance that had been collected and shipped by the Austrian people. This, in other words, is what we have described as a discourse of sympathy. After the initial phase of revolutionary events had run their course, politicians and so-called experts alike began to discuss more openly what should be done for and with these countries. The situation in Romania was estimated and evaluated by Austrian experts, and proposals were advanced in Austria on how best to inaugurate a 'real' democracy, but the opinions of those potentially affected by these decisions in Romania were seldom sought. This is what we have described as a discourse of tutelage. Chronologically, the third stage of the development towards a new quality of discourse was the period in which the population took notice of the fact that even after the 'liberation', Romanians were still coming to Austria seeking asylum. At this point, sympathy for the Romanians all but dissipated. They were no longer patronised as naive or immature; rather, in public discourse the Romanians began to be disparaged. This distant foreign group thus soon became the outgroup *par excellence*, inside Austria. From approximately the beginning of May 1990, then, it is possible to detect in public discourse increasingly hostile prejudiced attitudes and expressions towards Romanians, most of which appear in the form of what we have termed the discourses of defensive self-justification.

To illustrate these developments I would first like to present a few excerpts from that most public of media, the television news broadcasts of the Austrian national broadcasting company, ORF. The ORF is similar to the BBC in that it is a state-supported and viewer-funded institution that has a statutory commitment to 'objectivity' in the transmission of news. But, unlike the BBC, it has a monopoly on broadcasting in Austria (apart from cable) and Austrian television does run commercials, though not during programmes.

The first example of the discourse of sympathy is taken from a commentary on the news by Paul Lendvai, the ORF in-house expert on eastern European affairs, on 22 December 1989. Lendvai's comments typify the presentation of the foreign group as a humiliated, exploited, impoverished people, an image of a scapegoat was constructed: the Ceauşescu-clan. At one point Lendvai stated:

The long pent-up anger of a people who had been deprived of their rights, muzzled, spied upon and humiliated daily, has put paid to all predictions, to all cliches. In the common European home now emerging, Ceauşescu's Romania was a torture chamber in the truest sense of the word.

The second example contains two parts: a soundbite from the Austrian Chancellor Franz Vranitzky from 22 December 1989, and the text of the news itself two days later. Both illustrate the positive self-presentation of the ingroup, especially its sympathy and willingness to help. Vranitzky was shown on the news stating that 'it is certainly a very terrible thing that we [sic] are very probably going to have violence and dead and injured'. On the news on 24 December 1989, the newsreader stated, quite in the spirit of Christmas Eve, that 'Austria is helping the Romanian people. All sorts of aid are unreservedly being brought to collection points. ... Therefore please, do not give up donating, keep on proving your generous readiness to help.'

The third example, taken from the Lower Austrian local television news broadcast from 10 January 1990, again assigns guilt for all ills and evils to the Ceauşescu regime. The newsreader stated:

[In] Transylvania, Dracula's homeland, Ceauşescu and his wife system-atically sucked the blood out of the country ... Elena Ceauşescu is being represented as a modern zombie. ... The hatred of this dictator family [as well as] Ceauşescu's madness are omnipresent. Even in villages which are still partly idyllic.

What strikes one about this final example is the use of the allusion to Dracula ('evocation'/ switch to another genre) to ascribe sanguinary lust to Ceauşescu, from which followed the Romanians' thirst for vengeance. The motifs of hatred and revenge are continuously emphasised in the reporting; at the same time, understanding for these feelings on the part of Austrians (or at least on the part of the Austrian newsreader) is indi-cated by the description of the Romanians' miserable living conditions. This alleged motif of thirst for revenge, for which there was actually very little empirical evidence (for example, in the sense of spontaneous explo-sions of mass terror or lynch mobs), became a set-piece in the reporting on Romania, and was an important preparatory stage leading to the emergence of what we have termed the discourse of tutelage.

Before we turn to the discourse of tutelage, however, I would like to quote one example from the television news which is open to various interpretations in principle, applying our discourse-historical methodology however, narrows the possibilities considerably.

27.12.89, ZIB1. The citizens of Bucharest are being allowed to buy to their hearts' content certain kinds of meat that had previously been destined for export.

9.1.90, NÖ heute.... The children stand on the side of the street begging for a piece of chocolate or fruit. They only know about sweets from hearsay. The camera team has two kilograms of chocolate with them and wants to give it to the children.

One of the project associates, a German vegetarian who supports the Greens, thought that this was a textbook example of the arrogance and contempt of the Austrians towards the Romanians, thus an example for the discourse of tutelage. By reporting that children were eager to eat meat and would want something as unhealthy as chocolate would show, my colleague believed, that the ORF journalist conveyed the Romanian's backwardness. From his personal point of view and frame of reference, he read the report that way. However, if one relates this report to other reports after a war, when people are hungry, as well as to the ritual reporting of shortages of all consumer goods, but above all, meat, in countries like Romania, this report evokes a very typical scene: people standing in line for food, children with sparkling eyes, very happy to get meat and chocolate, which had been considered luxury items before the fall. And an approach which incorporates the context of the memory of postwar scarcities and contemporary images of communist deprivation, certainly promises more worthwhile interpretative results.[2]

The successor discourse to the discourse of sympathy, the discourse of tutelage, emphasised the (presumed) competence of Austrians in questions of democracy, while at the same time belittling the Romanians' own. If one examines the reports chronologically, there are, of course, numerous overlappings; however, the discourse of sympathy and helpfulness increasingly gave way to the discourse of tutelage.

In this discourse, the foreign group as a whole as well as individuals in it are presented as immature, naive, backward in questions of democracy, and either not at all, or not yet, suitable for the task of constructing a democratic community. The Austrians, who can 'tutor' the foreigners in proper civic behaviour, are portrayed as exhibiting democratic maturity and, more importantly, expert knowledge of the possibilities for democracy in Romania. These sentiments are realised linguistically principally in the form of contrived oppositions of good and bad and by means of discourse representation. Discourse representation can take the form of direct quotations (as well as the German subjunctive for indirect speech). Frequently, however, it takes the form of presenting the views of presumed Austrian experts on politics while neglecting to canvass the opinions of Romanians undergoing these upheavals, or of Romanian politicians or experts.

For example, the evening television news on 22 December 1989 contained an interview with former Austrian Chancellor Bruno Kreisky. The newsreader asked Kreisky, 'What would your personal advice to the population be at this moment in time? ... Do you think that the situation in the east is already stable enough that democracy could take root?' to which Kreisky replied, 'I think that there can be democracy there in the long term. But I wouldn't like to say that we are already over the mountain.'

Similarly, on the same programme, the ORF's own expert, Lendvai, was called upon for his views. To the newsreader's question, 'Professor Lendvai, back to Manescu, the new man. Do you think he is capable of leading his country into a better future?' Lendvai answered,

> Not at all. ... I met him in 1964 when he was foreign minister. He was, in fact, a very affable fellow, but he was a political lightweight. [An] extraordinarily handsome man, and the talk of the town in Bucharest was always to which reception would he be going with which girlfriend. ... He speaks excellent French ... but he could play a certain role as a symbol, as a figurehead, let us say, for the transition period.

If the reports in the electronic and print media treated the revolutionary events in Romania between December 1989 and February 1990 as foreign events, transmitting the images and messages outlined above, the character and (prejudiced) quality of reporting changed notably once increasing numbers of Romanians began making their way towards Austria. Romanians were no longer greeted with sympathy, but rather with open rejection. From around 1 March 1990, Romanians were perceived as representing a new threat (however conceived) to the Austrians. The break in the discourse pattern came, when the public became aware of the Interior Ministry's plan to house 800 young male Romanians seeking political asylum in an unused barracks located in Kaisersteinbruch, a small village of 200 inhabitants.

Emblematic of the prejudices identified with this new discursive 'turn' are the following passages taken from an article which appeared in Austria's leading tabloid, the *Neue Kronenzeitung*. I shall analyse this article along our three dimensions: the central theme of this article was the fear of Kaisersteinbruch residents that their women would be raped by the young Romanian men, although at the time of the article there was not a single Romanian male in the village. Particularly striking are the ways that the author's own opinion intrudes into the ostensible news article, either explicitly or by means of extremely vague discourse representation. The interspersing of direct quotations and indirect speech with the normal narrative indicative acts to transform the individual fears of some into a generalised panic among the entire village population, as the final sentence makes clear. The substantive content of the prejudice – the potential readiness of the Romanians to rape – is transmitted by means of a quote from an old village woman, who alludes to the relations between the local population and the Russian troops who occupied

Austria from 1945 to 1955. The groundwork for drawing the analogy between the Russians then and the Romanians now, however, is in fact laid by the author in the introductory section on the historical 'origins of fear':

> an old woman from the village, who will not forget that time for as long as she lives, recalled. 'Yeah, do you think things were done delicately back then? It was difficult for us women, alone, the men were away fighting, you know, or had been killed [in the war]. We knew [then] what it meant to be a sacrificial lamb. I can certainly understand that young women, who were only children back then, are afraid. Their husbands often work the night shift, and during the day there are only women around in the village. And now someone wants to bring in 800 robust, strong, young, immature men?'

The analogy between the past and present, in the form of an allusion, is unmistakable. The Russians, who were occupying the village, were not 'delicate'. The men were not there, the women became (sexual) sacrificial lambs. That the allusion is to sexual harassment or rape ostensibly experienced by the village women at the hands of the Russians, and not to non-sexual acts of violence, may be inferred from the adjectives used to describe the young Romanians. These latter were not described as violent, aggressive, etc., but rather as young, strong (stronger than women), robust (possibly positively connoted in the sense of well-developed?) but especially as immature (emotionally immature in the intended sense). Actual rapists, most of whom were presumably young Russian soldiers at the end of the Second World War, are equated with immature Romanian potential rapists. The comparison of the Russians, an occupying power in 1945 with these 800 Romanians, all of whom were seeking assistance and political asylum, represents an additional and especially crude distortion.

However, the fears, anxieties and cries for help of the women in the village, which the main headline, the lead and the text of the article help to generalise through the use of vague discourse representation, are in fact only legitimised in the final paragraph of the article, with the quote from the woman villager. Conveying this and similar specific substantive contents, especially in the form of discourse representations, are among the most favoured linguistic means of transmitting prejudiced attitudes in the reporting of the *Neue Kronenzeitung* (e.g. Bruck, 1991; Wodak *et al.*, 1994).

The attributes of laziness and disloyalty, which often appear in these contexts, refer principally to the belief that the Romanians who come to Austria should remain in and help rebuild their own country. The reference itself – as the historical analysis implies – alludes to the official Austrian ideology that after the Second World War, the Austrians stayed put and rebuilt their country from the ruins. The substantial aid which

Austria received from abroad after 1945 (under the Marshall Plan) is usually left out of the account, and other relevant facts are also frequently denied or distorted. Thus, those Romanians who come to Austria are believed to be taking flight for base motives, an attitude which received its linguistic christening as the dichotomy between genuine and 'economic' refugees. A not infrequent ancillary insinuation associated with the idea of Romanians fleeing their country is that they are doing so to escape a criminal past at home (the bad ones come, the good ones stay at home).

'Economic' discourse: the 'rational' justification discourse

Yet another strategy we found was that of rationalisation, the use of pseudo-economic arguments and terms, so-called hard facts, to underline and prove the necessity of keeping out 'economic refugees'.

I would like to quote four paragraphs from a newspaper article, with the title 'Refugee aid at home'. It was taken from the Austrian daily *Kurier*, the national paper with the second highest circulation. The article, a commentary, appeared approximately fourteen days after the demonstration in Kaisersteinbruch described earlier. I have selected it because the explicit argumentative text strategies associated with newspaper commentaries as a genre illustrate very effectively the way in which the choice of economic discourse expresses specific prejudiced contents. Although written by a journalist who specialises in economic affairs, the article is none the less representative of the socio-economic prejudiced discourse of this period.

On the Problem of Uncontrolled Immigration [Rubric]
REFUGEE AID AT HOME [Headline]
My Point of View [Regular Column Heading]
by Jens Tschebull

[Text: 5 columns, 101 lines]
(1) Romanian citizens have been required to obtain visas [to travel to Austria] for two days now. I hold the view that this is a justified and correct measure. On balance, it will avoid more conflicts, disappointments and tragedies than it will cause. For however unsatisfactory the living conditions in Romania are at the moment, the uncertain fate of an economic refugee with false expectations in a foreign country is not desirable, either.

(2) The [Austrian] 'federal assistance' resources [expended] for the housing and provisioning of economic refugees would be more sensibly allocated as aid aimed at self-help in Romania. For example in the form of a trading concern [*Gewerbehof*], financed by Austria, which would offer business and export opportunities to a few hundred small firms.

(3) By the way, the 'freedom to choose the place of one's residence/domicile' has been greeted by the peoples involved with a great deal of scepticism, even within the common market of the EC countries. One fears dirty competition from immigrants from poorer countries and/or displacement by more industrious neighbours. Even in both Germanys, this distrust of the settlers from the GDR or the buyers from the FRG dominates.

(4) A sober consideration also requires one coolly to scrutinise the 'immigrant assets' [*Zuwanderergut*] in terms of its usability to the economy and not to stint on naturalisation: the settlement of employable men and women and their families means not only additional workers, but also additional consumers who, especially in the initial phase, when they are setting themselves up, use up more [loans] that they [can] produce; thus rather than taking work away [from others], [they] create demand.

The problem for the author is the uncontrolled immigration of Romanians. The solution is to close Austria's borders to all Romanian immigrants and, if aid is to be provided, then in the form of economic aid directly to people in Romania.

In paragraph 1, the author unmistakably ascribes a certain amount of guilt for the introduction of the compulsory visa by Austria to the Romanians themselves, since they are 'economic refugees'. The perceived reasons for their leaving Romania (i.e. fleeing dire living conditions) are presented by the author as being clearly evident and understandable, yet at the same time the author recognises that the initial premises of these 'economic refugees' were mistaken: they came to Austria with 'false expectations'.

If we examine the hierarchical order of the various argumentation techniques of the discourses of sympathy, tutelage and justification employed here, it becomes clear that this text sequence unites several strategies of these discourse forms in a functional relationship. Initially, we recognise in the formulation 'unsatisfactory living conditions' an element of the discourse of sympathy. Further, the author's evaluation of the situation in Romania ('false expectations') is a typical instance of the discourse of tutelage.

However, self-justification is also a principal strategy: the introduction of restrictive measures is portrayed almost as a measure designed to protect Romanians, from the consequences of their disappointed hopes, from 'disappointments' and 'tragedies', as the author describes them. Compulsory visas are also portrayed as a defence against 'conflicts', that is to say, against friction between us and them.

Arguing, as does the author, that it is better to provide 'aid aimed at self-help', assumes that one has already acknowledged the Romanians to all be 'economic refugees'. The Romanians' problem is a purely economic one, and they should therefore remain at home: the solution to this problem is thus called economic aid to Romania.

In paragraph 3, the anxieties felt by Europeans about the planned 'freedom to choose the place of one's domicile' within the European Community are equated with the anxieties felt about the immigration from eastern Europe. This analogy underscores the proposition that the only motivation of Romanians who have come to Austria is that of fleeing the bleak economic conditions in their homeland. The connotations of the concept 'dirty competition' remain unclear at first. Apparently immigrants 'from poorer countries' who are unqualified according to economic criteria were meant (perhaps competition in the 'dirty occupations' such as building trade labourers or cleaners?). Other readings, however, suggest other connotations: for example, dirty competition in the sense of competitors from Romania driving out domestic businesses by means of unfair or illegal trade practices. At this point we find ourselves in the midst of an explicit economics discourse. The justification for the introduction of compulsory visas for Romanians (i.e. the rejection of Romanians) is the Austrians' fear of (unfair) economic competition.

The message of the article is rather explicit: the solution of the problem of immigration, for anyone prepared to think soberly, reasonably, thus economically, about it, is the introduction of the compulsory visa. But what should be done with the refugees already in Austria? The answer: the use by the state of 'foreign labour' as capital and factors of production.

The author's point of view becomes especially clear when he speaks of the 'sober consideration' of the 'immigrant assets' in terms of their 'utility to the economy', of his wish to 'scrutinise' these assets in terms of their 'usability', as though these people were comparable perhaps to bricks. In the succeeding sentence as well, the destinies of humans are not what is in the foreground, but rather again the economic cost-benefit analysis, thus economic discourse.

Let us summarise the strategies of justification employed in prejudiced discourse about Romanians which developed in 1989 and 1990. It served to defend the positive image of Austria as a 'traditional country of asylum' and the ostensibly tolerant and humanitarian attitude of the Austrians. At the same time, this positive self-presentation served to justify the refusal to accept these Romanian refugees, for though Austria is a traditional country of asylum, it is not a country to which 'economic refugees' might immigrate.

PERSPECTIVES

Whenever we speak about others, we at the same time also determine who we are. It follows that discourses about others, about foreign or hostile groups, are at the same time also reflections of our own self-image. If this is so, then the really interesting question becomes, just who are the genuine Austrians, anyway? Are they everything that the others are perceived not to be? If there are Austrians on one side and Jews, foreigners, refugees, Slovenes, Turks, now and then a Yugoslav building superintendent, then Austrians cannot be these. Many Austrians see themselves in this way, threatened with cultural extinction by the encroaching foreigners. The image of danger which outgroups represent and the emphasis on the Austrians as victims are tropes which recur incessantly in discourse about refugees or immigrants. As an expression of collective self-recognition, the role of victim seems to draw on the consensus history of the emergence of the Second Austrian Republic (Mitten, 1993; Wodak et al., 1994): first victim of National Socialism, a victim of a Jewish conspiracy during the Waldheim affair, and a victim of a changing political world at the end of the 1980s. Perhaps even the final victim of Communism, which now, *ex post facto*, unloads on the Austrians what it itself created: the 'masses' fleeing the poverty and destitution of the East.

Discourse about others is always connected with one's own identity, that is to say, with the question 'how do we see ourselves?'. The construction of identity is a process of differentiation, a description of one's own group and simultaneously a separation from the 'others'. Where better could this be observed than in speech about and dealings with the others, in other words, in discourse about foreigners?

Austria now seems to be torn by the extreme tension between its own ambivalent nationalism and its fear of becoming lost in a new unified Europe. Austrians, moreover, are trapped in a dilemma of searching for their own identity while trying to cope with their own history. At the same time, Austria is exposed to radical new developments through the migration from the East and through new tendencies which the end of the Cold War and the emergence of new structures in eastern Europe have thrown up. Fights about language always manifest other, deeper sociological and political problems. Mario Erdheim (1992) once described such tensions in a particularly apposite way:

Freud posits ... a contrast ... between aggression and culture. For him, culture, which increasingly binds people together, became a creation of Eros, while aggression isolates people from one another. From this perspective, hostility towards foreigners appears as a tendency which threatens culture as a whole. Violence against foreigners becomes a symptom which signifies the exhaustion of the culture's potential to change. This symptom is to be taken seriously, and one must investigate the preconditions for its emergence.

(Erdheim, 1992: 30)

NOTES

1 This paper came out of a project on 'Discrimination against foreigners', funded by the Austrian Ministry of Science and Research. Bernd Matouschek and Franz Januschek were co-workers on this research. I would also like to thank Richard Mitten for his important comments and his help with the English translation.

2 This is a good example of the importance of including the context in a more than intuitive way (e.g. Duranti and Goodwin, 1992); it also provides data for the discussion 'of how to find the right interpretation' (Kress, 1993; Wodak *et al.*, 1994).

REFERENCES

Bielefeld, U. (ed.) (1991) *Das Eigene und das Fremde: Neuer Rassismus in der Alten Welt?*, Hamburg: Junius.

Bruck, P. (ed.) (1991) *Das österreichische Format: Kulturkritische Beiträge zur Analyse des Medienerfolges 'Neue Kronen Zeitung'*, Vienna: Edition Atelier.

Burger, H. (1990) 'Uber das Problem der Staatssprache', in R. Wodak and F. Menz (eds) *Sprache in der Politik: Politik in der Sprache*, Klagenfurt: Drava, 13–19.

Duranti, G. and Goodwin, C. (1992) *Rethinking Context*, Cambridge: Cambridge University Press.

Erdheim, M. (1992) 'Fremdeln: Kulturelle Unverträglichkeit und Anziehung', *Kursbuch*, 107, 19–32.

Fassmann, H. and Münz, R. (1992) *Einwanderungsland Österreich? Gastarbeiter – Flüchtlinge – Immigranten*, Vienna: Österreichische Akademie der Wissenschaften.

GFK-Fessel (1991) *Meinungsumfrage zu Osterreich*, Vienna: Fessel Institute.

Guillaumin, C. (1991) 'Rasse: Das Wort und die Vorstellung' in U. Bielefeld (ed.) *Das Eigene und das Fremde: Neuer Rassismus in der Alten Welt?* Hamburg: Junius, 159–74.

Guillaumin, C. (1992) 'Zur Bedeutung des Begriffs Rasse', *Argument*, 201, 77–87.

Hall, S. (1989) *Ideologie, Kultur, Medien: Neue Rechte, Rassismus*, Hamburg: Argument.

Kress, G. (1993) 'Against arbitrariness: the social production of the sign as a foundational issue in critical discourse analysis', *Discourse and Society*, 4, 2, 169–92.

Matouschek, B., Wodak, R. and Januschek, F. (1995) *Notwendige Maßnahmen gegen Fremde?*, Vienna: Passagen.

Mitten, R. (1992) *The Politics of Antisemitic Prejudice: The Waldheim Phenomenon in Austria*, Boulder, CO: Westview Press.

Mitten, R. (1993) 'Die "Judenfrage" im Nachkriegsösterreich', *Zeitgeschichte*, 2 January, 14–34.

Mitten, R. and Wodak, R. (1993) 'On the discourse of racism and prejudice', *Folia Linguistica*, 27, 2/4, 191–215.

Plasser, F. and Ulram, P. A. (1991) 'Ausländerfeindlichkeit als Wahlmotiv: Daten und Trends', MS, University of Vienna.

Taguieff, P. A. (1991) 'Die Metamorphosen des Rassismus und die Krise des Antirassismus' in U. Bielefeld (ed.) *Das Eigene und das Fremde: Neuer Rassismus in der Alten Welt?*, Hamburg: Junius, 221–68.

van Dijk, T. A. (1989) *Communicating Racism*, Newbury Park, CA: Sage.

van Dijk, T. A. (1993) *Elite Discourse and Racism*, Newbury Park, CA: Sage.

Wodak, R. (1991) 'Turning the tables: antisemitic discourse in postwar Austria', *Discourse and Society*, 2, 1, 65–85.

Wodak, R. (1993) 'Unity and diversity: is there an Austrian German?' paper delivered at the conference on Unity and Diversity, Stanford University, CA, March.

Wodak, R. and Matouschek, B. (1993) '"We are dealing with people whose origins one can clearly tell just by looking": Critical Discourse Analysis and the study of neo-racism in contemporary Austria', *Discourse and Society*, 2, 4, 225–48.

Wodak, R. and Menz, F. (eds) (1990) *Sprache in der Politik: Politik in der Sprache*, Klagenfurt: Drava.

Wodak, R., Pelikan, J., Nowak, P., Gruber, H., De Cillia, R. and Mitten, R. (1990) *'Wir sind alle unschuldige Täter!' Diskurshistorische Studien zum Nachkriegsantisemitismus*, Frankfurt/Main: Suhrkamp.

Wodak, R., Menz, F., Mitten, R. and Stern, F. (1994) *Die Sprachen der Vergangenheiten: Öffentliches Gedenken in österreichischen und deutschen Medien*, Frankfurt/Main: Suhrkamp.

Chapter 7

Ethnic, racial and tribal: The language of racism?

Ramesh Krishnamurthy

Each one of us is exposed to a wide variety of language input in our daily lives, some of it of our own choosing and some not. This input helps to shape our knowledge and understanding of both the language and its users. However, the predominant attitudes and opinions expressed in the language may also shape our thinking.

This chapter is divided into three sections, reflecting three major language sources: the media, dictionaries, and a large language corpus. The media are responsible for enormous amounts of language output, which must have a substantial influence on the language community they serve. Written texts have a great impact because they can be read and re-read by the consumer, shared with friends and colleagues, photocopied or faxed, and once they are archived, acquire permanency and public accessibility. Spoken media – radio and television – are not as permanent or as readily accessible, though some resources do exist, such as sound archives, and television and film libraries. However, one cannot discount their influence: 20 million people in Britain might watch a popular television programme, whereas the best-selling national newspaper, the *Sun*, has daily sales of around 3.5 million (*Guardian*, 12 July 1993: 15). Another feature of spoken media is that, for example in news broadcasts, the same terminology and phraseology is often used several times a day, and may be further recycled in current affairs programmes, weekly reviews, and so on. Many programmes are repeated in their entirety, and their content, vocabulary and style are frequently the subject of both public discussion and private conversation. The first section of this chapter therefore looks at four newspaper articles, as a small sample of media output.

Dictionaries are widely regarded as arbiters of linguistic usage. Until the late 1980s, they were based largely on the intuitions of lexicographers, supplemented by reference to existing dictionaries, and sometimes bolstered by citational evidence. Lexicographers' judgements dictated the inclusion policy, the amount of space allotted to each entry, the division into discrete senses, etc. Most dictionaries are therefore far from being the objective records of the language that they are popularly conceived to be, although they may vary in the degree to which their editorial motivations are transparent or concealed, conscious or subconscious.

With the advent of large-scale computerised language corpora, lexicographers now have access to numerous examples of usage for thousands of the commonest words in the language. The *Collins COBUILD English Language Dictionary* (CCELD, 1987) made a start in this direction, using an 18-million-word corpus of modern English texts. However, the assumption that corpus-based dictionaries must of necessity be less subjective is open to question. From my own experience at COBUILD, I suspect that even with a large corpus no 'purely objective' account of a language is possible.

COBUILD quite openly adopted a non-neutral position on sexism and racism. Placing the 'homosexual' meaning of 'gay' first went against corpus frequency, but was felt to be appropriate, partly because corpus evidence is always slightly out of date, and partly because English language learners (at whom the dictionary was primarily aimed) needed to be warned off using the word in its older meaning. With contentious usages (such as 'hopefully' as a sentence adverb) the evidence was recorded neutrally, but a cautionary note was added to the effect that some people (especially teachers and examiners) might regard this as incorrect usage, however well-attested. However, as with the other dictionaries, many decisions on inclusion, space allocation, and sense discrimination were still a matter for personal lexicographic judgement by the editors.

The second section therefore looks at the entries in several dictionaries, both for learners and for native-speakers. The third section looks at a 121-million-word sample corpus from COBUILD's current Bank of English corpus-building initiative,[1] and the fourth section reviews the extent to which the newspaper articles and the dictionary entries conform to or deviate from patterns attested in the data.

NEWSPAPERS

The starting-point for this chapter was my initial reaction to two brief newspaper articles reporting on similar conflicts in former Yugoslavia and Kenya. The first was in a local Birmingham newspaper:

Belgrade civil war looms as crisis worsens
BELGRADE – Yugoslavia's leaders held a crisis meeting yesterday as the multi-ethnic state continued its slide toward anarchy and possible civil war.

It was a last-ditch bid to end a row over whether Yugoslavia should remain a federation dominated by Serbia or become a collection of independent states.

Nationalists in Croatia and Slovenia are threatening to break away and paramilitary units in the regions have refused to surrender arms, sparking fears of civil war.

A deadline of January 19 has now been set for the groups to lay down arms.

Dominated

Yugoslavia's eight-man presidential council, dominated by Communists, was appealing for unity combined with economic and political reform.

But it seemed a forlorn hope among the nation's 23 million people, who belong to six main ethnic groups and three major religions and are suffering economic hardship.

They were thrown together when the map of Europe was redefined at the end of the First World War.

There are fears of a civil war or a crackdown by the presidency's military, a bastion of hardline Marxism committed to a federation based on Socialism.

(*Birmingham Daily News*, 11 January 1991)

Several general journalistic features and devices are apparent even in this short text. Items like 'looms', 'crisis meeting', 'slide toward anarchy', 'last-ditch bid', 'sparking fears', and so on are typical of the genre. So is the way that the text of the headline is repeated in the following paragraphs. 'Civil war looms' is echoed by 'possible civil war', and two occurrences of 'fears of civil war'. Note that the journalistically mundane 'civil war' is repeated, whereas the more emotive 'looms' is re-lexicalised as 'possible' and 'fears of'.

The political orientation of the text is indicated in the way that 'dominated by Serbia' in the second paragraph is highlighted in the subheading, and then reapplied as 'dominated by Communists'. The message is underlined by 'a bastion of hardline Marxism' in the last line.

However, let us concentrate on the references to ethnicity. Yugoslavia is described as a 'multi-ethnic state', and of its people it is said that they 'belong to six main ethnic groups'. Unfortunately, the six groups are not listed, but note that the journalist specifically adds 'and three major religions'.

The following week, I came across this article in the *Guardian*:

Africa round-up
Weekend of tribal violence leaves 13 dead in Kenya

Thirteen people were killed in a weekend of renewed tribal fighting in western Kenya, local newspapers reported yesterday.

The Daily Nation said that eight people were killed on Sunday near Bungoma, 250 miles north-west of Nairobi, bringing the number of those killed in ethnic violence since Friday to 13. Police said 153 houses were burnt down in two separate areas and 45 cattle were stolen.

At least 120 people have been killed in recent months in Kenya's worst tribal fighting since independence.

Residents told reporters three of those killed were fellow Kalenjin tribesmen of President Daniel arap Moi, who have been blamed for fuelling the clashes.

(*Guardian*, 15 January 1991)

The final phrase, 'fuelling the clashes', is typical of the journalistic genre. 'Ethnic violence' is referred to once in the second paragraph, but the 'tribal violence' of the headline is repeated twice as 'tribal fighting' in the article and the reference is further strengthened by 'Kalenjin tribesmen'.

The alternation between 'ethnic' and 'tribal' gives rise to several questions. If the two terms are genuinely synonymous, is 'tribe' ever used of the people of former Yugoslavia? If the term for 'ethnic groups' in relation to Africa is 'tribe', why is 'ethnic' used here? Is 'ethnic' the superordinate term, with 'tribal' available only for subsets of the human population such as Africans? Are there other subsets to whom the term applies? These questions will be taken up in the final section of the chapter, as corpus data may provide some answers.

A reinspection of the local Birmingham newspaper yielded two further articles that seemed relevant. The first was about the British police force:

Police chiefs told to match city's ethnic recruiting rate
Britain's police chiefs have been condemned for their poor record on ethnic minority recruitment only days after West Midlands Police were praised for their own efforts.

The Commission for Racial Equality says forces up and down the country should implement a policy of 'positive action'.

West Midlands Police's campaign includes a careers caravan which visits inner city areas, leaflet drops and nationwide appeals for black recruits.

The CRE's employment officer, Jim Gribbin, said yesterday: 'We need to encourage and help applications from the ethnic minorities because they are severely under-represented at the moment'. Around 11 per cent of Britain's ethnic minority police officers serve with West Midlands Police, making it the force's highest employer of black and Asian people.

But that figure still only amounts to 192 officers from a total establishment of nearly 7,000 – a mere 2.7 per cent in an area where ethnic minorities account for around 20 per cent of the population.

(*Birmingham Daily News*, 11 January 1991)

The headline uses 'ethnic', and 'ethnic minority' occurs four times in this short article. Note that the term 'racial' is used in the name of the British institution 'The Commission for Racial Equality', but is not used by the journalist at all.

When talking about Britain, 'ethnic' seems to mean something different again. It certainly does not refer to indigenous minorities such as the Irish, the Scots or the Welsh, nor to any group of European origin, such as the Italian, Greek or Polish communities resident here. In Britain, according to the article, 'ethnic' means 'black' (as in 'black recruits', paragraph 3), or sometimes 'black and Asian' (paragraph 5).

The use of the abstract noun 'application', in the phrase 'encourage and help applications', is evidence of a depersonalised perspective, even though the speaker is an officer in the CRE. Why not encourage and help 'applicants'? The whole problem is seen very much from an impersonal stance: notice the emphasis on statistics rather than personalities. The aim is to 'boost the numbers', not to assist individuals against discrimination. In this context, compare also the significant use of numbers in the article on Kenya.

The second article in the *Daily News* was about South Africa. Below the caption 'An engaging smile' was a photograph of a young woman (one knee inexplicably raised nearly to her chin), and underneath that a very brief story introduced by a large bullet point:

● PRETORIA – Erica Adams (above), daughter of a prominent South African mixed-race politician, is rumoured to be engaged to a son of President F. W. de Klerk.

Cape Town newspapers said Ms Adams, aged 22, and Willem de Klerk, 24, met in college in the city.

Willem is the reformist president's second eldest son.

'I can't deny there has been a long-time friendship between Willem and myself, but I can't say we are engaged,' said Ms Adams.

Inter-racial marriage and sex was formerly a crime in South Africa and was only legalised in 1985.

(*Birmingham Daily News*, 11 January 1991)

Note the strikingly different focus here: the concentration on the human aspects, relationships, meeting-places, quotations, and so on. What is the rationale behind this shift of focus? Is it a matter of what journalists and editors consider to be of interest to the British public?

Although the report suggests a disapproving distance from apartheid ('was only legalised in 1985'), it slips into familiar South African usages such as 'mixed-race' and 'inter-racial'. Would similar reports about Britain use the same terms, or would they talk about 'mixed marriages'? Again, I shall return to this question later, when looking at COBUILD data.

On the basis of these four articles alone, one might sum up the evidence as follows:

1 Former Yugoslavia is definitely an 'ethnic' zone, with 'six main ethnic groups', and three major religions.
2 Kenya is equally definitely a 'tribal' zone, but its inhabitants may become victims of 'ethnic violence'.
3 Britain is an 'ethnic' zone, but not in the same way as Yugoslavia. In Britain, 'ethnic' means 'black' or 'black and Asian'.
4 South Africa is unequivocally a 'racial' zone, despite any recent reforms.

Thus three apparently near-synonymous terms are selected according to the part of the world that is being talked about.

DICTIONARIES

Let us now turn to the acknowledged authorities on language, dictionaries, and see whether they distinguish between these three terms, and if so, what criteria are involved.

> **ethnic** or **ethnical** adj. **1.** relating to or characteristic of a human group having racial, religious, linguistic, and certain other traits in common. **2.** relating to the classification of mankind into groups, esp. on the basis of racial characteristics. **3.** denoting or deriving from the cultural traditions of a group of people: *the ethnic dances of Bosnia.* **4.** characteristic of another culture, esp. a peasant culture: *the ethnic look*; *ethnic food.*
> (*Collins English Dictionary* (CED), 1991)

Note that two of the definitions use the word 'racial'. Unlike the news article about Yugoslavia, the entry includes religion as a component of 'ethnicity', and also linguistic identity. There follows the vague reference to 'certain other traits'. The example 'the ethnic dances of Bosnia' implies that the differences between the 'ethnic' groups in Yugoslavia is 'cultural'.

The entry later gives the noun ('used mainly in the US') and a brief etymology: entered English in the fourteenth century, via Late Latin, derived from Greek 'ethnos' (glossed as 'race'). The entry for 'ethnic minority' says: 'an immigrant or racial group regarded by those claiming to speak for the cultural majority as distinct and unassimilated'. Note the distancing devices employed: 'regarded as', 'claiming to speak for'.

The prefix 'ethno-' is defined as 'indicating race, people, or culture', and is followed mainly by technical, scientific and academic terms: 'ethnography' is 'the branch of anthropology that deals with the scientific description of individual human societies', and 'ethnomethodology' is 'a method of studying linguistic communication that emphasizes common-sense views of conversation and the world'. However, 'ethnocentrism' means 'belief in the intrinsic superiority of the nation, culture, or group to which one belongs, often accompanied by feelings of dislike and contempt for other groups'.

The range of terms used in these definitions is surely confusing, even to a sophisticated native-speaker of English. 'Race, religion, language, culture, immigration, distinctness, assimilation, nation, society' are concepts as difficult to fathom as 'ethnicity'. The variation in scale from 'mankind' at one end to 'groups' at the other, and distinctions as vague as 'certain other traits', sanction the use of the word in almost any context.

Let us look at some other native-speaker dictionaries:

1 of or being human races or large groups of people classed according to common traits and customs <~ *minorities*> <~ *group*> **2** (characteristic) of a traditional, esp. peasant, culture <~ *music*> <*the ~ look in fashion*> **3** *archaic* heathen

(*Longman Dictionary of the English Language* (LDEL), 1991)

concerning nations or races: pertaining to gentiles or the heathen: pertaining to the customs, dress, food, etc. of a particular racial group or cult: belonging to a particular racial group; foreign; exotic.

(*Chambers 20th Century Dictionary* (CTCD), 1983)

fr. Gk *ethnikos* national, gentile, fr. *ethnos* nation, people **1** HEATHEN **2 a:** of or relating to large groups of people classed according to common racial, national, tribal, religious, linguistic, or cultural origin or background < ~ minorities> <~enclaves> **b:** being a member of an ethnic group <~ Chinese in Vietnam> **c:** of, relating to, or characteristic of ethnics <~neighborhoods> <~ theater> <~ foods>

(*Webster's Ninth New Collegiate Dictionary* (W9), 1983)

1. Of or pertaining to a religious, racial, national, or cultural group. **2.** Pertaining to a people not Christian or Jewish; heathen . . . <*ethnos*, nation

(*American Heritage Dictionary* (AHD), 1982)

LDEL starts with a comprehensive, 'neutral' definition, invoking 'races', 'traits' and 'customs', and supplying the collocate 'minorities'. It then combines the 'traditional' with the 'peasant' sense (separated by CED), before listing the archaic use for 'heathen'. CTCD also begins 'neutrally' ('nations or races'), but has 'gentiles/heathen' next. It uses another difficult term: 'cult', and ends with the patronising 'exotic'. There are American/British differences: W9 has the noun first and glosses the Greek etymon as 'nation, people' rather than CED's 'race'. AHD gives the gloss 'nation' here, but 'people' at 'ethnical'. All the dictionaries suggest that the derived forms and compounds of 'ethnic' have a scientific, academic or technical status.

What about learners' dictionaries?

1 of a racial, national, or tribal group: *ethnic art/traditions – ethnic minority groups* **2** interestingly unusual because typical of such a group: *This music would sound more ethnic if you played it on steel drums*
(*Longman Dictionary of Contemporary English* (LDOCE), 1987)

1 Ethnic means connected with or relating to different racial groups of people, especially when referring to the native people of a particular region or to racial minorities within a particular country or city. EG *... the ethnic composition of the voters of New York ... ... ethnic minorities.* **2 Ethnic** clothes, music, food, etc., are characteristic of a particular ethnic group, and very different from what is usually found in modern Western culture; used showing approval. EG *She's really into ethnic music these days.*
(*Collins COBUILD English Language Dictionary* (CCELD), 1987)

1 of a national, racial, or tribal group that has a common cultural tradition: *ethnic minorities, groups, communities, etc.* **2** (typical) of a particular cultural group: *ethnic clothes, food, music, an ethnic restaurant.*
(*Oxford Advanced Learner's Dictionary* (OALD), 1990)

Unlike the native-speaker dictionaries, there are no references to the archaic use for 'heathen', and more emphasis on the 'exotic' connotations acquired since the mid-1970s. But general vagueness and synonymic definitions are common to both types: the frequent use of 'racial' and 'tribal' obscures any distinctions. The collocation with 'minorities' (noticed earlier in the article about Britain) is also generally supported: only CTCD and AHD omit it.

Let me give a more abbreviated overview of the entries for 'racial' and 'tribal'.

1 denoting or relating to the division of the human species into races on grounds of physical characteristics **2** characteristic of any such group **3** relating to or arising from differences between the races: *racial harmony* **4** of or relating to a subspecies ... from Italian *razza*, of uncertain origin

(CED)

1 of or connected with a person's race: *racial pride/customs* **2** existing or happening between different races of people: *racial violence/discrimination/harmony/segregation*

(LDOCE)

1 An unpleasant act that is **racial** is done to people because they belong to a particular race. EG *... the fight against racial discrimination ... ... the crudest kind of racial prejudice ... ... an alarming rise in racial harassment.* **2 Racial** is also used to describe **2.1** things that happen between people who belong to different races. EG *... our message of* *racial reconciliation* ...... *a struggle which transcended racial barriers* ...... *the racial inequality in our society.* **2.2** things that affect or relate to people who are members of a particular race. EG *An old racial memory is stirred in us.*

(CCELD)

characteristic of race[3] (1a); due to or resulting from race: *a racial feature, type, difference, etc – racial conflict, harmony, hatred, pride – racial discrimination.*

(OALD)

Although CED optimistically gives 'racial harmony' as its sole example, the learners' dictionaries include a large proportion of negative collocations: violence, discrimination, prejudice, harassment, conflict, hatred. Note that the etymon 'razza' is 'of uncertain origin' and relatively recent (Italian). Interestingly, 'race' is commonly found in less elevated combinations (race relations, race riots), rather than in scientific, academic and technical compounds like 'ethnic'. This pattern is not unusual: 'town, city, metropolis': the term from Greek is used for the greatest dimension or scope, and in more formal registers.

There are differences between the learner's dictionaries: CCELD puts the 'unpleasant' sense first, LDOCE and OALD give the 'neutral' meaning before the negative connotations. OALD relies on the entry for 'race' to explain 'racial'. A more detailed investigation would entail the entries for all the related forms: 'racism' and 'racist' would be obvious candidates.

In most dictionaries, 'tribal' requires reference to 'tribe':

1 a social division of people, esp preliterate, defined in terms of common descent, territory, culture, etc **2** an ethnic or ancestral division of ancient cultures (esp Rome, Israel, Greece) **3** *informal/humorous* large number of persons, animals, etc **4** Biology ... **5** Stockbreeding ... ~ tribal *adj* ... from Latin *tribus* probably related to Latin *tres* three

(CED)

of a tribe or tribes: *a tribal dance – a tribal chief – tribal warfare/ divisions* **1** a social group made up of people of the same race, beliefs, customs, language, etc., living in a particular area often under the leadership of a chief: *the tribes living in the Amazonian jungle – a member of the Zulu tribe* **2** a group of related plants or animals: *the cat tribe*

(LDOCE)

tribal is used to describe things relating to or belonging to tribes and to the way they are organized. EG ... *political and tribal leaders.... Her father had recently died in a tribal war.*

A **tribe** is **1** a group of people of the same race, who share the same customs, religion, language, or land, especially when they are not considered to have reached a very advanced level of civilization. EG *Mr Otunnu is a member of the Acholi tribe. . . . This attitude still remains in some primitive tribes.* **2** a group of related animals, especially ones that live or hunt together. EG *. . . the tribe of cheetahs.* **3** a group of people who do the same activities or job. EG *There was a tribe of schoolchildren coming up the path.* **4** a family; an informal and humorous use. EG *Good to see you, John! How's the tribe?*

(CCELD)

of a tribe or tribes: *tribal loyalties, dances, gods, wars.*
1 racial group (esp in a primitive or nomadic culture) united by language, religion, customs, etc and living as a community under one or more chiefs: *Zulu tribes – the twelve tribes of ancient Israel* **2** group of related animals or plants **3** (*infml esp joc*) large number of people: *tribes of holiday-makers – What a tribe* (ie large family) *they've got!* **4** (*usu derog*) set or class of people: *I hate the whole tribe of politicians.*

(OALD)

LDOCE's use of *chiefs* in both definition and example seems excessive. Do 'races' and 'ethnic groups' not have leaders? Oxford eschews the example, but agrees that 'chiefs' are essential. The dictionaries unanimously concede the pejorative connotations of 'tribal' and its related forms, both in its core meaning ('esp preliterate', 'not considered to have reached a very advanced level of civilization', 'esp primitive or nomadic') and in its extended meanings, which relate to plants and animals, stock-breeding, etc. CCELD tries to specify a 'neutral' and 'pejorative' meaning in the same definition, linked by 'especially', and the binary definition is matched by the examples. However, an unwary learner might well miss this subtlety and tar the Acholi with the 'primitive' brush.

The main point that emerges from these dictionary entries is that 'ethnic', 'racial' and 'tribal' do not have the same connotations. 'Ethnic' and 'racial' are not used pejoratively or humorously at all, so we cannot use 'tribal' derogatively and humorously to refer to 'politicians', 'schoolchildren' and 'overlarge families' on some occasions, and still expect it to be 'neutral' when we use it to refer to 'ethnic groups'. And if we use it only of some 'ethnic groups' and not others, this strengthens the suspicion of racism.

CORPUS DATA

COBUILD has been collecting data in the form of modern English written and spoken texts since 1980. In 1987, when the *Collins COBUILD English Language Dictionary* was published, COBUILD's core corpus data amounted to about 18 million words (for details see Sinclair, 1987).

The corpus in daily use at COBUILD now is a sample of the Bank of English, and stands at 121 million words. This is mostly post-1985, and includes British and American books, newspapers and magazines, and international and national radio broadcasts, as well as local radio phone-in programmes, informal conversations, lectures, meetings, and so on.

Note that in all the statistical evidence from corpus data, words with initial capital letters are standardly lower-cased for ease of programming.

Frequency

The first stage of corpus analysis is to assess the frequency of occurrence of the words under investigation. 'Ethnic' occurs 5,128 times in the 121-million-word corpus, 'racial' 2,924 times, and 'tribal' 1,362 times. So 'ethnic' is almost twice as common as 'racial', and four times as common as 'tribal'.

Comparing the rates of occurrence in the mainly pre-1985 18-million-word corpus and the mainly post-1985 121-million-word corpus, we find that 'ethnic' has increased in this respect since the mid-1980s. In the 1970s and early 1980s 'racial' was the predominant term. 'Tribal' has not changed much in rate of occurrence.

	18 million	121 million	
ethnic	9.33	42.73	occurrences per million words
racial	13.83	24.17	occurrences per million words
tribal	10.61	11.26	occurrences per million words

If we look at the number of forms associated with each word in the two corpora, we find that 'ethnic' had six related forms ('ethnic, ethnicity, ethnically, ethnics, multi-ethnic, inter-ethnic') in the 18-million and has eleven in the 121-million corpus (adding 'ethnical, ethnicide, ethnicisation', and so on). 'Racial' had seventeen related forms in the 18-million and has fifteen in the 121-million corpus. 'Tribal' had ten in the 18-million and has thirteen in the 121-million. So in morphological productivity, 'ethnic' has increased most, but still has fewer related forms than 'racial' or 'tribal'.

Distribution

The 121-million-word COBUILD corpus is divided into twelve sub-corpora, and the average rates of occurrence of the terms in these sub-corpora shows up some interesting 'genre' or 'text-type' differences. All three terms are least frequently used in the general spoken sub-corpus (local radio phone-ins, informal conversation, domestic phone calls, meetings, lectures): 'ethnic' occurs six times per million words, 'racial' four times, and 'tribal' only once per million. Most of the general spoken data is British in origin, so it would be interesting to compare it with similar American data, but as yet none is available.

However, we can compare other British and American data. Broadly speaking, the radio sub-corpora use the terms most frequently: the BBC World Service uses 'ethnic' 135 times per million words, 'racial' 38 times and 'tribal' 24 times. National Public Radio from Washington USA uses 'ethnic' 53 times per million words, 'racial' 56 times and 'tribal' only 11 times. So whereas British broadcasters overwhelmingly favour 'ethnic', US radio broadcasters prefer 'racial' to 'ethnic'. 'Tribal' is far less frequent in both, but the Americans seem to use it even less than their British counterparts. These two sub-corpora are almost identical in sample dates (1990–1), but the US data is mainly for domestic consumption, so that may have some influence.

Comparing *The Economist* with the *Wall Street Journal*, the British publication (like the BBC) favours 'ethnic' by a substantial margin: 61 per million, as compared with 37 for 'racial' and 21 for 'tribal'. The *Wall Street Journal* uses 'ethnic' and 'racial' almost equally (19 and 18 per million words), but rarely uses 'tribal' (3 per million). American books and British books seem to show a reversed distribution: both use 'tribal' 8 times per million words on average, but British books use 'racial' 17 times and 'ethnic' 14 times, whereas American books use 'ethnic' 18 times and 'racial' only 12. However, the ratio of fiction to non-fiction is substantially higher in the British books sub-corpus, so it may be that 'ethnic' is the prevalent term in non-fiction.

Comparisons can also be made within the same variety of English as well as within the same 'genre' or 'text-type'. Comparing three British newspapers, *The Times* heavily favours 'ethnic' (50 per million) over 'racial' (20 per million), the *Independent* is almost even-handed in its use (33 per million for 'ethnic' and 29 for 'racial'), but *Today* uses 'racial' slightly more than 'ethnic' (13 for 'racial', 10 for 'ethnic'). 'Tribal' is rare in all three (9 per million in *The Times* and *Independent*, and 2 per million in *Today*).

Surprisingly, the 'ephemera' sub-corpus (information leaflets, tourist brochures, 'junk mail', letters, diaries, etc.) has the highest incidence of 'tribal': 62 per million. These occurrences are mainly accounted for by travel brochures (informing us about trekking in remote areas of the world with the assistance of 'tribal' guides, and tourist attractions such as 'tribal' markets and 'tribal' dancing), and newsletters from environmental organisations (warning of the dangers to 'tribal' people of the rainforest timber trade). That is to say, 'tribal' is frequent only in these two topic-specific text-types.

Collocation

Finally, let us look at the collocational profiles of the three terms in the 121-million-word sample corpus from the Bank of English. There are several different statistical methods currently being used at COBUILD to indicate collocation, but I have selected just one ('T-scores') for the purpose of this chapter, and applied it to the three terms. Table 7.1 shows the 'top ten' strongest collocates for each, in order of their T-scores.

Table 7.1 Ordered list of collocates for *ethnic, racial* and *tribal*

ethnic	racial	tribal
groups	discrimination	assembly
minorities	non	grand
and	multi	leaders
minority	equality	chiefs
of	and	and
violence	of	groups
in	south	killings
cleansing	africa	navajo
group	commission	in
albanians	ethnic	a

Some clear differences are apparent: 'ethnic' collocates with 'group/s' and 'minority/ies', associated activities are 'violence' and 'cleansing', and major participants are 'Albanians'. 'Racial' has more abstract, ethical and bureaucratic associations (as suggested by the third newspaper article's reference to the Commission for Racial Equality): 'equality, non-racial, multi-racial, commission'. The principal related activity is 'discrimination' and the main geographical location is South Africa. 'Tribal' shares with 'ethnic' the collocate 'groups', but the focus is more on modes of organisation: 'assembly, leaders, chiefs'. The more abstract activity of 'violence' associated with 'ethnic' is replaced by the very specific term 'killings'. 'Navajo' are the featured peoples.

The presence of 'and' in all three lists suggests that each term is often accompanied by other adjectives indicating other taxonomic dimensions. Looking further down the list of collocates for 'ethnic', we find 'religious, political, racial'. For 'racial', 'ethnic' is in the top ten listed in the table, but there are also 'religious, sexual, cultural, political' lower down the order. For 'tribal', we also find 'religious, political, ethnic'.

Looking at the associated activities lower down the collocate lists, we see with 'ethnic': 'conflict/s, tension/s, unrest, clashes, problems' but also 'studies' (as the dictionaries suggested, 'ethnic' is the preferred term in academic contexts). With 'racial': 'tension/s, harassment, violence, prejudice, segregation, abuse, hatred, attacks, preferences, conflict' but also 'quotas, constitution, democratic, policies, law'. With 'tribal': 'conflict, fighting, violence, warfare'.

The nationalities and geographical areas that occur in collocation with each term also vary: with 'ethnic' we find, as well as 'Albanians', 'Germans, Serbs, Hungarians, Soviet, Turks, Yugoslavia, Chinese, Kosovo, Romanians, Serbians'. With 'racial' we find, in addition to South Africa, no other nationality or region! With 'tribal', after 'Navajo', we come across 'African, Western, Geneva'. This apparently rather strange set of collocates is explained by the prominence given by the newspapers that are included in the corpus to the arrival in Geneva of tribal chiefs from the Western Sahara for peace talks.

REVIEW

Let us now look briefly at the extent to which the usages in the newspaper items in the first section are reflected in a broader range of English texts, and the extent to which the information given in the dictionary entries in the second section can be considered to be reasonable summaries of actual usage as evidenced by the corpus. I shall also try and answer some of the questions I raised earlier in this chapter.

In the first newspaper article about Yugoslavia, featuring the word 'ethnic', the repetition of 'civil war' was noticed. Of the 5,128 concordance lines for 'ethnic' in the 121-million-word corpus, nine also mention 'civil war', referring to situations in Burma, Eritrea, Yugoslavia (three), Moldavia, the Soviet Union, and Sudan.

The collocation 'tribal fighting' highlighted in the second article is borne out by corpus evidence: 'fighting' is not a significant collocate of 'ethnic' or 'racial'. In fact there are twelve occurrences of 'ethnic fighting' in the corpus, but significantly none of them is connected with Africa. Georgia, Soviet Union, Croatia, Nagorno-Karabakh, Azerbaijan, Yugoslavia, even Pakistan, Afghanistan, and Sri Lanka, but not Africa.

Is 'tribe' ever used in the context of Yugoslavia? In nearly 9,000 lines for 'yugoslavia/-an/-ans', 'tribal' and 'tribe' do not occur even once. There is a solitary use of 'tribes' in *The Times*:

Serbian nationalist theory does not have much time for the remaining three tribes of Yugoslavia.

How common is 'ethnic' in connection with Africa? Of the 5,128 lines for 'ethnic', fifteen mention Africa, five of these are to do with South Africa, two with the West Indies, one with Britain, and five talk about ethnicity in global terms, with Africa one of several areas referred to. Two lines are for the 'exotic' sense of 'ethnic' mentioned in the dictionaries: 'ethnic fabrics' and 'ethnic-inspired clothes'.

What clues are there to the other principal subsets of humanity to whom the term 'tribe' can refer?

Sahara Krahn Venda Navajo Bedouin Chadian Mohawk Sumatra Liberia Afghanistan Kabul Indians Pakistan Africa African Indian American.

What does 'ethnic' mean in a British context? Let me quote a few of the forty-one lines for 'ethnic' that refer to Britain:

these findings don't vary much across different ethnic groups. Britons of Asian or Afro-Caribbean origin . . .

(BBC)

Mr Tebbit devised his famous cricket test when he asked which team was cheered for by West Indians and other ethnic minorities living in Britain.

(*Today*)

But in Britain we could not find one ethnic Father Christmas in Birmingham, Bradford or Manchester. So, is there really a black Santa?

(*Today*)

The term 'ethnic' extends beyond 'blacks and Asians' in a British context only when 'exotic' cultural items are under discussion: arts, music, food, clothing:

Its aim is to offer programmes specifically to listeners from ethnic backgrounds, immigrants to Britain, and their children – Italians, Hispanics, Greeks, Jews, Asians, Arabs, Chinese and Afro-Caribbeans.

(BBC)

One of the problems of cooking ethnic Italian dishes in Britain has always been to find the ingredients.

(*Vogue Magazine*)

Are 'mixed-race' and 'inter-racial' ever used in a British context? Of 102 occurrences of 'mixed-race' in the corpus, thirty-six from the BBC refer mainly to South Africa. Of the four from *The Times*, two relate to South Africa, but two are British references:

Police seek two men in their twenties, one white with a ponytail and the other of mixed race.

No MPs today would call some of their constituents 'half-casts' [*sic.*] They would say 'of mixed race', for 'half-caste' implies contempt.

Of the five in the *Independent*, two refer to South Africa, and the other three are from a play review (about adoption), a sociological/medical survey ('31 per cent of the white children and about half the Asian and mixed-race children'), and a clearly ironic usage:

> but we always pulled our weight when it came to glossy pictures for the annual report. Who could forget our three young people (mixed race, mixed gender) leaning over a computer print-out and smiling while one of them points to some key figure? Or, our two middle-aged executives (one dynamic, one thoughtful) studying a report carefully?

Ten from British books refer to South Africa, Nazi Germany, South America, and the USA. The twenty from US National Public Radio are all about South Africa or the USA, as are the eight from *The Economist*. The other sub-corpora reflect very similar patterns of usage. Basically, 'mixed-race' is primarily used about South Africa and the USA. The term is gradually increasing in a British context, partly because of American influence, and partly because the older term 'half-caste' is clearly seen as pejorative:

> When I said half-caste, she said the correct term was mixed race.
>
> *(Today)*

The British references to 'mixed-race' are usually to children, especially in the context of adoption. There are twenty-three occurrences of 'inter-racial', with a similar spread. Six refer to the USA, five to South Africa. There are actually ten occurrences that refer to Britain, but three are historical (one about the British in India), two are about adoption and child care, and one is from a 'new age' text exhorting peace and harmony. There is also one reference to North American Indians, and one to former Yugoslavia.

In my comments on the newspaper article, I suggested that in Britain we might more readily talk about 'mixed marriages'. There are thirty-two occurrences of 'mixed marriage(s)'. However, I had overlooked the historical dimension: most references to 'mixed marriages' are still concerned with inter-denominational and inter-faith relationships rather than inter-racial ones: marriages between Catholics and Protestants, Christians and Jews. So of the thirty-two, twelve are for this usage, eight are for marriages between blacks and whites in Britain, and the rest of the occurrences are very varied, referring to Nazi Germany, former Yugoslavia, the West Indies, South Africa, Russia, and France. Two refer to Shakespeare's *Othello*, and one jocularly to pig breeding.

This exercise has pointed up one limitation of COBUILD's current corpus tools: we need to know not only of whom a term is used, but also who uses it, and specific textual sources are not easy to pinpoint with the existing software.

The dictionaries' use of 'race' (as well as religion, language, culture, immigration, nation, society and other concepts) in their definitions of 'ethnic' is reflected by the frequent juxtaposition of the two terms in the corpus: ninety-four concordance lines have both, interestingly thirty have 'ethnic' before 'racial' ('ethnic and racial differences, ethnic or racial enmity', etc.), whereas sixty-five reverse the order ('racial or ethnic discrimination, racial and ethnic minorities', etc.). So the less frequent word is usually placed first.

The use of 'ethnic' rather than 'racial' in academic contexts has been noted above in the collocation with 'studies'. In both British and American sources, 'Ethnic Studies' refers mainly to an academic discipline in universities.

CED gave the examples 'the ethnic dances of Bosnia', 'the ethnic look' and 'ethnic food'. The 5,128 lines for 'ethnic' in the corpus reveal only one line for 'ethnic dance' ('Asian women are proud of the sari, . . . it is not merely a novelty piece to be taken out of the wardrobe only for national holidays and ethnic dances.'), three lines for 'ethnic look', and ten for 'ethnic food':

. . . lunch, and could it not be	ethnic food. He ate ethnic food . . .
. . . not be ethnic food. He ate	ethnic food all the time . . .
. . . is plenty of chi-chi and	ethnic food in Chicago. But the . . .
. . . has a range of books on	'ethnic' food and explained why . . .
. . . In the last 10 years	ethnic food sales soared by 400 . . .
. . . its way to being the new	ethnic food everyone turns to. . . .
. . . originally seen as sort of	ethnic food becomes more and . . .
. . . photograph. Scour markets,	ethnic food shops and . . .
. . . and – perhaps the least	ethnic food ever created – . . .
. . . in October and featuring	ethnic food, parades, and . . .

LDEL gave 'ethnic look' but also 'ethnic music'. This proves to be a stronger collocation in the corpus: there are eighteen lines for it. AHD offered 'enclaves, neighborhoods, theater'. Looking only at the American data in the corpus, out of 969 occurrences of 'ethnic', three are for 'enclaves', eight for 'neighborhoods', and one for 'theater'.

LDOCE gave 'ethnic art/traditions' and 'This music would sound more ethnic if you played it on steel drums'. There are no instances of 'ethnic art' in the corpus (but there is one for 'ethnic arts and crafts') and two occurrences of 'ethnic traditions'. The second example is very unusual: 'steel drums' and 'sound' are not found in the proximity of 'ethnic', it is normally used before a noun, and it is rarely qualified by 'more': there are two lines (both from American sources):

I mean, who is more ethnic and who is more American, Colin Powell or Frank Sinatra?

For more ethnic types of preparations, like baccala salad (page 101), you may wish to shorten the soaking period.

CCELD gives 'composition' and 'music': the first occurs eight times, the second twenty-one times. OALD adds 'clothes' and 'restaurant': there are no lines for 'ethnic clothes' (but there is one for 'ethnic-inspired clothes'), but there are eleven for 'restaurant', mainly from American books.

For 'racial', CED optimistically gives the example of 'racial harmony' (25 occurrences, against 202 for 'discrimination', plus all the other negative collocations noted earlier). LDOCE offers 'pride' (4 in corpus) and 'customs' (none), before the better-attested 'violence' (49), 'discrimination', 'harmony' and 'segregation' (66). CCELD cites 'discrimination', 'prejudice' (66), 'harassment' (63), 'reconciliation' (6), 'barriers' (8), 'inequality' (10) and 'memory' (5). OALD gives 'feature' (one line for 'features'), 'type' (3 – but 17 for 'stereotypes'), 'difference' (6 – but 14 for the plural form), then the more frequent 'conflict' (20), 'harmony', 'hatred' (45), the rarer 'pride' and, finally, the commonest collocate 'discrimination'.

LDOCE's collocates for 'tribal' are 'dance' (6), 'chief' (11 – but 44 for the plural), 'warfare' (11) and 'divisions' (1). CCELD offers 'leaders' (the commonest collocate, 45) and 'war' (15). OALD gives 'loyalties' (1), 'dances' (3), 'gods' (2) and 'wars' (2). My criticism of LDOCE's emphasis on 'chiefs' is not backed by the corpus evidence, but note that it is the plural form that is common (44), not the singular form (11) used in both definition and example. Also, 'leader' (22) and 'leaders' (45) taken together are commoner than 'chief' (11) and 'chiefs' (44).

At any rate, the pejorative connotations of 'tribal' are as clear in the corpus as in the newspapers and the dictionaries. 'Primitive' co-occurs with it six times, but never with 'ethnic' (which is four times as frequent) or 'racial' (which is twice as frequent). Similarly, 'tribal' attracts a higher proportion of 'insurgents' and 'rebels' than the other terms: 12 each, whereas 'racial' only has 1 and 2 respectively, and 'ethnic' only 15 and 19 (whereas proportionately, it should attract 48 of each).

The main area in which dictionaries other than CCELD (which was after all based on a corpus, though much smaller than the one being used in this chapter) seem to repeatedly miss the target is in their examples. Often, their examples are in the appropriate semantic environment, but fail to specify the most frequent lexical realisations. Sometimes, they select the appropriate word, but use the less common form (as with several instances cited above of using a singular when the plural is better-attested). Occasionally, the syntactic framework as well as the lexis is extremely marked (as, for instance, the example 'This music would sound more ethnic if you played it on steel drums.').

CONCLUSIONS

At the beginning of this chapter, I suggested that language not only affords us a means of understanding a language and its users, but also might cause us to unwittingly adopt their attitudes and opinions. The English word 'tribal' clearly has pejorative connotations, and if we continue to use it, and apply it only to certain groups of human beings, we are merely re-cycling the prejudices that the English-speaking culture has developed with regard to those groups. As English develops into a truly international language, one of the rites of passage must surely be for it to divest itself of these culture-bound terms. After all, for similarly organised small groups in the British Isles, we use the term 'clan'.

In his *Keywords*, subtitled 'A vocabulary of culture and society', Raymond Williams (1983) includes 'ethnic' and 'racial' in the headword list, but not 'tribal'. Of 'ethnic' he says:

> **Ethnic** has been in English since mC14. . . . It was widely used in the sense of heathen, pagan or Gentile, until C19, when this sense was gen-erally superseded by the sense of RACIAL (q.v.) characteristic. **Ethnics** came to be used in the United States as what was described in 1961 as 'a polite term for Jews, Italians, and other lesser breeds'. . . . The scien-tific uses are now specialized areas within anthropology. . . . Meanwhile in mC20 **ethnic** reappeared, probably with effect from the earlier American use of **ethnics**, in a sense close to FOLK (q.v.), as an available contemporary style, most commonly in dress, music, and food.
>
> (Williams, 1983: 119)

At the end of his lengthy article on 'race', he concludes:

> It is clear that the very vagueness of **race** in its modern social and polit-ical senses is one of the reasons for its loose and damaging influence. . . . Physical, cultural and socio-economic differences are taken up, projected and generalized, and so confused that different kinds of variation are made to stand for or imply each other. The prejudice and cruelty that then often follow, or that are rationalized by the confusions, are not only evil in themselves; they have also profoundly complicated, and in certain areas placed under threat, the necessary language of the (non-prejudicial) recognition of human diversity and its actual communities.
>
> (Williams, 1983: 250)

One aspect which has barely been touched upon in this chapter paper, except in the broadest sense, is the identity of the user. Who actually sponsors the usages of 'ethnic', 'racial' and 'tribal'? We need to know not only which particular text the term occurs in, but also the identity of the speaker or writer of the individual sentence in which the term occurs, whether authorial or fictional, and the degree to which the context reflects a deliberate choice, whether sincere or ironic. How many users of the terms might themselves be described as 'ethnic', 'racial' or 'tribal', and by whom?

The problems raised in this chapter are not new. The focus merely shifts from one term to another. Published on the eve of the Second World War, the frontispiece to a short text by Huxley (1939) reads:

The vague term 'race' has been much misused in modern pseudo-scientific writings and nationalist propaganda.

Huxley defines 'nation' in terms very similar to the dictionary entries for 'ethnic' and 'racial' quoted earlier:

Very many human activities, aspirations, and emotions have contributed, either naturally or artificially, to build up the great synthesis that we term a 'nation': language, religion, art, law, even food, gesture, table manners, clothing, and sport all play their part.

(Huxley, 1939: 1)

In a similar work of the same period by Walker (1940) we read:

Thirdly, there are the 6,600,000 Bantu, the Natives, who range from a still tribal majority to the few who have become thoroughly western-ized and even hold professional qualifications.

(Walker, 1940: 23)

Evidence more recent than the COBUILD corpus shows that the problems are becoming more acute, not less:

And the whole affair depended on the unspeakability of certain words. As Claudia Brodsky Lacour argues, Thomas's race was the essential factor in his nomination, but the word 'race' could not be mentioned, and opposition to Thomas would automatically be understood as 'racism': 'The word "racism" and not the thing ... was the object of concern.'

(Wendy Steiner, 'The witch, the judge and the Pepsi', *Independent on Sunday*, 21 February 1993: 28)

The terminology used with reference to adoptive children in Britain continues to be problematic:

As the (natural) mother of two children of mixed race, my heart went out to the Norfolk couple whose application for adoption was turned down because they were 'racially naive' ... a white single parent bringing up two mixed race children.... Because my ethnicity is in question ... I do indeed understand racism.

(Louise Gosnell, *Guardian*, 14 July 1993: 18)

Not 'ethnicity' but 'racism'; the term 'ethnicism' does not occur in the COBUILD corpus either.

'Tribe' and 'tribal' still strike me as raising a problem of a different dimension.

Tribes, states and empires are all agents of war. Purely tribal wars, however, are rare in the contemporary world. Ethnic and international conflicts are not reversions to the primitive, since they occur specifically in modern state and imperial structures. . . . The extreme violence of the post-Yugoslav conflict is therefore best understood by reference neither to tribal hatreds nor to a struggle between the primitive and the civilised.

(Michael Freeman, 'Death toll from the war in our midst', *Times Higher Education Supplement*, 5 March 1993: 23)

A new publication is listed in the *Bookseller* as:

Alexander Stuart
Tribes
Short, sharp, frightening tale of football hooliganism from the author of *The War Zone*.
(Sarah Broadhurst, 'Paperback Preview', *Bookseller*, 26 March 1993)

Yet journalists continue to see the 'humorous' side:

Essex, USA
The first in a series on British tribes looks at holidaymakers who find everything they like about America at Disney World
. . . I have always liked America, but I could never like it the way the Essex tribe do, with a fierce, transferred patriotism that admits no fault in the adopted nation and embraces even its prejudices.
(Martyn Harris, *Daily Telegraph*, 14 August 1993: 1)

NOTE

1 Readers wishing to know more about distance access to the COBUILD corpora should contact Mr Jeremy Clear, COBUILD, University of Birmingham, Egbaston, Birmingham B15 2TT, fax (44)121 414 6203, phone (44)121 414 3925.

REFERENCES

AHD *American Heritage Dictionary*, 1982
CCELD *Collins COBUILD English Language Dictionary*, 1987
CED *Collins English Dictionary*, 1991
CTCD *Chambers 20th Century Dictionary*, 1983
LDEL *Longman Dictionary of the English Language*, 1991
LDOCE *Longman Dictionary of Contemporary English*, 1987
OALD *Oxford Advanced Learner's Dictionary*, 1990
W9 *Webster's Ninth New Collegiate Dictionary*, 1983
Huxley, J. (1939) *Race in Europe, Oxford Pamphlets on World Affairs no. 5*, Oxford: Clarendon Press.
Sinclair, J. McH. (ed.) (1987) *Looking Up*, London: Collins ELT.
Walker, E. A. (1940) *South Africa, Oxford Pamphlets on World Affairs no. 32*, Oxford: Clarendon Press.
Williams, R. (1983) *Keywords*, London: Fontana.

Chapter 8

A clause-relational analysis of selected dictionary entries

Contrast and compatibility in the definitions of 'man' and 'woman'

Michael Hoey

This chapter begins by reconsidering a neglected class of texts that I have elsewhere termed 'colony' texts (Hoey, 1986). It was suggested in passing in that paper that the components of such texts might form strong semantic relations at a distance from each other. Although this claim has been tested on criminal statutes, it has never been tested on dictionaries, even though the claim was originally illustrated with a pair of dictionary definitions. This chapter seeks to show that the claim indeed holds for dictionaries as for statutes. In doing so, however, it uncovers a systematic bias in the dictionary definitions in preference of men, a bias that has arisen despite the explicit intentions to the contrary of the dictionary makers. It is argued that this is the result of their having worked with a corpus of the contemporary English language that gives undue representation to the male voice. The dictionary in this way not only reflects bias but also helps to perpetuate it.

THE NATURE OF 'COLONY' TEXTS

If you ask a group of students what texts they have read in the past few days, you get a varied response. Some will conscientiously recall the novels they have read, the articles they have pored over and the newspapers they have browsed. Others, more adventurous, will add the advertisement hoardings they have seen and the junk mail they have received through the post. A clever few, however, will challenge the constrained view of text that these examples imply and will mention bus tickets, timetables and shopping lists. Usually the mention of such items will then provoke a lively discussion about the nature of text and the kinds of reading we engage in.

Students are not alone in overlooking certain common kinds of texts. 'Cinderella' texts such as timetables and shopping lists have on the whole received short shrift from discourse analysts as well, if indeed they have been noticed at all. This is not a consequence of their low importance in our society but rather of a restricted notion of reading as a linear processing of text. This notion has led to an over-emphasis on the importance of cohesion as a coherence-creating feature and to a corresponding neglect of those texts that can only sensibly be read non-linearly. In 1986 I attempted a characterisation of a group of such texts (of which the shopping list was one) that seemed to share certain properties (Hoey, 1986). I labelled these texts 'colonies', taking the term from natural science where it is used to describe such phenomena as ant-hills, beehives and wasps' nests. If one jumbles the components of a colony, the utility of the colony may be radically affected but its meaning remains the same. So, if the sequence of the entries in a dictionary were to be randomised, we would find it extremely difficult to locate the entry we wanted, but our ability to understand the entry, once we located it, would (normally) be unaffected by its new location. A corollary property of colony text is that adjacent components do not normally form continuous prose. If they did, of course, the first-mentioned property would be inhibited.

SEMANTIC RELATIONS IN 'MAINSTREAM' TEXTS AND 'COLONY' TEXTS

'Mainstream' texts are of course characterised by the fact that adjacent components do normally form continuous prose. The coherence of this continuous prose has been accounted for (among other things) in terms of semantic relations that hold between the sentences or groups of sentences of the text (Beekman and Callow, 1974; Winter, 1974; and many others). These semantic relations are termed 'clause' relations by Winter, because the semantic relations that exist between clauses provide a model for the relations that can exist within a text; the term is not perfect because it implies that the relations are necessarily local rather than global but the other candidate terms have their defects also and so Winter's is the term adopted here for intra-textual semantic relations holding between clauses or groups of clauses.

Clause relations can, according to Winter, be divided into two major classes: the Sequence relations such as time sequence, cause-effect and instrument-purpose and the Matching relations such as contrast, compatibility and generalisation-example. Sequence relations are characteristically unidirectional and involve change in time or logic, while Matching relations are characteristically bidirectional and involve no temporal or logical change. Matching relations also differ from Sequence relations in their dependence on various kinds of repetition devices for their encoding. According to this view any particular two sentences may be read as representing contrasting positions or compatible ones (i.e. as Matching) or as reporting events that occurred in temporal succession or one as a result of the other (i.e. as Sequenced). Ample evidence has been produced that mainstream texts are amenable to analysis in terms of such relations (e.g. Hoey, 1983).

Matching relations are frequently marked by clear parallels of syntax and lexis. A fairly extreme but consequently clear example is the pair of sentences orthographically treated as one with which Dickens's *A Tale of Two Cities* closes:

It is a far, far better thing that I do, than I have ever done; it is a far, far better rest that I go to than I have ever known.

The compatibility of these sentences can be shown by setting them up in tabular form so as to highlight what is repeated and what replaced in the move from the first to the second (Hoey, 1983; Winter, 1979):

Table 8.1

| It is a far, far better | thing | that I do | than I have ever | done |
| It is a far, far better | rest | that I go to | than I have ever | known |

For many contrast relations, a similar parallelism may serve as a signal of the relation.

Fairly obviously, the colony text does not manifest this property of mainstream text; indeed it was partly the absence of obvious clause-relational connections between adjacent units of texts such as dictionaries, criminal statutes, encyclopedias and shopping lists that led me to investigate this kind of text in the first place. Less obviously, though, the absence of clear semantic relationships between adjacent units of a colony does not mean that there are no such relationships in the text as a whole. One feature of colonies mentioned in passing in the 1986 paper is that while there are normally no relations such as cause-consequence or contrast holding between adjacent components of a colony there may be strong relations holding between non-adjacent components. The following example drawn from *Chambers Universal Learner's Dictionary* was quoted in support of the claim:

easy *adj*   1. not difficult: *This is an easy job (to do); Those sums were easy.*

difficult *adj*   1. hard to do or understand; not easy: *He can't do difficult sums; It is a difficult task; It is difficult to know what is the best thing to do.*

There are a number of strong parallels between these two definitions, even though they appear at a considerable distance from each other in the dictionary. Most obviously the definition of *easy* and the second definition of *difficult* are parallel:

difficult

not

easy.

More interestingly we have an immediate parallel in one of the pairs of examples:

Table 8.2

This	is	an	easy	job
It	is	a	difficult	task

A further parallel exists between *Those sums were easy* and *He can't do difficult sums*, though this requires the operation of one of the lexical processes described in Hoey (1991) in order for the parallelism to be represented tabularly.

Examples such as this pair of definitions appear to give support to the idea that non-adjacent components of a colony may indeed be in a strong Matching or Sequence relation with each other. Evidence of a different kind is presented in Hoey (1988) where strong relations are found to hold among the sections of a criminal statute, but no further work has been done on the relations that may exist at a distance among the definitions in a dictionary.

In this chapter I present evidence to support the view that statutes are not alone among colony texts in permitting strong relations and that dictionary definitions do indeed manifest the strong relations posited for them in my initial work on colony texts. In the course of demonstrating this, I shall show that exploration of these relations is revealing ideologically about the state of the language (or the bias of the lexicographers) with regard to gender. Attention is not given to all possible relations but to the Matching relations of compatibility and contrast briefly discussed and illustrated above.

THE PRINCIPLES OF DATA SELECTION

Even with computational assistance, the task of analysing a complete dictionary, with a view to discovering whether and where clause-relations of contrast and compatibility occur within it, would be completely unmanageable. It would also be pointless since the objective is to test the claim that definitions in a relation of Matching may occur, not to provide a comprehensive description of any one text. The questions then are:

1 What kind of data should be selected?
2 How much data should be selected for examination?
3 From which dictionary should the data be selected?

The most appropriate kind of data to select is suggested by the definitions of the antonyms *easy* and *difficult* discussed above. The Matching relation noted between those definitions suggests that confirmatory evidence of the presence of Matching relations between non-adjacent components of a dictionary is most likely to be found among the definitions of antonymous, synonymous or co-hyponymous words.

Obviously, enough data should be analysed to preclude the possibility of a Matching relation being a chance occurrence; a single pairing such as that between *easy* and *difficult* can only be suggestive. So if satisfactory confirmation is to be found, Matching must be found either between the definitions of a number of pairs of related words (e.g. a representative selection of antonyms), or among the definitions of a group of related words (e.g. words from the same semantic field, such as *hot, warm, tepid, cool* and *cold*), or between the multiple definitions of a pair of polysemous words.

The *Collins COBUILD English Language Dictionary* has three features that commend it as a source of data. First, it was written from scratch making use of an extensive corpus of contemporary English and all its examples are drawn from that corpus; consequently any Matching found between definitions of words should reflect the state of the language as reflected in that corpus rather than the bias of the lexicographer. Of course this means that Matching cannot reasonably be expected between examples, only between definitions. Second, as Research Administrator on the dictionary project during the first three years of its preparation, I am aware of the policies that were adopted in its composition and can refer to these where the analysis requires it. One of the policies adopted by the team was that related words were defined at the same time. While this obviously makes the chance of finding Matching greater, it means that any Matching found may be assumed to be non-accidental. Third, it utilises full sentences in its definitions. These are easier to discuss and compare.

In the light of these considerations I decided to analyse the definitions of *man* and *woman* given in the Collins COBUILD Dictionary. These words meet the first requirement in that they are co-hyponyms and, for some purposes, antonyms. They also meet the second requirement in that both words are polysemous, occur in idiomatic expressions and have a range of typical collocations. The two (groups of) definitions are presented on pages 155–6 and 158–62 in their original typographical layout. The lines connecting the two entries indicate pairs of definitions that are discussed in this chapter.

DISCUSSION OF DATA: EXAMPLES OF CLEAR SYMMETRY

Despite striking dissimilarities in both the length and some of the detail of the entries for *man* and *woman*, there is ample confirmation across these entries of the claim that Matching relations occur between non-adjacent components of this particular type of colony text. All the sub-entries connected by lines in figure 8.1 on page 165 are closely matched and could be represented in tabular form as was used for the Dickens quotation (Table 8.1).

The pattern that exists for all the connected sub-entries can be illustrated from the first sections of the two entries. Here and in all subsequent examples, the bold-face is that of the original dictionary text; it is not a marker of emphasis:

Table 8.3

A man is . . .	an adult male	human being.
A woman is	an adult female	human being.

What this tells us is that wherever there is a lexical relation between the headwords of dictionary entries, there is highly likely to be a clause relation between the relevant non-adjacent components of the dictionary. It also provides support for the claim that lexical relations and clause relations mirror each other such that antonymy parallels matching contrast, co-hyponymy and synonymy in different ways parallel matching compatibility, hyponymy parallels generalisation-example relations, and meronymy parallels preview–detail relations. Presumably therefore a dictionary ordered on the principles of a thesaurus would come close to functioning like a mainstream text. In a sense, that is all we need to know. The dictionary proves to be like the statute in permitting closer connections to exist between distant components than exist between adjacent ones, though its special status as a record of lexis (and as we have discovered lexical relations) means that the claim that non-adjacent components of colonies may form strong clause relations needs further testing on other kinds of colonies before it can be confidently claimed for all kinds of colonies. However, to leave the matter here would be to neglect the most interesting feature of colony relations, namely that the pairs of sub-entries often do not form matching compatibility relations but other kinds of matching relations, which prove to be revealing about the way that the English language is used to discriminate against women.

We begin, though, by noting that there are a number of pairs of sub-entries where the relationship is the same as that between the pair presented in Table 8.3. Examples are:

*People sometimes refer to a man as **the man** instead of 'he' or 'him', especially when they do not like him; an informal use. (sub-entry 5)*

*People sometimes refer to a woman as **the woman** instead of 'she' or 'her', especially when they do not like her; an informal use. (2)*

*A **man** is also . . . a man who works for or represents a particular company or organization. (10.4)*

*A **woman** is also . . . a woman who works for or represents a particular company or organization. (7.1)*

*If you say that someone is his **own man**, you mean that he is able to make his own decisions and plans without having to obey other people. (13)*

*If you say that a woman is her **own woman**, you mean that she is able to make her own decisions and plans without having to obey other people. (11)*

Other exact matches will be found between 10.2 (man) and 7.2 (woman) and between 12 (man) and 10 (woman). In each of these pairs it is reasonable to argue that the use of the words 'man' and 'woman' is strictly symmetrical.

DISCUSSION OF DATA: EXAMPLES OF ASYMMETRY

There is, however, one apparently minor asymmetry in the last example that proves revealing. In the first definition the subject of the clause containing the usage to be defined is *someone*; in the second case the subject is *a woman*. So *someone* and *woman* are opposed as if they were of equivalent generality. There are no circumstances when it would seem natural to say 'She's her own man', so *someone* here is being used as a pseudo-synonym for *man*. This pseudo-synonymy seems to underpin a number of asymmetrical pairings, to which we now turn.

Whereas the discrepancy just mentioned is unlikely to have a bearing on the way the definition is understood, the discrepancies that follow have a direct bearing upon the definitions of the uses in question. When writing entries for the *COBUILD Dictionary*, the lexicographers attempted to provide a context for the word(s) being defined that would convey to the user of the dictionary something of the typical circumstances in which the word(s) would be used. Any discrepancies found in the contexts of otherwise symmetrical definitions are likely therefore to reflect the lexicographer's judgement that there is a systematic discrepancy in the way the two items are generally used in the language. They are unlikely to reflect sexist attitudes in the lexicographers themselves, who were at pains, for instance, to avoid stereotyping assumptions in their choice of examples. Two of the asymmetrical pairings are set out in tabular form so as to highlight the differences:

Table 8.4

If a group of	people	do something	**as one man**,	they do it at exactly the same time
If a group of	women	do something	**as one woman**,	they do it at exactly the same time
CONSTANT	VARIABLE	CONSTANT	VARIABLE	CONSTANT

Table 8.5

If people	talk to each other	**man to man**,	they talk honestly and openly, treating each other as equals.
If two women	talk to each other	**woman to woman**,	they talk honestly and openly, treating each other as equals.
VARIABLE 1	CONSTANT	VARIABLE 2	CONSTANT

In both cases variable 1 is one of generality rather than gender. This (mis-) match is summed up in the contrast between sub-entries 3 (man) and 6 (woman):

Table 8.6

You can refer to	human beings	in general as	**man**
You can refer to	women	in general as	**woman**
CONSTANT	VARIABLE 1	CONSTANT	VARIABLE 2

Given the antonymous interpretation of *man* and *woman* in variable 2, an available interpretation of variable 1 is that *women* are not, or are even the opposite of, human beings. This of course is not a correct interpretation since the whole point of the two definitions is that **man** is not symmetrical with **woman** in this usage, but the fact that it can be reached erroneously may lend support to those such as Spender (1985) who have argued that the English language is loaded against women. The correct interpretation is itself disturbing enough. The earlier definitions relied on the altogether uncontroversial hyponymy of *woman* to *human being* with *man* as co-hyponym. If, though, the exact parallelism of 1 (man) and **1** (woman) shown in Table 8.3 reflects the co-hyponymy and reverse antonymy of the words *man* and *woman*, the contrasts shown in Tables 8.4, 8.5 and 8.6 reflect the other use of *man* as superordinate with *woman* as its hyponym. Interestingly, had *men* been substituted for *people* in these definitions, they would have become ambiguous between the co-hyponymic and superordinate meanings of *men*.

DISCUSSION OF DATA: UNMATCHED DEFINITIONS

The imbalance in the uses of *man* and *woman* reflected in these pairs of definitions is highlighted by one definition of *man* that does not match with any element of the entry for *woman*:

*A **man** is . . . a human being of either sex. (1.2)*

This definition, it is worth noting, carries within it the seeds of its own dishonesty. First, were it strictly correct, there would be no need to specify *of either sex*. It is because *man* is automatically associated with the male sex that this association needs to be denied. Second, if this definition were correct, it would be offering *man* and *human being* as strictly synonymous. Were they so, it ought to be possible to reverse the elements in the definition without rendering it nonsensical. But this is not the case:

A human being is a man of either sex.

What the definition means, then, is that male human beings are some-times treated by users of the language as if they were the only human beings, and female human beings as if they were a sub-class of male human beings. To those who have undertaken a feminist critique of language, this will come as no surprise. The question begins to arise as to how a dictionary that its makers wanted to be non-sexist came to include such entries. A possible answer is given in the final section of this chapter.

Two of the other definitions of man that are not paralleled by any equivalent definition for woman lean on the same assumption as the definition we have just considered:

***The man in the street** is an ordinary person who is not especially rich or educated or famous, and who is therefore considered to be a typical representative of public taste and opinion. (2.1)*

***Modern man**, primitive **man**, etc means all modern people, primitive people, etc considered as a group. (4)*

It is worth noting that the democratic implications of the phrase **the man in the street** are replaced by sexual ones in the closely parallel phrase **a woman of the street**. It would appear that men can in the English language go about in the street and be regarded as normal, but that women go about the street at the peril of their reputations.

A third definition without parallel may be interpreted in the same way but seems to reflect a more complete exclusion of women:

*If a difficult or dangerous situation **separates the men from the boys** or **sorts the men from the boys**, it shows who can cope with difficulty or danger, and who cannot. (17)*

The absence of any equivalent idiom for *women* tells us that the users of the language represented in the corpus from which the COBUILD lexicographers worked have chosen to find no need to talk regularly of situations of courage and danger that might sort out the women from the girls, even though little historical or social knowledge is necessary for one to recognise that such situations occur.

A number of other unparalleled cases all reflect the same absence of interest in the woman's point of view:

*A **man about town** is a smart young man who goes to a lot of parties and is well-known in fashionable places; an old-fashioned expression. (unnumbered subcategory of 8)*

*If you describe a man as a **man's man**, you mean that he has qualities which make him popular with other men rather than with women. (14)*

*If something **makes a man out of** a young man, it causes him to behave like an adult man, rather than a boy; used showing approval. (15)*

*If you **are man enough** for something, you have the necessary courage or ability to do it; used showing approval. (16)*

Presumably the approval of women by other women is expressed in less stereotypical ways. Interestingly, although the dictionary does not include the expression *making a woman of her* I have heard it used in the context of a man's taking a girl's virginity (an expression itself loaded with asymmetries); such a use markedly contrasts with the equivalent expression for *man*.

There is only one definition in the *woman* entry that has no match in the *man* entry:

***Woman** and **women** are also used before other nouns EG We had one woman teacher . . . . . . women drivers . . . . . . a woman friend.*

This presumably needs little comment. The language treats man as the unmarked, woman as the marked (cf. Leech, 1981).

DISCUSSION OF DATA: SPECIAL EXAMPLES OF ASYMMETRY

We are left with a handful of matching pairs of definitions that we have not yet accounted for. They are all cases of asymmetrical matching relations but the explanation is different in each case. They are perhaps the most interesting of all the pairings thrown up by the analysis. The first of these is the pair of sub-entries 6 (man) and 3 (woman), presented in tabular form:

Table 8.7

People	sometimes talk about	**a man**	when they want to make a statement about	people in general
Women	sometimes say	**a woman**	when they want to make a general statement that applies especially to	themselves
VARIABLE 1	CONSTANT	VARIABLE 2	CONSTANT	VARIABLE 3

The first thing to notice about this pairing is that even the constants have varied wording, suggesting that these definitions may not have been written side by side. Notice for example that the entry for *woman* refers to *a general statement* while the entry for *man* refers to *a statement about people in general*, which can be paraphrased as *a general statement about people*. Such paraphrasing is quite normal in mainstream prose (Hoey, 1991), so it is unsurprising across components of a colony. Of real interest, though, are variables 1 and 3. Variable 1 contrasts *women* with *people* as hyponym to superordinate, the degree of generality being the point of the contrast. Variable 3 contrasts everybody with one person, namely the speaker.

If both definitions are taken at face value, they would suggest that women have a choice that men do not have. According to these definitions, women may either use the expression *a woman* when they refer to themselves or, since they are included in *people*, they may use the parallel expression *a man* when they wish to refer to people in general. Men have, it would follow, no such choice since the expression *a man* can refer only to *people in general* and not be an oblique reference to themselves. I think most readers would accept that this does not describe the real state of affairs. To begin with, a man may use the expression *a man* to refer to himself; one of the examples given to support the definition in 6 (man) is

You'd think they would at least leave a man in peace on a Sunday afternoon.

Out of context, one cannot be absolutely sure but it seems highly likely that this was originally said in a context in which the speaker was complaining about being disturbed on a Sunday afternoon. So men do have the choice that the above definitions imply is available only to women. On the other hand women do not in fact have such a choice. It is difficult if not impossible to imagine a woman saying one of the other examples given for 6 (man):

What else can a man do at a time like that?

and meaning by it 'What can anyone, male or female, do?'. What the two definitions in fact imply, then, is that when men refer to themselves, they assume the expression can be generalised to all men, but when a woman refers to herself using the parallel expression *a woman* she knows only too well that she is not permitted to generalise from that to all humankind.

The second matched pair of definitions that are not exactly symmetrical are those of 8 (man) and 4 (woman):

*A sporting **man**, outdoor **man**, etc. is a man who likes sport, outdoor activities, etc. (8)*

*A gardening **woman**, a dog **woman**, etc. is a woman who likes gardening, dogs, etc.; an informal use.(4)*

Note the subtle stereotyping that the contrasting sets of interests suggest; sport and outdoor activities are, if not public activities, at the very least activities open to public view, whereas gardening and dogs suggests that women operate in a private domain. (A connection might be made here with our earlier consideration of **the man in the street** and **a woman of the streets**.) I am not sure why it should be more informal to use such an expression of a woman than of a man. Could it be that men are conventionally expected to have interests and therefore men categorise other men in terms of them, but that women are not expected to have interests and therefore categorisation in terms of them smacks of the eccentric?

The last two matched pairs are slightly different from the others in that all the detail of one of the definitions is present in the other. The difference lies in the addition or omission of some point of detail. The first such pair is that of 7 (man) and 5 (woman):

*In informal English, a woman's **man** is her husband, lover or boyfriend. (7)*

*A man's **woman** is his lover or his wife; an informal usage. (5)*

The obvious point here is the omission of 'girlfriend' from the list for a *man's woman*. The implication is presumably that a man's possession of a woman is always sexual, whereas a woman's possession of a man need not be so. Perhaps, too, the fact that there is no alternative to 'girlfriend' for a man wishing to talk about such a friendship suggests that English categorises a woman in a non-sexual relationship with a man as immature (girl versus woman).

The second pair is that between 11 (man) and 8 (woman). Here it is the addition that is significant:

*People sometimes address a man as '**man**' when they are angry or impatient with him. (11)*

*People sometimes address a woman as '**woman**' when they are ordering her to do something or when they are angry or impatient with her; an offensive use. (8)*

The lexicographers were under an obligation to reflect the language as they found it in the 20-million-word corpus from which they worked. All they could do was indicate their dissatisfaction with a usage note such as the one attached to sub-entry (8).

CONCLUSIONS

In this chapter I began by asking a simple research question: does the dictionary, as a central instance of the text-type I have termed the 'colony', manifest the same propensity to form clause relations at a distance across non-adjacent components as the statute had been shown to have? The answer proved to be a resounding affirmative. But in examining the evidence it became apparent that the data could not be left there. The analysis of matching relations often reveals tensions or sleights of hand that are not immediately apparent; see for example an analysis of such relations in Brutus's speech to the citizens in *Julius Caesar* (Hoey and Winter, 1981) which reveals that Brutus's language is playing underhand games with his audience. So it proved here also.

The COBUILD lexicographers allowed us to see confirmed certain claims about gender bias that have been made in the literature. In addition, other features of gender bias were revealed. But how did it happen that this dictionary, one of whose principles was that there should be no reinforcement of sexist attitudes in and towards language, should end up reinforcing those attitudes at least as far as their definitions of **man** and **woman** are concerned. The answer lies in another, still more fundamental, principle that guided the dictionary's makers: that all definitions should be based on careful observations of the word's use in the large corpus of contemporary English created for the purpose of writing the dictionary. The problem is that no corpus is value-neutral. The corpus chosen had a predominance of written texts over spoken, and within the written corpus, there was a heavy predominance of published texts over unpublished, and within the published corpus, there was a predominance of male writers over female. Consequently what the corpus reflected – not exclusively but nevertheless strongly – was the value-system, as enshrined in their language, of the male-oriented establishment. The corpus was in large part a collection of instances of language being used as an instrument of power and control. In describing the usage of words on the basis of such a corpus, inevitable compromises with that ideology have occurred. Lest, however, it should be thought that I am blaming the lexicographers unduly, let me conclude this point by admitting that I was partly responsible for the creation of the corpus that was used. I played a full part in discussions as to what it should contain and an equally full part in its subsequent creation. The recognition that a corpus is never neutral has come to me much more recently.

Certain general conclusions can be drawn from this chapter. First, discourse analysis cannot avoid being Critical Discourse Analysis. Second, no text type is beneath our attention; sometimes the most unlikely kinds of text can be the most revealing. Third, our analysis has been parasitical on the detailed corpus study of the COBUILD lexicographers and such corpus study is not neutral, in that every corpus is value-loaded. With this awareness in mind, though, the more we can examine the facts of language use on a large scale, the more we shall uncover about how our language shapes our thinking for us.

REFERENCES

Beekman, J. and Callow, J. (1974) *Translating the Word of God*, Grand Rapids, MI: Zondervan.

Hoey, M. P. (1983) *On the Surface of Discourse*, London: Allen & Unwin. Reprinted by University of Nottingham, Nottingham.

Hoey, M. P. (1986) 'The discourse colony: a preliminary study of a neglected discourse type', in R. M. Coulthard (ed.) *Talking about Text*, Discourse Analysis Monographs, 13, English Language Research, University of Birmingham, 1–26.

Hoey, M. P. (1988) 'The discourse properties of the criminal statute', in C. Walter (ed.) *Computing Power and Legal Language*, Westport, CT: Quorum Books/Greenwood Press, 69–88.

Hoey, M. P. (1991) *Patterns of Lexis in Text*, Oxford: Oxford University Press.

Hoey, M. P. and Winter, E. O. (1981) 'Believe me for mine honour', *Language and Style*, 14, 315–39.

Spender, D. (1985) *Man Made Language*, London: Pandora.

Winter, E. O. (1974) 'Replacement as a function of repetition: a study of some of its principal features in the clause relations of contemporary English', unpub. PhD, University of London.

Winter, E. O. (1979) 'Replacement as a fundamental function of the sentence in context', *Forum Linguisticum*, 4, 2, 95–133.

man /mæn/, **men; mans, manning, manned. Men** is the plural of the noun. **Mans** is the 3rd person singular, present tense, of the verb. **1** A **man** is **1.1** an adult male human being. EG *Larry was a handsome man in his early fifties... He's a great President but a remarkably boring man... Every man, woman, and child will be taken care of... ...the first man on the moon, Armstrong wasn't it?* **1.2** a human being of either sex. EG *All men are born equal... Darwin concluded that men were descended from apes... ...a deserted island where no man could live.*
2 The word **man** is used in the following expressions. **2.1** The **man in the street** is an ordinary person who is not especially rich or educated or famous, and who is therefore considered to be a typical representative of public taste and opinion. EG *How will these changes affect the man in the street?* **2.2** If a group of people do something **as one man**, they do it at exactly the same time. EG *The whole crowd rose to its feet as one man.* **2.3** If a group of people think something, believe something, etc **to a man**, every one of them thinks or believes it. EG *Congress almost to a man thought that abstract art was undesirable.* **2.4** If people talk to each other **man to man**, they talk honestly and openly, treating each other as equals. EG *Few people are prepared to talk 'man to man' with the boss... She wanted to speak to her father 'man to man'.* ● See also **man-to-man**.
3 You can refer to human beings in general as **man**. EG *Why does man seem to have more diseases than animals?... ...the most dangerous substance known to man.*
4 Modern **man**, primitive **man**, etc means all modern people, primitive people, etc considered as a group. EG *Modern man refuses to acknowledge his need for mercy... ...neolithic man.*
5 People sometimes refer to a **man** as the man instead of 'he' or 'him', especially when they do not like him; an informal use. EG *The man must be mad!... I won't see him anyway. I don't like the man.*
6 People sometimes talk about a **man** when they want to make a statement about people in general; a fairly informal use. EG *How much can a man stand?... What else can a man do at a time like that?... You'd think they would at least leave a man in peace on a Sunday afternoon.*
7 In informal English, a woman's **man** is her husband, lover, or boyfriend. EG *The two women have abandoned their men and are going to spend the evening in town.*
8 A sporting **man**, outdoor **man**, etc is a man who likes sport, outdoor activities, etc. EG *I gather you're a sporting man... I'm an outdoor man.* ● A **man about town** is a smart young man who goes to a lot of parties and is well-known in fashionable places; an old-fashioned expression. EG *He's quite a man about town these days.* ● See also **ladies' man.**
9 An Oxford **man**, Cambridge **man**, etc is a man who is or was a student at Oxford University, Cambridge University, etc. EG *He liked the idea of his daughter marrying an Oxford man... He's a Reading University man, isn't he?*
10 A **man** is also **10.1** an ordinary soldier, as opposed to an officer. EG *They killed in all some 70,000 officers and men.* **10.2** a male worker. EG *The farmer can't get a new man... I never employ extra men, no matter how big the job.* **10.3** a servant; an old-fashioned use. ● See also **right-hand man. 10.4** a man who works for or represents a particular company or organization. EG *The man from the New York Times was here to interview us... They always had their trade union man telling them all their rights.* **10.5** one of the pieces that you move in a game of chess or draughts.
11 People sometimes address a man as **'man'** when they are angry or impatient with him. EG *Don't sit there talking, man. Get going!... For heaven's sake, man, can't you see she's had enough?*
12 People used to address a man as **my man** or **my good man** when they considered him to be socially inferior to themselves. EG *All right, my man, that will be all for today... Thank you very much, my good man.*
13 If you say that someone **is** his **own man**, you mean that he is able to make his own decisions and plans without having to obey other people. EG *Listen, I'm my own man and no one's going to tell me when to retire.*
14 If you describe a man as **a man's man**, you mean that he has qualities which make him popular with other men rather than with women. EG *Theodore Roosevelt was a man's man, through and through.*
15 If something **makes a man out of** a young man, it causes him to behave like an adult man, rather than a boy; used showing approval. EG *The army made a man out of little Arnold Sims.*
16 If you **are man enough** for something, you have the necessary courage or ability to do it; used showing approval. EG *He's not man enough for the job.*
17 If a difficult or dangerous situation **separates the men from the boys** or **sorts the men from the boys**, it shows who can cope with difficulty or danger, and who cannot. EG *Necessity separates the men from the boys.*
18 If you **man** something such as a machine, you are in charge of it or available to operate it. EG *They manned the phones all through the night... The rebels refused to man the barricades during the uprising.* ● See also **manned.**

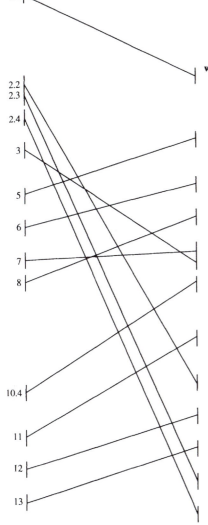

woman /wʊmən/, women. 1 A **woman** is an adult female human being. EG *...a tall, dark-eyed woman in a simple brown dress ... There were men and women working in the fields... Fifty women and children picketed the office.* ► **Woman** and **women** are also used before other nouns. EG *We had one woman teacher... ...women drivers... ...a woman friend.*

2 People sometimes refer to a woman as **the woman** instead of 'she' or 'her', especially when they do not like her; an informal use. EG *Drat the woman, she really gets on my nerves!... I've never even met the woman.*

3 Women sometimes say **a woman** when they want to make a general statement that applies especially to themselves; a fairly informal use. EG *A woman can only stand so much.*

4 A gardening **woman**, a dog **woman**, etc is a woman who likes gardening, dogs, etc; an informal use. EG *No, really, I'm not a drinking woman... I'm a small car woman, myself.*

5 A man's **woman** is his lover or his wife; an informal use.

6 You can refer to women in general as **woman**. EG *...man's inhumanity to woman.*

7 A **woman** is also 7.1 a woman who works for or represents a particular company or organization. EG *The publicity woman hand planned to take me there and show me around.* 7.2 a female worker. EG *You may be able to employ a woman to do the washing for you.*

8 People sometimes address a woman as **woman** when they are ordering her to do something or when they are angry or impatient with her; an offensive use. EG *Oh, for God's sake, woman, sit down!*

9 If a group of women do something **as one woman**, they do it at exactly the same time. EG *They turned on him as one woman.*

10 People used to address a woman as **my good woman** when they considered her to be socially inferior to themselves. EG *Thank you, my good woman, that will be all.*

11 If you say that a woman **is** her **own woman**, you mean that she is able to make her own decisions and plans without having to obey other people.

12 If a group of women think something, believe something, etc **to a woman**, every one of them thinks or believes it. EG *They believe to a woman that they will win.*

13 If two women talk to each other **woman to woman**, they talk honestly and openly, treating each other as equals. EG *I want to chat to her, woman to woman, on her own level.* ► used as an adjective. EG *You should approach her in a friendly woman to woman way.*

Figure 8.1 Matching relations between sub-sections of COBUILD Dictionary entries for *man* and *woman*

Chapter 9

The official version
Audience manipulation in police records of interviews with suspects

Malcolm Coulthard

We wouldn't have all these campaigns to get the Birmingham Six released if they'd been hanged. They'd have been forgotten and the whole community would be satisfied.

> (Lord Denning, liberal reforming judge and former
> Master of the Rolls, in August 1990)

As I look back I am very sorry, because I always thought that our police were splendid and first class and I am sorry that in this case it appears to be the contrary.

> (Lord Denning in February 1991 after the Director of Public
> Prosecutions made it clear that he no longer regarded the
> Birmingham Six convictions as safe)

In the English, Welsh and Northern Irish Courts, though not the Scottish, an unsigned confession is sufficient to convict, even if its authenticity is disputed and there is no other supporting forensic evidence. Thus the accuracy of the record of what an accused (is claimed to have) said while in custody can assume tremendous importance. Ideally the Court is presented with a complete verbatim record of what was said, in Austin's (1962) terms a *locutionary* record, and then it makes its own decision about the meaning and behavioural consequences of the crucial utterance(s), that is, their *illocutionary and perlocutionary forces*. However, for a whole series of reasons, the situation is rarely ideal.

Perhaps the most famous example of a problematic situation, the case of Derek Bentley and Chris Craig, dates from the 1950s. The two young men were apprehended by police as they were trying to break into a warehouse. Bentley, already under arrest at the time, was said to have shouted to Craig, who had a revolver, 'Let him have it, Chris'; shortly afterwards Craig fired several shots and killed a policeman. The debate in court over the interpretation of the ambiguous utterance was resolved in favour of the incriminating performative, 'I hereby urge you to shoot him', the perlocutionary effect of which, the death of a policeman, made Bentley an accessory to murder, for which he was convicted and subsequently hanged.

In his defence Bentley did not deny the Court's interpretation but rather, more radically, the fact that he had uttered the phrase at all: he asserted that it was a complete invention of the police officers involved in his arrest. Bentley's claim, that linguistic evidence had been in part or even totally invented by the police, was to be reiterated by many others down the years, although claims by the convicted that they had been 'verballed' were usually viewed with great scepticism by the general public – at least until 1989. This consensus began to change, however, following the case of one Paul Dandy, where it was irrefutably demonstrated, by means of Electro-Static Deposition Analysis (ESDA) – a technique which allows the analyst to read impressions and indentations which have been created on the particular sheet being examined by the pressure of the instrument used to write on the sheet above (see Davis, 1994) – that the final page of an otherwise authentic interview record had been rewritten to allow the insertion of the two incriminating utterances which are highlighted in italic in the extract below:[1]

1 Have you got a brother named Roy?
2 Yes.
3 On the 31st October 1986 you deposited £1,000 into the T.S.B. Where did that come from?
4 The sale of the GTi with 'Rabbit Injection' written on the back.
5 Will you sign an authority for us to look at your bank account?
6 No.
7 *I take it from your earlier reply that you are admitting been [sic] involved in the robbery at the M.E.B.*
8 *You're good. Thursday, Friday, Saturday, Sunday and you've caught me. Now you've got to prove it.*
9 Do you want to read over the notes and caption and sign them.
10 I'll initial the mistakes, but I won't sign them.
   (end of interview)

A rash of similar cases of 'verballing' followed and the disbelieving English public saw in quick succession the disbanding of the Birmingham-based West Midlands Serious Crime squad with the consequent suspension of fifty-one detectives, the quashing of the convictions of the 'Birmingham Six', the release of the 'Guildford Four' and the successful appeal of the 'Tottenham Three'. By the mid-1990s, the pendulum had swung so far that the tendency was rather to disbelieve the police in cases of disputed confessions and some 800 cases where it is claimed that there was some police interference with or actual falsification of evidence were currently under consideration by the Home Office for referral to the Court of Appeal.

As a result of the disquiet created by such cases the police system for recording interviews with an accused has changed significantly, at least in

England – now a significant proportion of interviews are video-recorded and almost all of the rest are audio-taped using stereo tapes with a voice announcing the time at 10-second intervals already pre-recorded on to one track, in order to prevent subsequent editing, deletion of expletives, and so on.

In this chapter, however, I do not propose to focus on cases of purported invented and incriminating evidence, but rather on more subtle examples where what was recorded and the ways in which it was recorded have introduced bias that could have affected the judge and jury's general impression of the character of the police officers and the accused. In so doing this bias created a frame within which other utterances which *were* incriminating were interpreted.

THE CREATION OF THE OFFICIAL VERSION

Within the English judicial system the communicative rights of the accused can be massively constrained in several ways and at several stages. The first information-gathering stage is almost always by interview. At the time of which I am writing the normal procedure was for two police officers to conduct an interview jointly, one would ask the questions and the other would write down in longhand both the colleague's questions and the responses given by the accused. At the end of the interview the accused would be asked first to read through the written record (or, if illiterate, to listen to the police officer/scribe read it aloud), then to initial any corrections he or she might wish to introduce and finally to sign each page confirming that the whole text was a true record of what had been said. Such records could be, and usually were, presented later in Court and used in evidence against the accused, even if the accused had in fact refused to sign them.

Obviously, this procedure put the police in a privileged position. They could, of course, as we have seen, invent utterances or even whole interviews and then claim that the accused, when invited, refused to sign; but, even when nothing was invented, the police remained in control of what was recorded. The interviewing officer was able to choose the interview topics through the questions, while the transcribing officer, though in principle required to write down verbatim what was said, had, at least in some forces, a substantial degree of freedom to decide what was and what was not recorded. It is very clear from a comparison of the predicted length of an interview, produced by dividing the number of words by the normal transcription speed of some 20–25 words per minute, which can be derived from unchallenged records, that, given the actual time taken, some written records are only partial; indeed some even contain an explicit acknowledgement of missing text 'at this point we discussed a series of unrelated matters'.

However, even when an officer scribe did set out to produce a full and verbatim record he remained in control of the language in which it was recorded and would thus, even with the best will in the world, produce what any linguist would regard as an inaccurate version, even if it was in no way a misrepresentation of the basic ideational *content* of the interview. Although the accused was (supposed to be) offered at the end of the interview the chance to make alterations, it is, as is well known, very difficult for anyone, let alone someone under stress, to remember exactly what has been said in an hour-long interview and then to challenge either the wording of individual questions and replies or occasional, but potentially significant omissions.

As we noted above, it is very surprising to the non-expert and even more so to the linguist to discover that, given the high significance attached by the Courts to verbal admissions, interview records could still be used as evidence when an accused had challenged their accuracy at the time of interview and refused to sign the notes. The legal justification was the accepted reliability of police officers as witnesses combined with the fact that, as there had been two of them present they could independently vouch for the truth and accuracy of the record. It was for this reason that police officers, rather than signing the same joint interview record, were required to waste an enormous amount of their own and their typists' time in producing two 'independent' typed versions of each and every interview, versions which were and obviously had to be, in reality verbally identical, except for the simple change of reference to the speaker – had they used any other strategy it would have been possible for the defence to challenge the accuracy of the record. Thus the scribe/officer would write 'DC Guile then asked Malone ... ' while Detective-Constable Guile, the interviewer, would report '*I* then asked Malone ... '. Of course, what in fact happened was that the scribe officers would produce their typed version first from their handwritten notes and then the interviewing officers would generate their version by copying the scribe's typewritten text, merely rephrasing the speaker reference. Occasionally performance errors would creep in, so in one authentic text we find DC Guile reporting 'DC Guile then said ... '.

Courts were willing to suspend their disbelief even further. Because verbatim evidence was so privileged, officers were pressured to produce it whenever possible, so much so that the police and the Courts collaborated in the pretence that police officers could remember what had been said in an interview or even during a house search and arrest so accurately that they could be relied upon to write up a *verbatim* record hours after the event. One of the incriminating and unsigned interviews I cite below lasts some 55 minutes, at the end of which the scribe reports that the prisoner was returned to his cell and then concludes his record with engaging honesty 'I *then* made up [*sic*] *contemporaneous* notes'. This at the end of some ten pages of transcript which are otherwise indistinguishable to the reader and certainly not distinguished in any linguistic way from authentic contemporaneous verbatim records – all the 'remembered' utterances are even placed in inverted commas.

ON TRANSCRIPTION

Converting the spoken to the written, as anyone who has attempted it is aware, is not an unproblematic task. However, there appear to have been in most police forces no explicit guidelines to officers about what they could or should legitimately omit and thus they had to reinvent the procedures for themselves. It is impossible to derive these procedures *post hoc* by comparing tape recordings of interviews with the written records because tape recordings were not made. So, in this context it is useful to consider Slembrouck's (1992) observations on the production of *Hansard* versions of proceedings in Parliament, where similarly linguistically naive scribes are charged with the creation of highly important verbatim records of what was said. In this case, however, Slembrouck was fortunate enough to have recordings to compare with *Hansard*. He notes that

> there is filtering out of 'disfluency' and other obvious properties of spokenness (e.g. intonation, stress). Repetitions, (even when strategically used ...), half-pronounced words, incomplete utterances, (un)filled pauses, false starts, reformulations, grammatical slips, etc. are equally absent,
>
> (Slembrouck, 1992: 104)

In addition

> Hansard does not represent ... accent or use of a regional variety. It also interferes with the level of formality ...: contracted verb forms are not used and informal variants are generally avoided.
>
> (Slembrouck, 1992: 105)

As Slembrouck observes none of these alterations are 'value-free', because they all affect the way the lay reader evaluates what is said. However, at the same time there is no suggestion that the records are biased in any other way – it appears that politicians of all parties, classes, nationalities and sexes are equally 'improved' and homogenised. In addition, Members of Parliament (MPs) who feel they have been misquoted or misrepresented by a scribe's reformulation are able to appeal after the event to the tape-recorded version and ask for a correction to be made to the official written record.

By contrast and in a different context, court stenographers, when asked about their procedures, report that their conscious strategy is (using Pitt

Corder's famous distinction) to correct the grammatical 'mistakes' made by judges and barristers who obviously know better, but to record the 'errors' produced by witnesses who don't. In other words, we see a transcription convention at work which on the one hand regards and therefore represents the educated professional as a speaker of standard English, whatever the objective evidence to the contrary, and on the other sees semi- or uneducated witnesses as speakers who may be characterised as such by the non-standard representation of their speech. In these situations, however, the witness, unlike the MP, never has access to, let alone the chance to correct, the written record.

Fortunately, the vast majority of police records seem to be, just like *Hansard*, linguistically unbiased. As we can see in the following and typical example, false starts, hesitations, filled pauses and even misunderstood questions are, quite reasonably, omitted. Equally, in this, as in most such records, there are no dialectal or other non-standard forms, no paralinguistic signals, no discourse markers, no terms of address. In other words, the transcription favours on the one hand the ideational and the textual over the interpersonal and on the other assumed competence over actual performance:

Q 'The robbery occurred at lunch-time yesterday, did you have anything to eat near the middle of the day?'
A 'No, I like to keep fit. I never have anything at dinner-time.'
Q 'What time did you leave home yesterday morning?'
A 'About 9.15.'
Q 'And what sort of property were you looking for?'
A 'Anything. I want older houses to do up.'
Q 'Is this what you do for a living, do old houses up?'
A 'No, not really.'
Q 'What do you do for a living?'
A 'I'm unemployed.'

THE MODULATION OF CONTENT

Not all police records, however, are equally neutral. There are two major ways in which a police record may affect the reception of its content:

1 by differentially modulating the perceived reliability of the speakers as witnesses;
2 by enhancing the verisimilitude of the interaction reported.

The attribution of non-prestige forms to the accused

Although the norm was to produce unmarked standard language in interview records, as exemplified in the extract above, there always existed the possibility of the police scribe choosing to record, or even mis-record, non-standard usage by the accused. The situation was compounded by the fact that this recording was invariably unilateral; that is, even when the police usage in terms of phonological, grammatical and discoursal choices was very similar to that of the accused, it could be differentially transcribed and thereby imply significant differences to the Court. We see a typical example in the short extracts below taken from a murder case, where a suspect with low intelligence is characterised by a few unremarkable spoken dialect choices, indeed choices which are not consistently maintained throughout the text and which fit oddly with the other full and standard forms he is simultaneously recorded as using:

CLAY   'I know what I did, I worked 11 to 8 and after work went straight home, had **me** tea, watched telly and didn't go out all night **me** mum and dad will tell you.'

CLAY   'I know what I've done and you are not pinning anything on me because I've done **nowt** wrong.'

At other times an accused would be assigned colloquial and slang forms:

MORLEY   replied 'I've already told your **blokes** because **I knock around** with John THORNTON and that **prat** McCARTHY, I get arrested for a robbery they have done, its **not on** because I was at work that day.'

and even obscenities:

DS   'Will you sign that?'
DA   **'Fuck off'**
DS   'We have finished for now. I will now read these notes back over to you and you may read them . . .'
DA   'Just **fuck off** put me back in the cell.'

This sprinkling of a text with obscenities, non-standard, colloquial and/or slang features to give a characterising flavour is a standard literary technique. In other words the police scribes were, consciously or unconsciously, operating in the same way as creative writers and using how people speak in part to characterise them – the classic example, of course, is *Lady Chatterley's Lover* where Mellor is at times represented as speaking an uneducated pseudo-dialectal form of the language by similar partial representation. Also, just as Lawrence makes no attempt to represent the usage of socially superior locals, whose pronunciation, if not grammar and vocabulary, would have sounded to an RP (received pronunciation) speaker almost as marked as Mellor's, so the local police record their own utterances in the standard form.

The suggestion that such linguistic features were considered to affect the way judges and juries perceived witnesses can be supported by the observation that, although the accused are at times recorded as swearing and uttering obscenities, I have never seen a police record of a police officer doing so. Thus, one might be permitted to speculate that this is, at least in part, due to self-editing. For example, one utterance extracted from an interaction with an amateur radio enthusiast who kept interfering with police calls on a police frequency was transcribed as follows in the official version:

Amateur: What are you all going ten ten, off duty is it? All right then, see about this, I'll tell you what, I'll go off at base station and I'll go onto just your mobiles. . . .

An independent transcription of this almost unintelligible utterance produced by an expert witness in phonetics called by the defence showed that the interaction in fact went as follows:

Amateur: What are you all going ten ten, off duty is it?
Police: **Shut up you pillock**
Amateur: **I'm a pillock am I**. All right then, see about this. I'll tell you what, I'll go off at base station and I'll go onto just your mobiles. . . .

Here the swearing had simply been omitted, with no trace, let alone overt indication, that there had been 'expletives deleted'.

The metalinguistic validation of the record

As was mentioned above unsigned incriminating interviews can be used as evidence in English courts, but they will of course be viewed with some suspicion by the judge and jury. It can therefore be very useful for the prosecution if there is some supporting text surrounding and even justifying or authenticating the unconfirmed confession. The following two extracts come from a case where the accused strongly denied ever having said any of the incriminating items (which are not reproduced below), let alone having been offered the chance to emend the text, yet he was subsequently convicted on the basis of the interview record:

> DS Smith said 'Listen **Roy**, we keep **true** records of what you've said, I speak for my colleague here Mr Jones when I say that we will be **completely honest and truthful** . . . but to **allay your suspicions** I could write down in question and answer form what is said and you can read it and then sign it, that way you would know it was a **true** record of what you have said, is that **fair**?'

There follows an incriminating record which ends with:

> DS Smith 'Right now **Roy**, DC Jones will read this over to you, then

you can read it yourself. You can **make any alterations you wish.** Is that being **fair** with you?
MORLEY replied 'Yes.'
DS Jones then read over to MORLEY the contemporaneous notes.
... MORLEY read them and was **invited** to sign them.
MORLEY then said 'No I can't. . . . **Nothing personal lads.**'
DS Jones said 'Look **Roy**, have we put anything down in these notes that you didn't say?'
MORLEY replied 'No, I can't sign the notes but at least you know the **truth.**'

These extracts display several devices used to reinforce an unsigned confession; the police officers are lexically constructed as reasonable, yea honourable, men: they make 'true records', they are 'completely honest and truthful', they want to 'allay suspicions', and produce a 'true record' which is also 'fair'. The text conveys an apparently friendly, non-threatening atmosphere through the repeated and reciprocal use of familiar forms of address, 'Roy' and 'lads', and a situation in which Morley is 'invited' to sign, feels sufficiently at ease with and linked to the officers to apologise for not signing, 'nothing personal lads' and wants them to 'know the truth', which he openly and helpfully admits he will later deny.

The metalinguistic creation of atmosphere and police character

Some records go further in the creation of a positive police image, probably because ultimately a witness statement has value and credibility only in so far as the witness has value and credibility. The following extracts, taken from three separate cases, are simply more marked examples of a general technique:

'if you were to give us your dealer it would be of assistance to society to stem the flow of this dangerous drug, heroin, onto the streets.'

'I believe that you were there and I think the strain of having to carry that knowledge of what you did and what you saw happen was so horrible that you almost convinced yourself it never happened, you would feel very much better in yourself if you got rid of that burden that you've carried for so long.'

'All that points to the fact that you committed this robbery and I must tell you that you have shown no remorse, you've shown no feelings and you have offered me no help in bringing these matters to a satisfactory conclusion. I feel very sorry that you have that dreadful disease of being a gambler and you stole that money to feed your habit.'

As we can see through the reporting of these utterances the speaker/police officer comes across as a socially aware, caring member of society.

The options discussed above are not, of course, mutually exclusive. The next extract comes from an interview in which the speech of the accused is filled with not only swearing and obscenities – 'bastard', 'fuck off', 'fucking pissed', 'piece of piss', 'any more shit', etc. – but also terms of address marking familiarity and solidarity – 'Frank', 'please boys', 'look boys', 'come off it boys' – and the odd mixture of the two 'Oh, fuck off, boys':

McCarthy said:	'Can't we do a deal. You obviously want Westwood and not me. Keep me out and I'll tell you who he is.'
DC Conran said:	'We can't make promises like that. We have got a job to do.'
McCarthy said:	'Fucking hell. I've got to be careful what I say then.'

Enhancing the verisimilitude of the interaction record

As noted above it was an accepted, though fortunately not particularly frequent practice for police officers to (re-)create a 'verbatim' record of an interview from memory after the event, indeed sometimes several hours afterwards. As no one can actually remember verbatim large chunks of speech (Hjelmquist, 1984), the police were in fact acting as amateur dramatists, putting (hopefully) accurately remembered content into a verbal form – and we must remember that absolute verbal accuracy can be vitally important. In a case in the Republic of Ireland, a man was convicted and sentenced to 40 years imprisonment on the basis of a single utterance which had been remembered by a police officer as 'I know you know I did it' but by the accused himself as 'I know you *think* I did it'.

Interestingly, if not paradoxically, some of the interview records produced from memory are formally more similar to linguists' verbatim transcriptions than are the authentic and supposedly verbatim records which have been produced contemporaneously. In other words when 'inventing' or 'composing' utterances police officers appear at times to have been more conscious of form and thus to have produced records that seem more 'authentic'. In such records we note the following features:

Discourse markers

One of the pervasive features of speech is the occurrence of discourse markers but these, as is evident in the extract on page 169), are typically edited out from the contemporaneous police records. However, as McCarthy (1993: 180) points out, 'spoken discourse markers ... play a major role in our judgement of the degree of spokenness present' in a written text and thus it may not be surprising that they occur with marked frequency in *remembered* records; indeed five times in a mere fourteen lines in the following remembered interview.

line 1   MORLEY said 'Well . . .
line 3   MORLEY thought for a moment and said 'Well . . .
line 6   I said 'Well . . .
line 12   DC JAMES said 'Well . . .
line 14   I said 'Look Roy . . .

Interruptions

As we noted above contemporaneous transcripts standardly omit performance features like interruptions, but these are the very stuff of drama. In the example below we note that not only was the interruption apparently successfully remembered and reported but also the interruption split a prepositional group:

MORLEY '. . . I then saw George CONLAN and John HURLEY just after 9, I played dominoes between 12.30 and 1.00 with . . .'

I interrupted him and said
'Hang on a minute, lets go through this slowly.'

Non-verbal features

Contemporaneous interview records rarely have reports of paralinguistic events, but remembered interviews frequently do:

'Hang on a minute, lets go through this slowly. It's amazing really, here we are on Thursday, 12 July, 1984, some 3 weeks after the robbery took place and you can remember specifically your movements for that morning?'

MORLEY *smiled* and made no reply.

In such cases the situation can be further complicated during the trial itself; some judges reinforce the deception by not reminding the members of the jury that the verbal report is only a remembered one, while others seem to forget the fact or at best to regard it as irrelevant and choose to treat the records as authentic and contemporaneous, texts from which they can extract direct quotes in their summings-up.

CODA

Critical Discourse Analysis . . . should describe and explain how power abuse is enacted, reproduced or legitimised by the text and talk of dominant groups or institutions.

(van Dijk, this volume: 84)

As is very evident from the small set of examples reproduced above the fairness of trials can be prejudiced by lay misunderstandings about the nature of discourse, its mental processing and the methods for recording it. Thus, the discourse analyst has perhaps more opportunities for critical action in the area of language and the law than in most other areas. Indeed the newly formed International Association of Forensic Linguists has, as one of its major aims, the informing of the legal profession on language matters.

This education is proceeding on two fronts, through publications aimed at lawyers and through linguists acting as expert witnesses in Court. The association has founded the journal *Forensic Linguistics: The International Journal of Speech, Language and the Law*, which includes lawyers as members of the editorial board and publishes articles by linguists both on case work and on theoretical problems and advances in analytic technique. In addition some of the members of the association are writing texts specifically for use by the legal profession, the most successful so far being Eades's (1992) handbook for Australian lawyers on how to deal with Aboriginal clients and witnesses.

Meanwhile linguists are growingly being asked to act as expert witnesses in Court cases when the authenticity, accuracy and interpretation of documents or the acceptability of police records of speech is being challenged. Useful summaries of what forensic linguists have achieved so far are Levi (1994), Eades (1994) and Coulthard (1992; 1993; 1994a; 1994b). In some cases there are still arguments over the admissibility of linguistic evidence in court and even when admitted linguists may find resistance to their claim that language is not always transparent, that meanings are not always readily available to the layman and that the transcription of speech is not unproblematic. The struggle continues ...

NOTE

1   All the examples in this article are taken from real cases, although in the majority of the extracts the names have been changed to preserve anonymity in case of any future appeal.

REFERENCES

Austin, J. L. (1962) *How to Do Things with Words*, London: Oxford University Press.

Coulthard, R. M. (1992) 'Forensic discourse analysis', in R. M. Coulthard (ed.) *Advances in Spoken Discourse Analysis*, London: Routledge, 242–57.

Coulthard, R. M. (1993) 'Beginning the study of forensic texts: corpus, concordance, collocation', in M. P. Hoey (ed.) *Data, Description, Discourse*, London: HarperCollins, 86–97.

Coulthard, R. M. (1994a) '*Power*ful evidence for the defence: an exercise in forensic discourse analysis', in J. Gibbons (ed.) *Language and the Law*, London: Longman, 414–42.

Coulthard, R. M. (1994b) 'On the use of corpora in the analysis of forensic texts', *Forensic Linguistics*, 1, 1, 27–43.

Davis, T. A. (1994) 'ESDA and the analysis of contested contemporaneous notes of police interviews', *Forensic Linguistics*, 1, 1, 71–89.

Eades, D. (1992) *Aboriginal English and the Law: Communicating with Aboriginal English Speaking Clients: A Handbook for Legal Practitioners*, Brisbane: Queensland Law Society.

Eades, D. (1994) 'Forensic linguistics in Australia', *Forensic Linguistics*, 1, 2, 113–32.

Hjelmquist, E. (1984) 'Memory for conversations', *Discourse Processes*, 7, 321–36.

Levi, J. (1994) 'Language as evidence: the linguist as expert witness in North American courts', *Forensic Linguistics*, 1, 1, 1–26.

McCarthy, M. (1993) 'Spoken discourse markers in written text', in J. M. Sinclair, M. P. Hoey and G. Fox (eds) *Techniques of Description: Spoken and Written Discourse. A Festschrift for Malcolm Coulthard*, London: Routledge, 170–82.

Slembrouck, S. (1992) 'The parliamentary *Hansard* "verbatim" report: the written construction of spoken discourse', *Language and Literature*, 1, 2, 101–19.

Chapter 10

Conflict talk in a psychiatric discharge interview
Struggling between personal and official footings

Branca Telles Ribeiro

> in talk it seems routine that, while firmly standing on two feet, we jump
> up and down on another.
>
> (Goffman, 1981a: 155)

The extract presented below comes from a psychiatric interview at a
mental institution; it is in fact the patient's discharge interview, after being
interned for twenty days. The patient, Jurema Cardozo, is a 61-year-old
Brazilian who had been institutionalised due to an acute psychotic crisis;
the treating psychiatrist, Doctor Edna Silva, is a 25-year-old who has only
recently graduated.[1]

	[acc]
(1) Doctor:	=why did you only have one child? ....
(2) Patient:	'because (it didn't), I didn-, *I suffered a lot*, I thought childbirth was terrible. the pain, ... y'know, [shakes head]
(3) Doctor:	[nods]
	[acc]
(4) Patient:	so that afterwards then I had a procedure so that I wouldn't have any more (children), [smiles, lowers head slightly] [dec] I avoi:ded it. [nods]
(5) Doctor:	/you were afraid to have children./= [short nods]
(6) Patient:	=yes. (1.7) [nods] because the pain is terrible, isn't it, doctor. (1.3)
(7) Doctor:	//mmm mmm// [nods]
(8) Patient:	/I don't know/ do you have children? [nods, bends forward and smiles] (2.0)

(9) Doctor:	/mmm./
	[short nod]
(10) Patient:	do you have children?=
	[bends further forward and smiles]
(11) Doctor:	=/yes, I do./=
	[nods, bends forward]
(12) Patient:	=yes, then you know that it is a terrible pain, right.
	then, because of that, you did not want any=
(13) Doctor:	the pain of childbirth is-
	[raises torso, raises head forward]
(14) Patient:	=/yes, it was, it was/ because of that that I did not want
	any more. (1.8)
	[nods, looks away to the right and down, long nod]
	because of the pain. (2.7)
	[looks away]
	[acc]
(15) Doctor:	//mmm, mmm.// 'and your son, do you- well::, go out often
	with him or does he come to visit= =you? ...

Generally, the purpose of the discharge interview is to evaluate the patient's overall well-being as well as her communicative performance. In this interview, as illustrated by the segment above, the patient in the main follows the expected interactional rules for medical interviews. For example, she provides the second parts of adjacency pairs, expands on the doctor's comments, and stays on topic, addressing the doctor's agenda for the interview. So if we look at topics and at the turn structure, the discourse coheres.

However, two conversational rules often described in the literature on doctor–patient communication are violated (Fisher, 1979; 1984; Frankel, 1984; Shuy, 1974; West, 1983; among others). First, the patient/interviewee at turns (8) and (10) asks the doctor a personal question, thus shifting discourse role. Second, this question concerns the doctor rather than the patient, and refers to an intimate matter – bearing children – a matter of interest to women. In performing this move, the patient steps out of her official role as patient and her addressee momentarily leaves the role of doctor to assume that of a younger woman conversing with an older woman. The interview is suspended. A subtle yet definite change in context takes place: rather than listening to an interaction between a doctor and a patient, we hear an older woman addressing a younger one.

This fleeting moment of intimacy soon fades. The doctor interrupts the patient (turns 12 and 13) and once again a contextual transformation takes place, whereby participants resume their official roles of doctor and patient (turns 14 and 15).

FOOTINGS AND INTERACTION

In everyday talk and interaction, speakers and listeners continuously step in and out of social roles. They choose from a wide range of official and non-official social attributes the ones which best fit the communicative situation they find themselves in. *Footing* is the term proposed by Goffman to refer to speakers' and hearers' *interactional stances, alignments* or *positions vis-à-vis* one another, as well as oneself, 'as expressed in the way [they] manage the production or reception of an utterance' (Goffman, 1981a: 128).

This chapter discusses some of the footings in the psychiatric interview. The discharge interview marks not simply the patient's release from the hospital, but also her transition from patient to person. We shall see how the prevailing institutional footings proposed by the doctor provide the context within which other activities come into being. We shall also see how personal stances on the part of the patient represent a necessary contextual transformation in bringing about a sense of self, of who the woman is, of the person behind the patient. The doctor, however, does not seem to be attuned to this situation.[2]

INSTITUTIONAL DISCOURSE: MEDICAL INTERVIEWS

Discourse in institutional contexts differs essentially from discourse in everyday life. Medical interviews are social events. They are structured in predictable ways and organised toward specific ends. They must comply with the organisational constraints of particular settings (Fisher, 1984: 202).

In doctor–patient face-to-face communication, certain contexts – institutional ones – prevail over others. Thus, talk which derives from medical concerns generally overshadows more personal talk (Mishler, 1984). In the psychiatric interview, for instance, participants display primarily their official roles of doctor and patient. They are viewed as 'social agents, located in a network of social relations, in specific places in a social structure' (Kress, 1989: 5).

Patients, however, often propose a departure from the institutional contexts (Mishler, 1984: 107). They attempt to interrupt the discourse of medicine by introducing a civilian repertoire, a set of informal footings salient to their own world of experience. Doctors seldom accept (or realise) this shift. More often than not, they interrupt the patients' talk, ignoring information which may otherwise have been important:

> discourse is revealed as a dialectic between the voices of the lifeworld [mostly done by patients] and of medicine [mostly done by doctors]; it involves conflict and struggle between two different domains of meaning.
>
> (Mishler, 1984: 121)

This discussion portrays a difference in the doctor's and the patient's expectations concerning events (such as a psychiatric interview) in institutional settings. Indeed it reveals a mismatch in expectations regarding participants' roles, ways to interact, topics and topic management, among other things. This mismatch also explains some of the frequent frustrations which characterise this type of encounter (Tannen and Wallat, 1987).

FRAMING TALK

A frame perspective to data analysis captures the inherent complexity of what goes on in the interview situation, where two major contexts of talk can be identified. I shall call these contexts of talk *frames* following Bateson (1981), Goffman (1974; 1981a), and Tannen and Wallat (1987).[3]

Briefly stated, a frame is the speaker's instructions to the listener on how to understand a discourse message. A frame is (or delimits) a set of messages (or meaningful actions) (Bateson, 1981: 186). It is a relational concept, since it indicates how the relationship between the participants is to be understood. As such it conveys a superordinate message – *a metamessage* – about the context of talk (Tannen, 1986).

Context, here, is to be understood in a dynamic way. It is interactionally constructed. Thus contextual information on who speaks to whom, about what, and in what circumstance is an ongoing joint creation and subject to micro-changes which may affect the interaction as a whole.

Since frames are hardly ever explicitly stated, participants use a variety of more subtle cues to signal them. Gumperz (1977; 1982) calls these features 'contextualisation cues'. They may be paralinguistic and prosodic features of speech (Goffman, 1981a; Gumperz 1977; 1982), or they may be non-verbal cues (Kendon 1979; 1990; Scheflen, 1973). They signal a qualitative change in context, triggering new interpretations about discourse and interaction. This being the case, while a reframing may alter the activity only slightly, it completely changes the participants' perception on the event (or what they would say was going on).

To complicate matters further 'simultaneous meanings are present in life as they are in language' (Goffman, 1974). That is, in a medical interview, the doctor's request to conduct a physical examination of the patient is a move embedded within the institutional frame of the interview. Bateson uses the analogy of the *mathematical set* to illustrate the logical relations which he applies to frames. One may have major or minor framings (sets), whose simultaneity reveals the complexity of contextual embeddings (Bateson, 1981: 188).

When a frame changes, participants' footings and ways of interaction change too. An entirely different reality comes into being (Goffman, 1974: 45). The one who proposes the frame (and has it ratified) establishes how talk is to be understood in that context (Tannen, 1986). It is not surprising therefore that often the person who controls the frame resists another participant's attempted change in frame and conflicting frames may thus result.

INSTITUTIONAL VS PERSONAL FRAMINGS

Two major framings emerge in the psychiatric interview discussed in the present study: the *institutional framings* (mostly proposed by the doctor) and the *personal framings* (mostly proposed by the patient). Both doctor and patient shift in and out of these framings. While participants may build talk in either of these contexts, each context has different sequential rules, different constraints on what talk should be about, and different underlying assumptions as to who controls the ongoing activity. The contextual transformations that take place follow the patterns described by Goffman (1974: 41; 1981a: 128).

The *institutional framings* of the psychiatric interview are by their very structure asymmetrical: the doctor controls the turn structure as well as the topic of discussion. This asymmetry can be seen in the sequential constraints of the interview procedure, which may involve a type of *sequential deference*. Frankel says that by asking a question, doctors impose the obligation of a response. This places a constraint on the patient's next move. Moreover it also places the responder in a secondary role, 'since responses always occur second and are limited in their appropriateness by actions which preceded them' (Frankel, 1984: 165).

A somewhat more balanced, conversational interaction is attempted in the personal framings. It is mostly the patient who proposes these framings and who strives to remain in these contexts. Shifting to personal framings introduces a more symmetrical relationship where the roles of patient and doctor remain largely in the background while a woman-to-woman relationship fleetingly emerges in the foreground. These shifts in frames have implications for the larger context of the interview. They alter the initial distance between the doctor and the patient. The doctor, however, shows resistance. She signals this underlying disagreement by shifting back to the institutional framings of the psychiatric interview.

THE POWER OF THE INSTITUTIONAL FRAMINGS

First and foremost, participants construct talk within the context of the psychiatric interview, where they display their official roles of doctor and patient in accordance with the norms set out by the institution. In a mental hospital, the institutional framings are proposed by doctors, nurses, administrative staff. Infringements on these framings by patients often produce what may be considered 'deviant behaviour' – unexpected responses (Goffman, 1961; 1974).[4]

Why do the participants (doctor and patient) remain mostly in these official framings? There are at least three reasons. First, these framings are proposed by *the gatekeeper*, the one who has the authority to make decisions on the patient's mobility within the institution (Erickson and Shultz, 1982). In the interview, the patient's future is at stake, dependent, at least in part, on the decisions being made at that very moment. In assuming the role of interviewer, the doctor sets the official framings. She is careful never to propose any other footings.

Second, the patient is compelled to participate in the frame proposed by the doctor, for fear of being evaluated as incompetent, or worse from a psychiatric point of view, incoherent (she is, after all, a psychiatric patient and incoherence is considered a serious disturbance in psychiatry). Hence, Mrs Cardozo accepts, even if reluctantly, the role of the respondent, what Goffman calls the dis-identifying role of patient (1961: 23). Most of the time she lets go of other possible footings, so as to be favourably evaluated by the doctor. Third, as Tannen says, most of us feel constrained to 'sail with the framing winds' (1986: 92). Jurema Cardozo, like everyone else, would rather yield to a frame than react, since resisting a frame or reframing talk requires additional effort. It requires alertness to framing, skill in shifting the conversational gears, as well as the power to do so.

So, in order not to rock the conversational boat, the patient, for the most part, stays in the official framings set by the doctor. Nowhere in the interview, for instance, does she ask any clarification questions; nor does she introduce any follow-up questions, which could redirect talk, thereby reframing the interaction. In the institutional framings her role is limited basically to answering questions.

THE PERSONAL FRAMINGS: MITIGATING THE ASYMMETRY

Shifts in framing, however, do occur throughout the interview since the patient often proposes a departure from the institutional contexts. She diverges from these contexts by discussing certain topics from the stance of her own personal experience. At times, the patient/interviewee footing fades into the background, giving way to a rather assertive older woman talking to a younger woman; at other times, we hear a gentle grandmother addressing a friendly listener; at yet other times, we hear an animated salesperson explaining sales activities. The following discussion portrays one of these instances.

AN ILLUSTRATION: THE NURTURING GRANDMOTHER

The extract below occurs at the opening of the interview. It illustrates two frame breaks: the patient shifts from the institutional to a non-institutional frame, and the doctor ratifies this shift; a few turns later, the doctor reframes the situation and shifts back to the institutional context.

	[acc]
(1) Doctor:	you were born on what date? ..
(2) Patient:	on January 11th ..
	[acc]
(3) Doctor:	of what year?
(4) Patient:	of 1921. ...
	[nods]
	I am sixty-one.=
	[nods] [smiles]
(5) Doctor:	[nods]
	[acc]
	=you have a son, [don't you?
(6) Patient:	[I have a son.
	[nods] [short smile]
	[acc]
(7) Doctor:	what's his name?
(8) Patient:	Francisco Ferreira de Souza.
	[dec]
(9) Doctor:	and he is how old now? ..
(10) Patient:	he's- about forty-two.
	[looks away, looks at doctor and smiles]
(11) Doctor:	/mmm/ ...
	you also have a granddaughter, don't you?=
(12) Patient:	=I've got a ((little)) sixteen-year old=
	=granddaughter. (1.4)
	[raises head and smiles]
Doctor:	//mmm//
Patient:	she's my li:fe.
	[raises head, looks up, big smile]
(13) Doctor:	do you- really?=
(14) Patient:	=really. I am crazy (about her).
	I like (her) [ve-
	[smiling] [
(15) Doctor:	[do you take care of her?=
(16) Patient:	=I don't take care of her because my daughter-in-law takes very good care, y'know ....
	[short smile]

		I just see her, and all that. (I don't)
(17) Doctor:	do you always <u>keep in touch</u> with them?
(18) Patient:	oh, yes, <u>always</u> . ..
		[nods]
		well as much as possible I do, y'know doctor. ...
		[nods and smiles, looks at doctor]
(19) Doctor:	'where do you live, Mrs Cardozo?
(20) Patient:	what?=
		[lips tighten and frowns]
(21) Doctor:	=//you-//
(22) Patient:	[I live with my sister. (1.2)
		[series of short nods]
		Ide:te, Tere:za,
		[series of short nods]
		161 Alvorada Avenue apartment 1001
		[series of short nods, smiles]
(23) Doctor:	you live with your two sisters, don't you?
(24) Patient:	yes, ...
		[nods and serious]
		the three of us live together . ..
		[nods, tightens lips and frowns]
(25) Doctor:	/mmm./ Mrs Cardozo, .. do you remember the day when you came to the hospital? to this hospital?

In analysing this segment, I take into consideration the turn-taking system and the moves that participants accomplish in each turn. A turn at talk refers to the process of holding the floor, not to 'what is said while holding it' (Goffman, 1981b: 23), while a move refers to the speech action taken during one's turn at talk (Coulthard, 1985). I also measure the amount of talk that goes on by the number of intonational units (Chafe, 1986) produced by the speaker.

The opening sequence of the discharge interview (turns 1 to 10) starts with the patient saying strictly what is required and no more. Thus, each turn has only one move and each move has only one intonational unit (1 move = 1 intonational unit), with the single exception of turn (4).

However, a change of topic at turn (11), when the doctor begins to ask the patient about her granddaughter, triggers a change in pattern. Mrs Cardozo provides more than the minimally required information. First, she not only agrees that she has a granddaughter but also states her age; she conveys involvement with the topic both by smiling and by adding a diminutive suffix to the word for 'granddaughter' in order to express affection. Then, she presents an evaluation: 'she's my life'. All these signals trigger a change in the doctor's questioning routine which can be seen in turns (13) to (18).

The patient's contributions become more informative than they were in turns (2) to (10). She presents a series of evaluations and also makes expressive use of a variety of lexical and syntactic forms and non-verbal cues.

First, she uses adverbs and adverbial clauses: 'my daughter-in-law takes *very good* care, (I) *always* (keep in touch)'; '*always, as much as possible*;'.

Second, she uses discourse markers, which were absent in the preceding segment, to indicate different aspects of communication. The marker 'y'know' in (16) and (18) signal an appeal to the hearer for co-operation (Schiffrin, 1985; 1987), and in the latter case 'y'know' gains stress as it is followed by the form 'doctor'. Also in (18) ('oh, yes, always. well, whenever it's possible I do, y'know doctor'.), as a response to a yes-no question, we see the patient doing four things: she uses the marker 'oh' to indicate familiar information and an expressive orientation (Schiffrin, 1985; 1987) to the new topic – family contacts – that the doctor has introduced; she then reinforces her positive answer with 'always'; she uses the marker 'well' to change the status of her prior contributions (Schiffrin, 1985), and modifies her previous assertion; and she closes her turn using 'y'know doctor' as a transitional device.[5]

Third, the pace of talk accelerates for both speakers as turns latch (13/14 and 15/16) and overlap (14/15); there is joint use of emphasis (in turn 17 for the doctor) 'you always *keep in touch* with them?' and (in 18 for the patient) '*always*'; and in Mrs Cardozo's talk there is vowel elongation in (turn 12) 'she's my li:fe'. These prosodic signals indicate the attitudinal aspects that underline expressed emotions. So does Mrs Cardozo's non-verbal behaviour. One sees the patient providing a series of non-verbal cues, such as raising her head, looking up to the doctor, smiling and nodding at different moments in this interaction. These verbal and non-verbal devices seem to cluster together to signal the change of footing.

It is small wonder, therefore, that when the doctor suddenly changes the topic of the interview and resumes the question-asking agenda, a misunderstanding occurs:

(19) Doctor: where do you live, Mrs Cardozo?
(20) Patient: what?

Here the doctor switches abruptly from a series of questions about relationships to a referential, factual request for information. As a consequence, a new footing must be negotiated. The doctor signals this shift by a rise in pitch. The patient, however, is taken by surprise. In line (20) she responds with what Goffman (1981b) calls a 'rerun signal', which indicates that she is addressing 'the process of communication, not what was communicated' (1981b: 34). The doctor, then, starts to restate her question and overlaps with the patient who provides an answer (turns 22 and 24).

This extract (turns 1 to 25) clearly shows that although both doctor and patient roles have been formally established by the official framing, changes in footing nevertheless do occur. The opening interaction is one of less involvement; this situation changes when a new footing between participants takes place, with the emphasis on evaluative devices and expressive language. This reframing triggers more talk from the patient while signalling a higher degree of co-operation, with the listener (the doctor) reinforcing the speaker's point, offering information and providing evaluation. From that point on, the conversation changes in strategy, until a new shift occurs at line (19), and the doctor returns to her official topic agenda. In changing the topic, the doctor regains control of the interview and reframes the interaction.

This extract is particularly interesting since it opens the interview. From the very start, we observe an underlying conflict between the way the doctor views the encounter (as a medical interview) and how the patient views it (as a personal talk). Thus the patient proposes reframings in the direction of the social encounter and the doctor shifts back, toward the medical encounter.

THE PERSONAL STRUGGLE

What takes place in this discharge interview has to do with the patient's own process of becoming a person again – an ongoing struggle between 'the patient' and 'the person', with the doctor reinforcing the patient persona.

Although, as we have seen above, the doctor sometimes accepts the patient's personal reframings in the direction of the social encounter, more often she interrupts the patient's talk, shifting back to the official context of the interview, towards the medical encounter. This conflict is often the result of mismatched expectations about what needs to be talked about and how talk needs to be constructed.

This conflict reveals a basic difference between the participants. Both are aware of the task that is to be accomplished: they must jointly create a medical encounter. However, each participant views her own role somewhat differently. While the patient approaches the encounter from a personal stance, one that says 'be friendly', 'be involved', the doctor approaches it from a strictly professional stance, one that says 'keep to the point (to the topic agenda of the interview)', 'be brief'.

This conflict gains even more relevance if one considers the larger frames of the institutional context: a medical psychiatric interview held at a mental hospital. Goffman (1961) discusses the work that patients perform in order to manage the tensions between the outside world and the institutional world. He says that institutionalised mental patients go through three main phases: *prepatient* (the period prior to entering the hospital), *inpatient* (the period in the hospital), and *ex-patient* (the period after discharge from the hospital.[6]

Jurema Cardozo's discharge interview takes place when she is completing her stay as an inpatient and beginning her transition to ex-patient. In such a position, she is caught in a double-bind situation as described by Gregory Bateson (1981). In order to play the official role of patient, Mrs Cardozo must take on what Goffman calls 'a dis-identifying role' (1961: 23) – that is, she must let go of each one of her social identities: the mother, the grandmother, the divorced woman, the retired saleswoman, etc. These unofficial roles are lost, says Goffman, given the barrier that separates (the patient) from the outside world.

On the other hand, to promote a transition from the inpatient phase to the ex-patient phase, that is in order to be able to leave the institution, Mrs Cardozo must recover her social roles. This is an essential step in gaining access to the outside world; that is, she must coherently perform her social identities (her several personal roles).

These unofficial reframings represent a necessary step for Jurema Cardozo to accomplish her *transition from patient to person*, and these reframings represent her effort toward an 'expansion of self'. As a consequence, the doctor's reluctance to manoeuvre the interaction within the patient's personal framings represents a major tension in the interview. Moreover, this reluctance imprints stiffness in the institutional framings, where the doctor never proposes (and seldom engages) in personal footings.

CONCLUSION: FRAMING AND POWER

A micro-analysis as used in the present study permits examination of issues of power as they relate to the cultural definitions of framing. While the doctor controls what happens in the institutional framings, it is the patient who proposes reframings and controls what takes place in the personal contexts. As a grandmother, she conveys rapport and camaraderie in her relationship with a very young doctor who reminds her of her granddaughter; in a woman-to-woman relationship, Jurema Cardozo tries to establish rapport with the doctor over her feelings regarding a personal matter (childbirth). In each reframing, Mrs Cardozo changes her communicative strategies from providing less information to providing more information; her communicative style changes from less involvement to more involvement (signalled by paralinguistic and linguistic cues); and a topic change or a change in focus on the ongoing topic occurs.

Jurema Cardozo's performance of her social roles represents *a gradual transition from patient to person*, a necessary process to re-enter the wider world, lest she remains subdued in a passive and dis-identifying role: the role of patient. Each personal reframing stages what I have called 'an expansion of self' (Ribeiro, 1994: 118). We have, therefore, an inverse movement from the one described by Goffman (1961), when a prepatient becomes an inpatient and curtailment of self occurs (1961: 14). The discharge interview represents Mrs Cardozo's transition from an inpatient to an ex-patient stance. Proposing and accomplishing social reframings is, therefore, a way of regaining control over her social identities. It is also a way of displaying a feeling of communion with the outside world.

A major frame tension, worthy of note, is the doctor's resistance to staying in the personal frame created by the patient. While Doctor Silva does ratify Mrs Cardozo's shifts (from the medical encounter to the social encounter), she does not stay for long in this frame of talk. Instead, she closes that segment, changes topic, and shifts back to the medical encounter. In doing so, the doctor repeatedly confines Jurema Cardozo to the single and limiting role of patient. The doctor's prevailing discourse strategy seems rather at odds with the rehabilitating purpose of a psychiatric treatment, which should not only allow but also support the enactment of personal footings on the part of the patient. These footings would inevitably bring about 'a sense of self' (and perhaps of self-esteem), of whom the woman Jurema Cardozo is, of the person behind the patient.

SPEECH TRANSCRIPTION CONVENTIONS

..	noticeable pause or break in rhythm, less than 0.5 second
...	half-second pause, as measured by stop-watch
....	one-second pause
(1.5)	numbers within brackets represent pauses in talk over one second, measured with a stop-watch
.	sentence-final falling intonation
?	sentence-final rising intonation
,	phrase-final intonation (indicating more talk to come)
' '	pitch shift on phrase, upwards, continuing till punctuation
À	pitch shift on phrase, lowered, continuing until punctuation
-	glottal stop or abrupt cutting off of sound
:	lengthened sound (extra colons indicate greater lengthening)
underline	emphatic stress
CAPS	very emphatic stress, loudness or shouting
/words/	spoken softly
//words//	spoken very softly
( )	transcription impossible
(words)	uncertain transcription
=	two utterances linked by = indicate no break in flow of talk (latching); = also links different parts of a single speaker's talk that has been carried over to another line of transcript.
[	overlapping speech: two people talking at the same time

[acc]   spoken quickly (appears over the line)
[dec]   spoken slowly (appears over the line)
[non-verbal]   description of non-verbal behaviour (changes in posture,
               orientation and eye gaze) appear below the segment of talk
               in square brackets

NOTES

1 All names have been changed to protect the confidentiality of the patient.
2 This interview was video-taped as part of a training programme developed by
   the Institute of Psychiatry of the School of Medicine at the Federal University
   of Rio de Janeiro, Brazil. Both participants are Brazilian; thus, the interview
   was conducted in Portuguese. I am grateful to Drs Eustaquio Portella and
   Jeremias Ferraz-Lima for providing me with the taped material. I am also
   grateful to the doctor who conducted the interview for her availability and
   interest in my work.
     In a larger study (Ribeiro, 1994), I looked at two psychiatric interviews: the
   admitting interview (with the patient in a psychotic crisis) and the discharge
   interview (with the patient out of the crisis). The study focuses on two types
   of discourse coherence. It uses frame analysis to examine the structure of social
   participation and topic analysis to examine the structure of the discourse.
3 Goffman's (1974; 1981a) comprehensive research in frame analysis stands out
   as a major reference for sociologic and sociolinguistic studies of interaction.
   He is concerned with close-up human interaction as it occurs in natural settings.
   The concepts that he develops for such a study derive from observations and
   descriptions.
4. Goffman (1974) provides various examples of patients' shifts of behaviour in
   mental institutions, indicating that behaviour is somewhat under the patients'
   control. He cites, for example, the patient 'who is mute in all daily interactions
   and steps off the sidewalk to avoid confrontation with the staff, yet at the
   patient dance becomes verbally facile and behaviorally full of address' (1974:
   246).
     On the same note, a Brazilian intern reports that a 65-year-old woman was
   admitted to the hospital under what was diagnosed as 'conversion hysteria'.
   She remained mute, in a semi-coma, pretending to be dead. For the next 24
   hours the staff was unable to remove her from this behaviour, though many
   approached her in a friendly way. The next day, there was a shift in staff. The
   doctor supervising the new team heard of the patient's behaviour as he walked
   through the ward. Upon approaching her, he informally tapped her shoulder
   saying out loud 'had too much to drink last night, ye grandma!' to which she
   immediately responded 'keep your mouth shut, young man; you better show
   some respect for your elders!'.
5 In this segment, the Portuguese markers ah ('oh'), bom ('well'), and não é
   ('y'know') seem to work in much the same way as their English equivalent,
   described in Schiffrin (1987).
6 A person admitted to a mental institution generally suffers several losses. To
   perform the official role of patient, s/he has her/his rights as a person suspended.
   Goffman's work on asylums describes this ongoing process. An individual
   gains (sometimes forcibly) not only a new social role; s/he actually begins a
   career of patient (Goffman, 1961: 14; Laing, 1974: 100). The end-result is role
   dispossession (Goffman, 1961: 14), since personal roles are suspended while

the individual remains in the institution. At this point, the individual's self is provided by the institution. A 'personal defacement' (1961: 20) takes place.

REFERENCES

Bateson, G. (1981) 'A theory of play and fantasy', in G. Bateson (ed.) *Steps to an Ecology of Mind*, New York: Ballantine, 177–93.

Chafe, W. (1986) 'How we know things about language: a plea for catholicism', in D. Tannen and J. E. Alatis (eds) *Language and Linguistics: The Interdependence of Theory, Data, and Application* (GURT 1985), Washington, DC: Georgetown University Press, 214–25.

Coulthard, R. M. (1985) *An Introduction to Discourse Analysis*, 2nd edn, London: Longman.

Erickson, F. and Rittenberg, W. (1987) 'Topic control and person control: a theory problem for foreign physicians in interaction with American patients', *Discourse Processes*, 10, 401–15.

Erickson, F. and Shultz, J. (1982) *The Counselor as Gatekeeper: Social Interaction in Interviews*, New York: Academic Press.

Fisher, S. (1979) 'The negotiation of treatment decisions in doctor/patient communications and their impact on the identity of women patients', doctoral dissertation, University of California, San Diego.

Fisher, S. (1984) 'Institutional authority and the structure of discourse', *Discourse Processes*, 7, 2, 201–24.

Frankel, R. M. (1984) 'From sentence to sequence: understanding the medical encounter through microinteractional analysis', *Discourse Processes*, 7, 2, 135–70.

Goffman, E. (1961) *Asylums*, New York: Anchor.

Goffman, E. (1974) *Frame Analysis*, New York: Harper & Row.

Goffman, E. (1981a) 'Footing', in E. Goffman (ed.) *Forms of Talk*, Philadelphia, PA: University of Pennsylvania Press, 124–59.

Goffman, E. (1981b) 'Replies and responses', in E. Goffman (ed.) *Forms of Talk*, Philadelphia, PA: University of Pennsylvania Press, 5–77.

Gumperz, J. (1977) 'Sociocultural knowledge in conversational inference' in M. Saville-Troike (ed.) *Linguistics and Anthropology* (GURT 77), Washington, DC: Georgetown University Press, 191–211.

Gumperz, J. (1982) *Discourse Strategies*, Cambridge: Cambridge University Press.

Gumperz, J. (1986) 'Interactional sociolinguistics in the study of schooling', in J. Cook-Gumperz (ed.) *The Social Construction of Literacy*, Cambridge: Cambridge University Press, 45–66.

Kendon, A. (1979) 'Some emerging features of face-to-face interaction studies', *Sign Language Studies*, 22, 7–22.

Kendon, A. (1990) *Conducting Interaction: Patterns of Behavior in Focused Encounters*, Cambridge: Cambridge University Press.

Kress, G. (1989a) *Linguistic Processes in Sociocultural Practice*, 2nd edn, Oxford: Oxford University Press.

Laing, R. D. (1974) *The Role of Experience and the Bird of Paradise*, Harmondsworth: Penguin.

Mishler, E. G. (1984) *The Discourse of Medicine: Dialectics of Medical Interviews*, Norwood, NJ: Ablex.

Ribeiro, B. T. (1993) 'Framing psychotic talk', in D. Tannen (ed.) *Framing in Discourse*, New York: Oxford University Press, 77–113.

Ribeiro, B. T. (1994). *Coherence in Psychotic Discourse*, New York: Oxford University Press.

Scheflen, A. E. (1973) *Communicational Structure: Analysis of a Psychotherapy Transaction*, Bloomington, IN: Indiana University Press.

Schiffrin, D. (1985) 'Conversational coherence: the role of "Well" ', *Language*, 61, 640–67.

Schiffrin, D. (1987) *Discourse Markers*, New York: Cambridge University Press.

Shuy, R. W. (1974) 'Problems in communication in the cross-cultural medical interview', *Working Papers in Sociolinguistics*, 19.

Tannen, D. (1986) *That's Not What I Meant!*, New York: William Morrow.

Tannen, D. and Wallat, C. (1987) 'Interactive frames and knowledge schemas in interaction: examples from a medical examination/interview', *Social Psychological Quarterly*, 50, 2, 205–16.

West, C. (1983) '"Ask me no questions": an analysis of queries and replies in physician–patient dialogues' in S. Fisher and A. Todd (eds) *The Social Organization of Doctor–Patient Communication*, Washington, DC: Center for Applied Linguistics, 75–106.

Chapter 11

Problems with the representation of face and its manifestations in the discourse of the 'old-old'

Dino Preti

INTRODUCTION

This work is based on examples taken from tape-recordings made for a project entitled 'Projeto da linguagem dos idosos velhos (LIV)' (The speech of the old-old), comprising some fifty studies involving the inter-action between young and old speakers in a wide variety of contexts – at home, in old people's homes and in rest homes. We have also used, exceptionally, some recordings from the 'Projeto de estudo da norma lingüística urbana culta de São Paulo (NURC/SP)' (Study of the educated urban linguistic norm of São Paulo, Brazil).

The subjects are all normal and lucid, and in general the topics chosen concern their past, a comparison between their youth and today, and an analysis of changes in customs. During the interviews, the young inter-viewers on many occasions became real interlocutors.

The interviews were recorded in rest homes, geriatric clinics or in the subjects' homes. Most of the subjects belonged to the middle class, had completed at least primary school and lived off their retirement pension or were helped by their families. No significant difference between male and female speakers could be detected at the level of discourse.

THE OLD-OLD AS A SOCIAL GROUP

First, we must consider up to what point the very old can be classified as a social group or category.

From the sociological point of view the word 'group' can be interpreted as 'a community of interests, as a casual gathering of individuals: a unitarian community in time and space, or the opposite, a scattered community which is conscious of itself or linked only by some character-istic purposes' (Horkheimer and Adorno, 1978: 61).

The idea of a 'community conscious of itself' is, perhaps, a point of approximation among these individuals, at least in terms of the aware-ness of old age, of the age factor as a limiter of social participation; or still better, of age as a stigma, 'an attribute that is deeply discrediting', marked by social prejudices (Goffman, 1973: 13).

One of the difficulties in characterising this 'group' is the fact that the idea of old age contains a strong psychological component: a person is as old as he/she thinks he/she is (Preti, 1991: 26) and for this reason social psychologists make a distinction between the 'young-old', those between 60 or 65 and 80 years old, and the 'old-old', those who are over 80.

We must recognise that it is very difficult to characterise the very old, if we consider that old age 'is never a total fact', since there are elderly people who assume only certain aspects of old age. Some, for example, re-establish their affective lives, others plan trips; some set up businesses with which they can support themselves economically; still others develop their artistic talents. 'In other words, on the one hand, they are defined as elderly and are considered as such; on the other hand, they carry out projects which are apparently incongruent with that condition' (Debert, 1988: 62).

But the elderly people who are over 80 (the 'old-old') assume more easily the awareness of old age, since they suffer more acutely the action of the psycho-physical factors which indicate ageing, notably those transformations which affect their communicative ability, that is, those which affect their memory and their hearing, and within this latter category lies the most serious factor, 'the loss of hearing for speech, particularly when the speech signal is degraded or is in competition with other sounds' (Ryan et al., 1986: 3).

This awareness is reflected in how the old-old relate socially with different age groups, affecting their activities, their psychic reactions, their power of reflection and analysis, their communicative and receptive capacity and their conversational ability. Hence, this scattered social group, which is identifiable through its common problems and which, up to a certain point, is conscious of itself, begins to live the difficult conditions that modern society imposes upon it. In urban communities, for example, they might integrate what are usually classified as 'dis-esteemed groups', those formed by people whose characteristics (in this specific case, old age, with its psycho-physical markers, such as deafness, for example) are already known and discriminated by the community.

The stigma of old age brings as immediate consequences a feeling of insecurity and the continual sensation of not knowing what others think about one, and that can result in an attitude of withdrawal or aggressiveness, which shows clearly in face-to-face verbal interaction. In the context within which elderly people live, withdrawal may contribute to their being ignored as 'non-persons', physically present but without the right to opinions, like the class of servants, for example (Goffman, 1973: 30, 34).

Conversation may reveal some of these problems, at the moment when elderly people 'act' their way of being before others, when they try to define for their observers the social role that ageing has reserved for them, when they project an image of themselves by means of which they are valorised, and they try to make their interlocutors treat them in the way that the members of their 'group' have the right to expect to be treated. Or they try to adjust to the level of the younger person, when expressing their ideas, by renouncing their social image, and making concessions in order to be better accepted socially.

On the other hand, in urban societies (such as that of São Paulo, Brazil's biggest city, where the research was conducted), elderly people feel deprived of power, uncertain as to their real social role, estranged from any form of command, isolated in their homes or in geriatric institutions where they are sent by their families.

The problem of isolation is reflected mainly in family conversation or in interaction in rest homes, where each of them is locked up in the silence of his or her own world. Their discourse, when it is listened to, generates disinterest on the basis of the presupposition that it embodies outdated ideas and hence the lack of credibility attributed to the opinions they express.

THE ELDERLY AND THEIR SOCIAL ROLE

Goffman (1967) has compared social behaviour to a 'performance for the benefit of other people', and in this *theatre of life*, the social roles are distributed according to a variety of *situations*, among which verbal communication, conversation, is the most important. Defining roles in a face-to-face dialogue has become an important starting-point for people to 'negotiate' their participation in the conversational act. Normally it is the responsibility of the speakers to 'introduce themselves' when, for example, the interlocutors are not known to them. It is their responsibility, through their conduct and appearance, to impart their social image, the role which they play or intend to play in the conversation, that is, the 'front' or 'the expressive equipment of a standard kind intentionally or unwittingly used by the individual during his performance' (Goffman, 1959: 22). If they do not do this, their interlocutors may make use of clues 'that allow them to apply their previous experience with individuals roughly similar' to those with whom they intend to converse, or, in the absence of these signs, they may rely on already presupposed, although unproven, stereotypes (Goffman, 1959: 1). It is, therefore, convenient that the speakers make themselves known at the beginning of the conversational act, or better still, that they define the situation.

During a 'performance', speakers try to appear to their interlocutors a little better than they really are and take care to preserve their social image, so that a discourse from off-stage does not suddenly interfere with their performance, causing them to lose the credibility of their listeners.

To a certain extent, this social 'performance' serves as one of the masks which we often wear to play roles which we would, in fact, like to perform in society, but which, for various reasons, we cannot.

> It is probably no mere historical accident that the word person, in its first meaning meant mask.... In a sense, and in so far as this mask represents the conception we have formed of ourselves – the role that we are striving to live up to – this mask is our truer self, the self we would like to be.
>
> (Park, 1950, cited in Goffman, 1959: 19)

For the elderly person, for example, to speak like younger people do, to use up-to-date slang, to wear showier clothes than the discretion of age would recommend, to take on affective behaviour more suited to young people, could be social masks, 'front' strategies used to try to play social roles no longer attributed to them, which means, in short, a false social 'performance'.

It is interesting that we can say that such roles 'are not suitable', if, as we have said before, old age, up to a certain point, may be a psychological attitude and, therefore, nothing can prevent individuals from retarding the ageing process as much as possible, prolonging their youth, if they wish to do so. In principle, this possibility seems reasonable, if we do not think that society is deeply concerned with keeping people stable in their social role, as if there were a pre-established location on the 'stage' where they would act out their part. Thus, a servant is a servant, and is not allowed by society to adopt masks that may reveal that the servant has stopped performing the role of servant or 'non-person', during a performance that is usually mute. In the same way, old people are old people, and at times this situation, brought about by ageing, robs them of their very individuality. Society has also reserved for elderly people the role that it expects them to perform. There is not much freedom of choice, despite attempts to change masks, since the ideal for all is that the established social norms be respected.

In the 1950s, the existentialists, led by Sartre, fought against this threat to the individual liberty of human beings to alter their social role. 'There are indeed,' wrote Sartre, 'many precautions to imprison a man in what he is, as if we lived in perpetual fear that he might escape from it, that he might break away and, suddenly, elude his condition' (Sartre, 1956: 59, cited in Goffman, 1959: 76).

In the case of elderly people, the preservation of their social image signifies a struggle, which they lose bit by bit with the passing of time and the natural degeneration caused by ageing.

Even within the family setting it is not easy for the old-old to maintain this image, which they see threatened by new social behaviour, by the evolution of ideas, by the cultural transformations that are imposed on the phenomenon of old age. In fact, the removal of elderly people to sanatoriums, old people's homes and rest homes, or their progressive degradation within the family setting, itself, hampering the maintenance of a social image which harmonises with the new times and which may be accepted by the younger generations, has become completely normal behaviour in the large urban communities, where it is commonly claimed, that 'the elderly have already lived their life' or that 'we, the young, have to live our lives, and why should we be inconvenienced by those who have already lived theirs?'.

Elderly people, however, try, at times indirectly, to make it understood that if they cannot assume the same condition and the same roles as a young person in their 'performance' (which can be understood), they can, at least, understand it or even contest it in their values in the sense of maintaining their own social image.

Our research, however, has shown that elderly people not infrequently forgo their values, demeaning themselves and considering themselves incapable of debating the new values that are presented to them.

Conversation as an image of this social performance which Goffman (1959) refers to, is an expressive phenomenon for us to observe how the 'old-old' act in relation to the problem of defending their image in public or, in other words, how they try, at all costs, 'to save face', which is constantly threatened because of the stigma of age.

THE PROBLEM OF MAINTAINING THE SOCIAL IMAGE

The concept of *face* studied by Goffman (1967) and by Brown and Levinson (1978) is linked, in social 'performance', with the the self-image each one has of oneself and which one tries to maintain in conversation. As Brown and Levinson (1978: 61) recognise, this concept is tied to the notion of embarrassment and humiliation or, as we could say, 'losing face' during a verbal interaction.

We cannot forget that maintaining our social image often signifies a form of making ourselves known to our interlocutors, trying, for example, to show that we do or do not have certain prejudices, that our values are or are not the same as theirs. As the authors recognise, 'face is something that is emotionally invested, and that can be lost, maintained or enhanced and must be constantly attended to in interaction' (Brown and Levinson, 1978: 61).

But 'the simple fact of entering in contact with others in society upsets a pre-existing ritual balance and potentially threatens the public self-image built up by the members of the group' says Rosa (1992: 20), based once more on Goffman's theories. Thus conversation 'by being an activity in which permanent negotiations between the individuals are developed, always presents a potential threat of loss of face to the interlocutors' (Marcuschi, 1989: 284).

In no way, however, should it be imagined that the problem of saving face necessarily leads the interlocutors who take turns in the conversation to a verbal dispute (which may occur), since generally there exists an attempt at consensus or an 'operational consensus' (Goffman, 1959: 10) which contributes to a joint definition of the situation in which the conversational act takes place. This interactional *modus vivendi* is the implicit recognition by the interlocutors that the saving of face by one often depends on the saving of face by the other, since to threaten the social image of an interlocutor in an interaction may lead him or her to use defence mechanisms and vice versa. Because of this operational consensus, it is not unusual for the conversational act to amount to a breakdown in the face-saving mechanism. This can be observed in interactions with elderly people.

A further specification of this phenomenon of face was made by Brown and Levinson (1978: 61), making a distinction between *positive face* ('self-image or "personality", crucially including the desire that this self-image be appreciated and approved of') and *negative face* ('the basic claim to territories, personal preserves, rights to non-distraction').

Considering these various aspects of the phenomenon of face, there are verbal means (forms of politeness, conversational markers of attenuation, affective language resources, etc.) and prosodic elements (change in tone of voice) which take care of preserving or saving face.

Example 1

A change in voice is enough in the following dialogue for Speaker 2 to save face, when he makes it clear to his interlocutor that he has no sex or colour prejudices.

S.2   oh eu acho que em termos de:: ... centro por
oh I think that in terms of ... centre for

exemplo está começando a acontecer um negócio
example something is beginning to happen

que ... você vê em cidade americana grande
that ... you see in large American cities

Washington Nova Iorque ... que é:: ...
Washington New York ... that is ...

pessoal mais classe alta ir para o subúrbio ...
people of higher class go to the suburbs ...

e o:: centro bom:: em Washington por exemplo
and the centre well in Washington for example

é gueto ... né? em Nova Iorque também ...
is a ghetto isn't it? in New York also ...

S.1   uhn::
uhm

S.2   então a Tatá estava contando outra dia né? que::
so Tatá was saying the other day wasn't she? that

depois das seis horas da noite você andar na
after   six o'clock at night you walk in the

cidade e o jeito dela 'só tem preto ...
city and the way she says it, 'there are only blacks ...

só tem preto e bicha né? e::: e realmente
there's only blacks and queers aren't there? and and really I

acho que ne/ muito pouca gente ainda mora lá
think that very few people still live there

assim de nível sócio-econômico mais alto né?
like from the upper socio-economic levels isn't that right?

(NURC/SP 343)

We can see in this extract that Speaker 2 makes use of the opinion of an absent third person (Tatá) to say that the centres of large cities at night are frequented only by Negroes and homosexuals. He does it by stressing 'the way she says it' and changing his tone of voice. To save his positive face, Speaker 2 uses an attenuation process to say that in the centre of São Paulo 'very few people from the upper socio-economic levels still live there', from which we can conclude that he is indirectly implying that blacks and homosexuals belong to the lower, marginal levels of the population. But this attenuation protects his public image in the expression of sexual and colour prejudices which might give a bad impression to his interlocutor.

THE PRESENTATION OF *FACE* IN THE DISCOURSE OF THE ELDERLY

The situation of separating the 'old-old' from society is reflected in their preservation mechanisms, which neutralise threats or save face. But it also shows how such speakers at times abandon these mechanisms and risk their social image to allow the normal continuation of the interaction.

Evidently such mechanisms employed by elderly people can also be present in the speech of speakers from other age groups. But the strategies employed by the elderly will occur only in contexts where the factor *age group* is at stake. In other words, there is threat to face in the reference to 'things and customs of the past' as outdated, in disuse, or of no prestige nowadays. And in so far as elderly speakers are concerned this occurs as a consequence of a natural clash of generations, as in the dialogue below. Therefore, safeguarding their past, defending 'their time', amounts to preserving their social prestige in conversation.

Let us examine some processes of the presentation of face in the discourse of old-old people.

Example 2

The positive face of the elderly interlocutor is threatened by the young speaker. The young person tries to make fun of old customs. Saving face, the old person balances the interaction by means of an approximation between old and modern customs. It is a process of negotiation aiming at 'operational consensus'.

> (S.1, a young, 24-year-old speaker, and S.2, an elderly person of 84, are discussing fashion.)

S.2   (. . .) eu já tive um vestido assim:: eu já tive
       I once had a dress like this I once had

       eu fico lembrando minha mocidade viu?
       I keep remembering my youth you know

S.1   mas a roupa era assim justi::nha como a gente
       but the clothes were like this tight like we

       usa hoje em dia ou era mais aquela saia assim . . .
       wear them nowadays or more like that skirt . . .

       redonDO::na
       really full

S.2   não não no meu tempo não no meu tempo era
       no no in my time no in my time they were

       justinha . . . era:: era . . . bem bem moderninha como
       tight . . . they were were . . . very very modern like

       é hoje sabe
       they are today you know

S.1   ah é?
       ah yes

S.2   é sim
       oh yes

S.1 puts the positive face of the listener (S.2) at risk when expressing doubt about the old dresses, the disapproval of the skirt 'assim redonDO::na' (*really full*), in comparison with the elegance of the modern 'justinha' (*tight*) skirt. The Portuguese diminutive ('-inha') and augmentative ('-ona') suffixes mark this opposition, reinforced by an overstressed and lengthened vowel. Speaker 2 saves face by affirming that the clothes she used to wear in her time were 'justinha' (*tight*) and 'moderninha' (*modern*) and in this way parries the idea that the garments of her youth could seem ridiculous in the eyes of her interlocutor. Therefore, in order to save face, Speaker 2, on retaking the turn, incorporates today's values (tight skirts), likening them to those of the past. Note that in her intervention the young speaker uses intonational resources in the marker 'assim' (*like this*), which presupposes accompanying gestures.

Example 3

The elderly speaker humbles herself, shows reserve and places her positive face at risk.

(S.1, an elderly woman of 89; S.2, a young 20-year-old woman.)

S.2 que que a senhora acha ... dessas ... dessa atitude
what what do you think of ... there ... this attitude

do seu neto?
of your grandson

S.1 eu () me conformo o que que eu ia fazer ...
I'm resigned to what what I was going to do ...

eu agora não tenho mais ... (laughter) não tenho
now I have nothing more ... (laughter) I have nothing

mais que falar éh:::(laughter) éh:::. ... o tempo,
more to say it's (laughter) it's ... the time

que eu falava ... se foi ... eu agora não tenho
that I spoke about ... has gone ... now I don't have to

mais que falar são os pais ... ()
speak anymore it is the parents

S.2 e ... e os pais dele aceita::ram também como a
and ... and did his parents also accepted it like

senhora? não ...
you did? they didn't ...

S.1   os pais
        the parents

S.2   os pais do do do seu bisneto
        the parents of of of your great-grandson

S.1   sim ... não é:: é meu neto
        yes ... no he isn't he's my grandson

S.2   é:: seu neto
        he's your grandson

(LIV 27)

The elderly speaker finds herself in the precise position of a 'non-person', whose opinion is worth nothing within the family setting, hence her self-abasement in the presence of her young interlocutor. We could say that the speaker 'lost face' and we can observe this in the hesitation and repetition of the same idea.

This is a clear example of an elderly person accepting the stigma of old age, of her insecurity, through not having the self-conviction to hold an interesting discourse. It is a bitter process of self-depreciation, of under-estimating oneself which constitutes one of the most characteristic stereo-types of ageing (Preti, 1991: 28).

Example 4

The elderly speaker invades the personal territory of the interlocutor, threatening the negative face of the young listener through her praise of modern customs and her concurrence with new patterns of behaviour.

> (Two elderly people and two young people are discussing the contrast between present-day customs and those of yesteryear. The speech is of S.1, an 80-year-old woman.)

S.1   agora é livre agora vocês são livres coisa
        now it is free now you are free it is a beautiful

        linda ... e se fosse naquele tempo ... hoje fosse
        thing ... and if it were at that time ... if today were

        naque/eu não casava ... e sabe por que?
        then I wouldn't marry ... and do you know why?

        porque eu I::a estudar ... ia trabalhar ter meu
        would study ... I would work to have my own

        dinheiro ... ser livre e:: independente e não preci-
        money ... to be free and independent and I wouldn't

sava casar . . . porque eu acho que a mulher
need to get married . . . because I think that women

hoje em dia não precisa casar . . . elas casam quando
nowadays don't have to marry . . . they marry when

elas querem casar . . .
they want to get married . . .

(LIV 40)

The elderly speaker addresses the two young speakers, praising the liberty that they have today, as opposed to the strict customs of her time. (The theme preceding the text quoted here.) This praise represents an invasion of the listeners' territory, threatening their negative face. It is an act which attributes a desire of the speaker in relation to the young listeners, with expressions that indicate that Speaker 1 would like to have something which belongs to the terrritory of the young people with whom she is talking (cf. Brown and Levinson, 1978: 66).

The opposition between past and present is processed with the adverbial variation of *hoje* (*today*) / *naquele tempo* (*at that time*). Exceptionally, *hoje* is preferred by the elderly speaker.

One of the tactics of the discourse of the elderly person, with the aim of trying to get closer to the young interlocutor, is to demonstrate that she agrees with modern customs and, at the same time, to condemn, exceptionally, the old customs, under which she was brought up. This attitude enables an 'operational consensus' to be reached in the conversation.

Example 5

The elderly speaker acts aggressively, putting at risk the positive face of the young interlocutor, through valorising the past to the detriment of the present. As a consequence the positive face of the elderly person is strengthened.

> (S.4, who is 22, is conversing with S.1, who is 100, S.2, who is 81, and S.3, who is 82, about cooking.)

S.4   ah . . . na festa ontem com sua irmã
       ah . . . at the party yesterday with your sister

S.2   ah na festa estava todos d/
       ah at the party there were all/

       todos os irmãos . . . tudo à moda antiga . . .
       all my brothers and sisters . . . like in the old days . . .

       agora não . . . a mulher não gosta de cozinha . . .
       not now . . . women don't like cooking

S.4	éh::: that's true
S.2	e é pior de que ... – – você gosta? ((laughter)) and it's worse than ... do you like it? ((laughter))
S.4	não ... no
S.2	você não entende nada de cozinha? ... don't you know anything about cooking? ...
S.4	eu entendo ... eu sou casada ... I do I'm married
S.2	ah você é casada? ah you're married?
S.4	eu sou casada ... eu tenho uma filhinha ... e eu I'm married . . . I have a little daughter . . . and I faço alguma coisa ... mas se eu comparar com minha can cook a little but compared with my mãe ... nossa eu não sei fazer nada mother . . . gee I don't know how to do anything
S.2	sua mãe está viva? is your mother still alive?
S.4	está ... está sim she is . . . she is yes
S.2	não tem comparação ... eu quando casei ... já sabia there's no comparison . . . when I got married . . . I already cozinhar ... porque::: meu marido escolheu porque knew how to cook . . . because my husband chose (me) because eu sabia cozinhar ... então ... I could cook . . . so ...

(LIV 44)

Speaker 2 provokes S.4 to turn the conversation to 'cooking' and, taking advantage of the young woman's indecision, challenges her with a direct question ('você gosta?' *do you like it?*), and then with another which is even more aggressive in terms of S.4's positive face ('você não entende nada de cozinha? ...' (*don't you know anything about cooking?*)). S.4 tries to preserve her image with a hesitant reply ('eu entendo ... eu sou casada' (*I do, I'm married*)), in which she implicitly admits that a married woman should know how to cook. In view of this reply S.2 rushes in with another question which reinforces the idea of her disapproval of the fact that S.4 is married and does not like cooking. S.4 feels the threat to her positive face in this disapproval of her values (cf. Brown and Levinson, 1978: 68) and tries to justify her behaviour through a process of attenuation ('e eu faço alguma coisa' (*I can cook a little*) but ends up falling back on comparisons with values of the past ('mas se eu comparar com minha mãe . . . nossa eu não sei fazer nada' (*but compared with my mother gee I don't know how to do anything*)) and definitively exposing her face, since S.2 takes advantage to conclude with an argument that valorises her positive face, when she expounds a basic necessity which is desirable for her interlocutor (cf. Brown and Levinson, 1978: 62): 'não tem comparação . . . eu quando casei . . . já sabia cozinhar . . . porque::: meu marido escolheu porque eu sabia cozinhar . . .' (*there's no comparison me when I got married I could already cook because my husband chose me because I could cook*). There is a tone of pride in this affirmation which causes S.4 'to lose face'.

In this passage, therefore, we can observe how the elderly woman skilfully finds arguments which can valorise her social image, revealing that she wants her skill (knowing how to cook) to be appreciated (directly or indirectly) by her young interlocutor, who admits that it was her mother who cooked well, in comparison with whom, she says: 'nossa eu não sei fazer nada' (*gee I don't know how to do anything*).

A strategy is employed by the elderly speaker to maintain her positive face, to the detriment of the interlocutor. The topic is handled by S.2 in such a way as to valorise the past and, therefore, her social image.

Aggressiveness is not typical behaviour for the social 'performance' of an elderly person, but it may occur, and may include discursive devices, like irony, which have a devastating effect on the young interlocutor's positive face. In the example, S.2 alludes to the fact that she had had the honour of being chosen by her husband because she knew how to cook and ironically says, 'não tem comparação' (*there's no comparison*).

Example 6

Still on the subject of irony as a threat to the interlocutor's face, consider the following example, a dialogue between two elderly people (81 and 85 years old) and a young woman (22 years old), who is both interviewer and interlocutor at the same time.

> (S.1, an old man of 81, helped by S.2, an old woman of 85, converse with S.3, a young woman of 22, about the clothing worn in the olden days. S.1 talks about the custom in those days for men to wear discretely coloured suits made from fine, imported cashmere, while, today, the fashionable cloth is a strong, cotton fabric – denim. But S.1 had had a blue suit, the colour of denim,

made for him and because of this, was made fun of by the girls
who knew him.)

S.1   (...) e eu mandei fazer uma:: ficou mais ou menos
      (...)and I had one made   it was more or less

      a cor é ... uma cor azulada assim ... que regra
      the colour is ... a bluish colour like this ... as a

      geral as co/as casimiras eram mais discretas que
      general rule the col/the cashmeres were more discreet than

      hoje mas eu mandei fazer um:: ... então:: umas
      today but I had one made ... well some

      moças me puseram o apelido de zuarte ... ((ri)) as
      girls nicknamed me denim ... (he laughs) the

      as moças da Escola Normal onde eu ia esperar ...
      girls from the Normal School where I went to wait ...

      'lá vem o zuarte' ... ((ri)) quer dizer achavam que
      'here comes denim' ... (he laughs) that's to say they

      eu estava muito mal vestido ... era o zuarte hoje
      thought I was very badly dressed ... it was the denim

      eu ta/me lembrei disso porque:: ...
      today I I remember this because ...

S.3   ( )

S.1   o zuar/ o zuarte hoje é o forte ...
      den/ denim today is the fashion

S.2   hoje
      today

S.3   é:::
      it is

S.1   hoje o forte é roupa des-co-ra-da ...
      today the fashion is faded clothing

S.3   é:::
      yeah

S.1   quando é que a gente vestia uma roupa
      when   would we   wear clothes

      descorada? ... né? quando? ...
      that were faded? ... eh? when? ...

S.3   mas é...
       but it is

S.1   nesse nesse tem::po a gente...
       in this in this time we ...

                                    (NURC/SP 396)

Besides strengthening the positive face of the old man, the text illustrates
S.1's discursive tactic of ridiculing the modern custom of wearing clothes
made of faded denim with a rhetorical question ('quando é que a gente
vestia uma roupa descorada? ... né? quando? ...' (*when would we wear
faded clothing? eh? when?*)). This is marked as an obvious threat to the
young speaker's positive face. The young speaker limits herself to just
listening and, when she tries to argue back ('mas é...' (*but it is*)), the
speaker steals her turn and continues to hold the floor. Hence S.3 does
not manage to neutralise the threat to her social image.

Example 7

The elderly person uses the tactic of reproach, putting the negative face
of the young speaker at risk. In conversations covering more polemic
themes, depending also on the type of interlocutors, it may happen that
the greater agility of the young speaker confuses the older person. One
of the tactics used on such occasions to re-establish the conversational
modus vivendi is to appeal to the young speaker to put the conversation
in order, not to move away from the theme under discussion, and to be
more objective. That amounts to a clear threat to the young person's negative face, as can be seen in this dialogue between an elderly man (S.2,
who is 84 years old) and a young man (S.1, who is 21).

S.1   só que eu acho que a criança tem que crescer
       just that I think a child has to grow up

       com os dois desde criança ela já tem que crescer
       with both since (it is) a child it has to grow up

       com a criação familiar ... e com a criação
       brought up by its family and with a social

       social ... porque senão quando ela começa a viver
       upbringing ... because otherwise when it begins

       a viver a vi/ ela ela leva um choque tão grande se ela ...
       to live to li/ it it gets such a great shock if it ...

       ela ... que ela vai ver 'meu Deus na minha familia
       it ... that it is going to see 'my God in my family it

tudo bonitinho era tudo certo de repente eu
everything was nice, all was all right, suddenly I

conheço que o mundo não é assim ... aí ela
realise that the world is not like this then it

leva um BAque e ela não conse::gue enfrentar os
suffers a blow and it can't face up to the

problemas do mundo ... que de repente é a mesma
problems of the world which suddenly is the same

coisa que o senhor criar uma pessoa pra fazer tal
thing as you bringing up a person to do a certain

coisa ... o senhor joga ela no mundo e fala 'agora
thing ... you toss him into the world and say 'now

se vira'
get on with it'

S.2   não eu entendo ... eu sei
      no I understand I know

S.1   então ... o senhor entende?
      then ... you understand?

S.2   mas não é esse o ponto que nós
      but this is not the point that

      estamos ... nós estamos desconversando ...
      we are ... we are changing the subject ...

      sobre a diferença de vivência de costume ... de
      about the difference in the experiencing of customs ... of

      de respeito ... de romantismo ... agora a sociedade é difícil
      of respect,   of romanticism,   now society is difficult

S.1   é eu sei ... é meio difícil
      yes I know it's rather difficult

S.2   responder....
      to reply

(LIV 34)

Notice that S.2 reminds S.1 to keep to the theme proposed at the start
of the conversation. This is a clear type of threat to the young speaker's
negative face, an invasion of his personal territory which results in S.1's
concordance ('é eu sei ... é meio difícil' (*it is I know it's quite difficult*)).
You could say, therefore, that the situation intervenes to affect both faces

of the young speaker, who has no arguments to oppose the reproach (a threat to his negative face) and ends up agreeing with S.2's argument, in the sense that he had diverted the course of the conversation (loss of positive face).

Example 8

The elderly speaker shows acquiescence which results in a serious threat to her positive face.

> (Four speakers, three old women and a young woman (see Example 5) are talking about the change in customs. This extract highlights the participation of S.3, who is 82, and S.4, who is 22.)

S.3   (...) porque as coisas têm que se modificar ...
       because things have to be changed

       agora nós que somos de outra época a gente
       now   we who are from a different time we

       esTRAnha muito ... estranha certas coisas né? ...
       find it very strange ... find certain things strange

       né? ... a gente não ... quer dizer a gente tem que
       eh? ... and we don't ... that's to say we have to

       aceitar porque a gente está no mundo não somos
       accept because we are in this world we are not

       nós que vamos modificar as coisas né? ...
       the ones who are going to change things is it? ...

S.4   é verdade
       that's true

S.3   agora ... a gente aceita mas a gente não/não se
       now ... we accept this but we don't don't get

       acostuma compreende? a gente não se acostuma ...
       used to it do you see? we don't get used to it

                                                        (LIV 44)

Speaker S.4 shows resignation toward the new, different times. The construction of her topic in the conversation, however, is adroit, because, despite accepting the facts in view of the impossibility of changing them (loss of positive face), *the speaker exhibits a certain tacit reaction* ('agora ... a gente aceita mas a gente não se costuma ...' (*now we accept this but we don't get used to it*)) which, in a certain manner, strengthens her face.

It is important, also, to note that the discourse in S.3's first turn is hesitant, because the speaker does not want to be humiliated, she does not want to show her impotence in the face of the changes brought about by the new times. In the second turn, there is a timid reaction, indicated by the marker 'agora' (*now*) and it constitutes an attenuation to the loss of face, in spite of the hesitation, present in the repetitions.

CONCLUSION

In summary, we can say that the presentation of face in the discourse of elderly people, in conversation with young people, presents some characteristics which are repeated, with greater or lesser intensity and which can be summed up as follows:

1 Defence of positive face, threatened by the young interlocutor who pokes fun at old customs (see Example 2).
2 Threat to the young interlocutor's negative face, by invasion of her territory, with the old person manifesting the desire that he would like to belong to this territory (see Example 4).
3 Condemnation of old customs and loss of positive face (see Example 4).
4 Self-humiliation, withdrawal, being placed in the situation of a 'nonperson', subject to prejudices and stereotyping. Destruction of his/her 'front' in his/her social performance in the conversation. 'Loss of face' (see Examples 3 and 8).
5 Abandonment of face-saving mechanisms, in an attempt to balance the conversation, maintaining the 'operational consensus' (see Examples 5 and 6).
6 Aggressiveness, putting at risk the young interlocutor's positive face. Use of ironic discourse (see Examples 5 and 6).
7 Disguised disagreement in accepting the lack of means to fight back. Reaction by means of attenuation processes at discourse level. Loss of positive face (see Example 8).
8 Use of warnings to the speaker, putting at risk the young speaker's negative face (see Example 7).
9 Preservation of face of both the interlocutors, in an ideal balance for the *modus vivendi* in conversation (see Example 9).

If we analyse these characteristics, we shall see that, as in the case of their social 'performance', when they oscillate between past and present values, trying, at one moment to strengthen 'their' time, and at another to passively accept their discredited situation, the old-old mark their presence in the conversation with discourse which is also hesitant, and in which, invited to reveal themselves, they hesitate between withdrawal and aggressiveness, continually placing their faces at risk.

In spite of their not being accepted, they strive to establish an 'operational consensus' during the interaction, in which, at times skilfully, they try to approximate present values with those of the past. After all, for them, the ideal would be to show that time has passed, customs have changed, but they have not changed so much that certain values might not have remained, reconciling them with their interlocutors at certain moments of the conversation.

Example 9

S.2   (...) eu namorei o meu o meu namoRADO cinco
         I went out with my my boyfriend for five

         quatro anos e meio ... depois eu casei ... mas
         four and a half years then I got married but

         eu não permiti nunca que ele me desse beijo ...
         I never allowed him to give me a kiss ...

         porque os homens são atrevidos né? Não são
         because men are bold-faced aren't they? Aren't they

         atrevidos?
         bold-faced?

S.4   são ...
         yes they are

                                                      (LIV 44)

Here the face of both the interlocutors (S.2, who is 81, and S.4, who is 22) is preserved.

SPEECH TRANSCRIPTION CONVENTIONS

Incomprehensible words or utterances	()
Hypothesis as to what was heard	(hypothesis)
Uncompleted word	/
Emphatic intonation	CAPITAL LETTERS
Lengthening	:: (may be increased to ::: or more)
Syllabification	–
Interrogation	?
Pause of any duration	...
Descriptive comments by the transcriber	((laughter))
Thematic sequence breaks or deviations	– –

Indication that the speech was taken up
at a determined point, and not at
the beginning, for example   (. . .)
Literal quotation, reproduction of
direct speech   " "

REFERENCES

Brown, P. and Levinson, S. C. (1978) *Politeness: Some Universals in Language Usage*, Cambridge: Cambridge University Press.
Debert, G. G. (1988) 'Envelhecimento e representação da velhice', *Ciência Hoje*, São Paulo, 8, 44, 60–8.
Goffman, E. (1959) *The Presentation of Self in Everyday Life*, New York: Doubleday.
Goffman, E. (1967) *Interaction Ritual: Essays on Face to Face Behavior*, New York: Doubleday.
Goffman, E. (1973) *Stigma: Notes on the Management of Spoiled Identity*, Harmondsworth: Penguin.
Horkheimer, M. and Adorno, T. (1978) *Temas Básicos da Sociologia*, 2nd edn, trans. by A. Cabral, São Paulo: Cultrix.
Marcuschi, L. A. (1989) 'Marcadores conversacionais do português brasileiro: formas, posições e funções', in A. T. Castilho (ed.) *Português Culto Falado no Brasil*, Campinas: Editora da UNICAMP, 281–318.
Preti, D. (1991) *A Linguagem dos Idosos*, São Paulo: Contexto.
Rosa, M. (1992) *Marcadores de Atenuação*, São Paulo: Contexto.
Ryan, E. B., Giles, H., Bartolluc, G. and Henwood, K. (1986) 'Psycholinguistic and psychological components of communication by and with the elderly', *Language and Communication*, 6, 1/2, 1–24.
Sartre, J-P. (1956) *Being and Nothingness*, trans. by H. E. Barnes, New York: Philosophical Library.

Chapter 12

'Guilt over games boys play'

Coherence as a focus for examining the constitution of heterosexual subjectivity on a problem page

Val Gough and Mary Talbot

In this chapter coherence is presented as a focus for attending to the constitution of subjectivity. We critically examine the distinction between 'surface' and 'underlying' coherence, arguing that it misleadingly implies that textually cued coherence is a purely textual phenomenon. We propose that the points at which a reader needs to construct coherence can be used as a focus for critical language analysis. Our sample analysis investigates Marje Proops' problem page in the *Sunday Mirror* newspaper. We attend principally to a single problem page reply: its 'liberal' message is that homosexual experiences are legitimate, in the context of a development towards confirmed heterosexuality. Our analysis concentrates on the construction of the letter writer and problem page reader as unambiguously heterosexual and on the range of (sometimes contradictory) ideological assumptions required for that construction.

The notion of coherence is used to cover a wide range of topics in linguistics in general and we have no intention of attempting to review them all exhaustively.[1] Instead we limit ourselves to a general discussion of the field with reference to some contributions with potential for examining the constitution of subjectivity in the act of constructing coherence. The search for points of focus for attention to identity-construction in discourse is intended to contribute to developments in Critical Language Study. This is a body of collaborative, synthesising work with the explicitly emancipatory objective of consciousness-raising (e.g. Clark *et al.*, 1987; Fairclough, 1989, 1992; Ivanič, 1988; Talbot, 1990).

In our discussion we attend principally to a particular letter and its reply which appeared on Marje Proops' problem page in the *Sunday Mirror* newspaper (see Figure 12.1), entitled 'Guilt Over Games Boys Play'. The letter is from a confused man (henceforth referred to as C) who writes that he is anxious about some homoerotic experiences he shared years ago with his best friend when they were schoolboys. C is now married, and his friend has a girlfriend, but he still feels both guilty and curious about gay sex. In Marje's reply, C is reassured that he is 'normal', precisely because he has turned out to be, according to Marje, unambiguously

Guilt over games boys play

Dear Marje

FOR years I have been very uneasy about what happened between me and my best friend when we were schoolboys.

We were about seven when we started mucking about and playing rude kids' games.

We showed each other our private parts and, young as we were, we compared sizes.

We touched each other up and as we got into our teens, we masturbated each other.

Then we both started taking a healthy interest in girls.

After we left school, we went our separate ways and lost touch until a couple of years ago when we met again by chance.

He was living with a girl and I was engaged.

We see each other quite often but I feel awful when we meet. It stirs up all the old guilt.

I love my wife. We have great sex but this cloud hangs over me.

Sometimes I wonder if I am secretly perverted because although I've never had sex with another male, frankly I am curious about it.

I'm really mixed up and I hope you can help me.

✱ YOU are no more mixed-up than countless other men. The main difference, though, between you and them is that you are honest enough to confront your feelings and your guilt. That's a healthy attitude.

There can't be many men who when young have never mucked about with each other behind the bike shed. Girls do it, too.

Your experiments with your school friend were as important a part of your learning process as geography and history and maths.

Those youthful playground larks prepared you for the manhood you are now enjoying. Or would be enjoying if it wasn't for the unnecessary guilt you still feel.

Many heterosexual men have a passing curiosity about homosexuality, and that isn't such a bad thing. It compels you to make choices.

You made yours many years ago when you began to pursue women and married the one you love.

I think you were lucky to meet your old friend again, despite the feelings you describe. You feel awful because you are ashamed of those youthful fumblings.

If you could be as frank with each other now as you were when you were schoolboys, I guarantee he'd confess to similar guilt.

It's interesting that comparing size has always been a male obsession. A perfectly harmless one, in my view.

It's like the way women compare breast sizes and it's simply because penises and breasts are symbols of sexuality and performance.

You are performing OK. You'd get 10 out of 10 and a gold star, I bet, from a wife who is satisfied her husband is all man.

I hope my observations will help to lift that cloud.

Why don't you fix up a foursome dinner date with your pal and his girl and drink a toast to the good old days – the days that changed you from a boy into a manly man? I'll drink to that with you.

READ MARJE AGAIN IN THE DAILY MIRROR ON TUESDAY

Figure 12.1 Problem page of the *Sunday Mirror*, 17 January 1983

heterosexual. The overall message is that homosexual experiences are legitimate provided that they occur in the context of a development towards confirmed heterosexuality. In our discussion, we have a two-fold purpose: to revise existing theoretical models of coherence, and to demonstrate how coherence is a useful focus of attention in the examination of identity-construction in discourse.

GUILT OVER GAMES BOYS PLAY

Dear Marje

(1) FOR years I have been very uneasy about what happened between me and my best friend when we were schoolboys.

(2) We were about seven when we started mucking about and playing rude kids' games.

(3) We showed each other our private parts and, young as we were, we compared sizes.

(4) We touched each other up and as we got into our teens, we masturbated each other. Then we both started taking a healthy interest in girls.

(5) After we left school, we went our separate ways and lost touch until a couple of years ago when we met again by chance.

(6) He was living with a girl and I was engaged.

(7) We see each other quite often but I feel awful when we meet. It stirs up all the old guilt.

(8) I love my wife. We have great sex but this cloud hangs over me.

(9) Sometimes I wonder if I am secretly perverted because although I've never had sex with another male, frankly I am curious about it.

(10) I'm really mixed up and I hope you can help me.

(11) YOU are no more mixed-up than countless other men. The main difference, though, between you and them is that you are honest enough to confront your feelings and your guilt. That's a healthy attitude.

(12) There can't be many men who when young have never mucked about with each other behind the bike shed. Girls do it, too.

(13) Your experiments with your school friend were as important a part of your learning process as geography and history and maths.

(14) Those youthful playground larks prepared you for the manhood you are now enjoying. Or would be enjoying if it wasn't for the unnecessary guilt you still feel.

(15) Many heterosexual men have a passing curiosity about homosexuality, and that isn't such a bad thing. It compels you to make choices.

(16) You made yours many years ago when you began to pursue women and married the one you love.

(17) I think you were lucky to meet your old friend again, despite the feelings you describe. You feel awful because you are ashamed of those youthful fumblings.

(18) If you could be as frank with each other now as you were when you were schoolboys, I guarantee he'd confess to similar guilt.

(19) It's interesting that comparing size has always been a male obsession. A perfectly harmless one, in my view.

(20) It's like the way women compare breast sizes and it's simply because penises are symbols of sexuality and performance.

(21) You are performing OK. You'd get 10 out of 10 and a gold star, I bet, from a wife who is satisfied her husband is all man.

(22) I hope my observations will help to lift that cloud.

(23) Why don't you fix up a foursome dinner date with your pal and his girl and drink a toast to the good old days – the days that changed you from a boy into a manly man? I'll drink to that with you.

A FALSE DIVIDE: 'SURFACE' AND 'UNDERLYING' COHERENCE

Michael Stubbs (1983) identifies discourse analysis as the study of the principles governing coherence:

> People are quite able to distinguish between a random list of sentences and a coherent text, and it is the principles which underlie this recognition of coherence which are the topic of study for discourse analysts.
>
> (Stubbs, 1983: 15)

He refers to discourse analysis as 'the study of connected discourse in natural situations' (1983: 7). Like other linguists, he sees the objective of discourse analysis as an explanation for the possibility of 'well-formed' discourse beyond the scope of theoretical linguistics. As a result, the tendency is to approach the problem in terms of how to account for meaningful discourse when textual cues cannot be found. Many studies of coherence in discourse analysis distinguish between 'surface' and 'underlying' coherence (Craig and Tracy, 1983; Tannen, 1984b; Widdowson, 1979). This distinction is implicit in the work of Gillian Brown and George Yule, in their contrast between 'coherence discussable in terms of formal linkage providing grammatical wellformedness' and 'the other extreme' where formal linkage is absent (Brown and Yule, 1983: 223–4). As an example of the second 'extreme', they refer to Sinclair and Coulthard's (1975) model of classroom discourse. Starting with the inability to account for coherence grammatically, Sinclair and Coulthard pose the problem of how language users can identify sequences of utterances as coherent discourse despite the absence of formal linkage. Formal properties are given primacy: what is thought to be in need of explanation is how coherence is possible in their absence.[2] The problem is posed as how people can identify sequences of utterances as coherent discourse without formal cues. Brown and Yule quote Labov's (1970) much-quoted statement that there are rules of interpretation relating 'what is said to what is done' and observe:

> it is on the basis of such social, but not linguistic, rules that we interpret some conversational sequences as coherent and others as non-coherent.
>
> (quoted in Brown and Yule, 1983: 226)

In this view, connections between the actions performed in utterances are what make discourse coherent. In discourse analysis and pragmatics, which identify the functions of utterances and how they connect together to form coherent discourse, these actions tend to be viewed solely as purposive interventions in the world by individuals.

This distinction between 'surface' and 'underlying' coherence used by discourse analysts seems to us to be a misleading one. It suggests that we only need to have recourse to context to interpret a text in the absence of explicit cues to coherence, thereby misleadingly implying the appropriacy of an 'economy principle' in accounting for coherence. This would mean looking at 'surface' coherence first, at the most explicit cues, and then, if (and only if) explicit 'surface' cues are not to be found in the text, turning to some solitary element of the surrounding context (such as a writer's intention, or a reader's inference) for 'underlying' coherence. Our analysis of 'Guilt Over Games Boys Play' will demonstrate how misleading this distinction is. We begin by attending to the contribution of formal linkage (grammar, cohesion) to coherence. We shall show that, in accounting for coherence by focusing on the observable textual properties contributing to it, one relies heavily on details not provided by textual cues themselves and that for both 'surface' and 'underlying' coherence other resources for interpreting discourse as coherent need consideration. We shall then turn to the characterisation of 'world-knowledge' brought in for interpretation in work on coherence, presenting first a distinction between sequential 'text-text' connections and other 'text-world' connections made for coherence, and giving specific attention to prior knowledge of frames, to presupposition, automatic gap-filling and inferencing. Through attention to inferencing and so on, we shall bring into focus resources from beyond the text more usually brought to bear unreflectively, and, if thought of at all, considered to be matters of simple 'common sense'.

FORMAL PROPERTIES AS CUES TO COHERENCE

Surface coherence is sometimes referred to as 'cohesion' (e.g. Stubbs, 1983; Tannen, 1984b). Halliday and Hasan (1976) use the term to refer to the range of features which bind together clauses and sentences indicated in Figure 12.2. This kind of cohesion in general is characterised as a 'presuppositional' relation. The presence of a cohesive tie 'presupposes' something to which it connects.

Cohesive ties are 'directives indicating that information is to be retrieved from elsewhere' (Halliday and Hasan, 1976: 31). The cohesive cues in Halliday and Hasan's inventory are presented as 'systematic resources' from which speakers/writers select options. We want to stress the view implicitly held here that these formal features do not create the continuity that texts display, but cue it. Halliday and Hasan do not go into the implications of this. They give no indication of where/who the 'directive' in the cue comes from, or how/why it leads to one connection rather than another. But an example from our sample text shows that formal features cue coherence rather than create it: a 'reversed causal' connector, *because*, in the problem page reply is on the face of it very straightforward:

You feel awful because you are ashamed of those youthful fumblings. (17)

Cohesion

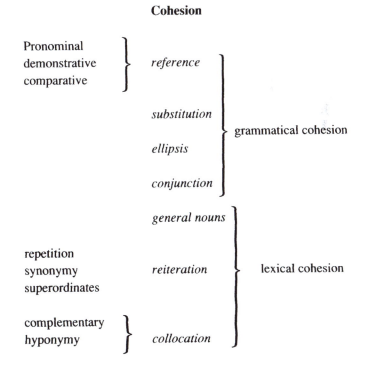

Figure 12.2 Cohesion

The connector cues the information in the second clause as the cause of the condition in the first. But the 'reversed causal' can serve all kinds of different functions in utterances; it operates in the way indicated only because of additional information, as we shall see in a moment. First, consider the following example, from a *Jackie* magazine interview with a soap opera star (*Jackie* is a British publication for young teenage girls):

> I use ... Clinique and Almay which are good for my skin because it's quite sensitive.

In order to achieve a coherent interpretation of this clause complex, we need to know that skin is classified into different types, that some products have harmful effects on 'sensitive' skin, others are hypo-allergenic, etc. We also have to fill in what kind of causal relation is being cued by the conjunction *because*. In the soap-star interview example it cues the grounding of an assertion. Elsewhere it may be functioning to cue a reason for, for instance, a request for information (e.g. 'What's the time because I have to leave at eight') or the cause of an emotional state, as in the Marje example above. We can read the cohesive link cued by the causal connector in Marje's reply only with the help of additional information. We need to understand that Marje is setting herself up as an 'analyst' and making a diagnosis of the symptoms reported by her 'client'.

Halliday (1985) groups all these functions together as types of expansion. Subordinate clauses with connectors cuing a causal relation (and some non-finites) are grouped together in a subcategory of *enhancements: Cause*, which covers a range of reasons and purposes. The structural generalisation is functional, but not sufficient alone to interpret what kind of causal relation is cued. For this we need to draw on other resources. For the contextual information about discourse conventions, such as the classification schemes and act of grounding assertions needed for the Almay example above, we need knowledge not of grammar but of the world (a causal relation within a clause complex may not be formally cued and depend entirely upon the reading subject's complicity: cf. Pêcheux, 1982).

Similarly, causal links without any textual cue may combine sentences. For example, Marje says:

> Many heterosexual men have a passing curiosity about homosexuality, and that isn't such a bad thing. It compels you to make choices. (15)

The causal link which is needed to coherently combine these two sentences is not cued by any formal element. This is a point where the reader's complicity must be complete for any sense to be made of the two sentences as they stand together. We need to infer that heterosexuality and homosexuality are separate sexualities and that interest in homosexuality is useful inasmuch as it reinforces this separate heterosexual identity. And to construct coherence, the pronoun 'you' which functions both as a singular pronoun referring specifically to C, and as a generic pronoun referring to people in general, must be taken to refer to a heterosexual male subject. Otherwise, the construction of a causal connection between the two sentences cannot occur. So for coherence to be constructed, both C and the reader must be constituted as heterosexual. Note that here it is the ('underlying') world-knowledge being drawn upon that is permitting the ('surface') cohesive link between 'many heterosexual men' and 'you'.

In the next example, there is formal linkage providing a textual cue for coherence in the form of a comparative clause:

Your experiments with your school friend were as important a part of your learning process as geography and history and maths. (13)

However, recognition of this formal cue must be supplemented by the following resources beyond the text: learning is natural, youth is an appropriate time for sexual experimentation, the sexual experiences of youth function as experiments rather than primarily as sexual gratification. 'Surface' coherence, then, is dependent on the language-user's ability to make connections 'outside' the text. In the act of constructing coherence by making these connections the reader is him/herself constructed as a subject. In the sample text we have chosen, the act of constructing coherence constructs the reader as heterosexual.

One contributor to the global coherence of Marje's reply is lexical cohesion. This is partly produced by two quite distinct lexical sets:

mucked about	your manhood
your experiments	all manly
youthful playground larks	manly man
passing curiosity	
those youthful fumblings	

As we said above, the construction of coherence relies heavily on the ability of the reader to fill in details not provided by textual cues themselves. In other words, the reader must draw upon what is thought of as 'common sense'. In the first lexical set, the vocabulary items which create the cohesive ties serve to distance C's homoerotic experiences in the past. This discoursal 'common sense' includes the assumption that childhood and adolescent sexual experiences are innocent, transient, and that they form a legitimate phase of sexual development, a kind of sexual training for the 'real stuff' later. This is a body of assumptions which is partly provided by the reply-text itself, in Marje's reference to the 'good old days', for example; thus the reply itself provides a textual context upon which the reader draws when constructing coherence. Other texts on the same problem page provide a similar context upon which the reader may draw, for example repetition of the phrase 'playground larks' in the reply to another letter. Both replies draw on the assumption that childhood experiences of a mythical past (as opposed to the experiences of present-day, supposedly streetwise children) were 'innocent' and based harmlessly on sexual ignorance. They thus rely on the assumption of the separateness of and differences between childhood and adulthood. Thus the coherence of both these replies relies on the same resources of background knowledge. This demonstrates how texts on the same problem page provide mutually reinforcing knowledge.

Contrasting with the vocabulary of youth, innocence and triviality is a second lexical set, encoding maturity, masculinity and virility. Marje uses a series of euphemisms which form extended cohesive ties through reiteration. Though 'all manly' and 'manly man' clearly refer back to 'the manhood you are now enjoying', to make this cohesive tie coherent and to make sense of the contrast between the two lexical sets, heterosexist assumptions are drawn upon: the reader needs the homophobic assumptions that to be gay is to be girlish, immature, feminine, impotent and emasculated, and therefore that to be heterosexual is to be the opposite of that. Clearly the ideology of 'manliness' is crucial to the homophobic message.

Focus on how coherence is cued by another lexical set exposes the nature of C's problem as a site of ideological struggle. The establishment of what 'the problem' is in Marje's eyes is important in constituting the subjectivity of the reader. In paragraph 8, C uses the image of a 'cloud' to establish the existence and nature of his 'problem': 'this cloud hangs over me'. It is one item in a lexical chain:

uneasy ... feel awful ... the old guilt ... this cloud ... mixed up

To this the reader must bring knowledge of the way that metaphor works and read the cloud non-literally, in order to include it in this chain. As a metaphor, C's cloud brings with it an indeterminate set of associations relating to doubt and depression, but also blurring of vision, or of limits, and confusion. Marje picks up the metaphor in her reply, reiterating it in paragraph 22: 'I hope my observations will help to lift that cloud'. However, the chain she produces links C's problem less to confusion and more to guilt:

your guilt ... similar guilt ... that cloud

This link has of course already been strongly forged in the first word of the heading 'Guilt Over Games Boys Play', and in her reply, Marje has already dismissed sexual confusion as a real problem: 'You are no more mixed up than countless other men'. Thus C's potential sexual curiosity is ignored in Marje's reply. The nature of the problem as Marje sees it is much less potentially disruptive of heterosexist assumptions. To admit that a seemingly happily heterosexual man also feels curious about gay sex or confused about sexual orientation would challenge the assumed separateness of sexual realms, the dichotomisation of sexual orientation which underpins the ideology of her reply. The definition of C's problem as a 'cloud' of guilt rather than of confusion or curiosity enables Marje's project of reassurance of C's (and the reader's) heterosexual identity. For this project to make any sense, we need to draw upon, among other things, a conventional, generic relationship between the letter and the reply. We need to assume that reinterpretation and reassurance are in themselves effective ways of solving someone's problem.

RESOURCES BEYOND THE TEXT

Generic conventions: 'I'm really mixed up because . . .'

In systemic linguistics, Paul Thibault (1988) extends the functional grammar description of the cause type of enhancement within a clause complex to cover connections in activity-structure manifested across groups of clause complexes. Thibault's article consists of an analysis of a letter and response from the problem page of a magazine for young women. Since his data and purposes coincide with ours to a high degree, this article merits some detailed attention here. He applies the function of enhancement to a 'discourse-level' relation between the actions: Reason for Request – Request, realised by three clause complexes. We have already seen a single clause complex which can be interpreted as a sequence of two causally related acts of this kind: 'What's the time' (Request) 'because I have to leave at eight' (Reason for Request). On the analogy of grammatical enhancement, Thibault describes a causal relation between actions manifested in groups of clause complexes. The first two clause complexes of the letter realise the Reason for Request:

> I am a 17 year old virgin and very scared. I have never been brave enough to try sexual intercourse.

The third clause complex realises the Request itself:

> Could you please give me some idea as to how I will feel, what will happen and what to expect when I finally share my body with another?

Like the enhancing clause 'because I have to leave at eight', the first two clause complexes realise an act which functions as an 'enhancement' in an activity-structure. The Reason for Request qualifies the Request. As Thibault says, 'The clause complex relations . . . contribute to the major structural boundaries of the text as social activity structure' (Thibault, 1988: 211). Prior knowledge of a conventional kind of activity is needed to read the passage as coherent, that is, a reader needs a particular item of knowledge as a resource in order to interpret the actions embodied in the discourse as a coherent activity. The correspondent writes for advice about some condition seen as a 'problem'. The 'problem' condition is established in a confession: some kind of divulgence before (or, alternatively, after) the request for advice. In our Marje sample, the single sentence paragraph concluding the letter contains a similar activity-structure. The second clause is functioning as a Request; the first clause functions as the Reason for Request:

I'm really mixed up and I hope you can help me. (10)

In this Reason for Request, C is formulating his divulgence in the rest of the letter. In the 'gist' type of formulation he provides,[3] he identifies his 'problem' as one of confusion. As we have seen, Marje explicitly refutes this interpretation.

Problem page letters and replies contain conventional activity-structures such as the Request – Reason for Request and constitute a generic activity-type. Another activity structure – setting up specific subject positions and relations between them – is in Marje's diagnostic utterance in paragraph 17, establishing herself as analyst and C as client. Problem page letters offer specific kinds of social identity and relationship to writers and readers:

> They are a distinct sub-genre which both invites women to confess their 'inner' feelings and sexual problems ... as well as co-opting this genre in the service of a normative matching of the positions of social agents with dominant schemas of actions, knowledge and belief about gender-differentiated heterosexual relations.
>
> (Thibault, 1988: 205)

Top-down and bottom-up processing

Both textual properties and actions, then, depend heavily on the interpreter's own resources for interpretation. A text itself is only the trace of the meaningful action of discourse. This action is meaningful only because the reader has expectations about who people are, what they are like and the kinds of social practices they engage in. Knowledge and expectations about human actions in and surrounding discourse are needed for coherence globally and locally. All discourse takes place in a social context and has a history.

Fairclough (1989) uses the term 'coherence' to cover two broad kinds of connection made by an interpreter; namely:

> (i) between the sequential parts of a text; and (ii) between (parts of) a text and 'the world'.
>
> (Fairclough, 1989: 78)

He uses the notion of frames to account for the second of these: 'text-world' connections. We have already noted Thibault's observation that the discourse-level causal relation between the Reason for Request and the Request itself can be interpreted only given specific knowledge relating to the kinds of activity enacted in problem pages in the press. In Fairclough's model of text interpretation, drawing on schemata, cognitive representation of conventional kinds of activity is a form of 'top-down' processing, which a reader does to build both global and local coherence. In other words, we draw on knowledge of the world to make sense of a text 'as a whole' as well as to make connections between adjacent sentences in it. Other resources drawn upon for top-down processing are assumptions and expectations. In Fairclough's model these assumptions and expectations are elements of socially/discursively constituted knowledge that are drawn upon for coherent interpretation. They are represented cognitively in frames.[4]

The problem page correspondents write for advice about some condition seen as a 'problem'. Top-down processing is needed throughout our Marje example. To demonstrate, we'll return to just one of the examples we considered earlier:

You feel awful because you are ashamed of those youthful fumblings. (17)

A frame of knowledge relating to diagnostic practices enacted by problem page 'agony aunts' must be drawn on for interpretation of the specific functioning of the reversed causal connector, 'because', as a cue to a cause (rather than, for example, a justification, reason, or authority claim).

For Thibault's sample Reason for Request we need to draw upon implicit frames to know that the writer's problem is fear of sexual involvement and her own perceived cowardice (and probably have no difficulty in doing so). These frames relate to a range of assumptions and expectations about 'normal' behaviour among young people; the pressures of 'teenage bravado', etc. To highlight how much of our recognition of the writer's problem relies on 'unspoken' knowledge in frames, try imposing a fictional frame relating to the sacrifice of virgins as the root of her problem. This would, among other things, impose a causal connection (in this case more explicitly realisable by 'so') between the first and second clauses of her opening sentence (this being our own perverse first reading of it). Other 'unspoken' knowledge contributing to coherence is more explicitly established by presupposition 'triggers'. For recognition of the 'problem', one of the resources available to a reader is an assumption which is set up as presupposed: 'you have to be brave to try sexual intercourse'.[5]

The first kind of connection for coherence Fairclough refers to relates to local coherence between segments of text: 'text-text' connections. Along similar lines to those followed by Brown and Yule, he attends to this local, linear coherence using the notions of automatic 'gap-filling' and inferencing. Unlike them, he stresses that the distinction between automatic provision of a 'missing link' and a connection requiring inferential work on the part of the interpreter is not clearcut. The amount of inferential work required of an interpreter depends on who he/she is (what discourses he/she has access to).

The apparently un-cued causal connection between two adjacent sentences of Marje's reply is an example of what is probably automatic 'gap-filling' for most readers:

> Many heterosexual men have a passing curiosity about homosexuality, and that isn't such a bad thing. It compels you to make choices. (15)

As we said earlier, the causal link which is needed to coherently combine these two sentences is not cued by any formal element, and this is a point where the reader's complicity is required if the two sentences as they stand together are to make sense. The 'missing link' we need to supply is that heterosexuality and homosexuality are separate sexualities and that interest in homosexuality is useful inasmuch as it reinforces this separate heterosexual identity. For some readers it may require inferential work.

Thibault's sample text, and his analysis, provides another example. There is a connection between the propositions in the first clause complex which is not made explicit. The additive connector 'and' alone is not sufficient to account for what we take to be a reader's interpretation; namely that the two clauses form part of what Thibault calls a 'set of circumstantial relations' (1988: 211) preceding the writer's request for advice. Following Fairclough's approach, this interpretation would be accounted for using the notion of automatic 'gap-filling' between explicit propositions. A reader who is unfamiliar with problem pages (such as the perverse reader we pretended to be earlier) would need to engage in a good deal of inferential work to make this kind of connection.

We feel that the twin notions of automatic connections and inferencing need to be used in conjunction with conceptions intended to capture text-world considerations, such as frames and activity-types. Turning to the problem page letters for an example again: the connection between the Reason for Request and the Request in each of them is likely to be commonsensical for a regular reader of problem pages: an 'automatic' connection a reader makes by drawing on knowledge of a specific activity-type. For a less expert reader it might require inferential work.

Frames, automatic connections, presupposed ideas and inferences are each part of the 'discoursal common sense' a reader needs to draw upon in order to construct coherence. They are assumptions about the social world that are set up in such a way that they are not asserted, but readers still need to supply them to read a text as coherent. Fairclough observes that persuasive discourse and propaganda make use of these features, but stresses that readers are not deterministically positioned by them. Attempts to position an addressee as someone with particular common-sensical assumptions can be easy to spot and contest: as in the following example, where we need to draw on assumptions about the predatory nature of male heterosexuality:

> You made [your choice] many years ago when you began to pursue women . . . (16)

An addressee is necessarily complicit in constructing a text's coherence. But he/she can resist interpellation, that is, positioning as a person with certain beliefs, schemas of action, etc., if he/she has access to an opposi-tional discourse. Commonsense assumptions attributed to an addressee in presuppositions (like the one in the *when*-clause above) are probably more readily retrievable, and hence contestable, than those in 'missing links' or frames, as Fairclough implies. Nevertheless the manipulative presupposi-tion is only 'obvious' to someone already critical of such assumptions about the male sexual drive (or a linguist accustomed to picking out presuppositions!), who is able to resist interpellation.[6]

CONCLUSIONS

So the ability to construct coherence is dependent upon the resources readers have access to: their social identity. The cultural variability of language users' expectations about activities has been examined by various linguists, among them Tannen (1984a), and Jarrett (1984). Jarrett for instance examines the pragmatic coherence of blues lyrics, requiring knowledge of oral traditions in the blues and other genres:

> one must be familiar with a number of Afro-American traditions, some of which mainly exist in speech-community activities other than the blues, others of which are commonly found in blues lyrics.
>
> (Jarrett, 1984: 163)

Listeners construct the coherence of blues lyrics, drawing on frames relating to knowledge of genres. Ethnocentric white listeners lack the necessary frames to interpret the lyrics as coherent. This implies that the ability to construct coherence is dependent upon the social identity of the interpreter. The claim we wish to make goes one step further: people take up subject positions in constructing, or failing to construct, coherence, and are thereby constituted as social subjects.

Focusing on coherence construction can reveal ideological contra-dictions. At one point in Marje's reply, the reader must draw upon a knowledge frame which contradicts the frame relating to dichotomised sexual realms brought in elsewhere. The assumptions of dichotomised, supposedly exclusive or opposing realms of youth and maturity, and by implication homosexuality and heterosexuality, must be suspended to make sense of the following:

> You'd get 10 out of 10 and a gold star, I bet, from a wife who is satisfied her husband is all man. (21)

Here the language of the (homoerotic) schoolroom invades that of the heterosexual bedroom and requires a momentary unconscious suspension of the assumption that the two are necessarily separate. The subjectivity of C must be constituted as dual, the very feature which elsewhere the construction of coherence has repressed. The reader must understand C as a metaphorical 'boy' in order to be reassured that he is a 'man'. Thus the subjectivity of C must be constituted simultaneously as virile, mature, masculine heterosexual male and as an immature 'schoolboy', seeking reassurance and reward. This latter image contradicts the understanding that it has been left behind.

In conclusion, coherence offers a focus for attending specifically to the constitution of subjectivity in discourse. It provides this focus because subjectivity is constituted as coherent interpretation is made, that is, the reader is positioned as a subject in the act of interpreting discourse. It is the points at which a reader needs to construct coherence which provide a focus of attention for a critical language analysis.

NOTES

1   A particular body of work not given specific attention which must be noted is that of Teun van Dijk and associates.
2   Marilda Cavalcanti (1983: 31) makes a similar observation with regard to the use of the prior knowledge as a last resort in text-linguistic approaches to text comprehension.
3   See Jenny Thomas (1985) for the distinction between 'gist' and 'upshot', two different rewordings of what has gone before.
4   The interrelated concepts of *activity*, *schema*, *frame* and *script* have been proposed to account for 'world knowledge' contributing to coherence. Cavalcanti (1983) has already provided an extensive and detailed review of these and other related concepts, with particular attention to prior knowledge-based research on text comprehension. As she remarks, there is 'a plethora of terms used variously in the literature namely SCHEMA, FRAME, SCRIPT, SCENARIO, inter alia' (Cavalcanti, 1983: 25). These are used in a variety of ways. Working in Artificial Intelligence (AI), Schank and Abelson (1977) devised the notion of 'script' to refer to stereotypical knowledge of an action structure. These scripts simulate a language user's expectations about sequences of action. They provide the encyclopedic background information necessary to make inferential leaps from one sentence to another. We can think of this encyclopedic knowledge as part of language user's 'practical consciousness' of activities; of what it is to go into a restaurant, take a bus ride, travel by train, etc. According to Abelson (1981) scripts involve two kinds of constraints: event sequence, 'the causal chaining of enablements and results for physical events

and of initiations and reasons for mental events', and a notion of 'stereotype and familiarity' (Abelson, 1981: 3).

In this approach, the bare minimum of cultural context is introduced to fill in gaps in the 'surface' text. As Quinn and Holland (1987) say, they tend to attribute their own culture-specific knowledge of action sequences to 'pan-human experience of how the world works' (Quinn and Holland, 1987: 20). Since the objective of AI is to simulate human language processes on a machine their view of people's 'standard' expectations is not subjected to critical examination. In recognising an action (such as an utterance), an inferential connection is made between the action and its actor's intention or reason for doing it: a teleological explanation is constructed for it. In constructing teleological explanations for another's action, an interactant or an analyst is commonsensically assuming access to the same interpretative resources as the actor.

Minsky's (1975) notion of a 'frame', from which Shank and Abelson developed their 'script', suffers from similar problems.

5 In Thibault's (1988) problem page text, the 'Agony Aunt' picks out the presupposition *you have to be brave to try sexual intercourse* in her reply, contesting it with the explicit assertion: 'There is nothing brave about trying sex'.

6 Wendy Hollway (1984) critically examines discourses which construct sexuality.

REFERENCES

Abelson, R. P. (1981) 'Psychological status of the script concept', *American Psychologist*, 36(7), 715–30.

Brown, G. and Yule, G. (1983) *Discourse Analysis*, Cambridge: Cambridge University Press.

Cavalcanti, M. (1983) 'The pragmatics of FL reader–text interaction: key lexical items as a source of potential reading problems', unpub. PhD, University of Lancaster.

Clark, R., Fairclough, N., Ivanič, R. and Martin-Jones, M. (1987) *Critical Language Awareness*, Centre for Language in Social Life Working Paper Series no. 1, University of Lancaster.

Craig, R. T. and Tracy, K. (eds) (1983) *Conversational Coherence: Form, Structure, and Strategy*, New York: Sage.

Fairclough, N. (1989) *Language and Power*, London: Longman.

Fairclough, N. (ed.) (1992) *Language Awareness: Critical Perspectives*, London: Longman.

Halliday, M. A. K. (1985) *An Introduction to Functional Grammar*, London: Edward Arnold.

Halliday, M. A. K. and Hasan, R. (1976) *Cohesion in English*, London: Longman.

Hollway, W. (1984) 'Gender difference and the production of subjectivity', in J. Henriques, W. Hollway, C. Urwin, C. Venn and V. Walkerdine (eds), *Changing the Subject: Psychology, Social Regulation and Subjectivity*, London: Methuen, 227–63.

Ivanič, R. (1988) 'Critical language awareness in action', *Language Issues*, 2, 2, 2–7.

Jarrett, D. (1984) 'Pragmatic coherence in an oral formulaic tradition: I can read you letters / sure can't read your mind', in D. Tannen (ed.) *Coherence in Spoken and Written Discourse*, Norwood, NJ: Ablex, 155–71.

Labov, W. (1970) 'The study of language in its social context', *Studium Generale*, 23, 30–87.

Minsky, J. (1975) 'Framework for representing knowledge', in P. H. Winston (ed.) *The Psychology of Computer Vision*, New York: McGraw-Hill, 211–77.

Pêcheux, M. (1982) *Language, Semantics and Ideology: Stating the Obvious*, trans. by H. Nagpal, London: Macmillan.

Quinn, N. and Holland, D. (1987) 'Culture and cognition', in D. Holland and N. Quinn (eds) *Cultural Models in Language and Thought*, Cambridge: Cambridge University Press, 3–40.

Schank, R. and Abelson, R. (1977) *Scripts, Plans, Goals and Understanding*, Hillsdale, NJ: Erlbaum.

Sinclair, J. McH. and Coulthard, R. M. (1975) *Towards an Analysis of Discourse*, Oxford: Oxford University Press.

Stubbs, M. (1983) *Discourse Analysis: The Sociolinguistic Analysis of Natural Language*, Oxford: Blackwell.

Talbot, M. (1990) 'Language, intertextuality and subjectivity: voices in the construction of consumer femininity', unpub. PhD, University of Lancaster.

Tannen, D. (1984a) 'Spoken and written narrative in English and Greek', in D. Tannen (ed.), *Coherence in Spoken and Written Discourse*, Norwood, NJ: Ablex, 21–41.

Tannen, D. (ed.) (1984b) *Coherence in Spoken and Written Discourse*, Norwood, NJ: Ablex.

Thibault, P. J. (1988) 'Knowing what you're told by Agony Aunts: language function, gender difference and the structure of knowledge and belief in the personal columns', in D. Birch and M. O'Toole (eds), *Functions of Style*, London: Frances Pinter, 205–33.

Thomas, J. (1985) 'The language of power: towards a dynamic pragmatics', *Journal of Pragmatics*, 9, 765–83.

Widdowson, H. (1979) *Explorations in Applied Linguistics*, Oxford: Oxford University Press.

Chapter 13

Barking up the wrong tree?

Male hegemony, discrimination against women and the reporting of bestiality in the Zimbabwean press

Andrew Morrison

Bestiality rarely appears in the litany of sex 'scandals' involving soccer stars, vicars, princesses and politicians typical of tabloid newspapers. Although tabloid-style journalism does not often occur within the predominantly state-controlled press in Zimbabwe, there have been occasions when sensationalist material has appeared. Since Independence in 1980 the main government-owned newspaper group has chiefly been concerned to champion the development needs of a predominantly rural population. The group has also exercised considerable control over the content and nature of reporting and has patently promoted the goals and achievements of the elected government.[1] Such practice needs to be seen in the context of the military struggle through which the state of Zimbabwe was created and the continued aggression and destabilisation policies of South Africa. Privately owned newspapers and magazines were published throughout this period and during the 1980s became increasingly critical of the government's policies. In the early 1990s, with the establishment of a more open economy, newspapers and magazines became more competitive in their search for an audience. It is against this backdrop that a leading Sunday newspaper reported an alleged incident of bestiality.[2] This initial report became the focus for numerous responses through which the alleged act of bestiality was attacked, often on strongly moralistic grounds. However, the responses from readers and editors established a discourse which not only discriminated against the women who allegedly took part in acts of bestiality, but also was extended cumulatively and through dense intertextuality to Zimbabwean women in general.

The allegations were that black women had been paid by a white man to have sexual intercourse with a dog and that these acts had been videotaped for sale abroad. Given Zimbabwe's history, subsequent material in the press reacted against the inherent racism of a situation in which black women were paid by a white man to enter into prostitution involving bestiality. However, much of the material which appeared not only moralised against female commercial sex workers, but also criticised women in general and was at odds with positive developments in law relating to women since Independence (e.g. Stewart and Armstrong, 1990).

In the initial report and the many texts responding to it – in a range of genres (Threadgold, 1989) from lead articles, to letters to the editor, editorials, commentaries and cartoons – one woman in particular was portrayed as having doubly 'sold herself'. First, she had sold herself to another man who was described as white, and, in historical terms, the colonial thief. Second, in entering into this economic relationship, the woman had exchanged a black man for a dog as her sexual partner. In doing this she threatened dominant sexual relations between men and women, and violated her role as a reproductive agent (see e.g. Heng and Devan, 1992).

Bestiality involving women introduced a new dimension to the reporting of sexual offences. As with other sexual offences, bestiality is characterised as an affront to moral and social propriety.[3] In the letter of the law such an act is 'against the law of nature'. It is, in Sumner's (1990) terms, met with social censure:

> Social censures combine with forms of power and economy to provide distinct and important features of practices of domination and social regulation. These ideological categories of morality and politics help both to *explain* and to *mystify* the routine targeting of the practices of surveillance and regulation: explain because their surrounding, constitutive discourse tells us something about the specific offence; and mystify, because censures are often expressed in universalistic language which appeals to general moral principles.
>
> (Sumner, 1990: 35; my emphasis)

The press coverage of this incident indicated the extent to which the social censure against bestiality could be publicly constituted through expression of male hegemony. Under law it was required that the alleged act be investigated. However, the 'constitutive discourse' revealed,[4] through activating earlier practices of surveillance and regulation concerning women,[5] an assertion of ideological categories of morality and sexual politics grounded in male hegemony. The discourse which emerged revealed fundamental differences from other instances of bestiality reported in the press. This alleged incident involved women as opposed to men. It was carried out for financial gain and not sexual gratification.

The alleged incident of bestiality became a site of contest where male hegemony (Craig, 1992a; Croteau and Hoynes, 1992; Hanke, 1992) was asserted and through which individual women, women's bodies, and the body of Zimbabwean women could be castigated, contained and claimed (see McFadden, 1992). This discourse which discriminated against women (see Clark, 1992) also revealed that the state-controlled press did not give voice to women's organisations and repeatedly printed material which served to reconstitute the original assertion thereby revealing its editorial position (see Love and Morrison, 1991; Saunders, 1991). As the volume of published texts relating to the issue increased, it became clear that publications were uncertain how to critically handle such a taboo topic as bestiality and as a result exposed their own gender ideology.

THE FIRST ACCUSATION

Discriminatory discourse has been a central concern for Critical Discourse Analysis. As van Leeuwen (1993a) argues

> Critical discourse analysis is, or should be, concerned with . . . discourse as the instrument of power and control as well as with discourse as the instrument of the social construction of reality.
>
> (van Leeuwen, 1993a: 193)

The initial report functioned as the framing move (see e.g. Swales, 1992) for the generation of a discourse of discrimination which became possible because of three main features of the initial report. First, the topic was itself problematic. Commercial sex carried out by women had been widely covered in the press. Brief reports of convictions of men for acts of bestiality had also been reported in daily newspapers. However, bestiality involving women rather than men introduced an unknown dimension into an already taboo area. This became even more marked because it was allegedly instigated for the production of pornographic video material in a country with very strict censorship laws on pornography. Second, the allegation of such an incident even without material proof was in itself enough to generate the hybridisation of facticity and speculation typical of tabloid reporting (Fiske, 1992: 48). Third, the initial report was voiced from the position of a man who had been living with one of the women alleged to have taken part in the incident.

The resulting discourse created a fictional world (Sinclair, 1986) in which evaluation and judgement were constructed through a mixture of rumour, moralising and the characterisation of women as unclean, untrustworthy and guilty (see e.g. Frank, 1990; Gilman, 1985; Treichler, 1987). The status of the alleged event and the moralistic responses to it resulted in it being labelled a 'saga' and a 'parable' and indicated how such a discourse might need to be examined in terms similar to those Bowers and Iwi (1993) refer to in examining the relationships between discourse and the construction of 'society'. Bowers and Iwi draw on the work of Latour:

> in reconceiving society *performatively*, as the outcome of a multiplicity of struggles to define the social and make definitions endure. The suggestion we have from Latour is that society itself is constructed in these struggles which are happening '*now*, before our very eyes (Latour, 1986: 271)'.
>
> (Bowers and Iwi, 1993)

The labelling of the alleged incident condensed the processes through which that incident was reconstructed and regenerated in the context of a news environment in a 'developing country' in which rumour and oral discourse are significant means of communication.[6] The range of genres and the high level of intertextuality (Fairclough, 1992a; Lemke, 1985) in the corpus of fifty-nine verbal and visual texts related to the incident are indicative of the orders of discourse (Fairclough, 1989a) through which the incident was repositioned and the interdiscursivity of written and spoken discourse in the creation of news values.[7]

The initial text was entitled 'Inhuman sex acts: women arrested' and appeared in the *Sunday Mail*, 29 September 1991.[8] This text articulated many of the problems which would be reproduced in subsequent discourse but did not address these analytically. A distinction was not made between men as seekers of pleasure in paying for sex and female commercial sex workers as having to work to make a living, not pay for their own sexual gratification. As a result, it was not the employers – the men – but the women who faced criticism. The women were criticised for committing bestiality when it was the male clients who required it and a white man who arranged the video-recording.

Furthermore, the focus on the women drew attention away from the white man and magnified a discourse which negatively evaluated Zimbabwean women.

The headline identified women with bestiality by not naming bestiality itself, but thematising 'inhuman sex acts' thereby giving prominence to the judgement which followed. 'Women arrested' signalled the assigning of blame but also new information: bestiality involving women.

The first agentless clause 'In what can be described as a bizarre and inhuman sex activity' thematised the alleged event as 'bizarre and inhuman' and this evaluation was authenticated through reference to the police as having 'confirmed the arrest of some women'. Although arrests had been made only on the basis of allegations, the report nevertheless attributed blame to women (see Cameron, 1985; Clark, 1992). Women were also connected with bestiality in this opening paragraph, whereas the man who allegedly organised the event was introduced subsequently. The man allegedly involved is first described as 'the owner of the animal' and then later in parenthesis is presented as a white man. The police were positioned as having 'confirmed the arrest' of 'some women' before a statement of the problem was given. At this point the women were implicated in an alleged event which the 'Sunday Mail understands' to have taken place and which was presented in scare quotes as 'sex sessions'.

The attempt to present the report as a piece of objective journalism implied that there were grounds for the allegations but such a tactic obscures the source or sources behind the use of this mental process verb 'understands'. The reference to sources was delayed narratively to allow the writer to refer first to the taboo event which was described at first using euphemism. The acts of bestiality were referred to as sex sessions. The nature of the alleged acts was introduced through reference to the women being paid 'depending on the "quality" of performance'. The use of 'quality' of performance foregrounded the description of the physical details of the act which were given in a later paragraph and introduced to readers a speculation about the physicality and alleged value of the acts. Many readers, as subsequent texts would indicate, reacted in support of the seemingly objective reporting taken in this text, while the nature of their responses suggested that they had consumed the publication of material covering such a topic with considerable interest. In terms of news values, the 'novelty' of the alleged event appeared for the reporter to blur the boundaries between reporting the allegations and presenting them in terms of a sensationalist style of reporting which accentuated the 'novelty' and expressed a prurience in the details of the alleged physical act of bestiality.

The report implicitly accepted the likelihood of the event having occurred by referring to a police spokesperson who was reported as saying that the activity had been 'going on for some time'. The reiteration of 'police say' reinforced the first reporting of the views of the police. The mention that some of the women 'were still at large' strongly suggested that 'the other criminal women' had been brought under police control and that there was clear basis for that action. However, the man had not been located.

Rather than referring to the women for a statement, the writer then positioned the discourse according to the man who alleged that the incident had taken place. While this might be a reasonable move, this man is labelled 'A former boyfriend of one of the dog's "mistresses", a gardener in the suburb'. This served to contrast the man not only with the owner of the dog and by implication a lush garden, but also in relation to one of the women implicated. This phrase contained traces of the problems of the report: the premodification 'former' not only established the status of their relationship, but also prefigured the reasons for that status having arisen as is subsequently portrayed.

In addition, this man was presented as the 'wounded party' in the following string which introduced his testimony: 'A former boyfriend of one of the dog's "mistresses", a gardener in the suburb'. Not only was this man once connected with the woman, but also his occupation contrasts sharply with the white owner of the house and video equipment. This labelling suggested an attempt at irony: the journalist suggested infidelity, but the effect of this labelling was to accentuate the innocence of the man. The man as accuser had knowledge based on an intimate sexual relationship. This provided the physical and medical link for his allegation: the woman had given him a sexually transmitted disease which took months to heal. There was no question whether this man had other sexual partners. His version was presented as verifiable because he had extracted a confession from the woman, and, by implication, because he consulted the police to report the 'crime'. This provided him with the justification to describe the alleged acts and was used by the writer to provide details. His words were quoted in the article: 'I threw her out with her belongings when she went further to tell me that as part of the contract a women would first indulge in other unnatural sex acts with the dog before doing the "actual thing".' In particular he mentioned that the woman had reported to him that 'the dog's owner would put gloves on its forequarters to protect the women from being clawed during the session'. In addition to reporting this detail, the journalist also noted that the woman had mentioned to the aggrieved man that 'she had almost passed out after having an hour long session with the dog but she was given anti-depressants and some pain-killers'. This relating presented a man's perspective on an event of which he had knowledge only through the alleged 'confession' of his former partner. Details were given of the preparations for the sexual act itself thereby drawing readers into speculating about the mechanics of undertaking an act deviating from traditional sexual negotiation between men and women. The mentioning of the dog being made to wear gloves sensationalised the act itself in a way which had not occurred previously in the reporting of bestiality by men. Furthermore, mention was made of the duration of an alleged 'session' and that considerable pain had occurred for the women allegedly involved. No such details appeared in the reports relating to bestiality involving men for men's pleasure. Here, a woman needed both physical and chemical protection in order to go through with the alleged event in an attempt to earn money rather than sexual gratification.

Having provided details of the act, this man then referred to the way in which he had come to be labelled 'uncle of the dog' at his local drinking spot. This man presented himself as having been rejected and dispossessed by asking where he would now be able to buy his beer. His need for satisfaction had been displaced.

Only when the thematisation of the words, views and experience of this man as diseased through the fault of a woman had been established were the views of a woman presented. This woman was described as 'a friend of one of the women involved in the affair', thereby reinforcing the presupposition that this and other women took part. No premodification was used. Comment on the clothing of one woman was linked with the accounts of eyewitnesses, referred to only as 'some' and not according to gender, who had seen the women smartly dressed. The women's friend commented that 'All I used to ask her was where she was getting the money to buy her expensive dresses and make-up.' The implication was that these women were poor and that such goods might well have been financed through prostitution.

In the penultimate paragraph this depiction of the woman was reasserted in the following clause:

> The women, according to some residents, were over a long period seen by beerhall patrons in the suburb's shopping centre smartly dressed, waiting for the man or his gardener to pick them up.

The women are 'smartly dressed' implying that they have 'dressed up' – prefigured in the earlier description of the 'gloves'. However, this view is attributed to 'some residents' whose eyewitness accounts extend only as far as reporting who collected the women. Perhaps 'pick them up' was used neutrally, but given the tone of the text, connotations of sexual exchange cannot be entirely ignored.

The final move in the article presented the alleged event within the context of sexual negotiation: 'The women were understood to be shunning men in the suburb, saying they had better offers elsewhere.' The implication here was that the women were 'prostitutes' and that men in the area felt that they had been rejected by the women for more lucrative acts of commercial sex. However, this move presented the problems of voice which were to appear in later texts. It was not necessarily the case that women uttered this themselves or whose view was being presented. The *Sunday Mail* therefore closed with its own semblance of objectivity.

TRIAL BY MEDIA

The initial report mixed allegations of fact with evaluation of the alleged event, but the text nevertheless presented two accused parties – the women and the white man. However, prominence was given to the women. The negative labelling of women and the assigning of blame established in this initial text were re-articulated in the variety of texts which appeared in newspapers and magazines. Selected examples are given below. As Mawerera (*Africa South*, December 1991: 50) later argued, men structured the discourse relating to the incident and thereby articulated their hegemony. Women were not allowed to voice their comments in the initial report and this was largely perpetuated in the 'saga' which followed:

> The attacks have been primarily by men, who have the high-profile jobs on mass-circulation newspapers. The women have been rendered impotent by their lack of an effective public voice: they are, in the context of the debate, virtually speechless.

Many of the published texts were letters to the editor (see Love and Morrison, 1993).

One letter writer presented women as deceptive and unclean in commenting that he had always suspected that behind those dainty looks, and behind that insatiable craving for stylish cultures which are not entirely known, there must be some cunning and insanitary behaviour which cannot be detected easily, and I was right.

('Shameless harlots of Borrowdale', *Chronicle*, 5 October 1991)[9]

Furthermore, this writer equated the behaviour of the women with that of dogs, saying that they were 'wagging their bottoms like dogs'. The writer continued his invective through over-lexicalisation:

If you think of women's merry talk, pathetic absurdities, women's whims, and female foibles that we have heard of before, nothing has been as infuriating as the behaviour of these smothered harlots of Borrowdale.

This writer also found it necessary to moralise, introducing the first of several Christian references in adjudging: 'Although I do not attend church, I am seriously considering doing that now, so that when God destroys this world of shameless fornicators, I could be spared.'

In another letter to the editor, 'What a disgrace' commented:

It is unfortunate that a male member of our society contracted a venereal disease from one of these prostitutes (maybe the appropriate term is 'bitch' in this case, since a dog is involved). I sympathise with him because he was unsuspecting.

Here, the women were directly called prostitutes, but the man was 'unsuspecting', and therefore presented as innocent. In addition, the woman was labelled 'bitch', an informal term used by men in Zimbabwe to refer to female commercial sex workers. This writer then mentioned that the man might have had to 'maintain a "litter" of up to twelve "babies", (should I say puppies?)'. This writer inverted his discrimination against women by presenting men as the 'real victims' when he commented that, 'What disturbs me most is that if women can have relations with dogs for money, will they ever stop victimising men when it comes to claiming maintenance.'

Metaphor was used to reposition the discourse in an attempt to satirise claims for their rights by women. In 'Get the dog's side' (C: 15 October 1991), 'The Wag' attempted to satirise the issue in asking why the dog had not been consulted, whether it was over the age of consent and how it had been enticed into 'starring'. This further marginalised the way in which women had been presented, and revealed a fascination with the physical details of the alleged event. Reference was made to the original description of the alleged act, once again visually taking readers back to the 'scene of the crime', but also linking the description of the apparel of the alleged participants with the Economic Structural Adjustment

Programme: 'Fashion also entered into this quagmire. No more fishnet nylons and suspender belts, but a mere pair of gloves. Does this indicate the effects of ESAP?'

A letter entitled 'Shocking story' (C: 12 October 1991) was evidence of the extent to which the event was presented in terms of two metaphors of economic exploitation. The writer judged the white man as most culpable. He referred to a colonial 'master–servant' relationship and that of the newly instigated economic reform programme in describing the dog as having 'succumbed to the wishes of its white master and the nearest Ever Servicing African Prostitute (ESAP)'. This re-lexicalisation of the acronym of the World Bank–IMF programme indicates the extent to which the incident was re-articulated in terms of wider economic structures. The writer drew further on idiom in asking, 'Is this what they meant by a man's best friend being his dog?' and signed the letter 'Bosopo Lo Inja' (Beware of the dog), parodying the sign frequently used on the gates of white suburban homes prior to Independence and which still remain a feature of suburbia in Zimbabwe.

'They were victimised' (C: 22 October 1991), written by 'Dog Eat Dog', used the incident to comment on the nature of racism and capitalism. The writer imaged the role of race in the hierarchy of the society in 'We still see whites driving their vehicle with a dog in front while a black person sits in the back of the truck.' The author closed the letter by saying that people who blamed the women were 'not aware of how in one way or the other they too continue to be victimised by a racist capitalist system whose motto is Dog Eat Dog'. Other than these letters, little comment was made about the lack of identity of the white man and the inability of police to locate him.

A competing discourse between women and the state press emerged. 'Wag sees red' (SM: 3 November 1991) reported a protest demonstration by the Women's Action Group (WAG) and others against the reporting by the *Sunday Mail*. The report presented for the first time the comments and criticisms of women as a group rather than the views of individual women which had appeared in articles and letters. The women were reported as condemning the paper for printing a page of 'letters insulting and defamatory to women'. In a counter-move, the paper set about containing this critique in saying it had published letters opposed to the incident. It then quoted Minister Mahachi as saying that: 'With the evidence already in hand, there is no use denying or trying to hide that the women did commit an act of bestiality as alleged.' This prior judgement contributed to the continued publication of material.

The accompanying editorial 'Let sleeping dogs lie' (SM: 3 November 1991) specifically presented the rationale for running the intitial report and denied that the original report had aimed to 'hold women up to contempt' and went on to 'condemn the barking men just as we condemn those women and men who are pressuring us to be silent'.[10] The editorial continued to argue for right of publication: 'We also discern in their attitude, determined efforts to manipulate, terrorise and intimidate the media into silence over issues they may regard as taboo.' The paper's judgement was presented as refined in the tone of the verb selected: 'discern'. The editorial asked whose interests the organisations were serving with reference to the bestiality issue. It also argued that the paper had broken the story because 'we sincerely believed we were fighting a possible evil which had the hallmarks of degrading Zimbabweans'. In contrast to this self-defined crusading role, the editorial evaluated the criticisms of the women's groups as follows:

> The attitude we are encountering instead, is that we should let sleeping dogs lie. This is most unfortunate because we could never have imagined the press in this country which was free to hound glorious figures in the history of the liberation of this country should come under pressure from some women, to cover up for dogs.

This assertion of freedom of the press from a state-run newspaper needs to be seen in the light of its not having given space for the views and responses of women's organisations and representatives to be voiced. Once again, lexis – 'hound' – was transferred from the discourse relating to the alleged incident to justify the action of the national press. The national press was now in a position to 'hound' the responses of women to an issue which had been extended by the media to refer to the body of women in Zimbabwe. At no point was there comment on the manner of reporting and the terms used to refer to women. Everjoyce Win, the then head of the Women's Action Group, commented on the position of women in the news:

> women do not make news. At least not ordinary women. It is raped women who usually make news on page 6 or 7. Or the occasional woman who can dose a cow in front of the Minister of Agriculture who makes it to page one.
>
> (*Parade*, December 1991: 74–5)

In response to the reports of the 'Borrowdale saga', as she labelled it, Win commented that 'women want to tell their own story' rather than have it articulated for them by newspapers which did not represent their views and argued that 'morals depend on who is defining them'.

The three cartoons which appeared in the state-controlled press reinforced the labelling and stereotyping of verbal texts (see e.g. McLoughlin, 1989; Wernick, 1991). Each of the cartoons incorporated images of women which positioned them as objects of ridicule.

The first cartoon (*People's Voice*, 6–12 October 1991) presented two male dogs in the guise of popular images of criminals.[11] One of these dog-criminals clearly has its tongue hanging out and is wagging its tail at three women who are walking by. The three women are stereotype images of prostitutes with short skirts, high heels and permed hair. Two of the women are imaged as wearing heavy make-up. One of the women is showing her navel and is wearing fishnet stockings, the second woman wears a T-shirt reading 'Zvino naka zvinodhura' (Taste now, pay now), while the third woman has long and painted fingernails. The caption 'No matter how much money they have girls, let's stick to human beings' could be attributed to one of the women in the cartoon, but also echoes the voice of the editorial in the same issue of this paper. The women are imaged as 'prostitutes' and the implication is that they should stick to male human partners, and presumably be paid by them.

Following a march by women's organisations protesting the coverage in the press of the alleged incident, a cartoon was published in the largest selling daily newspaper (*Herald*, 4 November 1991).[12] This cartoon contrasted a female journalist in business suit, with notebook and high heels with a large, aggressive woman with hairy legs and laced-up shoes. Such was the response of the leading daily to an organised protest by women against the style of reporting and continued publication of material which they claimed discriminated against women. The paper's presentation of its own sense of 'professionalism' through such gender imaging does not sit comfortably with the images of the women allegedly involved in the act of bestiality presented in the first cartoon and the one which followed.

The third cartoon incorporated the negative presentation of women in the first cartoon and sought to reinforce the position that the *Sunday Mail* had taken in response to the organised protest by women (SM: 10 November 1991).[13] In this cartoon a group of women have set their dogs upon the male embodiment of the *Sunday Mail*. This man is placed at the centre of the cartoon. With his large stomach emblazoned with the newspaper's name, he is lifted on to the tips of his two-tone shoes by the act of spearing an attacking dog with a sabre.

A second sabre, raised above his head, has broken in two. This defender has behind him four women who are crying out, presumably against the four dogs who are being encouraged to attack by the three women who are on the opposite side of the picture. Three of the women crying for defence are dressed in miniskirts and are wearing extremely high stiletto heels. The women encouraging the dogs to attack are led by a woman in a miniskirt, dark stockings and high heels. She is carrying a small handbag and has three dogs around her feet. It appears to be daylight. These women are visually and narratively linked with the women of the original report and the discourse through and in which they were discriminated against. It is therefore no surprise that the man in the cartoon is defending another group of women, presumably the virtuous women of the nation, from the dogs set loose by the 'other' group of women. This tableau reveals the way in which a process of rearticulation took place. The women protesting the reporting by the *Sunday Mail* were now equated with the women alleged to have been involved in the original incident. The newspaper is now the moral defender.

Relationships between gender and bestiality were discussed in the only piece of serious and analytical journalism to appear in newspapers which was entitled 'Bestiality – "let's put on some brakes" ' (*Sunday Times*, 13 October 1991). Simomo Mubi, female host of a television discussion show, acknowledged that the incident may have taken place for monetary gain, but related the incident to other instances of bestiality involving men for which convictions had been obtained. She was the only writer to refer to a legal expert in her analysis. Geoff Feltoe, a specialist in criminal law, differentiated the case from others involving men and was quoted by Mubi as follows: 'If the facts of the incident as reported in the Press are proven, then this particular case is unique and entirely different from other bestiality crimes which tend to occur for perverse sexual gratification.' This key distinction – between sexual gratification on the part of men and economic need on the part of the women – was not examined in the state press. Instances of bestiality involving men were reported as legal judgments without journalistic evaluation.

Four legal judgments relating to bestiality were reported in the press in the nine months between the initial report and the report of the legal judgment relating to the case. The first concerned two women who had been assaulted by two men and three referred to convictions of men for acts of bestiality. 'Two women beaten "over dog affair" ' (H: 30 October 1991) related a judgment of assault of two women by two men. The women alleged that they had been called 'women of dogs' when they refused to listen to commands the men had made to them. While admitting they had assaulted the women, the men did not agree that they had hit them with bricks nor accused them of bestiality as the women had argued. This matter was also reported in the *Sunday News* (3 November 1991). Neither paper chose to comment any further on the matter. There was no statement about the condition of the morals of the nation. Comment from legal, human rights or women's groups were not included. This incident and judgment were not discussed in any further newspaper texts. Two legal convictions relating to bestiality appeared (H: 20 December 1991 and *Mutare Post*, 25 December 1991). The first reported the conviction of a 17-year-old male domestic worker who admitted he had committed an act of bestiality with his employer's dog 'out of curiosity' and had been witnessed by the employer's son. The second report was of the conviction of a man for an act of bestiality with a dog. This man also admitted he had committed such an act. He was named and described as a 'father of four' and his age (53) given. In both cases the reports were presented in legalistic language and only the facts and legal judgment given. There was no statement about the number of such incidents in the year, nor any discussion of morality in terms voiced earlier in relation to women. The reports of legal judgments are notable for their lack of context and commentary. A decision by the court was presented and left to stand on its own terms without evaluation by the journalist.

Evaluation did appear in magazines and due to their publication after a considerable number of letters and articles had appeared in newspapers, they were able to view the alleged with a certain element of cynicism although this was not always successfully crafted. The comment column in *Horizon* (December 1991: 50) was entitled 'Beware of the shaggy dog' with the subheading '... and newshounds who bark up the wrong tree'.[14] In addition to this play on words, the columnist attempted to undercut the credibility of the incident through what may have been intended as humorous reference to the physical unlikelihood of the sexual act ever having taken place.

> A dog is a noble creature that certainly is not going to jump all over a $150 hooker just because she gets down on her hands and knees. More to the point, a dog's arousal response is triggered by smell and though a $150 hooker may smell pretty bad if she has been standing out in the hot sun all day, it is not the right sort of smell.

Although the writer questioned the credibility of the entire event, the woman involved was given a premodifying price tag and was labelled 'hooker' and was degraded in the way in which the dog was presented as unlikely to disregard its instinctual sense of arousal. The woman was further humiliated by the way in which she was imaged as 'down on her hands and knees'. The use of 'just' both trivialised the woman and obscured the likely economic reason for a woman to have been a part of such an act, should this incident ever have occurred. This quotation also revealed interest in the physicality of the alleged act itself. The writer went even further, though, in presenting the dog as 'noble' by placing the woman in the sun and reducing her to a bad odour. In so doing, the writer incorporated other male prejudices in the labelling of women as 'meat' and here implied that the woman was rotten. This magazine has a good reputation as an alternative and analytical monthly and this article suggests the extent to which the unusual nature of the alleged bestiality involving women drew forth an unsavoury mixture of interest and unfounded judgement.

THE FINAL JUDGEMENT

After December 1991 the 'story' was no longer newsworthy and dropped out of the public gaze. In the *Weekend Gazette* (10 July 1992) the legal outcome of the case was finally made public.[15]

The narrative sequence of events relating to the alleged incident was not reported in this final text. There was presupposition that readers knew the legal procedures which had been followed. The report concerned charges being dropped against a man who had 'spread the rumour'; no link was made for readers as to how a charge was laid against the man rather than the women who had been 'cross-examined' in the press. The text used formulaic legal language and contrasted markedly with the sensationalist tone of the text which had initiated the 'news event'. This highlighted that an apocryphal story had been created and believed because it reinforced the very stereotypes it evoked.

The final text related how the woman had moved out of the room she was renting from the man after he had demanded sex as a condition to her keeping the room without payment. When the woman refused this demand, the man had allegedly spread the story as originally cited. Police investigations 'revealed that the woman did not have venereal disease, and that neither the white man nor the dogs existed'. However, the woman did exist. It is implied that she underwent a different kind of 'investigation' as a result of the allegations. Not only were the allegations shown to be malicious rumours, but also the woman is reported as not having venereal disease. The implications are twofold: first, that she asserted this herself and was believed, and second, and more sinisterly, that she was made to undergo medical examination. These implications are all the general readership had for information. This, therefore, reinforced the pattern of the earlier discourse in denying women their own voice and presenting them, even in the final published judgment, as potential sites for disease. It is as if the woman's innocence finally rested on the rights of others to determine whether she was of sound body. Given this imaging of the woman, it is not surprising that the article did not comment in any way about the discrimination against this woman and other women of Zimbabwe. Comments from women's organisations were absent in this article.

Mawerera was the only writer who explicitly noted that the man alleged to be involved in the case seemed to have been forgotten (*Africa South*, December 1991: 50). He also labelled the media event as a parable, thus highlighting its moral yet fictional status:

> Whatever the truth behind it may be, Zimbabwe's parable of five foolish women, a wicked man and a dog must stand as a lesson that the activities of a handful can be used as mud to throw at the whole. Society is quick to condemn and slow to learn or change. Our bestiality scandal bears sad witness to this fact.

An attempt to enter into a 'popular' style of journalism can result, as Sparks (1988; 1992) suggests, in reactionary discourse which defeats the intention of challenging boundaries and conventions of staid institutionalised forms of reporting and publication. Whereas Zimbabwean politicians have been strong advocates of media in which Africans are not negatively stereotyped, the construction through the media of this alleged instance of bestiality is a testament to a self-inflicted negative representation and imaging of Zimbabwean women.

In a time of severe drought and changing economic policies, this incident became a metonymic frame for the emergence of discourse moves motivated by other areas of conflict and uncertainty (Fairclough, 1992b). Particularly in the letters to the editor, writers expressed concern at the state of morals in the country. They shifted the focus of the initial report to commentary on the conditions and constraints of the economic structural adjustment programme. Writers also drew on the incident as a means of commenting on racism in the society, although on the basis of all reported material the white man who allegedly arranged the videotaping was not identified. The topic bestiality and the alleged involvement of women motivated writers to produce a variety of speculations and judgements and the publication of such speculative material suggested that the mainstream press was operating at odds with professed social and legal policy advocating improved working and living conditions for women. That such material continued to be written by readers and was then printed and again consumed by readers suggests that there was interest in such a taboo topic which went beyond the specific allegations.

In attempting to analyse the construction of discrimination in these texts it has become clear that Critical Discourse Analysis needs to delve more deeply into news media in which the interrelationships between verbal, visual and spoken discourse are complex (see e.g. Morrison, 1993) and where established notions of tabloid and objective reporting are intermingled with rumour and moral judgement. This is particularly important in development-oriented contexts where communication strategies for the creation, circulation and evaluation of news draw on performative dimensions of oral discourse and principles of formal, written news discourse (Fowler, 1991).

Since the early 1990s, the press in Zimbabwe has become increasingly critical of the performance of both the public and the private sector. As the material suggests, the incident became not only a site of contest concerning gender, but also an indicator of how a sexually taboo topic came to be presented and evaluated in state-supported newspapers and privately owned magazines. Inter-textuality between spoken and written discourse contributed to this evaluation. Speculation, rumour and the visual rearticulation of the alleged event occurred in the absence of material evidence. This resulted in the production and reproduction of a discourse in the press which frequently negatively evaluated women while at the same time sidestepping the occurrence of bestiality involving men discoursally which was contained in legal reporting. There was no mention

246 Texts and practices

of the potential legal actions which might be considered on the part of the woman and no commentary or comparison with the occurrence of bestiality committed by men for sexual gratification or curiosity.[16]

ACKNOWLEDGEMENT

I am grateful for suggestions and comments from Hilde Arntsen, Everjoyce Win, Alison Love, David Kaulem, Edward Antonio, Jennifer Mohamed, Julie Stewart and the editors.

NOTES

1 Saunders (1991) documents in detail the mass media in Zimbabwe in the first decade of Independence.
2 *Sunday Mail*, 29 September 1991.
3 In Zimbabwean law bestiality is defined as 'Unlawful and intentional vaginal or anal intercourse with an animal' (Feltoe, 1989).
4 Bowers and Iwi (1993: 389) comment on the way in which the assertion of the notion of 'society' may result in an embodiment of society:

> An argument is a heterogeneous textual assembly with many different kinds of element associated with one another. If the associations stay in place or – better still – multiply in number, the rhetoric may be convincing. If the associations are weak and can easily be broken, it may not be. Either way what is being offered through the deployment of 'society' is a set of associations which if found convincing and acted in accordance with could be(come) society.

5 The imaging and construction of women as bearers of disease (Frank, 1990; Gilman, 1985) has been significant in shaping the experience of women both before and after Independence. Jackson (1991) has traced the way in which the construct of the 'stray woman' was employed in Rhodesia as a means of containing black women both economically and culturally within the colonial system. Single or unmarried women were subjected to laws which restricted their physical movement (Schmidt, 1991) and which provided the state with the means to examine them for venereal disease. As has been documented in the portrayal of women in Zimbabwean literature (Gaidzanwa, 1985), individual women standing outside the scope of traditional family structures, particularly in urban areas, were seen as contaminated and thus threats to moral and physical health. The 'clean-up' campagins of the 1980s revealed how this construct was extended to seeing 'stray women' as prostitutes, and prostitutes as deviants who threaten both the physical and moral fabric of the nation with disease.
6 Critical discourse studies have been concerned with both process and product in news discourse (Bell, 1991; Fowler, 1991; van Dijk, 1988; 1991a; 1991b) but have yet to seriously deconstruct the formation and operation of news values in the production of news discourse in a context where oral communication channels are still an important means of conveying information (see Melkote, 1992).
7 The material on which this chapter is based was drawn from both the state-controlled and the private press between 29 September and 24 November 1991,

with one final article appearing on 10 July 1992. The topic was covered in the October and December 1991 issues of the major national magazines. Newspapers contained seventeen articles, three editorials, twenty-two letters and seven cartoons. Magazines carried six articles, one editorial, one letter and one cartoon.

8 The Zimbabwe Newspapers group refused permission for this text to be reprinted for research purposes. Hereafter the *Sunday Mail* is referred to as 'SM'.

9 Hereafter referred to as 'C'.

10 There were several reported instances of men barking at women from car and bus windows.

11 The *People's Voice* is the newspaper of the political party in office.

12 Hereafter referred to as 'H'.

13 Permission to reproduce this cartoon for research purposes was denied by Zimbabwe Newspapers.

14 *Horizon* is one of few magazines in the country which has a reputation for investigative journalism.

15 The *Weekend Gazette* is a new paper, part of a 'stable' of independent papers which are privately owned and which have begun to compete with the leading government newspapers.

16 The woman's claim to legal compensation (defamation, iniuria, malicious prosecution) would depend on whether it could be shown that her identity had been established. As she was not named in the press, her action would be contestable.

REFERENCES

Bell, A. (1991) *The Language of the News Media*, Oxford: Blackwell.

Bowers, J. and Iwi, K. (1993) 'The discursive construction of society', *Discourse and Society*, 4, 3, 357–93.

Cameron, D. (1985) *Feminism and Linguistic Theory*, London: Macmillan.

Clark, K. (1992) 'The linguistics of blame: representations of women in *The Sun*'s reporting of crimes of sexual violence', in M. Toolan (ed.) *Language, Text and Context*, London: Routledge, 208–24.

Craig, S. (1992a) 'Considering men and the media', in S. Craig (ed.) *Men, Masculinity and the Media*, London: Sage, 1–7.

Croteau, D. and Hoynes, W. (1992) 'Men and the news media: the male presence and its effects', in S. Craig (ed.) *Men, Masculinity and the Media*, London: Sage, 154–67.

Fairclough, N. (1989a) *Language and Power*, London: Longman.

Fairclough, N. (1992a) 'Discourse and text: linguistic and intertextual analysis within discourse analysis', *Discourse and Society*, 3, 2, 193–217.

Fairclough, N. (1992b) *Discourse and Social Change*, Cambridge: Polity.

Feltoe, G. (1989) *A Guide to Zimbabwean Criminal Law*, Harare: Zimbabwean Legal Resources Foundation.

Fiske, J. (1992) 'Popularity and the politics of information', in P. Dahlgren and C. Sparks (eds) *Journalism and Popular Culture*, London: Sage, 45–63.

Fowler, R. (1991) *Language in the News: Discourse and Ideology in the Press*, London: Routledge.

Frank, A. (1990) 'Bringing bodies back: a decade review', *Media, Culture and Society* 7, 131–62.

Gaidzanwa, R. (1985) *Images of Women in Zimbabwean Literature*, Harare: College Press.

Gilman, S. (1985) *Difference and Pathology: Stereotypes of Sexuality, Race and Madness*, Ithaca, NY: Cornell University Press.

Hanke, R. (1992) 'Redesigning men: hegemonic masculinity in transition', in S. Craig (ed.) *Men, Masculinity and the Media*, London: Sage, 185–98.

Heng, G. and Devan, J. (1992) 'State fatherhood: the politics of nationalism, sexuality and race in Singapore', in A. Parker, M. Russo, D. Sommer and P. Yaeger (eds) *Nationalisms and Sexualities*, New York: Routledge, 343–64.

Jackson, J. (1992) 'Honesty in investigative journalism', in A. Belsey and R. Chadwick (eds) *Ethical Issues in Journalism and the Media*, London: Routledge, 93–111.

Jackson, L. (1991) '"Stray Women" on the colonial mind: African women and the disease metaphor in colonial Zimbabwe 1890–1949', MS, Department of Sociology, University of Zimbabwe.

Latour, B. (1986) 'The powers of association', in J. Law (ed.) *Power, Action and Belief: A New Sociology of Knowledge*, Sociological Review Monograph 32, London: Routledge & Kegan Paul.

Lemke, J. L. (1985) 'Ideology, intertextuality, and the notion of register', in J. D. Benson and W. S. Greaves (eds) *Systemic Perspectives on Discourse, vol. 1*, Norwood, NJ: Ablex, 275–94.

Love, A. and Morrison, A. (1991) 'Readers' obligations: an examination of some features of Zimbabwean newspaper editorials', *English Language Research Journal*, University of Birmingham, 3, 137–72.

Love, A. and Morrison, A. (1993) ' "Now the question is . . .": questions in letters to the editor in two Zimbabwean magazines in 1990', paper presented at 10th Congress of the International Association of Applied Linguistics (AILA), Amsterdam, August.

McFadden, P. (1992) 'Sex, sexuality and problems of AIDS in Africa', in R. Meena (ed.) *Gender and Ideology*, Harare: Sapes, 157–95.

McLoughlin, T. O. (1989) 'The comic strip and Zimbabwe's development', in E. A. Ngara and A. Morrison (eds) *Literature, Language and the Nation*, Harare: Baobab, 120–9.

Melkote, S. (1992) *Development Communication*, London: Sage.

Morrison, A. (1993) 'Some observations on news photography in Zimbabwe', in H. Arnsten (ed.) *Media, Culture and Development*, I, Oslo: University of Oslo, 137–54.

Saunders, R. (1991) 'Information in the Interregnum: the press, state and civil society in struggles for hegemony, Zimbabwe 1980–1990', unpub. PhD, Carleton University, Ontario, Canada.

Schmidt, E. (1991) 'Patriarchy, capitalism, and the colonial state in Zimbabwe', *SIGNS*, 16, 4.

Sinclair, J. McH. (1986) 'Fictional worlds', in R. M. Coulthard (ed.) *Talking about Text*, Discourse Analysis Monographs, 13, English Language Research, University of Birmingham, 43–60.

Sparks, C. (1988) 'The popular press and political democracy', *Media, Culture and Society*, 10, 209–23.

Sparks, C. (1992) 'Popular journalism: theories and practice', in P. Dahlgren and C. Sparks (eds) *Journalism and Popular Culture*, London: Sage, 24–44.

Stewart, J. and Armstrong, A. (eds) (1990) *The Legal Situation of Women in Southern Africa*, Harare: University of Zimbabwe Publications.

Sumner, C. (1990) 'Rethinking deviance: towards a sociology of censure', in C. Sumner (ed.) *Censure, Politics and Criminal Justice*, Milton Keynes: Open University Press.

Swales, J. (1992) 'Genre and engagement', paper presented at conference on

Discourse and the Professions, Uppsala, July.

Threadgold, T. (1989) 'Talking about genre: ideologies and incompatible discourses', *Cultural Studies*, 3, 1, 101–27.

Treichler, P. (1987) 'Aids, homophobia and biomedical discourse: an epidemic of signification', *Cultural Studies*, 1, 3, 263–305.

van Dijk, T. (1988) *News as Discourse*, Hillsdale, NJ: Erlbaum.

van Dijk, T. (1991a) *Racism and the Press*, London: Routledge.

van Dijk, T. (1991b) 'The interdisciplinary study of news as discourse', in K. B. Jensen and N. W. Jankowski (eds) *A Handbook of Qualitative Methodologies for Mass Communication Research*, London: Routledge, 108–20.

van Leeuwen, T. (1993a) 'Genre and field in Critical Discourse Analysis: a synopsis', *Discourse and Society*, 4, 2, 193–225.

Wernick, A. (1991) '(Re-)imaging gender: the case of men', in A. Wernick, *Promotional Culture*, London: Sage, 47–66.

Chapter 14

'Women who pay for sex. And enjoy it'

Transgression versus morality in women's magazines

Carmen Rosa Caldas-Coulthard

Women's magazines are increasingly the object of critical sociological and cultural analysis (Ballaster *et al.*, 1991; Ferguson, 1983; McCracken, 1993; Winship, 1987). As mass culture texts they are pervasive in modern societies, and, as the studies prove, are a continuing presence in many women's lives. They have a highly important role in the maintenance of cultural values, since they construct an 'ideal' reader who is at the same time both produced and in a sense imprisoned by the text.

I examine here, from a textual perspective, a very popular genre in women's magazines: first-person narratives concerned with one of the most private parts of the private life – sex. Giddens argues that sexuality is essential to the 'regime of truth', and texts about sexuality are seen as a form of access to the truth: 'since women are historically linked to the private world, sexuality as a topic is directly connected to women's "truth"' (Giddens, 1992: 30). The real self is the self revealed in personal intimacy and in the modern women's magazines this real self is understood as sexual behaviour.

The personal narratives I concentrate on provide an entrance point to the lives of others, exactly because they deal with sex. They are there to provoke a vicarious participation, since most of them are about transgression. Voyeurism is an opportunity to see the 'truth' of someone else's life.

I want to argue that writers create, through first-person testimonies, a fictionalised world that helps to construct and maintain a contradictory ideology of femininity and sexuality. First-person narratives project a fallacious idea of modernity, which as McCracken suggests, 'covers up a system of domination and praises tradition and accepted values' (1993: 37). In mass culture, as Jameson (1981) points out, there is a compensatory exchange process, where people are offered a series of gratifications in return for their passivity. The cultural forms touch on, but at the same time neutralise, social problems.

I also argue, by focusing on the narrative analysis categories of orientation and evaluation, that the narrator, although apparently transgressive, in fact reinforces moral values in the report of her sexual practices. Women's magazines ultimately reaffirm traditional views of the role of women in society. Through evaluative structures that link positive images to ideas of inadequate and insecure women, these texts put an emphasis on themes of social asymmetries. Transgressive pleasure and social punishment are closely associated.

READING PLEASURE: CONTRASTS AND CONTRADICTIONS

Women's magazines are enjoyed daily by thousands of people who enthusiastically read them in their private spaces or in such public places as doctors' surgeries, hairdressers' salons, baby clinics and dental waiting-rooms. The glossy monthly *Marie Claire* (the magazine from which I extracted the texts for analysis here) was first published in France, but now appears in twenty-two separate country editions and according to its Brazilian editor, Sergio Vaz (personal communication), *Marie Claire* is now read by 10 million people worldwide each month. The English editor, Glenda Bailey, says that people enjoy *Marie Claire* (MC) because

> we are a magazine of contrasts and contradictions. We do not stereo-type women as interested either in the way they look or what is going on in the world. We know most women are interested in both. The MC reader is a little older and wiser than some and if she's reading about men's sex lives for example, she wants to hear it as it is. The women who buy our magazine want to read something they've never read before, *with a fresh approach*. If it's new and it's sexual we should have it.
> (Interviewed by Lisa O'Kelley, *Guardian*, 6 January 1993; my emphasis)

Reading women's magazines involves an undeniable number of pleasures of participation and action. Indeed it is very difficult to resist reading them because they deal with women's lives and desires, they show ideal bodies, represent ideal careers and ideal relationships. They also offer advice and hope through many voices which range from topic specialists to the person like 'you and me' – the 'I' narrator.

They are targeted at a particular audience – women. This reflects the conventional division of periodical genres along gender lines. Newspaper analysts claim that journalistic reporting is based on factuality and analytical forms of reporting and therefore produces texts basically written for men (see Caldas-Coulthard, 1992; 1993). Women's magazines, by contrast, are characteristically 'female' because of the emphasis on the ideal and emotive novelisation of events. They report on individual experiences women can easily identify with. Narrative (mostly fictional) and procedural structures are the forms most frequently chosen to convey femininity. A problem here, however, is that magazines, since their first appearance in the late seventeenth century in England, address women readers as if they were a homogeneous group with similar practices, shared experiences and patterns of behaviour. A set of images and representations construct an imaginary world and an ideal reader which is basically heterosexual, white and middle class, in other words, women who are interested in and can afford to buy the goods offered.

'Men' are constructed as the natural opposite. As Ballaster *et al.* suggest (1991: 9), in all magazines, 'there is an evident tension between the need to confirm the centrality and desirability of men in all women's lives and the equally insistent recognition of men as a problem for and threat to women'. Although the two sexes are always struggling, they are always also in pursuit of each other. Winship (1987: 6) points out that these divides mark the boundaries of femininity and masculinity in the culture. She suggests that 'those versions of two genders are still profoundly influential in our experiences of growing up'.

In essence, women's magazines are attractive to women because they are about being female and about the problems of being female. Femininity is presented in texts that are easy to process and interpret. Visual pleasure is stimulated through beautiful pictures of people and things. In fact, lots of people buy the magazines just to look at the pictures. The contents are diversified and cater for many tastes. Winship says that reading can engross readers in different ways:

> It is either the peeping at the lives and loves of the rich and famous or at the disasters of the less fortunate, it can be the pleasurable conversation with a friend, or the identification with heroines whose problems satisfyingly unfold and are resolved. The contents can mentally stimulate or excite creativity, but magazines are bought primarily for relaxation.
>
> (Winship, 1987: 52)

Textual expectations are set up for the issues yet to come, and the different magazines create and select a loyal group of readers. The monthly issues have the same structural format with the same set agenda for internal sections. The presentation and continuity in format are powerful persuasive strategies which subtly persuade the faithful to buy more of the same. *Marie Claire*, for instance, has a fixed structure made up of eight major features:

1 Reportage – an article inspired by women's daily lives in other cultures
2 Profile – a celebrity interview
3 Emotional – a writer is commissioned to interview people about an emotional situation

4 Society – a slice of the social life
5 First person – a raw first-hand account of something that has happened to someone
6 Designer profile – a fashion story
7 Life stories – a mini-biography of a famous dead person
8 Review section – films, books, music, etc.

Although the magazines differ in content, narrative, as represented by first-person accounts or biographies, is, as we can see from the list above, crucial in defining what it is to be female. Most important of all, projected personas, like the Cosmo Girl, are created and based on the agendas and definitions set up by the magazines. The readers should aim to be like her.

Apart from the undeniable pleasure, reading a magazine is an institutionalised and rule-governed practice which is essentially conflictive. Magazines are bearers of particular discourses of femininity (maternity, domesticity and beauty), but they also present a combination of other discourses (apparently feminist, progressive and mainly transgressive). The more traditional magazines (like *Woman's Own* and *Women's Weekly*, for example) work with a definition of femininity which constructs women as passive and preoccupied with personal and individual achievements. The rhetoric of romance underlines and structures them. The topics without exception situate women either in the domestic sphere or in close proximity to it. The concept of femininity offered is bound to family ideals of affection, loyalty and obligation and domestic production or housekeeping. That is why features on cookery, decoration and motherhood are present in most of these texts.

In the newer glossy ones (*Cosmopolitan, New Woman, Marie Claire, Vogue, Elle*), on the other hand, there seems to have been an acceptance and incorporation of some basic feminist and liberal principles: there is some criticism of misogyny and prejudice, and women are encouraged to stand up for their rights. The conservative discourse of separate spheres between men and women and of female passivity, however, continue to coexist with a liberal discourse of the independent woman. Sexuality, as the textual analysis will demonstrate, is constructed both by a Christian discourse of distaste and fear which makes sex dangerous and punishable, and by progressive discourses which construct sex as autonomous from other forms of relationship such as love and friendship. Domesticity, however, is defined through the home as the feminine place. There is an insistence that women's primary duty and orientation is to men.

Magazines are based on paradoxes. While their main purpose is to inform and entertain, they also function as a commercial vehicle. Ballaster *et al.* (1991) suggest that the magazine is at the same time a medium for the sale of commodities to an identifiable market group, women, and itself [sic] a commodity, a product sold in the capitalist market place for profit. It is also a text, a set of images and representations which construct an imaginary world and an imaginary reader.

(Ballaster *et al.*, 1991: 2)

Entertainment is constructed by this media discourse as inextricably bound up with consumption. The different magazines situate readers according to different buying practices. The weekly magazines address women as domestic consumers, the glossies appeal to individualistic values. In all, identities are achieved through consumption.

Because women are seen by this institutionalised discourse as the main buyers of goods, everything revolves around market forces. Femininity and sexuality are defined through consumerism. Sex is one of the most attractive products to be sold. That is why sex-as-topic is present in almost all magazines. Some of the cover headlines exemplify this point

Women who pay for sex. And enjoy it (Brazilian *Marie Claire*, December 1993)
'I pay men for sex'– Ten women explain why (English *Marie Claire*, February 1994)
Men talk about their mistresses (*Marie Claire*, March 1993)
I know he has a mistress (*Marie Claire*, December 1993)
How many lovers have you had? (*Cosmopolitan*, December 1993)
Orgasm school (*Marie Claire*, December 1993)
Female Ejaculation – another fine mess we've got ourselves into (*Cosmopolitan*, December 1993)
Suck up to your man – Why oral sex will thrill him more than practically anything else (*Cosmopolitan*, February 1993)
On your back – here's a sneaky sex trick which (almost) always guarantees an orgasm (*Cosmopolitan*, August 1993)
Could you handle SEX with – a boomerang penis, the man who has two (*Cosmopolitan*, March 1993)
Attention please! Why he wants you to grab him by the, er … (*New Woman*, August 1992)
Do you dream about three in bed? (*19*, December 1993)
Boys on Condoms – caps and other squidgy things (*19*, October 1993)

Here, sex is sold as a commodity (the magazine itself). Texts about sexual practices, like the institution itself, also involve a number of contradictory readings. On the one hand, it gives readers a sense of powerful knowledge and a sense of modernity (the modern liberated woman not only should 'know' about sex and sexual techniques, but also should be able to perform). On the other hand, it involves being in accordance with prescribed social rules and behaviour, generally of a traditional and patriarchal kind: the sexually attractive woman is the beautiful one who, to please men, is persuaded to buy the products being advertised in the magazine. Editorial and advertising material are thus inseparable.

Although the 'trendy' magazine apparently represents women as independent financially and with a free sexual life, the implicit agenda is based on the prioritising of only certain forms of heterosexual relationship as the determining force in human relations, and traditional sexual role models. Femininity is a goal to be worked for. Women are designed as objects of male desire. Ballaster *et al.* (1991) suggest that the discourse of sexual liberation draws on the male-dominated sex manual. Relationships are women's responsibility and part of their work.

> The assumption of femininity as simultaneously natural and culturally acquired through labour sets up a complex tension for the reader. On the one hand she is addressed as already 'woman' – this is, after all, the ground on which she is identified as a reader. On the other hand, there is a clear gap between what is and what the magazines claim she 'ought' to desire to be. Femininity, therefore, becomes both a source of anxiety and a source of pleasure because it can never be fully achieved. The magazines perpetuate this myth of femininity and offer themselves as a solution. The magazine will be friend, advisor and instructor in the difficult tasks of being woman.
>
> (Ballaster *et al.*, 1991: 143)

Constructed thus on the ideology of consumerism and on formulas of advice and hope, the private world is directly accessed either through procedural discourses ('you should do this or that') or through first-person narratives of personal experience ('I am twice divorced ...'). Consequently people's identities are reassured when they identify themselves with the myths and utopias offered.

The first-person narratives (from now on the 'sex narratives') I want to discuss here contagiously provide for the reader vicarious and transgressive pleasures linked to the prohibited and the utopian. That is why they are so exciting. Who would stop reading, for instance, after this beginning?

JANE, 51, HOUSEWIFE
For the past two years, I've been seeing young men in the afternoons.

These pleasures offer fantasy and an escape from routine and daily life. The sad part, however, is that a deeper discussion of gender politics and power relations is totally absent from these magazines and the oppositions of masculine and feminine, public and private, production and consumption continue to structure the magazine text. Sexuality is merely an object of consumption.

NARRATIVES OF TRANSGRESSION: THE 'FRESH APPROACH'

Narratives about sexual encounters or experiences, especially of a transgressive kind, are the modern version of the romance stories. Sex narratives are small reports retold by different voices and put together under a general heading ('Why Women Go to Male Prostitutes', 'Men Talk about their Mistresses').

Although popular magazines have changed in their visual representations over time, they preserve a basic macro-narrative which is an articulation of the world centred on the woman and retold supposedly from a woman's perspective. Constructed from an explicit point of view (the voice who tells the story), sex narratives are a crucial sub-genre in the articulation of sexuality and femininity.

In organisational terms, each text is voiced by a supposedly real person who, prior to the recounting act, has undergone some kind of personal experience. Labov and Waletsky (1967), when they put forward their theory of narrative, refer to the concept of 'reportability'. For any narrative to be successfully encoded by the participants of the interaction, it needs to have a 'point' and a reason to be told. The sexual component makes the report exciting, but the transgressive is the reason for the story to be told.

Because narrative or storytelling is one of the most attractive and vivid representation of experience through language, first-person narratives are, as I pointed out above, one of the preferred organisational patterns found in female magazines. In *Marie Claire*, for instance, there is a massive concentration on narrative – from the eight sections (see pp. 250–1) that together constitute the magazine, five consist of narratives – reportage, emotional issues, first person, life stories, fashion story.

Like any other kind of narrative, sex narratives have the general characteristics that Longacre (1983) suggests:

1 narrative discourse is usually in the first or third person
2 narrative discourse is actor-oriented
3 narrative discourse encodes accomplished time, and chronological linkage is necessary
4 narrative is also distinct from other genres because of 'plot'.

Labov and Waletsky (1967) suggest that narratives of personal experience are composed of the following structural categories:

1 abstract
2 orientation
3 complicating action
4 evaluation
5 result
6 coda.

Coming from a different perspective, Hoey (1979; 1983) views narratives as linguistic patterns organised in terms of a situation, a problem and a response (or solution), which can be evaluated positively or negatively. If negatively, there is a tendency to expect a further response. Alternatively, within a situation, a goal may be identified for which a response is necessary.

In the particular sex narratives from *Marie Claire* chosen for analysis (ten from the February 1994 issue – **'I pay men for sex'** – **Ten women explain why**), the headlines function as the abstract or the summary of what is yet to come. The abstract summarises the central action and it is used to answer the questions: what is this about, why is this story being told. Orientation sets the scene: the who, when, where and what of the story. It establishes the 'situation' of the narrative.

In newspapers the *headline* and the *lead* (the first paragraph of the text), in most cases, fulfil the dual function of the abstract and the orientation. The lead is the most important paragraph of the story. It establishes the main theme and gives information about the basic facts and people involved in the event. Orientation, on the other hand, can also continue through the story, and characters can be introduced as the events develop.

By contrast, in other written narratives the title, which corresponds to the headline in the written media, does not necessarily give the listener/ reader a clue to the topic to be developed. The title of a film, for example, *Best Intentions* (directed by Bille August, winner of the 1992 Cannes Film Festival and about the early married life of Ingmar Bergman's parents) tells us nothing about the theme of the narrative. In magazines the head-line is crucial: it not only contains basic information about the topic but also has to be catchy and sometimes poetic.

Headlines are the most powerful persuasive and auto-promotional tool used to attract magazine readers. Just as in the newspapers, they have the purpose of selling the magazine and attracting readers. In fact, many read-ers choose to read a story only if the headline attracts their attention.

Headlines appear three times: on the cover, on the feature page and framing the actual text, where they are rearticulated and expanded. This is an interesting feature of this kind of text and differs from newspaper news, where the headline only appears once and then is followed by a summary of the story, the lead paragraph. The following headline, for example, appears on the cover of the February issue of *Marie Claire*:

'I pay men for sex' – Ten women explain why

It is rewritten on the feature page as:

Why Women Go to Male Prostitutes – Ten women talk to Clare Campbell about hiring men for sex

and, once again, inside the magazine heading the actual narrative:

Why women go to Male Prostitutes.
Men who charge for sex can be found in hotel bars, or through escort
agencies, personal columns and ads in newsagent's windows. Clare
Campbell talks to ten women who have hired male prostitutes.

The transformations are meaningful in terms of the fictionalisation of the
events and also in terms of power relations. In the examples above, a
series of linguistic strategies are used. In the cover headline voice is given
to a supposedly 'real' person who will reveal her sexual activities. This
narrator is a persona created to be exactly like you and me, through the
device of reported speech which dramatises the recounting and supposedly gives veracity to it. Quote is the final layer in a hierarchy of narrative levels, since it is the introduction of one text into another. Halliday
(1985) refers to the notion of projection: 'the logical-semantic relationship whereby a clause comes to function not as a direct representation of
(non-linguistic) experience, but as a representation of a (linguistic) representation' (1985: 287–8). The recursive potentiality of the syntactic structure of report allows speakers and writers to create different layers of
narration. This is the case in the example

First layer narration: **I** (person/writer in the real world) tell
                          you (reader in the real world)
                          that
Second layer narration: **someone** (identified only as an 'I') told **me**
                          that
Third layer narration: QUOTE

The use of the quote on the cover is a strategy of authorial detachment
and approximation of reader and character. Although quoted material
represents interaction, the represented speech is always mediated and
indirect, since it is produced by someone (in this case the writer of the
article, who interprets the speech acts represented according to her point
of view (see Caldas-Coulthard, 1987; 1994). The apparent 'factuality' is a
fiction.

The problem (why women pay for sex) is only suggested in the headline and raises expectations. The explanation will be given inside the magazine – Ten women explain why. This is a powerful strategy used to make
readers continue reading. It is the basic technique used by all episodic
narrative: the action is suspended to be continued later on.

The feature page introduces a new headline where the problem is now
mediated through an omniscient voice, thereby establishing distance
between text and reader and changing the perspective of the telling. It
also introduces a very important participant in the creation of the story
– Clare Campbell, the receiver of the verbal process. In fact, she is the
explicit name through whose point of view the events will be retold. The

clauses are constructed in such a way, however, that Clare is in the receiving position and the women narrators are the *sayers*. The feature page headline also reclassifies the 'men' of the cover as 'male prostitutes'.

Finally, inside the magazine, the headline is expanded to an orientative section – 'men can be found in certain places or through certain agents'. The male participants, who are given theme position in the sentences, are once again reclassified as 'men who charge for sex'. They are now the actors in charge of the action, and Clare Campbell from receiver of the message in the previous headline becomes the sayer of the process. In this last headline, the meaning of the text has changed. Power is attributed to men. The writer of supposedly 'real' events is given voice.

Another interesting fact is that the quote reported in the cover headline never reappears in the ten short narratives that make up the section *Emotional Issues*. This is another of the signs of the fictionalisation of the supposedly factual tellings.

Other headlines employ different linguistic strategies like the use of the imperative to summon the reader to action ('Suck up to your man', 'On your back') or the use of questions that will be answered in the inside text ('Could you handle sex with . . .', 'How many lovers have you had?').

These techniques give the tone of intimacy which is pervasive in all women's magazines. The idea of the magazine as friend, giving advice or solution to common problems, implicitly addresses the question of femininity as one shared by all women.

In the text itself, the macro-narrative is framed by the reporter, whose name appears in the headline and who introduces the subnarratives and describes the narrators by first name plus age. The age information is ideologically interesting – Irene, 37, Yasmin, 44, Louise, 47, Ann, 64, Jane, 51 – because age here is attached to transgression. The implicit message is that these middle-aged women should not be doing what we are about to read. The macro-narrative is subsequently layered, and the women are given voice to recount their personal experiences.

All the sex narratives follow basically the same structures as the one below:

IRENE, 37, HOUSEWIFE AND MOTHER
Richard, my husband, hasn't made love to me for ten years. We have a lovely twelve-year-old son called Liam, so I wouldn't dream of breaking up my marriage by having an affair or leaving Richard for another man. I have tried to get him to go for marriage guidance or some sort of sex therapy, but he absolutely refuses. I ended up going on my own and I realised afterwards that I either had to learn to live without sex or find an alternative way of living.

Then I read an article about gigolos in a women's magazine. I didn't do anything about it immediately, but I began to think about it and eventually even told Richard what I was considering. Even at that stage, I think I was still hoping that he would be so outraged that it would make him do something. But it didn't.

He said that as long as I didn't do it in the house and Liam never found out, it was all right by him. He justified this by saying that he didn't want to lose me, and that maybe this was the only way of finding a compromise. He also said he never, never wanted me to tell him the details.

I have now been going with paid men for over a year. It isn't that expensive – about £100 a time – and I only do it about once a month at the most. The agency regard me as a regular now and have been very good about finding us a place to go each time. The only aspect that worries Richard is when I see the same man too often. Otherwise I think he has got quite used to it. I felt guilty about the expense at first, but I now look on it as an extended mortgage – certainly cheaper and less upsetting than a divorce.

All texts examined follow the same formulaic pattern: there is a situation, which indicates a problem:

Richard, my husband, hasn't made love to me for ten years. (Irene)

I'm twice divorced ... I don't want any more relationships with men especially gold diggers. The only thing lacking in my life is regular and uncomplicated sex. (Yasmin)

Until about two years ago ... I had never questioned whether my husband and I were happy. It was only then that I began to recognise the huge gap between us. (Louise)

Two years ago I had a hysterectomy. I am not married and have no children, but until that time I had been in an eleven-year relationship I believed to be a happy one. Then my partner left me – just like that, a fortnight after my operation. (Nicole)

My husband went off with another woman six years ago. (Jean)

In the orientation (discussed in more detail below), the women narrators are classified through the representation of family actors – husbands, daughters and sons.

I have a beautiful and successful daughter of 24. .... My daughter, who is terribly Sloane these days, despite her Asian origins ... (Yasmin)

[My husband] has got a demanding job as a sales director, and he has hobbies like gardening and model making. (Louise)

My husband Leo died four years ago. (Ann)

My husband Derek is the managing director of a large chemical company. (Jane)

The idea of going to a gigolo horrified me at first. But I love my husband, Gary, very much and he *wanted me to do it.* (Julie)

After the problem is introduced, responses are proposed but are negatively evaluated by the narrators:

I have tried to get him to go for marriage guidance or some sort of sex therapy, but he absolutely refuses. (Irene)

I do still love [my husband] and we make love at least twice a month. But he never talks to me like he used to and sex is no fun without the pillow talk. (Louise)

I am terribly fond of Derek [my husband] but he is often away and never really listens to anything I say when he is here. (Jane)

Because the responses to the problems are negatively evaluated, further responses are sought:

I realised afterwards that I either had to learn to live without sex or find an alternative way of living. (Irene)

Hiring a man for sex was my equivalent of finding a hobby. (Nicole)

For the past two years, I've been seeing young men in the afternoons. I don't really know why I do it – the most obvious reason is sheer boredom. (Jane)

Then a series of dynamic actions make up the complicating action, which is the essence of the narrative. For Labov (1972), complicating action answers the question 'what happened'. Complicating action brings in the elements which disrupt the equilibrium which will be finally restored by the resolution: in our case, the narrator becomes attracted to the idea of hiring a male prostitute, then finds one and reports on the sometimes ludicrous details. It is interesting to note that in the narrative quoted above, this section is introduced by self-referentiality:

Then I read an article about gigolos in a *women's magazine.* (Irene)
(my emphasis)

This points to the fact that the autopromotional discourse is subtly inserted in the different sections of the text.

The actions are extensively evaluated (discussed below) through the text, and we come to the end of the stories with some odd/funny/cynical resolutions (finally what happened?) and codas (explicit signal of the end of the report):

I felt guilty about the expense at first, but I now look on it as an extended mortgage – certainly cheaper and less upsetting then a divorce. (Irene)

I can't say there isn't a certain satisfaction in knowing that the money I pay comes out of my husband's pocket. (Jane)

After all, you only get one life, don't you? (Louise)

All these sex narratives have not only the main components that Longacre, Labov and Hoey all refer to, but also some structural variations. Source attributions, actors, time and place are also important features of all sex narratives. In fact, according to Bell (1991: 175), journalists have a short list of what should go in a story, 'the five W's and a H' – who, when, where, what, why and how. In the sex narratives the emphasis, however, falls on orientation and evaluation, which I shall discuss below.

Another important characteristic of sex narratives is that women readers are addressed as a large group undefined by political, or ideological allegiance and undifferentiated at personal level. There is an assumption that 'all' women are interested in the sexual activities reported.

I want now to concentrate on how social actors are constructed through voice, orientation and evaluation.

WHOSE VOICE?

Facts and fictions

The question of voice is an interesting one in sex narratives. First-person accounts in media discourse make pretensions to factuality. 'I' narrators are put forward as real people. The Brazilian *Marie Claire*, for instance, introduces first-person narratives with:

This space belongs to *Marie Claire* readers. If you have an unusual story write to . . .

and ends with

Report collected by Aida Veiga.
(Brazilian *Marie Claire*, March 1994, my translation)

Another formula used by both the Brazilian and the English *Marie Claire*s is

Clare Campbell *talks* to ten women who have hired male prostitutes.

Or

Marie Claire *listened* to married and single men, who told her why they continue to pay for sex.

These statements make the authorship very problematic. In the written press in general, narratives are not produced by a single source. According to Bell (1991) a factual newspaper report for instance is a text produced by multiple parties: principal sources of information, agencies, institutions, other media and authors, editors, copy editors, reporters, and others.

The 'copy' – the actual written text – is handled by many people and undergoes transformations as it follows its way to printing. Bell (1991) also points out that the copy follows a path which is itself a narrative of changes: from chief reporter to journalist (the first writer), to sub-editor and finally to the editor. Thus the number of people involved in the production of a newspaper text is quite large. This naturally accounts for one of the major characteristics of media narrative texts – embedding. Version 1 is embedded in version 2 which is embedded in version 3 and so on. The text therefore undergoes many modifications, and authorship and responsibility for the text is diluted in the process. Ultimately, the magazine editor is responsible for what is said, although all the versions are based on other authors, including the unknown ones who write for the agencies.

In classical narratives, by contrast, there are tellers who are somehow identifiable and who can choose to *aver*, in other words, to be responsible for what they recount or to detach themselves from the responsibility of what is being uttered by transferring the averral to other tellers and creating other narrators.

The sex narratives are a composite of these two sub-genres: the appearance of factuality is due to the fact that there seems to be a person out there in the world who is recounting events from her/his life. However, if we start examining the textualisations of this narrator, we find many traces of fictionality. The narrators are presented by their first name; age and some kind of 'occupation' are attached to it:

> Irene, 37, housewife and mother
> Yasmin, 44, charity fund-raiser
> Louise, 47, housing officer
> Ann, 64, housewife
> Jane, 51, housewife
> Jean, 39, teacher

First names do not in fact identify real people, and most of the professional glossing attached to the names fails to place the women in any recognisable space. There are no addresses or further indications of where the activities are being developed. Naturally, the activity of being a housewife and mother does not need any other development – women are attached here to the domestic space.

By contrast, when men are described, particularly in the press (see Caldas-Coulthard, 1993), they are glossed by their professional designations or positions in the government or in some kind of public institution:

Keith Wafter, medical director of Cilag
Sir Charles Tidbury, former chairman of Whitbread brewers
(examples taken from the COBUILD newspaper corpora)

By contrast, the sex narrators cannot be factually identified. Although the magazine wants the readers to believe that the stories are real the texts are not produced by the 'I' narrator that appears in the text, but by a series of people that put the text together, ultimately Clare Campbell or Aida Veiga. Even if there was a primary report by a Yasmin or a Louise, the media writers are in charge of selecting, ordering and organising the sequence in which events will be recounted. There is always a choice and a construction since events are interpreted and then recounted by tellers who live in a particular society at a given time and have possibly different ideological values for the supposed women who 'recount' their sad stories.

Another important element that signals fictionalisation is the visual presentation of the articles. According to Kress and van Leeuwen (1990), images, illustrations and text interplay and combine to produce meanings. Texts cannot be analysed without taking into consideration the pictures that come with them. Magazines explore the visual interaction as much as possible. If the text is about some celebrity, a photograph will be presented. However, there are no photographs of the narrators in the sex narrative texts. Obviously there is the question of anonymity, but other gossipy texts, especially in newspapers, present photographs of the participants. What we have instead are illustrations of the type shown in Figure 14.1.

The sex narratives work with fantasy and imagination. Transgression is possible if set in an imaginary world. A picture of a real Ann, 64, could have a negative impact on the readers, because by her age all the physical attributes proposed by the beautification discourse and so very important to both the advertisers and the sales of the magazine would have disappeared, and the confrontation with reality could be costly.

According to Theo van Leeuwen (Chapter 3, this volume) a given culture or a given context in the culture has specific ways of representing the social world, and meaning can be realised verbally as well as visually. My reading of the picture in Figure 14.1 is that it is the representation of the 'talkative' (gossipy, perhaps) woman who tells others about her sexual encounters. The phone is an instrument and also a semiotic sign of the interaction. It is interesting to notice that the woman is not addressing the reader: her gaze is not directed frontwards. The men in the picture, columns supporting a discourse, have no importance: important is to speak. Once again, the stereotype of the woman talker is reinforced here. The texts add additional layers of meaning to the graphic meaning. Who are the women who tell their friends about sexual encounters?

Figure 14.1 Brazilian *Marie Claire*, December 1993

Orientation, evaluation and guilt

As I have indicated, the orientation section of the narrative specifies the participants and the circumstances – place and time. In a linear narrative, orientation is generally placed after the abstract and before the complicating action. However, very commonly, orientative clauses can be found embedded throughout the text. The most interesting uses of orientation are when parts of it are strategically delayed, and surprising effects are created because important information is recounted later in the telling. This is the case in the sex narratives. One of their major characteristics is that the women narrators have to describe their family links in order to define their own identities. So we have descriptions like:

> [My husband] has got a demanding job as a sales director, and he has hobbies like gardening and model making. (Louise)

> My husband Leo died four years ago. We had been married for nearly 40 years and his death was a terrible shock. I recently moved next door to my daughter and I have lots of women friends and have a very good pension from my husband's company. (Ann)

> My husband Derek is the managing director of a large chemical company. We own a lovely house with a swimming-pool, as well as holiday homes both in France and the US. (Jane)

> I'm twice divorced. I have a beautiful and successful daughter of 24, plenty of money in my own right and many women friends. (Yasmin)

> We have a lovely twelve-year-old son called Liam. (Irene)

The identities of the narrators are constructed through their relationships with husbands and children and through the money that they spend on their lovers:

> It isn't that expensive – about £100 a time. (Irene, 37)

> I paid him £150 for the afternoon – which was much more than I expected, and also more than I had in cash in the house. I was worried about writing a cheque for so much in case Colin [my husband] questioned it. (Louise, 47)

> We went back to my cabin together and he told me it would cost £300 for him to stay all night. I agreed. (Ann, 64)

The older the woman, the more expensive the encounter becomes! Ann, 64, in fact says:

> I wouldn't expect a man to want to do it with a woman of my age for nothing.

The lovers, by contrast with the husbands and family, are unnamed. They are labelled as 'lovers', 'gigolos', 'men' or by reference to their youth or physical attributes:

> He looked like one of the Chippendales – he was a young Australian with huge muscles and lovely blond hair. (Jane, 51)

> Suddenly I noticed a very handsome young man staring hard in my direction. At first I tried to ignore him. Then he came over. (Yasmin, 44)

> I have now been going with paid men for over a year. (Irene, 37)

> I rang [an escort agency] and asked them to send a young man round to see if I liked him. (Jane, 51)

> I have only had sex with three men in my life – one of whom is Colin [my husband], one I met after answering an advertisement in the personal column, and the other one was from an escort agency. (Louise, 47)

Van Leeuwen (Chapter 3, this volume) suggests, in his discussion of how social practices are transformed into discourses, that there is an 'array of choices' or a system network that people choose from for representing other social actors. If we analyse the choices found in the examples above according to his categories, we notice that husbands and children are *included*, *personalised*, *determined* and *nominalised* (husband + name, children + name). The narrator's identity is shaped by the ways these other actors appear in the text. Lovers, on the other hand, are included in the discourse, but are sometimes *undetermined* (the one, the other one), explicitly differentiated from the family group and they are not *nominated*. In terms of functionalisation (the activities or roles people have in society) husbands are classified in terms of their professional status whereas lovers are classified by their looks.

Husbands and children are classified in the text to establish relational identification, while lovers are classified according to their physical identification. Van Leeuwen (ibid.) observes that physical identification is always overdetermined since physical attributes have special connotations. We can see that in the sex narratives, lovers are reduced to bodies, while husbands and children are integral parts of the narrator's identification.

Finally, I want to examine the question of how the narrators evaluate their actions and how they contribute to reinforcing moral and traditional values and practices.

Evaluation is a very important category in all kinds of narratives. It can appear at any point in a story. It is through evaluation that narrators reveal their degree of involvement in the action and show their recognition of the audience's expectation of reportability. It is also through evaluation that ideological values are conveyed. In media discourse in general, evaluation is a crucial entrance point to the hidden discourse. In the sex narratives under analysis, the women narrators always evaluate their transgression negatively:

I felt *guilty* about the expense at first. (Irene)

It made me feel good about myself for a short time, but *very bad* later. I am deeply *ashamed* of doing it. (Louise)

Maybe if Derek and I had had children of our own I *wouldn't be doing* this. I am sure Derek would leave me if he ever found out. Yet part of me blames him for leaving me on my own. (Jane)

The sex was very good, but I felt *miserable* about it afterwards. Whenever I have paid other men for sex, I have always been left with that same *feeling of loss*. (Barbara)

These utterances are examples of what Labov (1972: 366) calls external evaluation. The narrator breaks the frame of the report to address the reader directly and interrupts the actions to express her general evaluation of the distant events. The lexical items chosen in all the narratives are part of the same lexical field: guilt, shame, misery, loss. The actions are therefore evaluated negatively with obvious connotations. The women transgressors regret and repent afterwards. The ambiguous message, based on the contradictory nature of the narratives, is either 'don't do it' or 'if you do it you will feel guilty afterwards'. The transgressive pleasure leads to social punishment.

CONCLUSIONS

I have tried to show that narrative structures and subjects are like working apparatuses of ideology, repositories for the meanings by which we live. Without any doubts, the sex narratives I have analysed here testify to 'the pervasive power of narrative and in particular romance narrative as the structuring agent or generic continuity of the women's magazines' (Ballaster *et al.*, 1991: 172).

The paradox to be noted, however, is that the sex narratives provide readers with forms of sexual deviance and prohibited love affairs but maintain a moral attitude of condemnation towards the facts portrayed. The combination of reporting and condemning is a commercial formula adopted by the press to attract more readers. All texts code the ideological position of their producers. 'The everyday, innocent and innocuous, mundane text is as ideologically saturated as a text which wears its ideological constitution overtly' (Kress, 1993: 174). Consumerism and traditional values are the underlining ideology of these texts.

The first-person narratives that are supposedly transgressive are transgressive only in terms of a traditional view of human sexuality and sexual relationships: to be happy a woman should be in a long-term heterosexual relationship. The analysis of how the social actors are included and named in the sex narratives proves this point. The women are identified by their family links and the most important actors are the husbands. The report of the deviations in the heterosexual marriage is a spectacle which may be glimpsed without any reader involvement. As Chibnall (1977: 32) suggests, 'the reader can sit over her cornflakes in mild moral indignation while today's shock horror probe into yesterday's sex, drugs/orgy unfolds its unseemly content'. The topic of 'sexual practices' examined here shows women who are apparently liberated, but are intrinsically subordinated to kinship evaluation. This evaluation, however, implies social punishment.

In constructing a fictionalised world, sex narratives do not challenge the hegemonic power of middle-class values. The texts analysed prove that women's magazines cannot offer political resolutions to what they consistently define as personal problems. There is a pervasive 'personalised politics' structuring the magazines.

Women's magazines are an institution produced for profit sold all over the world and consequently they are potent cultural forms. It is sad to acknowledge that many women read them, not for intellectual or political challenge, but only for relaxation and 'easy' pleasure. It is also sad to notice the mis-appropriation of the feminist discourse of sexual liberation. The transgressive woman of *Marie Claire* is not very different from the first readers of the early women's magazines.

Sex narratives as cultural texts and discourses are responsible for maintaining a state of affairs which feminism has fought hard to change: inadequate and insecure women who, to have a voice, have to tell of their secret affairs even though they feel guilty.

ACKNOWLEDGEMENT

I am grateful to Susana Funck, Philippe Humblé and Luiz Paulo Moita Lopes for their valuable comments on earlier versions of this chapter, needless to say any remaining deficiencies are my own.

REFERENCES

Ballaster, R., Beetham, E., Fraser, E. and Hebron, S. (1991) *Women's Worlds: Ideology, Femininity and the Woman's Magazine*, London: Macmillan.

Bell, A. (1991) *The Language of the News Media*, Oxford: Blackwell.

Caldas-Coulthard, C. R. (1987) 'Reporting speech in narrative written texts', in R. M. Coulthard (ed.) *Discussing Discourse*, Discourse Analysis Monographs, 14, English Language Research, University of Birmingham, 149–67.

Caldas-Coulthard, C. R. (1992) *News as Social Practice*, Florianópolis, Brazil: Universidade Federal de Santa Catarina.

Caldas-Coulthard, C. R. (1993) 'From discourse analysis to Critical Discourse Analysis: the differential re-presentation of women and men speaking in written news', in J. McH. Sinclair, M. Hoey and G. Fox (eds) *Techniques of Description: Spoken and Written Discourse*, London: Routledge, 196–208.

Caldas-Coulthard, C. R. (1994) 'On reporting reporting: the representation of speech in factual and factional narratives', in R. M. Coulthard (ed.) *Advances in Written Text Analysis*, London: Routledge, 295–308.

Chibnall, S. (1977) *Law and Order News: An Analysis of Crime Reporting in the British Press*, London: Tavistock.

Ferguson, M. (1983) *Forever Feminine: Women's Magazines and the Cult of Femininity*, London: Heinemann.

Fowler, R. (1991) *Language in the News: Discourse and Ideology in the Press*, London: Routledge.

Giddens, A. (1992) *A Transformação da Sociedade; Sexualidade, Amor e Erotismo nas Sociedades Modernas* (Portuguese trans.), São Paulo: Editora da UNESP.

Halliday, M. A. K. (1985) *An Introduction to Functional Grammar*, London: Edward Arnold.

Hoey, M. P. (1979) *Signalling in Discourse*, Discourse Analysis Monographs, 6, English Language Research, University of Birmingham.

Hoey, M. P. (1983) *On the Surface of Discourse*, London: Allen & Unwin.

Jameson, F. (1981) *The Political Unconscious: Narrative as a Socially Symbolic Act*, London: Methuen.

Kress, G. (1993) 'Against arbitrariness: the social production of the sign as a foundational issue in Critical Discourse Analysis', *Discourse and Society*, 4, 2, 169–91.

Kress, G. and van Leeuwen, T. (1990) *Reading Images*, Victoria: Deakin University Press.

Labov, W. (1972) 'The transformation of experience in narrative syntax', in his *Language in the Inner City*, University Park, PA: University of Pennsylvania Press, 354–96.

Labov, W. and Waletsky, J. (1967) 'Narrative analysis: oral versions of personal experience', in J. Helm (ed.) *Essays on the Verbal and Visual Arts*, Seattle, WA: University of Washington Press, 12–44.

Longacre, R. E. (1983) *The Grammar of Discourse*, New York: Plenum.

McCracken, E. (1993) *Decoding Women's Magazines: From Mademoiselle to MS*, London: Macmillan.

Winship, J. (1987) *Inside Women's Magazines*, London: Pandora.

Bibliography

Abelson, R. P. (1981) 'Psychological status of the script concept', *American Psychologist* 36(7), 715–30.

Anderson, D. A., Milner, J. W. and Galician, M. L. (1988) 'How editors view legal issues and the Rehnquist Court', *Journalism Quarterly*, 65, 294–8.

Argyle, M. (1978) *The Psychology of Interpersonal Behaviour*, 3rd edn, Harmondsworth: Penguin.

Armstrong, I. (ed.) (1992) *New Feminist Discourses: Critical Essays on Theories and Texts*, London: Routledge.

Aronowitz, S. (1988) *Science as Power: Discourse and Ideology in Modern Society*, Minneapolis, MN: University of Minnesota Press.

Atkinson, M. and Drew, P. (1979) *Order in Court: The Organisation of Verbal Interaction in Judicial Settings*, London: Macmillan.

Aufderheide, P. (1992) *Beyond PC: Toward a Politics of Understanding*, Saint Paul, MN: Graywolf Press.

Austin, J. L. (1962) *How to Do Things with Words*, London: Oxford University Press.

Baker, W. (1991) 'Recent work in critical theory', *Style*, 25, 4, 571–615.

Ballaster, R., Beetham, E., Fraser, E. and Hebron, S. (1991) *Women's Worlds: Ideology, Femininity and the Woman's Magazine*, London: Macmillan.

Barker, M. (1989) *Comics, Ideology, Power and the Critics*, Manchester: Manchester University Press.

Barthes, R. (1967) *Elements of Semiology*, New York: Hill & Wang.

Barthes, R. (1970) *Mythologies*, London: Paladin.

Barthes, R. (1977) *Image-Music-Text*, London: Fontana.

Bateson, G. (1981) 'A theory of play and fantasy', in G. Bateson (ed.) *Steps to an Ecology of Mind*, New York: Ballantine, 177–93.

Beekman, J. and Callow, J. (1974) *Translating the Word of God*, Grand Rapids, MI: Zondervan.

Bell, A. (1985) 'One rule of news English: geographical, social and historical spread', *Te Reo*, 28, 95–117.

Bell, A. (1991) *The Language of the News Media*, Oxford: Blackwell.

Belsey, C. (1980) *Critical Practice*, London: Methuen.

Ben-Tovim, G., Gabriel, J., Law, I. and Stredder, K. (1986) *The Local Politics of Race*, London: Macmillan.

Berger, J. (1972) *Ways of Seeing*, Harmondsworth: Penguin.

Berger, P. L. (1966) *Invitation to Sociology*, Harmondsworth: Penguin.

Berman, P. (1992) *Debating PC: The Controversy over Political Correctness on College Campuses*, New York: Bantam-Dell.

Bernstein, B. (1971) *Class, Codes and Control, vol. 1, Theoretical Studies towards a Sociology of Language*, London: Routledge.

Bettelheim, B. (1979) *The Uses of Enchantment*, Harmondsworth: Penguin.

Bielefeld, U. (ed.) (1991) *Das Eigene und das Fremde: Neuer Rassismus in der Alten Welt?*, Hamburg: Junius.

Billig, M., Condor, S., Edwards, D., Gane, M. and Middleton, D. (1988) *Ideological Dilemmas*, London: Sage.

Blair, J. A. (1987) 'Everyday argumentation from an informal logic perspective', in J. P. Wenzel (ed.) *Argumentation and Critical Practices*, Annandale, VA: Speech Communication Association, 177–83.

Boltz, C. J. and Seyler, D. U. (eds) (1982) *Language Power*, New York: Random House.

Borzeix, A. and Linhart, D. (1988) 'La participation un clair-obscur', *Sociologie du Travail*, 88, 1, 37–48.

Bourdieu, P. (1986) *Distinction: A Social Critique of the Judgement of Taste*, Cambridge: Polity.

Bourdieu, P. (1988) *Language and Symbolic Power*, Cambridge: Polity.

Bowers, G. and Iwi, K. (1993) 'The discursive construction of society', *Discourse and Society*, 4, 3, 357–93.

Brown, G. and Yule, G. (1983) *Discourse Analysis*, Cambridge: Cambridge University Press.

Brown, P. and Levinson, S. C. (1978) *Politeness: Some Universals in Language Usage*, Cambridge: Cambridge University Press.

Bruck, P. (ed.) (1991) *Das österreichische Format: Kulturkritische Beiträge zur Analyse des Medienerfolges 'Neue Kronen Zeitung'*, Vienna: Edition Atelier.

Burger, H. (1990) 'Über das Problem der Staatssprache', in R. Wodak and F. Menz (eds), *Sprache in der Politik: Politik in der Sprache*, Klagenfurt: Drava, 13–19.

Caldas-Coulthard, C. R. (1987) 'Reporting speech in narrative written texts', in R. M. Coulthard (ed.) *Discussing Discourse*, Discourse Analysis Monographs, 14, English Language Research, University of Birmingham, 149–67.

Caldas-Coulthard, C. R. (1992) *News as Social Practice*, Florianópolis, Brazil: Universidade Federal de Santa Catarina.

Caldas-Coulthard, C. R. (1993) 'From discourse analysis to critical discourse analysis: the differential re-presentation of women and men speaking in written news', in J. Sinclair, M. Hoey and G. Fox (eds) *Techniques of Description: Spoken and Written Discourse*, London: Routledge, 196–208.

Caldas-Coulthard, C. R. (1994) 'On reporting reporting: the representation of speech in factual and factional narratives', in R. M. Coulthard (ed.) *Advances in Written Text Analysis*, London: Routledge, 295–308.

Cameron, D. (1985) *Feminism and Linguistic Theory*, London: Macmillan.

Cameron, D. (ed.) (1990) *The Feminist Critique of Language*, London: Routledge.

Cameron, D., Frazer, F., Harvey, P., Rampton, N. M. H. and Richardson, K. (1992) *Researching Language: Issues of Power and Method*, London: Routledge.

Candlin, C. and Lucas, J. L. (1986) 'Interpretation and explanation in discourse: modes of "advising" in family planning', in T. Ensink, A. van Essen and T. van der Geest (eds) *Discourse Analysis and Public Life*, Dordrecht: Foris, 13–38.

Cavalcanti, M. (1983) 'The pragmatics of FL reader–text interaction: key lexical items as a source of potential reading problems', unpub. PhD, University of Lancaster.

Chafe, W. (1986) 'How we know things about language: a plea for Catholicism', in D. Tannen and J. E. Alatis (eds) *Language and Linguistics: The Inter-*

dependence of Theory, Data, and Application (GURT 1985), Washington, DC: Georgetown University Press, 214–25.

Chibnall, S. (1977) *Law and Order News: An Analysis of Crime Reporting in the British Press*, London: Tavistock.

Chilton, P. (1984) 'Orwell, language and linguistics', *Language and Communication* 4, 2, 129–46.

Chilton, P. (ed.) (1985) *Language and the Nuclear Arms Debate: Nukespeak Today*, London: Frances Pinter.

Chilton, P. (1988) *Orwellian Language and the Media*, London: Pluto.

Clark, K. (1992) 'The linguistics of blame: representations of women in the *Sun's* reporting of crimes of sexual violence', in M. Toolan (ed.) *Language, Text and Context*, London: Routledge, 208–24.

Clark, R., Fairclough, N., Ivanič, R. and Martin-Jones, M. (1987) *Critical Language Awareness*, Centre for Language in Social Life Working Paper Series no. 1, University of Lancaster.

Clegg, S. R. (1989) *Frameworks of Power*, London: Sage.

Connerton, P. (ed.) (1976) *Critical Sociology*, Harmondsworth: Penguin.

Coulthard, R. M. (1985) *An Introduction to Discourse Analysis*, 2nd edn, London: Longman.

Coulthard, R. M. (ed.) (1986) *Talking about Text*, Discourse Analysis Monographs, 13, English Language Research, University of Birmingham.

Coulthard, R. M. (ed.) (1987) *Discussing Discourse*, Discourse Analysis Monographs, 14, English Language Research, University of Birmingham.

Coulthard, R. M. (ed.) (1992a) *Advances in Spoken Discourse Analysis*, London: Routledge.

Coulthard, R. M. (1992b) 'Forensic discourse analysis', in R. M. Coulthard (ed.) *Advances in Spoken Discourse Analysis*, London: Routledge, 242–57.

Coulthard, R. M. (1993) 'Beginning the study of forensic texts: corpus, concordance, collocation', in M. P. Hoey (ed.) *Data, Description, Discourse*, London: Harper Collins, 86–97.

Coulthard, R. M. (1994a) '*Power*ful evidence for the defence: an exercise in forensic discourse analysis', in J. Gibbons (ed.) *Language and the Law*, London: Longman, 414–42.

Coulthard, R. M. (1994b) 'On the use of corpora in the analysis of forensic texts', *Forensic Linguistics*, 1, 1, 27–43.

Coulthard, R. M. (ed.) (1994c) *Advances in Written Text Analysis*, London: Routledge.

Craig, R. T. and Tracy, K. (eds) (1983) *Conversational Coherence: Form, Structure, and Strategy*, New York: Sage.

Craig, S. (1992a) 'Considering men and the media', in S. Craig (ed.) *Men, Masculinity and the Media*, London: Sage, 1–7.

Craig, S. (ed.) (1992b) *Men, Masculinity and the Media*, London: Sage.

Crombie, W. (1985) *Process and Relation in Discourse and Language Learning*, Oxford: Oxford University Press.

Croteau, D. and Hoynes, W. (1992) 'Men and the news media: the male presence and its effects', in S. Craig (ed.) *Men, Masculinity and the Media*, London: Sage, 154–67.

Curthoys, A. and Docker, J. (1989) 'In praise of prisoner', in J. Tulloch and G. Turner (eds) *Australian Television: Programs, Pleasures and Politics*, Sydney: Allen & Unwin.

Davis, H. and Walton, P. (eds) (1983) *Language, Image and the Media*, Oxford: Blackwell.

Davis, M. (1990) *Miles: The Autobiography*, London: Macmillan.

Davis, T. A. (1994) 'ESDA and the analysis of contested contemporaneous notes of police interviews', *Forensic Linguistics*, 1, 1, 71–89.

Debert, G. G. (1988) 'Envelhecimento e representação da velhice', *Ciência Hoje*, São Paulo, 8, 44, 60–8.

Department of Education and Science (1989) *English for Ages 5 to 16* (Cox Report), London: HMSO.

Downes, W. (1978) 'Language, belief and verbal action in a historical process', *University of East Anglia Papers in Linguistics*, 8, 1–43.

Downing, J. D. H. (1980) *The Media Machine*, London: Pluto.

Duranti, G. and Goodwin, C. (1992) *Rethinking Context*, Cambridge: Cambridge University Press.

Eades, D. (1992) *Aboriginal English and the Law: Communicating with Aboriginal English Speaking Clients: A Handbook for Legal Practitioners*, Brisbane: Queensland Law Society.

Eades, D. (1994) 'Forensic linguistics in Australia', *Forensic Linguistics*, 1, 2, 113–32.

Eagleton, T. (1976) *Criticism and Ideology*, London: New Left Books.

Elshtain, J. B. (1982) 'Feminist discourse and its discontents: language, power, and meaning', *Signs*, 7, 3, 603–21.

Erdheim, M. (1992) 'Fremdel: Kulturelle Unverträglichkeit und Anziehung', *Kursbuch*, 107, 19–32.

Erickson, B., Lind, A. A., Johnson, B. C. and O'Barr, W. M. (1978) 'Speech style and impression formation in a court setting: the effects of "powerful" and "powerless" speech', *Journal of Experimental Social Psychology*, 14, 266–79.

Erickson, F. and Rittenberg, W. (1987) 'Topic control and person control: a theory problem for foreign physicians in interaction with American patients', *Discourse Processes*, 10, 401–15.

Erickson, F. and Shultz, J. (1982) *The Counselor as Gatekeeper: Social Interaction in Interviews*, New York: Academic Press.

Ervin-Tripp, S. M., O'Connor, M. C. and Rosenberg, J. (1984) 'Language and power in the family', in C. Kramarae, M. Schulz and W. M. O'Barr (eds) *Language and Power*, Beverly Hills, CA: Sage, 116–35.

Essed, P. J. M. (1987) *Academic Racism: Common Sense in the Social Sciences*, University of Amsterdam: Centre for Race and Ethnic Studies, CRES Publications, no. 5.

Essed, P. J. M. (1991) *Understanding Everyday Racism*, Newbury Park, CA: Sage.

Fairclough, N. (1985) 'Critical and descriptive goals in discourse analysis', *Journal of Pragmatics*, 9, 739–63.

Fairclough, N. (1988) 'Register, power and sociosemantic change', in D. Birch and M. O'Toole (eds) *Functions of Style*, London: Frances Pinter, 111–25.

Fairclough, N. (1989a) *Language and Power*, London: Longman.

Fairclough, N. (1989b) 'Language and ideology', *English Language Research Journal*, University of Birmingham, 3, 9–28.

Fairclough, N. (1989c) 'Discourse and social change: a conflictual view', paper delivered at ISA RCS (International Sociological Association Research Committee on Sociolinguistics) conference, Dublin.

Fairclough, N. (1992a) 'Discourse and text: linguistic and intertextual analysis within discourse analysis', *Discourse and Society*, 3, 2, 193–217.

Fairclough, N. (1992b) 'The appropriacy of "appropriateness"', in N. Fairclough (ed.) *Critical Language Awareness*, London: Longman, 33–56.

Fairclough, N. (1992c) *Discourse and Social Change*, Cambridge: Polity.

Fairclough, N. (ed.) (1992d) *Critical Language Awareness*, London: Longman.

Fairclough, N. (1993) 'Critical Discourse Analysis and the marketization of public discourse: the universities', *Discourse and Society*, 4, 2, 133–59.

Fassmann, H. and Münz, R. (1992) *Einwanderungsland Österreich? Gastarbeiter – Flüchtlinge – Immigranten*, Vienna: Österreichische Akademie der Wissenschaften.

Fedler, F. (1973) 'The media and minority groups: a study of adequacy of access', *Journalism Quarterly*, 50, 1, 109–17.

Feltoe, G. (1989) *A Guide to Zimbabwean Criminal Law*, Harare: Zimbabwean Legal Resources Foundation.

Ferguson, M. (1983) *Forever Feminine: Women's Magazines and the Cult of Femininity*, London: Heinemann.

Fernandez, J. P. (1981) *Racism and Sexism in Corporate Life*, Lexington, MA: Lexington Books.

Fisher, S. (1979) 'The negotiation of treatment decisions in doctor/patient communications and their impact on the identity of women patients', doctoral dissertation, University of California, San Diego.

Fisher, S. (1984) 'Institutional authority and the strufture of discourse', *Discourse Processes*, 7, 2, 201–24.

Fisher, S. and Todd, A. D. (eds) (1986) *Discourse and Institutional Authority: Medicine, Education, and Law*, Norwood, NJ: Ablex.

Fisher, S. and Todd, A. D. (eds) (1988) *Gender and Discourse: The Power of Talk*, Norwood, NJ: Ablex.

Fiske, J. (1992) 'Popularity and the politics of information', in P. Dahlgren and C. Sparks (eds) *Journalism and Popular Culture*, London: Sage, 45–63.

Fiske, S. T. and Taylor, S. E. (1991) *Social Cognition*, 2nd edn, New York: McGraw–Hill.

Foucault, M. (1979) 'Governmentality', *Ideology and Consciousness*, 6, 5–21.

Foucault, M. (1981) *A History of Sexuality*, vol. I, Harmondsworth: Penguin.

Fowler, R. (1985) 'Power', in T. A. van Dijk (ed.) *Handbook of Discourse Analysis, vol. IV, Discourse Analysis in Society*, London: Academic Press, 61–82.

Fowler, R. (1987a) 'People in the news: discourse and discrimination', in J. Swann (ed.) *Study Guide to Open University Course EH207, Communication and Education Unit 8, Bias in the System?, Block 3 Language and Inequality*, Milton Keynes: Open University Press, 17–24.

Fowler, R. (1987b) 'The intervention of the media in the reproduction of power', in I. M. Zavala, T. A. van Dijk and M. Diaz–Diocaretz (eds) *Approaches to Discourse, Poetics and Psychiatry*, Amsterdam: Benjamins, 67–80.

Fowler, R. (1991) *Language in the News: Discourse and Ideology in the Press*, London: Routledge.

Fowler, R. and Marshall, T. (1985) 'The war against peacemongering: language and ideology', in P. Chilton (ed.), *Language and the Nuclear Arms Debate: Nukespeak Today*, London: Frances Pinter, 3–22.

Fowler, R., Hodge, R., Kress, G. and Trew, T. (1979) *Language and Control*, London: Routledge & Kegan Paul.

Frank, A. (1990) 'Bringing bodies back: a decade review', *Media, Culture and Society* 7, 131–62.

Frankel, R. M. (1983) 'The laying-on of hands: aspects of the organization of gaze, touch, and talk in a medical encounter', in S. Fisher and A. D. Todd (eds) *The Social Organization of Doctor–Patient Communication*, Washington, DC: Center for Applied Linguistics.

Frankel, R. M. (1984) 'From sentence to sequence: understanding the medical encounter through micro-interactional analysis; *Discourse Processes*, 7, 2, 135–70.

Fraser, N. (1989) *Unruly Practices: Power, Discourse and Gender in Contemporary Social Theory*, Minneapolis, MN: University of Minnesota Press.

Further Education Unit (1987) *Relevance, Flexibility and Competence*, London: HMSO.

Gaidzanwa, R. (1985) *Images of Women in Zimbabwean Literature*, Harare: College Press.

Galtung, J. and Ruge, M. H. (1965) 'The structure of foreign news', *Journal of Peace Research*, 2, 1, 64–91.

GFK-Fessel (1991) *Meinungsumfrage zu Österreich*, Vienna: Fessel Institute.

Giddens, A. (1992) *A Transformação da Sociedade: Sexualidade, Amor e Erotismo nas Sociedades Modernas* (Portuguese trans.), São Paulo: Editora da UNESP.

Gilman, S. (1985) *Difference and Pathology: Stereotypes of Sexuality, Race and Madness*, Ithaca, NY: Cornell University Press.

Goffman, E. (1959) *The Presentation of Self in Everyday Life*, New York: Doubleday.

Goffman, E. (1961) *Asylums*, New York: Anchor.

Goffman, E. (1967) *Interaction Ritual: Essays on Face to Face Behavior*, New York: Doubleday.

Goffman, E. (1973) *Stigma: Notes on the Management of Spoiled Identity*, Harmondsworth: Penguin.

Goffman, E. (1974) *Frame Analysis*, New York: Harper & Row.

Goffman, E. (1981a) 'Footing', in E. Goffman (ed.) *Forms of Talk*, Philadelphia, PA: University of Pennsylvania Press, 124–59.

Goffman, E. (1981b) 'Replies and responses', in E. Goffman (ed.) *Forms of Talk*, Philadelphia, PA: University of Pennsylvania Press, 5–77.

Goldberg, J. A. (1990) 'Interrupting the discourse on interruptions: an analysis in terms of relationally neutral, power- and rapport-oriented acts', *Journal of Pragmatics*, 14, 6, 883–903.

Graber, D. A. (1980) *Crime News and the Public*, New York: Praeger.

Graustein, G. and Thiele, W. (1987) *Properties of English Texts*, Leipzig: VEB Verlag Enzyklopädie.

Grice, H. P. (1975) 'Logic and conversation', in P. Cole and J. L. Morgan (eds) *Syntax and Semantics, vol. 3, Speech Acts*, New York: Academic Press, 41–58.

Grimshaw, A. D. (ed.) (1990) *Conflict Talk: Sociolinguistic Investigations of Arguments in Conversation*, Cambridge: Cambridge University Press.

Guillaumin, C. (1991) 'Rasse: Das Wort und die Vorstellung', in U. Bielefeld (ed.) *Das Eigene und das Fremde: Neuer Rassismus in der Alten Welt?*, Hamburg: Junius, 159–74.

Guillaumin, C. (1992) 'Zur Bedeutung des Begriffs Rasse', *Argument*, 201, 77–87.

Gumperz, J. (1977) 'Sociocultural knowledge in conversational inference', in M. Saville-Troike (ed.) *Linguistics and Anthropology* (GURT 77), Washington, DC: Georgetown University Press, 191–211.

Gumperz, J. (1982) *Discourse Strategies*, Cambridge: Cambridge University Press.

Gumperz, J. (1986) 'Interactional sociolinguistics in the study of schooling', in J. Cook-Gumperz (ed.) *The Social Construction of Literacy*, Cambridge: Cambridge University Press, 45–66.

Hall, S. (1989) *Ideologie, Kultur, Medien: Neue Rechte, Rassismus*, Hamburg: Argument.

Halliday, M. A. K. (1973) *Explorations in the Functions of Language*, London: Edward Arnold.

Halliday, M. A. K. (1978) *Language as Social Semiotic*, London: Edward Arnold.

Halliday, M. A. K. (1985) *An Introduction to Functional Grammar*, London: Edward Arnold.

Halliday, M. A. K. and Hasan, R. (1976) *Cohesion in English*, London: Longman.

Hanke, R. (1992) 'Redesigning men: hegemonic masculinity in transition', in S. Craig (ed.) *Men, Masculinity and the Media*, London: Sage, 185–98.

Harari, J. V. (ed.) (1979) *Textual Strategies: Perspectives in Post-Structuralist Criticism*, Ithaca, NY: Cornell University Press.

Hariman, R. (ed.) (1990) *Popular Trials: Rhetoric, Mass Media, and the Law*, Tuscaloosa, AL: University of Alabama Press.

Hartmann, P. and Husband, C. (1974) *Racism and the Mass Media*, London: Davis-Poynter.

Heng, G. and Devan, J. (1992) 'State fatherhood: the politics of nationalism, sexuality and race in Singapore', in A. Parker, M. Russo, D. Sommer and P. Yaeger (eds) *Nationalisms and Sexualities*, New York: Routledge, 343–64.

Herman, E. S. and Chomsky, N. (1988) *Manufacturing Consent: The Political Economy of the Mass Media*, New York: Pantheon.

Hjelmquist, E. (1984) 'Memory for conversations', *Discourse Processes*, 7, 321–36.

Hoey, M. P. (1979) *Signalling in Discourse*, Discourse Analysis Monographs, 6, English Language Research, University of Birmingham.

Hoey, M. P. (1983) *On the Surface of Discourse*, London: Allen & Unwin.

Hoey, M. P. (1986) 'The discourse colony: a preliminary study of a neglected discourse type', in R. M. Coulthard (ed.) *Talking about Text*, Discourse Analysis Monographs, 13, English Language Research, University of Birmingham, 1–26.

Hoey, M. P. (1988) 'The discourse properties of the criminal statute', in C. Walter (ed.) *Computing Power and Legal Language*, Westport, CT: Quorum Books/Greenwood Press, 69–88.

Hoey, M. P. (1991) *Patterns of Lexis in Text*, Oxford: Oxford University Press.

Hoey, M. P. and Winter, E. O. (1981) 'Believe me for mine honour', *Language and Style*, 14, 315–39.

Hollway, W. (1984) 'Gender difference and the production of subjectivity', in J. Henriques, W. Hollway, C. Urwin, C. Venn and V. Walkerdine, (eds) *Changing the Subject: Psychology, Social Regulation and Subjectivity*, London: Methuen, 227–63.

Horkheimer, M. and Adorno, T. (1978) *Temas Básicos da Sociologia*, trans. by A. Cabral, São Paulo: Cultrix.

Hujanen, T. (ed.) (1984) *The Role of Information in the Realization of the Human Rights of Migrant Workers*, report of international conference, Tampere (Finland), University of Tampere: Dept of Journalism and Mass Communication.

Huxley, J. (1939) *Race in Europe*, Oxford Pamphlets on World Affairs no. 5, Oxford: Clarendon Press.

Illich, I. (1971) *Deschooling Society*, Harmondsworth: Penguin.

Ivanič, R. (1988) 'Critical language awareness in action', *Language Issues*, 2, 2, 2–7.

Jackson, J. (1992) 'Honesty in investigative journalism', in A. Belsey and R. Chadwick (eds) *Ethical Issues in Journalism and the Media*, London: Routledge, 93–111.

Jackson, L. (1991) ' "Stray Women" on the colonial mind: African women and the disease metaphor in colonial Zimbabwe 1890–1949', MS, Department of Sociology, University of Zimbabwe.

Jameson, F. (1981) *The Political Unconscious: Narrative as a Socially Symbolic Act*, London: Methuen.

Jarrett, D. (1984) 'Pragmatic coherence in an oral formulaic tradition: I can read your letters / sure can't read your mind', in D. Tannen (ed.) *Coherence in Spoken and Written Discourse*, Norwood, NJ: Ablex, 155–71.

Jaworski, A. (1993) *The Power of Silence: Social and Pragmatic Perspectives*, Newbury Park, CA: Sage.

Jaynes, G. D. and Williams, R. M. (eds) (1989) *A Common Destiny: Blacks and American Society*, Washington, DC: National Academy Press.

Jenkins, R. (1986) *Racism and Recruitment: Managers, Organisations and Equal Opportunity in the Labour Market*, Cambridge: Cambridge University Press.

Johnson, C. E. (1987) 'An introduction to powerful and powerless talk in the classroom', *Communication Education*, 36, 2, 167–72.

Johnson, K. A. (1987) *Media Images of Boston's Black Community*, William Monroe Trotter Institute, Research Report, Boston, MA: University of Massachusetts.

Jones, C. (1989) *The Search for Meaning*, Sydney: ABC Publications.

Jordan, M. P. (1984) *Rhetoric of Everyday English Texts*, London: Allen & Unwin.

Kedar, L. (ed.) (1987) *Power through Discourse*, Norwood, NJ: Ablex.

Kendon, A. (1979) 'Some emerging features of face-to-face interaction studies', *Sign Language Studies*, 22, 7–22.

Kendon, A. (1981) *Non-verbal Communication, Interaction and Gesture*, The Hague: Mouton.

Kendon, A. (1990) *Conducting Interaction: Patterns of Behavior in Focused Encounters*, Cambridge: Cambridge University Press.

Kochman, T. (1981) *Black and White Styles in Conflict*, Chicago: University of Chicago Press.

Kress, G. (1983a) 'Linguistic and ideological transformations in newspaper language', in H. Davis and P. Walton (eds) *Language, Image and the Media*, Oxford: Blackwell.

Kress, G. (1983b) 'The politics of newspaper language', *International Journal of the Sociology of Language*, 32, 43–58.

Kress, G. (1985a) 'Discourses, texts, readers and the pro-nuclear arguments', in P. Chilton (ed.) *Language and the Nuclear Arms Debate: Nukespeal Today*, London: Frances Pinter, 65–87.

Kress, G. (1985b; 1989) *Linguistic Processes in Sociocultural Practices*, 1st edn, Victoria: Deakin University Press; 2nd edn, Oxford: Oxford University Press.

Kress, G. (1986a) 'Language in the media: the construction of the domains of public and private', *Media, Culture and Society*, 8, 395–419.

Kress, G. (1986b) 'Interrelations of reading and writing', in A. Wilkinson (ed.) *The Writing of Writing*, Milton Keynes: Open University Press.

Kress, G. (1989a) *Linguistic Processes in Sociocultural Practice*, Oxford: Oxford University Press.

Kress, G. (1989b) 'History and language: towards a social account of linguistic change', *Journal of Pragmatics*, 13, 445–66.

Kress, G. (1990) 'Critical Discourse Analysis', *Annual Review of Applied Linguistics*, 11, 84–99.

Kress, G. (1993) 'Against arbitrariness: the social production of the sign as a foundational issue in Critical Discourse Analysis', *Discourse and Society*, 4, 2, 169–91.

Kress, G. and Hodge, R. (1979/1994) *Language as Ideology*, London: Routledge.

Kress, G. and van Leeuwen, T. (1990) *Reading Images*, Victoria: Deakin University Press.

Labov, W. (1970) 'The study of language in its social context', *Studium Generale*, 23, 30–87.

Labov, W. (1972) 'The transformation of experience in narrative syntax', in his *Language in the Inner City*, University Park, PA: University of Pennsylvania Press, 354–96.

Labov, W. and Fanshel, D. (1977) *Therapeutic Discourse: Psychotherapy as Conversation*, New York: Academic Press.

Labov, W. and Waletsky, J. (1967) 'Narrative analysis: oral versions of personal experience', in J. Helm (ed.) *Essays on the Verbal and Visual Arts*, Seattle, WA: University of Washington Press, 12–44.

Laing, R. D. (1974) *The Role of Experience and the Bird of Paradise*, Harmondsworth: Penguin.

Lakoff, R. T. (1990) *Talking Power: The Politics of Language*, New York: Basic Books.

Latour, B. (1986) 'The powers of association', in J. Law (ed.) *Power, Action and Brlief: A New Sociology of Knowledge*, Sociological Review Monograph 32, London: Routledge & Kegan Paul..

Leech, G. (1981) *Semantics: The Study of Meaning*, 2nd edn, Harmondsworth: Penguin.

Lemke, J. L. (1985) 'Ideology, intertextuality, and the notion of register', in J. D. Benson and W. Greaves (eds) *Systemic Perspectives on Discourse, vol. 1*, Norwood, NJ: Ablex, 275–94.

Lerman, C. L. (1983) 'Dominant discourse: the institutional voice and control of topic', in H. Davis and P. Walton (eds) *Language, Image and the Media*, Oxford: Blackwell, 75–103.

Levi, J. (1994) 'Language as evidence: the linguist as Expert Witness in North American courts', *Forensic Linguistics*, 1, 1, 1–26.

Longacre, R. E. (1983) *The Grammar of Discourse*, New York: Plenum.

Love, A. and Morrison, A. (1991) 'Readers' obligations: an examination of some features of Zimbabwean newspaper editorials', *English Language Research Journal*, University of Birmingham, 3, 137–72.

Love, A. and Morrison, A. (1993) ' "Now the question is . . .": questions in letters to the editor in two Zimbabwean magazines in 1990', paper presented at 10th Congress of International Association of Applied Linguistics (AILA), Amsterdam, August.

Lukes, S. (1974) *Power: A Radical View*, London: Macmillan.

Lukes, S. (ed.) (1986) *Power*, Oxford: Blackwell.

McCarthy, M. (1993) 'Spoken discourse markers in written text', in J. M. Sinclair, M. P. Hoey and G. Fox (eds) *Techniques of Description: Spoken and Written Discourse. A Festschrift for Malcolm Coulthard*, London: Routledge, 170–82.

McCracken, E. (1993) *Decoding Women's Magazines: From Mademoiselle to MS*, London: Macmillan.

McFadden, P. (1992) 'Sex, sexuality and problems of AIDS in Africa', in R. Meena (ed.) *Gender and Ideology*, Harare: Sapes, 157–95.

McLoughlin, T. O. (1989) 'The comic strip and Zimbabwe's development', in E. A. Ngara and A. Morrison (eds) *Literature, Language and the Nation*, Harare: Baobab, 120–9.

Malmkjær, K. L. (ed.) (1992) *The Linguistics Encyclopaedia*, London: Routledge.

Mann, W. C. and Thompson, S. A. (1987) *Rhetorical Structure Theory: A Theory of Text Organization*, Monica del Rey, CA: Information Science Institute/ University of Southern California.

Marable, M. (1985) *Black American Politics*, London: Verso.

Marcuschi, L. A. (1989) 'Marcadores conversacionais do português brasileiro: formas, posições e funções', in A. T. Castilho (ed.) *Português Culto Falado no Brasil*, Campinas: Editora da UNICAMP, 281–318.

Martin, J. R. (1992) *English Text: System and Structure*, Amsterdam: Benjamins.

Martindale, C. (1986) *The White Press and Black America*, New York: Greenwood Press.

Matouschek, B., Wodak, R. and Januschek, F. (1995) *Notwendige Maßnahmen gegen Fremde?*, Vienna: Passagen.

Matthiessen, C. (1992) *Lexicogrammatical Cartography: English Systems*, Sydney: Department of Linguistics, University of Sydney.

Mazingo, S. (1988) 'Minorities and social control in the newsroom: thirty years after Breed', in G. Smitherman-Donaldson and T. A. van Dijk (eds) *Discourse and Discrimination*, Detroit, MI: Wayne State University Press, 93–130.

Mehan, H. (1987) 'Language and power in organisational process', *Discourse Processes*, 10, 291–301.

Mehan, H. (1990) 'Oracular reasoning in a psychiatric exam: the resolution of conflict in language', in A. D. Grimshaw (ed.) *Conflict Talk*, Cambridge: Cambridge University Press, 160–77.

Melkote, S. (1992) *Development Communication*, London: Sage.

Menz, F., Wodak, R., Gruber, H., and Lutz, B. (1988) 'Power struggles in the media: a case study', *Folia Linguistica*, 23, 3–4, 439–57.

Milroy, J. and Milroy, L. (1985) *Authority in Language*, London: Routledge & Kegan Paul.

Milroy, L. (1987) *Observing and Analysing Natural Language: A Critical Account of Sociolinguistic Method*, Oxford: Blackwell.

Minority Participation in the Media (1983) Hearings before the Subcommittee on Telecommunications, Consumer Protection and Finance, of the Committee on Energy and Commerce, House of Representatives, 98th Congress, 19 and 23 September 1983.

Minsky, M. L. (1975) 'Framework for representing knowledge', in P. H. Winston (ed.) *The Psychology of Computer Vision*, New York: McGraw-Hill, 211–77.

Mishler, E. G. (1984) *The Discourse of Medicine: Dialectics of Medical Interviews*, Norwood, NJ: Ablex.

Mitten, R. (1992) *The Politics of Antisemitic Prejudice: The Waldheim Phenomenon in Austria*, Boulder, CO: Westview Press.

Mitten, R. (1993) 'Die "Judenfrage" im Nachkriegsösterreich', *Zeitgeschichte*, 2 January, 14–34.

Mitten, R. and Wodak, R. (1993) 'On the discourse of racism and prejudice', *Folia Linguistica*, 27, 2/4, 191–215.

Morrison, A. (1993) 'Some observations on news photography in Zimbabwe', in H. Arnsten (ed.) *Media, Culture and Development*, 1, Oslo: University of Oslo, 137–54.

Mumby, D. K. (1988) *Communication and Power in Organisations: Discourse, Ideology, and Domination*, Norwood, NJ: Ablex.

Ng, S. H. and Bradac, J. J. (1993) *Power in Language: Verbal Communication and Social Influence,* Newbury Park, CA: Sage.

Norris, C. (1982) *Deconstruction: Theory and Practice*, London: Methuen.

O'Barr, W. M. (1982) *Linguistic Evidence: Language, Power and Strategy in the Courtroom*, New York: Academic Press.

O'Barr, W. M. (1984) 'Asking the right questions about language and power', in C. Kramarae, M. Schulz and W. M. O'Barr (eds) *Language and Power*, Beverly Hills, CA: Sage, 260–80.

Pateman, T. (1981) 'Linguistics as a branch of critical theory', *University of East Anglia Papers in Linguistics*, 14–15, 1–29.

Pêcheux, M. (1982) *Language, Semantics and Ideology: Stating the Obvious*, trans. by H. Nagpal, London: Macmillan.

Plasser, F. and Ulram, P. A. (1991) 'Ausländerfeindlichkeit als Wahlmotiv: Daten und Trends', MS, University of Vienna.

Preti, D. (1991) *A Linguagem dos Idosos*, São Paulo: Contexto.

Quinn, N. and Holland, D. (1987) 'Culture and cognition', in D. Holland and N. Quinn (eds) *Cultural Models in Language and Thought*, Cambridge: Cambridge University Press, 3–40.

Quirk, R., Greenbaum, S., Leech, G. and Svartvik, J. (1972) *A Grammar of Contemporary English*, London: Longman.

Ribeiro, B. T. (1993) 'Framing psychotic talk', in D. Tannen (ed.) *Framing in Discourse*, New York: Oxford University Press, 77–113.

Ribeiro, B. T. (1994) *Coherence in Psychotic Discourse*, New York: Oxford University Press.

Richardson, K. (1987) 'Critical linguistics and textual diagnosis', *TEXT*, 7, 2, 145–63.

Rosa, M. (1992) *Marcadores de Atenuação*, São Paulo: Contexto.

Rosch, E. (1975) 'Cognitive representation of semantic categories', *Journal of Experimental Psychology*, 104, 3, 192–233.

Rose, N. (1989) 'Governing the enterprising self', paper given at conference on Values of the Enterprise Culture, University of Lancaster, September.

Rose, N. and Miller, R. (1989) 'Rethinking the state; governing economic, social and personal life', MS, University of Lancaster.

Rumelhart, D. E. (1980) 'Schemata: the building blocks of cognition', in R. J. Spiro, B. C. Bruce and W. F. Brewe (eds) *Theoretical Issues in Reading Comprehension*, Hillsdale, NJ: Erlbaum.

Ryan, E. B., Giles, H., Bartolluc, G. and Henwood, K. (1986) 'Psycholinguistic and psychological components of communication by and with the elderly', *Language and Communication*, 6, 1/2, 1–24.

Sartre, J-P. (1956) *Being and Nothingness*, trans. by H. E. Barnes, New York: Philosophical Library.

Saunders, R. G. (1991) 'Information in the Interregnum: the press, state and civil society in struggles for hegemony, Zimbabwe 1980–1990', unpub. PhD, Carleton University, Ontario, Canada.

Schank, R. and Ableson, R. (1977) *Scripts, Plans, Goals and Understanding*, Hillsdale, NJ: Erlbaum.

Scheflen, A. E. (1973) *Communicational Structure: Analysis of a Psychotherapy Transaction*, Bloomington, IN: Indiana University Press.

Schiffrin, D. (1985) 'Conversational coherence: the role of "Well"', *Language*, 61, 640–67.

Schiffrin, D. (1987) *Discourse Markers*, New York: Cambridge University Press.

Schmidt, E. (1991) 'Patriarchy, capitalism, and the colonial state in Zimbabwe', *SIGNS*, 16, 4.

Seyler, D. U. and Boltz, C. J. (eds) (1986) *Language Power*, New York: Random House.

Shuy, R. W. (1974) 'Problems in communication in the cross-cultural medical interview', *Working Papers in Sociolinguistics*, 19.

Simpson, P. (1993) *Language, Ideology and Point of View*, London: Routledge

Sinclair, J. McH. (1986) 'Fictional worlds', in R. M. Coulthard (ed.) *Talking about Text*, Discourse Analysis Monographs, 13, English Language Research, University of Birmingham, 43–60.

Sinclair, J. McH. (1987) *Looking Up*, London: Collins ELT.
Sinclair, J. McH. and Coulthard, R. M. (1975) *Towards an Analysis of Discourse*, Oxford: Oxford University Press.
Slembrouck S. (1992) 'The parliamentary *Hansard* "verbatim" report: the written construction of spoken discourse', *Language and Literature*, 1, 2, 101–19.
Smitherman-Donaldson, G. and van Dijk, T. A. (eds) (1988) *Discourse and Discrimination*, Detroit, MI: Wayne State University Press.
Solomos, J. (1989) *Race and Racism in Contemporary Britain*, London: Macmillan.
Sparks, C. (1988) 'The popular press and political democracy', *Media, Culture and Society*, 10, 209–23.
Sparks, C. (1992) 'Popular journalism: theories and practice', in P. Dahlgren and C. Sparks (eds) *Journalism and Popular Culture*, London: Sage, 24–44.
Spender, D. (1985) *Man Made Language*, London: Pandora.
Sperber, D. and Wilson, D. (1986) *Relevance: Communication and Cognition*, Oxford: Blackwell.
Steiner, E. (1985) 'Towards a critical linguistics', in P. Chilton (ed.) *Language and the Nuclear Arms Debate: Nukespeak Today*, London: Frances Pinter, 213–30.
Stewart, J. and Armstrong, A. (eds) (1990) *The Legal Situation of Women in Southern Africa*, Harare: University of Zimbabwe Publications.
Stubbs, M. (1983) *Discourse Analysis: The Sociolinguistic Analysis of Natural Language*, Oxford: Blackwell.
Sumner, C. (1990) 'Rethinking deviance: towards a sociology of censure', in C. Sumner (ed.) *Censure, Politics and Criminal Justice*, Milton Keynes: Open University Press.
Swales, J. (1992) 'Genre and engagement', paper presented at conference on Discourse and the Professions, Uppsala, July.
Taguieff, P. A. (1991) 'Die Metamorphosen des Rassismus und die Krise des Antirassismus', in U. Bielefeld (ed.) *Das Eigene und das Fremde: Neuer Rassismus in der Alten Welt?*, Hamburg: Junius, 221–68.
Talbot, M. (1990) 'Language, intertextuality and subjectivity: voices in the construction of consumer femininity', unpub. PhD, University of Lancaster.
Tannen, D. (1984a) 'Spoken and written narrative in English and Greek', in D. Tannen (ed.) *Coherence in Spoken and Written Discourse*, Norwood, NJ: Ablex, 21–41.
Tannen, D. (ed.) (1984b) *Coherence in Spoken and Written Discourse*, Norwood, NJ: Ablex.
Tannen, D. (1986) *That's Not What I Meant!* New York: William Morrow.
Tannen, D. (1990) *You Just Don't Understand: Women and Men in Conversation*, New York: William Morrow.
Tannen, D. (ed.) (1993a) *Framing Discourse*, New York: Oxford University Press.
Tannen, D. (ed.) (1993b) *Gender and Conversational Interaction*, New York: Oxford University Press.
Tannen, D. and Wallat, C. (1987) 'Interactive frames and knowledge schemas in interaction: examples from a medical examination interview', *Social Psychology Quarterly*, 50, 2, 205–16.
Thibault, P. J. (1988) 'Knowing what you're told by Agony Aunts: language function, gender difference and the structure of knowledge and belief in the personal columns', in D. Birch and M. O'Toole (eds) *Functions of Style*, London: Frances Pinter, 205–33.
Thomas, J. (1985) 'The language of power: towards a dynamic pragmatics', *Journal of Pragmatics*, 9, 765–83.
Thompson, J. (1991) *Ideology and Modern Culture*, Cambridge: Polity.

Threadgold, T. (1989) 'Talking about genre: ideologies and incompatible discourses', *Cultural Studies*, 3, 1, 101–27.

Toffler, A. (1970) *Futureshock*, London: Bodley Head.

Treichler, P. (1987) 'Aids, homophobia and biomedical discourse: an epidemic of signification', *Cultural Studies*, 1, 3, 263–305.

Trew, T. (1979) 'Theory and ideology at work', in R. Fowler, R. Hodge, G. Kress and T. Trew, *Language and Control*, London: Routledge & Kegan Paul, 94–116.

Tuchman, G. (1978) *Making News: A Study in the Construction of Reality*, New York: Free Press.

Tuchman, G., Kaplan Daniels, A. and Benet, J. (1978) *Hearth and Home: Images of Women in the Mass Media*, New York: Oxford University Press.

van Dijk, T. A. (1977) *Text and Context: Explorations in the Semantics and Pragmatics of Discourse*, London: Longman.

van Dijk, T. A. (1984) *Prejudice in Discourse*, Amsterdam: Benjamins.

van Dijk, T. A. (1987) *Communicating Racism*, Newbury Park, CA: Sage.

van Dijk, T. A. (1988) *News as Discourse*, Hillsdale, NJ: Erlbaum.

van Dijk, T. A. (1989a) 'Critical news analysis', *Critical Studies*, 1, 1, 103–26.

van Dijk, T. A. (1989b) 'Structures of discourse and structures of power', in J. A. Anderson (ed.) *Communication Yearbook*, 12, Newbury Park, CA: Sage, 18–59.

van Dijk, T. A. (1990) 'Social cognition and discourse', in H. Giles and R. P. Robinson (eds) *Handbook of Social Psychology and Language*, Chichester: Wiley, 163–83.

van Dijk, T. A. (1991a) *Racism and the Press*, London: Routledge.

van Dijk, T. A. (1991b) 'The interdisciplinary study of news as discourse', in K. B. Jensen and N. W. Jankowski (eds) *A Handbook of Qualitative Methodologies for Mass Communication Research*, London: Routledge, 108–20.

van Dijk, T. A. (1992) 'Discourse and the denial of racism', *Discourse and Society*, 3, 87–118.

van Dijk, T. A. (1993a) *Elite Discourse and Racism*, Newbury Park, CA: Sage.

van Dijk, T. A. (1993b) 'Discourse and cognition in society', in D. Crowley and D. Mitchell (eds) *Communication Theory Today*, Oxford: Pergamon, 104–26.

van Dijk, T. A. (1993c) 'Principles of critical discourse analysis', *Discourse and Society*, 4, 249–83.

van Dijk, T. A. and Kintsch, W. (1983) *Strategies of Discourse Comprehension*, New York: Academic Press.

van Leeuwen, J. (1981) *De Metro van Magnus*, The Hague: Omniboek.

van Leeuwen, T. (1987) 'Music and ideology: notes towards a sociosemiotics of mass media music', Sydney Association for the Study of Society and Culture, *SASSC Working Papers*, 2, 1–2, 19–45.

van Leeuwen, T. (1993a) 'Genre and field in Critical Discourse Analysis: a synopsis', *Discourse and Society*, 4, 2, 193–225.

van Leeuwen, T. (1993b) 'Language and representation: the recontextualization of participants, activities and reactions', unpub. PhD, University of Sydney.

von Sturmer, J. (1981) 'Talking with Aborigines', *Australian Institute of Aboriginal Studies Newsletter*, 15, 13–30.

Walker, A. G. (1987) 'Linguistic manipulation, power and the legal setting', in L. Kedar (ed.) *Power through Discourse*, Norwood, NJ: Ablex, 57–80.

Walker, E. A. (1940) *South Africa, Oxford Pamphlets on World Affairs no. 32*, Oxford: Clarendon Press.

Watney, S. (1987) *Policing Desire: Pornography, AIDS and the Media*. London: Methuen.

Watts, R. J. (1991) *Power in Family Discourse*, Berlin: Mouton de Gruyter.

Wernick, A. (1991) '(Re)-imaging gender: the case of men', in A. Wernick, *Promotional Culture*, London: Sage, 47–66.

West, C. (1983) ' "Ask me no questions": an analysis of queries and replies in physician–patient dialogues', in S. Fisher and A. Todd (eds) *The Social Organisation of Doctor–Patient Communication*, Washington, DC: Center for Applied Linguistics, 75–106.

Widdowson, H. (1979) *Explorations in Applied Linguistics*, Oxford: Oxford University Press.

Williams, R. (1983) *Keywords*, London: Fontana.

Wilson, C. C. and Gutiérrez, F. (1985) *Minorities and the Media*, London: Sage.

Winship, J. (1987) *Inside Women's Magazines*, London: Pandora.

Winter, E. O. (1974) 'Replacement as a function of repetition: a study of some of its principal features in the clause relations of contemporary English', unpub. PhD, University of London.

Winter, E. O. (1977) 'A clause relational approach to English texts: a study of some predictive lexical items in written discourse', *Instructional Science*, 6, 1, 1–92.

Winter, E. O. (1979) 'Replacement as a fundamental function of the sentence in context', *Forum Linguisticum*, 4, 2, 95–133.

Wodak, R. (1985) 'The interaction between judge and defendant', in T. A. van Dijk (ed.) *Handbook of Discourse Analysis, vol. 4, Discourse Analysis in Society*, London: Academic Press, 181–91.

Wodak, R. (ed.) (1989) *Language, Power and Ideology*, Amsterdam: Benjamins.

Wodak, R. (1991) 'Turning the tables: antisemitic discourse in postwar Austria', *Discourse and Society*, 2, 1, 65–85.

Wodak, R. (1993) 'Unity and diversity: is there an Austrian German?', paper delivered at the conference on Unity and Diversity Stanford University, CA, March.

Wodak, R. and Matouschek, B. (1993) ' "We are dealing with people whose origins one can clearly tell just by looking": Critical Discourse Analysis and the study of neo-racism in contemporary Austria', *Discourse and Society*, 2, 4, 225–48.

Wodak, R. and Menz, F. (eds) (1990) *Sprache in der Politik: Politik in der Sprache*, Klagenfurt: Drava.

Wodak, R., Menz, F., Mitten, R. and Stern, F. (1990) '*Wir sind alle unschuldige Täter!' Diskurshistorische Studien zum Nachkriegsantisemitismus*, Frankfurt/Main: Suhrkamp.

Wodak, R., Menz, F., Mitten, R. and Stern, F. (1994) *Sprachen der Vergangenheiten: Öffentliches Gedenken in österreichischen und deutschen Medien*, Frankfurt/Main: Suhrkamp.

Wright, W. (1975) *Sixguns and Society: A Structural Study of the Western*, Berkeley, CA: University of California Press.

Wrong, D. H. (1979) *Power: Its Forms, Bases and Uses*, Oxford: Blackwell.

Index

Numbers in bold denote chapter/major section devoted to subject

ABC (Australian Broadcasting
    Corporation): radio programme
    'Offspring' 48–9; *The Search for
    Meaning*, 55
Abelson, R. P. 228–9n
abstraction 59, 60, 61
academia: lack of access to by ethnic
    minorities 94–5
access to discourse **84–102**; dimensions
    87–90; ethnic minorities lack of
    91–5, 102: in academia 94–5; in
    business 95; in media 92–4; in
    politics 92; judges and 90;
    newspaper articles on immigration
    96–102; power based on 85–6;
    various domains 86–7
activation 43, 44, 45
agency 32, 33 *see also* social actors,
    representation of
aggregation 49
AI (Artificial Intelligence) 11, 229,
    230
American Heritage Dictionary (AHD)
    135, 136, 145
anachronism 64
anonymity: in media discourse 116–17
anti-semitism 113
appraisement: of social actors 58
argumentation, strategies of in
    prejudiced discourse **116–25**:
    development of discourse of
    sympathy, tutelage and justification
    117–23; economic discourse 123–5
Argyle, M. 72–3, 74
Artificial Intelligence (AI) 11, 229,
    230

assimilation 48–50
association: realisation of 50–1
asymmetry: institutional framings of
    psychiatric interview 183; in
    'man/woman' dictionary definitions
    156–7, 160–2
Australia 36–8, 47; representation of
    immigration in 'Our Race Odyssey'
    35–8, 40, 41–2, 45, 49–51, 52, 54,
    58–61, 67–9
Australian Aborigines: and relational
    identification 56–7
Australian Broadcasting Corporation
    see ABC
Austria, racist discourse in **107–26**;
    change in attitude towards East
    Central European neighbours 111,
    114–15; development of discourse of
    sympathy, tutelage and justification
    114, 116–25; and falling of iron
    curtain 109, 114; FPO propaganda
    poster on foreigners 114–15;
    historical background 108–9;
    immigration laws 107–8, 114; Jews
    in 113; language conflicts 110; media
    discourse on Romania/Romanians
    116–25; self-image 126
authors *see* writing
'autonomous linguistics' 3, 5

backgrounding 39, 41
Ballaster, R. *et al.* 252, 253–4, 255,
    268
Barthes, R. 63
Bateson, G. 182, 189
Bell, A. 54, 262, 263

beneficialisation 44–5
Bentley, Derek 166–7
Berger, J. 63
Berger, P. L. 55
Bernstein, B. 47
Best Intentions (film) 257
bestiality case, **231–46**; consequences
of 245; discrimination against
women in initial text 231–2, 233–7,
243, 244; lack of commentary of
reported legal judgements 242–3;
legal outcome 243–4; protest
demonstration by Women's Action
Group 239–40; re-articulation of
negative labelling of women in
press 237–43, 245–6; report of
incident in Zimbabwean press
231–3
Bettelheim, B. 62–3
Bild 29, 31
Billig, M. *et al.* 78
Birmingham Daily News 131, 132–3
blues lyrics: coherence of 227
Borzeix, A. and Linhart, D. 76
Bourdieu, P. 17, 46–7
Bowers, G. and Iwi, K. 233
Britain: and immigration 100–2;
meaning of 'ethnic' in 132–3, 143–4;
newspaper article on police force
132–3; use of 'ethnic', 'racial',
'tribal' compared to United States
140
Brown, G. and Yule, G. 217, 218,
226
Brown, P. and Levinson, S. C. 198,
199, 206
Burger, H. 109
business: lack of access to by ethnic
minorities 95

Candlin, C. and Lucas, J. L. 81
car: drawing of 20-2
categorisation 11, 52–3; choice
between types 55–6; in 'Race
Odyssey' text 58–9; types of:
functionalisation 54, 56;
identification 54–5, 56–8
causation: linguistic analysis of
ideology 11
Cavalcanti, M. 228n
CCELD (Collins COBUILD English
Language Dictionary) 156;
definitions of 'ethnic', 'racial' and

'tribal' 130, 136, 137, 138, 146;
source of data for clause relations
154; writing entries for 156
Ceauşecu: reporting on fall of
118–19
CED (*Collins English Dictionary*) 134,
135, 136, 137, 145, 146
Certificate of Pre-Vocational
Education 81
Chafe, W. 186
Chambers 20th Century Dictionary
(CTCD) 135, 136
*Chambers Universal Learner's
Dictionary* 152–3
Chibnall, S. 269
children: represented as groups 48–9;
television example for role
allocation 43
children's stories: associations in 51;
categorisation and nomination used
53, 54; example of realisation of
indetermination 51–2; exclusion in
39; first day at school 52, 64–5; over
determination in *De Metro van
Magnus* 61, 62
Chilton, P.: nukespeak volume 6, 9
Chronicle (Zimbabwean newspaper)
237–9
church: de-legitimation of 64
'Cinderella' texts 150–1
class(es): and difference between the
Sun and *Frankfurter Allgemeine* 31;
and representation of social actors
46–8
classification: and social actors 54–5,
56, 58, 63
classroom discourse 217
clause relations 151–2
COBUILD 138–9; gender bias 162–3;
limitation of 144; methods to
indicate collocation 141; on sexism
and racism 130
coherence **214–28**; and blues lyrics
227; contribution of world
knowledge to 218, 224–6, 228–9n;
dependent on readers' social
identity 227–8; distinction between
'surface' and 'underlying' 214,
217–18; formal linkage 218–19;
'gap filling' and inferencing 218,
226; heterosexuality and
construction of 214, 220–3, 226,
227–8; reliance on common sense

for construction of 220–2, 226–7;
Thibault's Reason for Request –
Request 223–4, 225, 226
collectivisation 49
*Collins COBUILD English Language
Dictionary see* CCELD
Collins English Dictionary see CED
'colony' texts: matching relations in
dictionaries 151, **152–6**, 162; nature
of 150–1; semantic relations in 151,
152–3
common sense 11; and construction of
coherence 220–2, 226–7
conflict talk: in psychiatric discharge
interview **179–91**
Connerton, P. 4–5, 11
connotation 63
conversation 86
conversationalisation: and
technologisation of discourse 74,
76–7
corporate discourse: lack of access to
by ethnic minorities 95
corpus data 130, **138–42**; collocation
141–2, 145, 146; distribution and
frequency of words 139–40; *see also*
COBUILD
Coulthard, R. M. 186
court stenographers 170–1
courts: access to 87, 88, 89–90; judges'
power of access 90; need for
education in language matters 177;
and police interview records 169
Cox Report (1989) 82
Craig, Chris 166–7
criminal statutes: and clause relations
150, 152, 153
critical language projects 15; move
towards productive activity 15–16,
19; and texts 20
Critical Language Study 214
critical linguistics **3–13**; 'critique' and
'criticism' 4–5; form of
historiography 10; goal of 5; and
ideology 3, 8, 9, 10–12; importance
in development of original model
6–7, 8–9, 12–13; and increased
power to reader 7–8;
interdependence of language and
context 9–10; interest in 5; origin
3–4, 6; problems with 9; theory 4;
and theory and practice of
representation 4–5, 10

criticism 4–5
critique: defined 4
CTCD (*Chambers Twentieth Century
Dictionary*) 135, 136
Curhoys, A. and Docker, J. 43
curriculum 27; view of 16–17
Czechs: in Austria 109, 110

Daily Mail: article on immigration
100, 101
Daily Telegraph 47, 101, 149
Dandy, Paul 167
Davis, Miles 58
Debert, G. G. 195
Denning, Lord: quoted 166
Deschooling Society (Illich) 63–4
deviation: form of inversion 64–5
dictionaries: arbiters of linguistic
usage 129–30; bias in preference to
men in definitions 150, 155, 157,
158–9, 160–3; distinction between
'racial', 'tribal' and 'ethnic' **134–8**,
144–6; matching relations in 151,
152–6, 162
differentiation 51, 52
discharge interview *see* psychiatric
discharge interview
discourse: defined 7
discourse-historical approach 108–9,
111
discourse markers: edited out in
police records 175–6; used by
patient in psychiatric discharge
interviews 187
'discourses of difference', theory of
108, 111–13
discriminatory discourse 233; and
bestiality report 231–2, 233–6,
245–6
dispositions: and Bourdieu's habitus
17
distillation 63–4
doctor–patient communication 180;
conflict in perception of encounter
182, 188–9, 190; institutional and
personal framings 181–2, 183–4,
185–8
dominance *see* social power, abuse of
Downes, W. 12
Downing, J. D. H. 93

economic discourse: and immigration
of Romanians 123–5

Economist, The 140

education: access to 86, 87; changes in language 81–2; and curriculum 16–17; lack of access to by ethnic minorities 94; *see also* schooling; universities

elderly **194–213**; consequences of stigma attached to 195; conversation and saving of face 198–200; difficulty in characterising 195; preservation of social image 196–212; as a social group 194–6; social role 196–8; society's view of role of 197–8

Electro-Static Deposition Analysis (ESDA) 167

equity, issue of 18–19

Erdheim, M. 126

Erickson, F. and Schultz, J. 184

ESDA (Electro-Static Deposition Analysis) 167

Essed, P. J. M. 91, 94

'ethnic': collocations 135, 141–2, 145; distinction between 'racial', 'tribal' and: in corpus data 138–42; in dictionaries 134–8, 145–6; in newspapers 130–4, 140, 142; in texts 140, 143–4; meaning of in British context 132–3, 143; Williamson on 147

ethnic minorities: change in Austrian attitude towards 111, 114–15, 116–25; and issue of equity 18–19; lack of access to discourse **90–102**: academia 94–5; business 95; media 92–4; newspaper examples 95–102; politics 92; *see also* immigrants; racist discourse

exclusion **38–42**; backgrounding 39, 41; and inclusion in 'Race Odyssey' text 41–2; methods of 40–1; and realisation of suppression 39–40; in schooling texts 39

face, saving of: in discourse of elderly 200–11; problems of for elderly 198–200

Fairclough, N. 71, 74, 81, 82, 80, 224–7, 234, 245

fairy tales 63

Fedler, F. 93

femininity: in women's magazines 252, 253, 254, 255

first-person narratives 250, 256, 262, 268–9

Fisher, S. 181

Fiske, J. 233

Fiske, S. T. and Taylor, S. E. 85

Flintstones, The 62, 64

Folha de São Paulo 30, 31

footings: defined 181

Foucault, M. 72, 75; discourse of sexology 55

Fowler, R. 245; and Marshall, T. 12; *et al.* 3

FPO (Freedom Party of Austria) 114–15

framings 182–3; expansion of self in personal 189–90; institutional and personal 181–2, 183–4; shifts in 183, 184–8

Frankel, R. M. 183

Frankfurt School 4

Frankfurter Allgemeine 31; contrast between *Sun* and 25, 27, 31; subjectivity 25; typographical and layout features 23–5

Freedom Party of Austria (FPO) 114–15

functional linguistics 8: and critical linguistics 5; defined 3

functionalisation 54, 57, 59, 63; choice between identification and 55–6

Futureshock (Toffler) 57

genericisation: and representation of social actors 46–8

geriatrics *see* elderly

Germany 113

Giddens, A. 250

Goffman, E.: on elderly 195, 196, 197, 198, 199; forms of talk 179, 181, 183, 186, 187, 191n; on mental patients 188–9, 190, 191n

government: and technologies of discourse 72, 75, 76

Graff, Michael 108

grammatical metaphor 33

Grice, H. P. 8, 11

Guardian 53, 148; article on Kenya 131–2, 134

Guillaumin, C. 112–13

Gumperz, J. 182

habitus 31, 46; defined 17; formation of 18–19

Haider, Jörg 115

Hall, S. 111, 113

Halliday, M. A. K. 11; *Explorations in the Functions of Language* 3, 12; and Hasan, R. 218–19; *Introduction to Functional Grammar* 8, 32, 40, 44, 45, 51, 54, 67, 220, 258; *Language as Social Semiotic* 7, 9, 74; theory of grammatical metaphor 33

Hansard 170

headlines: content in news reports 93–4; importance of 257–8; in sex narratives 257

Herald: cartoon in 241

Herman, E. S. and Chomsky, N. 85

heterosexuality: and construction of coherence 214, 220–3, 226, 227–8

history: and critical linguistics 10; discourse-historical approach 108–9, 111

Hjelmquist, E. 175

Hoey, M. P. 150, 151, 153, 160, 257; and Winter, E. O. 162

homosexuality: and construction of coherence 214–16, 220, 226, 228

Horizon 243

Horkheimer, M. and Adorno, T. 194

Hungarians: in Austria 109, 110

Huxley, J. 148

identification 54; choice between functionalisation and 55–6; classification 54–5, 56, 58, 63; physical 57–8; relational 56–7, 59

ideology: and critical linguistics 3, 4, 6, 8, 9, 10–12

Illich, I.: *Deschooling Society* 63–4

immigrants (immigration); Austrian laws on 107–8; lack of access to discourse **91–5**; presented in negative way in media 93, 95–101; representation of in 'Race Odyssey' 35–8, 40, 41–2, 45, 49–51, 52, 54, 58–61, 67–9

impersonalisation **59–61**; effects of 60; types of: abstraction 59; objectivation 59–60

inclusion 41–2; *see also* exclusion

Independent 140, 143

Independent on Sunday 148

indetermination 51–2

individualisation 48, 49, 52, 62

industry: 'post-Fordist' developments in 75

institutional discourse: conversation-alisation of 74, 76–7

institutional framings: defined 183; power of 183–4; shifts between personal and 181–2, 183, 184–8; stiffness in 189

instrumental linguistics 3, 10

instrumentalisation 60

'inter-racial': use of term 133, 143–4

interest: and sign-making 20–2

International Association of Forensic Linguists 177

interviews: conflict talk in psychiatric discharge **179–91**; personnel 72–3, 74; police system for recording 167–70; transcription of 170–1

Introduction to Functional Grammar (Halliday) 8, 32, 40, 44, 45, 51, 54, 67, 220, 258

inversion 62; forms of: anachronism 64; deviation 64–5

Jackie magazine 220

Jameson, F. 250

Jarrett, D. 227

journalistic reporting: contrasted with women's magazines 251; *see also* newspapers

judges: power of access 90

Julius Caesar 162

justification, discourse of 114, 116, 118, 124–5

Kaisersteinbruch: report of Romanians in 121–2

Kenya: newspaper article 131–2, 134

kinship relations 56–7

Kochman, T. 93

Kreisky, Chancellor Bruno 120–1

Kress, G. 9, 20, 181; and Hodge, R. 3, 46; linguistic theory and texts 6–7, 8, 268; on metaphor 11, 12; and van Leeuven, T. 264

Kurier: 'Refugee aid at home' article 123–5

Labov, W. 218, 261, 268; and Fanshel, D. 11; and Waletsky, J. 256

Lady Chatterley's Lover 172

Language and Control 5, 6, 8

Language and Symbolic Power 17

Latour, B. 233

Lawrence, D. H.: *Lady Chatterley's Lover* 172
LDEL (*Longman Dictionary of the English Language*) 135, 145
LDOCE (*Longman Dictionary of Contemporary English*) 136, 137, 138, 145, 146
legal profession: language education 177
Lemke, J. L. 234
Lendvai, Paul 118–19, 121
linguistic criticism *see* critical linguistics
Longacre, R. E. 256
Longman Dictionary of Contemporary English see LDOCE
Longman Dictionary of the English Language (LDEL) 135, 145

McCarthy, M. 175
McCraken, E. 250
magazines, women's *see* women's magazines
'mainstream' texts: clause relations in 151–2
male hegemony: and press report of bestiality 232, 233–6, 237, 238
Malmkjaer, K. 5
'man', dictionary definitions of **150–63**; bias towards 150, 155, 157, 158–9, 160–3; examples of asymmetry 156–7, 160–2; matching relations between 'woman' and 154–6; unmatched relations between 'woman' and 158–9
Marcuschi, L. A. 199
Marie Claire: attraction of 251; concentration on narrative 256; sex narratives 257–62; structure 252–3
matching relations: asymmetrical examples 156–7, 160–2; in 'colony' texts 152, 153; data selection for study of 153–4; defined 151–2; 'man' and 'woman' 154–6
Matouschek, B. *et al.* 111
Matthiessen, C. 67
media: access to 86, 87, 88, 102; access to by ethnic minorities 92–4; active role in representation of social actors 69; discourse on Romania/Romanians 116–25; evaluation in discourse of 267–8; influence of 129; issue of

immigration 93; judges access to 90; and reinforcement of prejudicial discourse 109; *see also* newspapers
medical discourse 86, 87; *see also* doctor–patient communication
medical interviews 181–2; *see also* doctor–patient communication
mental patients 188–9, 191n
'metaphor', concept of 11, 12, 33
Metro van Magnus, De 61, 62
minority groups *see* ethnic minorities
Minsky, J. 11, 229n
Mishler, E. G. 181
Mitten, R. 108, 126
'mixed marriages': term of 144
'mixed race': use of term in British context 133, 143–4
Mubi, Simomo 242
Muslims 100, 101–2

narratives 256–7, 263; first-person 250, 256, 262, 268–9; importance of evaluation 267–9; *see also* sex narratives
Nazis: and anti-semitism 113
Netherlands: and access to discourse 92, 94
Neue Kronenzeitung 121–2
news media 245
news reports 129; headline content 93–4
newspapers: description of men 263–4; distinction of 'ethnic', 'tribal' and 'racial' in 130–4, 140, 142; embedding of narrative text 263; headlines in 93–4, 257; on immigration 95–102; lack of access to by ethnic minorities 92, 93, 100; representation of social actors 47, 48, 53, 54; representation and subjectivity 23–31; *see also* individual papers; Zimbabwean press
nominalisation 40, 44, 45, 60, 67
nomination 34, 52–4, 56, 57
nukespeak 6, 9, 12

OALD (*Oxford Advanced Learner's Dictionary*) 136, 137, 138, 146
objectivation 59–60
old-old people *see* elderly
ORF 118–19, 121

'Our Race Odyssey' see 'Race Odyssey'
overdetermination 57–8, **61–5**;
  categories: connotation 63;
  distillation 63–4; inversion 62, 64–5;
  symbolisation 62–3
*Oxford Advanced Learner's
  Dictionary* (OALD) 136, 137, 138,
  146

passivation 43–4, 45
passive agent deletion 39, 60
patient–doctor communication *see*
  doctor–patient communication
People's Voice: cartoon in 240–1
personal framings 183; expansion of
  self in 189–90; and institutional
  framings 184–8
personal relations 56–7
personnel interviews 72–3, 74
physical identification 57–8
Plasser, F. and Ulram, P. A. 115
police force, British: newspaper article
  on 132–3
police records **166–77**; Craig and
  Bentley case 166–7; devices used to
  manipulate audience 171–6: creation
  of positive police character 174–5;
  discourse markers 175–6;
  interruptions 176; non-verbal
  features 176; production of non-
  standard usage of language 171–3;
  re-creation of 'verbatim' record
  produced from memory 169–70, 175,
  176; reinforcement of unsigned
  confession 173–4: interviewing
  167–70; transcription of interview
  tape recordings 170–1; 'verballing'
  cases 167
politics: access to 86; lack of access to
  by ethnic minorities 92
possessivation 44, 45, 56
possessive pronouns 32, 44, 51, 53, 60
power: and framing 189–90
power, abuse of social **84–102**; and
  access to discourse in various
  domains 85–7, 102; cognitive
  dimension of control 85; defined
  84–5; dimensions of access 87–90;
  ethnic minorities' lack of access to
  discourse 90–5; and judges 90;
  mentally mediated control as
  ultimate form of 88–9; preferential
  access to media and 96–102

prejudiced discourse: and anonymous
  letters 116–17; argumentation
  strategies 116, discourses of
  sympathy, tutelage and justification
  117–23; reinforcement of by media
  109; *see also* discriminatory
  discourse; racist discourse
press *see* newspapers
Preti, D. 195
problem page letters 214–16; activity
  structures in 224, 225
process nouns 40, 45; realisation of
  activation 44
'productive consumption' 7, 9
Proops, Marge 214–16, 222, 224
proper nouns: realisation of
  nomination 53
prospectus, university 78–80
'prototype', notion of 11, 12
psychiatric discharge interview **179–91**;
  conflict in perception of encounter
  by patient/doctor 182, 183, 188–9,
  190; process of transition from
  patent to person 188–90; purpose of
  180; reasons for staying within
  official framings 184; shift in
  institutional and personal framings
  181–2, 183, 184–8

Quinn, N. and Holland, D. 229n
Quirk, R. *et al.* 46

'race': distinguishing features of
  112–13; entry in dictionaries 137;
  Huxley on 148; Williams on 147
'Race Odyssey, Our' 48, 67–9;
  associations 51; categorisation 58–9;
  differentiation 52; exclusion and
  inclusion 38, 39–40, 41–2; generic
  reference 48; impersonalisation
  59–61; individualisation of racism 50;
  nomination 54; overdetermination
  65; representation of immigration
  35–8, 40, 41–2, 45, 54, 58–61, 67–9,
  49–51, 52; role allocation 44–6;
  summary of treatment of social
  actors 67–9; text of 35–8
'racial': collocations 137, 141–2;
  distinction between 'tribal', 'ethnic'
  and: in corpus data 139–42;
  in dictionaries 135–8, 145, 146;
  in newspapers 132–4, 140, 142;
  in texts 140, 143–4

racist discourse: argumentation
strategies 116–25; change in
Austrian attitude towards East
Central European neighbours 111,
114–15; defined 111–12;
development of discourses of
sympathy, tutelage and justification
117–25; different types of 112–13;
and discourse-historical approach
108–9, 111; Guillaumin's features of
race 112–13; origin of in Austria
109–10; in Romania *see* Romania;
see also immigrants
radio 129
reading: distinction between writing
and 19, 20; and linguistic theory
6–7, 11, 16; processes of 7–8
Reason for Request – Request 223–4,
225, 226
records, police *see* police records
register: Halliday's formulation of 7
relational identification 56–7, 59
relationships: change in social at
workplace due to technologisation
of discourse 76–7
representational processes 19
representational resources 18; and
distinction between *Sun* and
Frankfurter Allgemeine 23–7, 31;
and formation of habitus 18, 31;
need for ethnography of in
multicultural society 18–19; and
subjectivity 18, 22–3, 25, 27
residency laws (Austrian) 107–8, 114
Rhodesian Herald 38
Ribeiro, B. T. 190
role allocation: and representation of
social actors 42–6
Romania (Romanians) 109, **116–25**;
analogy between Russians and 122;
anonymous letter 116–17; article on
Kaisersteinbruch 121–2; change in
discourse pattern after revolution
121–3; discourse of justification 118,
124–5; discourse of sympathy 117,
118–19, 120; discourse of tutelage
114, 118, 119–21, 124; economic
discourse 123–5; increase in hostile
prejudice since 1990 118; perceived
as threat 121; reporting on fall of
Ceauşescu 118; and television news
broadcasts 118–19, 120–1
Rosa, M. 198

Rosch, E. 11
Rose, N. 76; and Miller, R. 72
Ruxton, Bruce 68
Ryan, E. B. *et al.* 195

São Paulo: elderly people in 196
Sartre, J-P. 197
Schank, R. and Abelson, R. 11, 228n
schooling texts: and assimilation 48–9;
inclusion/exclusion of fathers in 39
schools: de-legitimation of 64
science fiction: example of
anachronism 64
scripts 228–9n
Search for Meaning, The (ABC radio
programme) 55
self-justification, discourse of 114, 116,
118, 124–5
sex narratives 250, 255, **256–69**;
characteristics of 256, 262;
evaluation 267–8; fictionalisation of
250, 263–4, 269; headlines in 257–9;
orientation 227, 260–1, 266–7;
266–7; structures 259–61
sexuality: defined through
consumerism 254–5; Giddens on
250; portrayed in women's
magazines, 255; *see also* sex
narratives
Shakespeare, William 33, 34
shopping lists 151, 152
signs, motivation of 20–2, 23
simulation: and redesigned discourse
techniques 74, 76
Sinclair, J. McH. 138, 233; and
Coulthard, R. M. 217
Slembrouck, S. 170
social actors, representation of **32–69**;
appraisement 58; blurring of
boundaries in 67; [categorisation
52–3, 54–9: functionalisation 54;
identification: (classification) 54–5;
(physical) 57–8; (relational) 56–7];
choice between generic and
specific reference 46–8; in different
sectors of press 47, 48, 53, 54;
differentiation 52; [exclusion and
inclusion **38–42**: deletion of
beneficiaries 40; distinction between
suppression and backgrounding
39–41; retrievable of suppressed by
readers 41; through nominalisation
and process nouns 40]; [as groups:

assimilation 48–9, 50; association
50–1]; [impersonalisation **59–61**:
(abstraction) 59; (effects of) 60;
(objectivation) 59–60]; indetermination 51–2; individualisation 48, 49,
50; nomination 52, 53; [overdeter-
mination **61–5**: (connotation) 63;
(distillation) 63–4; (inversion) 62,
64–5; (symbolisation) 62–3]; [role
allocation **42–6**: activation 43, 44;
passivation 43–4: (beneficialisation)
44–5; (subjection) 44–5]; role as
'Sayers' 33; summary of principal
ways 65, 66 (fig.), 67; treatment in
'Race Odyssey' *see* 'Race Odyssey'
social group: defined 194; elderly as
194–6
social skills training 72
Socialist Worker 27, 28
somatisation 60
South Africa: newspaper article 133,
134
Sparks, C. 244
spatialisation 59–60
specification: and representation of
social actors 46–8
speech functions: in relation to
university prospectus 78–80
speech transcription conventions
190–1, 212–13
Spender, D. 157
Sperber, D. and Wilson, D. 11
staff appraisal 73
staff development 73
statutes, criminal *see* criminal statutes
stenographers 170–1
Stubbs, M. 217
subjection 44–5
subjectivity: constitution of in art of
constructing coherence 214–28; and
curriculum 16–17, 27; *Frankfurter
Allgemeine* and *Sun* 23–7, 31;
production of 15–16;
representational resources and 18,
22–3; sign-making 20–2;
transformation of 17–18, 22–3, 27
Süddeutsche Zeitung 25
Sumner, C. 232
Sun 129; articles on immigration
96–100; contrast between
Frankfurter Allgemeine and 25, 27,
31; and reader 25–6, 31; and visual
25

Sunday Mail (Zimbabwean): article on
bestiality 234–7; cartoon 241–2;
protest by Women's Action Group
on reporting of incident 239–40
Sunday Mirror: problem page 214–16
suppression: distinction between
backgrounding and 39; realisation of
39–40; retrievable of actors by
readers 41
Sydney Morning Herald 47
symbolisation 62–3
sympathy, discourse of 114, 117,
118–19, 120, 124

Taguieff, P. A. 112, 113
Tale of Two Cities, A (Dickens) 152
Tannen, D. 183, 227; and Wallat, C.
182, 184
teachers 63, 64; decrease in autonomy
at universities 77; and discourse
access 86; necessity for openness
that linguistics is not a discovery
procedure 9–10
technologisation of discourse **71–82**;
changes in language education and
training 81–2; and changing
workplace culture 71, 75–7;
characteristics 71, 72–5; design of
discoursal techniques 73, 74, 75;
effect on university prospectus
78–80; emergence of expert
discourse technologists 74, 75, 77;
impetus towards standardisation 73,
74–5, 81; pathological consequences
77; reaction to change emanating
from 77–8; shift in location of
policing of 73–4, 75; upheavals in
industry 75; upheavals in
universities 75–6
technologists of discourse: emergence
of experts 73, 74, 75, 77
television: influence of 129; lack of
access to by ethnic minorities 92–3;
news broadcasts on Romania
(Austrian) 118–19, 120–1
Thatcher, Margaret 98, 101
therapy/therapist: taxonomy on 63–4
Thibault, P. J. 223, 224, 226
Thompson, J. 17
Threadgold, T. 232
Times, The 38, 140
Times Higher Education Supplement
149

Today 140, 143, 144
training 73, 74; and language
    education 75, 81–2; social skills 72
transcribing 170–1; conventions of
    190–1, 212–13
Trew, T. 38–9
'tribal': collocations 137, 141–2, 146;
    distinction between 'racial', 'ethnic'
    and: in corpus data 139–42; in
    dictionaries 136–8, 146; in
    newspapers 132, 134, 140, 142; in
    texts 140, 143–4; in 'ephemera' sub
    corpus 140; pejorative connotations
    to 138, 146, 147; problems with
    using 148–9
Tuchman, G. *et al.* 43, 93
tutelage, discourse of 114, 118, 119–21,
    124

United States 95; access to politics by
    ethnic minorities 92; use of words
    'ethnic', 'racial' compared to Britain
    140
universities: decrease in autonomy for
    teachers at 77; emergence of expert
    discourse technologists 73;
    prospectus 78–80; shift in policing
    73–4; upheavals due to increase in
    discourse technologisation 75–6
Unknown Soldier, The: character in
    Dutch children's story 61
utterance autonomisation 34, 60, 61

van Dijk, T. A. 91, 92, 93, 94, 97, 108;
    on Critical Discourse Analysis 176;
    on prejudiced discourse 109; on
    representation of social actors 264,
    267; theory of discourse 19
van Leeuwen, T. 34, 35, 39, 48, 52,
    265; on Critical Discourse Analysis
    233; on *De Metro van Magnus*
    61
visual: dominance of over verbal 20;
    increase in representation of 34; in
    the *Sun* 25
von Sturmer, J. 56–7
Vranitzky, Chancellor Franz 119

Walker, E. A. 148
Wall Street Journal 140
*Webster's Ninth New Collegiate
    Dictionary* (W9) 135
Weekend Gazette 243–4

Westerns: transition from individual-
    isation to collectivisation in 62
Williams, R. 147
Win, Everjoyce 240
Winship, J. 252
Winter, E. O. 151
Wodak *et al.* 108, 110, 111, 116, 126
'woman', dictionary definitions of;
    discrimination through 150, 155,
    157, 158–9, 160–3; examples of
    asymmetry 156–7, 160–2; matching
    relations between 'man' and 154–6;
    stereotyping in language 161;
    unmatched relations between 'man'
    and 158–9
women: discrimination against in
    Zimbabwean Press *see* bestiality
    case
Women's Action Group 239–40
women's magazines **250–69**; attraction
    of 252; concept of femininity 252,
    253, 254, 255; conflict in 253;
    construction of men in 252; contrast
    with journalistic reporting 251;
    important role 250; pleasure in
    reading 251, 252; presentation and
    structure 252–3; sex narratives *see*
    sex narratives; sexuality defined
    through consumerism 254–5;
    targeted for women 251–2; use of
    headlines 257–9; use of quote 258
Woolf, Virginia 46–7
workplace culture: changes in due to
    technologisation of discourse 71,
    75–7
Wright, W. 62
writing 6–7; distinction between
    reading and 19, 20

Yugoslavia: newspaper article 130–1,
    142

Zimbabwean press (bestiality case)
    231–46; cartoons 240–2; discourse
    between women and 239–40;
    discrimination against women in
    initial article 231–2, 233–7, 243, 244;
    incident of bestiality 231–3; lack
    of commentary of reported legal
    judgements 242–3; legal outcome
    of case 243–4; re-articulation of
    negative labelling of women in other
    texts 237–43, 245–6